Deutsche Mark Politics

Deutsche Mark Politics

Germany in the European Monetary System

Peter Henning Loedel

LYNNE
RIENNER
PUBLISHERS

BOULDER
LONDON

Published in the United States of America in 1999 by
Lynne Rienner Publishers, Inc.
1800 30th Street, Boulder, Colorado 80301

and in the United Kingdom by
Lynne Rienner Publishers, Inc.
3 Henrietta Street, Covent Garden, London WC2E 8LU

© 1999 by Lynne Rienner Publishers, Inc. All rights reserved

Library of Congress Cataloging-in-Publication Data
Loedel, Peter H., 1965–
  Deutsche mark politics : Germany in the European monetary system / Peter Henning Loedel.
      p.   cm.
  Includes bibliographical references and index.
  ISBN 1-55587-835-0 (hc. : alk. paper)
  1. Monetary policy—Germany. 2. Monetary unions—European Union countries. 3. European Union—Germany. I. Title.
HG999.5.L6 1999
332.4'943—dc21   98-47375
                                                                      CIP

British Cataloguing in Publication Data
A Cataloguing in Publication record for this book
is available from the British Library.

Printed and bound in the United States of America

∞ The paper used in this publication meets the requirements
   of the American National Standard for Permanence of
   Paper for Printed Library Materials Z39.48-1984.

    5 4 3 2 1

Contents

List of Tables and Figures		vii
Preface		ix
1	The Political Economy of Deutsche Mark Politics	1
2	Bundesbank Preeminent, Not Predominant	35
3	From Plaza to Black October: The Europeanization of Deutsche Mark Politics, 1985–1987	67
4	Exporting the Deutsche Mark to Europe, 1989–1991	93
5	Bundesbank Under Pressure, 1992–1993	143
6	Dollar Crises and Halting Steps Toward Economic Monetary Union, 1994–1995	179
7	Economic Monetary Union for Europe? 1996–1998	207
8	Conclusion: The Lessons of Deutsche Mark Politics	235
Selected Bibliography		253
Index		257
About the Book		261

Tables and Figures

Tables

1.1 Bundesbank and Government Monetary Objectives: Domestic, European, and International   10

1.2 Final Bargaining Strategy of the Government   27

4.1 Chronology of German Economic and Monetary Union (GEMU), November 1989–July 1990   113

Figure

1.1 The Triangulation of Deutsche Mark Politics   8

Preface

Lenin was certainly right. There is no subtler, no surer means of overturning the existing basis of society than to debauch the currency.

—John Maynard Keynes,
Essays in Persuasion

The central banker's field of action is the ever changing stream of economic history, where every day may pose new problems requiring new solutions. He will use economic science as a commander of armies uses military science, namely as collected pieces of information and wisdom that, though often useful and sometimes indispensable, can never provide a recipe for victory. In fact, such a recipe would be a contradiction in terms, because opposing armies could use it, but only one can win. . . . In monetary policy, as on the battlefield, it is the unexpected that counts most. This treatise may thus end on a note of humility: however far monetary theory progresses, central banking is likely to remain an art.

—Jörg Niehans,
A Theory of Money

What justifies state intervention in monetary matters? If one believes Keynes, there appears to be some justification for the state to intervene in monetary affairs. The state is responsible for securing the stability of the currency, and thereby securing the overall stability of society. However, on further reading of Keynes, one finds that he appears to give some justification for minimizing the role of the state in monetary affairs. When the state becomes too involved or plays an overtly political role in monetary decisions, the value and stability of a nation's currency, and its societal foundations, may suffer. One need only examine the impact on German society of the hyperinflationary period during the Weimar Republic to understand this point. Yet, leaving a nation's currency to find its value in the global financial markets may not be a desirable option for some states.

From Indonesia to Mexico, allowing currency to float in the markets has produced dramatic social upheaval.

To draw a fine balance between these two interpretations, states created central banks that would supervise, regulate, and protect the value of a nation's money. However, central banks have never been immune to political pressures—whether domestic or international—and their powers, both theoretical and institutional, are not insurmountable. Indeed, monetary policy remains more an art than a science and more an instrument of state power than a neutral, apolitical, determination of central bankers. Undeniably, there exists a politics of monetary policy that necessitates a political examination of governmental authority, power, and interest centering on monetary policy. At bottom, most economic and monetary issues are political issues.

For political scientists to understand the complexities of political decisions such as those surrounding the processes of European monetary integration, or the deeply political negotiations surrounding the Group of Seven (G7) finance minister meetings, we must study the institutions, actors, and interests that influence monetary policy. Interest rates, exchange rates, and money supply targets, however technical, all have serious impacts on elections, politicians, interest groups, and the processes of international cooperation, among many other things. It was this awareness that attracted me to examine German monetary policy. Having witnessed the monumental monetary reform in Germany during the summer of 1990, there appeared to be tremendous opportunities to explore this challenging and engaging topic. Understanding deutsche mark (DM) politics—the politics of German monetary policy—became the central objective of this study.

The decision to examine deutsche mark politics returned me to some personal roots as well. My father owned a small assembly plant that imported goods and parts from a moderate-sized German electronics and lighting firm during the 1970s and early 1980s. I worked closely with him during my high school and early college years, gaining an appreciation for running an internationally minded business. In particular, I was fascinated that we could gain or lose a large amount of money based on the current value of the U.S. dollar to the DM. The cost of items that we would import from Germany fluctuated wildly during this period (the era of benign neglect, double-digit inflation rates, interest rates at or around 20 percent, Paul Volcker, and so on). I scanned the currency quotations in the newspapers daily to gain some further understanding, often in vain, of the phenomenon. Not only would the currency fluctuations affect our planning and our competitiveness here in the United States, but we would also play the currency odds, hoping to land a more favorable exchange rate, perhaps waiting an extra week to pay our German account. I never knew then what forces were exerting pressure on the DM. *Deutsche Mark Politics* is my attempt to develop a comprehensive account of such forces.

Nowhere is the politics of monetary policy more pronounced than in Germany. The DM has become a powerful symbol for the German nation; Germans are proud of their economic wealth and economic and political stability, and it is the DM that is the source and focus of this respect. The DM has also gained the admiration of other nations, though at the same time Germany's political and economic partners often negatively perceive Germany's ability to translate political power demands into more respectable avenues of economic discourse and monetary diplomacy. This ambivalence poses unique difficulties for Germany's monetary authorities, and understanding how Germany attempts to resolve them is one important part of the story that is deutsche mark politics.

Given these themes, the overarching question guiding this study is, Why was Germany prepared to sacrifice the DM for European Monetary Union (EMU)? Seeking an answer, I propose that what is needed is an analysis both of the institutional relationship between the Bundesbank and the federal government and of Germany's bargaining strategies toward European and global monetary governance structures. Thus, *Deutsche Mark Politics* examines the powerful integrating forces of the interdependent international political economy on the one hand, and the almost heroic attempt by political-economic actors within Germany to retain some measure of domestic sovereignty and autonomy on the other. Although the book does at times focus on the minutiae of monetary and exchange rate policy, deutsche mark politics is translated for the most part into the language of foreign policy and monetary diplomacy.

The organization of the book reflects both practical and theoretical purposes. The first two chapters set forth the analytical and theoretical foundations for the empirical analysis to follow. Chapter 1 develops a basic model of deutsche mark politics and a theoretical model of bargaining. Chapter 2 examines the relationship between the Bundesbank and the federal government in the constant tug-of-war over the direction of and influence over deutsche mark politics; special attention is given to the concept of central bank independence and its relationship to monetary policy credibility.

The next five chapters proceed chronologically, addressing the substantive issues of deutsche mark politics. Chapter 3 examines the level of interest rate and exchange rate coordination and intervention pursued by the Germans with the Europeans and by the G7 with the United States between 1985 and 1987. Chapter 4 examines the period 1989–1991, an extremely active stage of German monetary policy best characterized as the export of the DM to Europe (as codified in the Maastricht Treaty of December 1991) and the protection of the DM from the benign dollar neglect of the U.S. administration. Chapter 5 demonstrates the limitations to policy accommodation and cooperation illustrated by the dramatic turmoil within the EMS during 1992 and 1993 and the divergent G7 views on addressing a global recession.

Chapter 6 analyzes the period 1994–1995, notable for the dissolution of G7 consensus and monetary coordination and for the dramatic U.S. dollar volatility brought on by the Mexican peso crisis and renewed dollar neglect; on the European front, the future of EMU remained on unstable footing. Chapter 7 covers 1996–1998, illuminating the critical variables of negotiation heading toward the final stages of EMU, as well as possible changes in G7 summitry. As the DM proceeded toward its fiftieth anniversary in 1998, the Bundesbank undertook one "last stand" against a gold revaluation scheme proposed by the government.

Finally, in Chapter 8, which summarizes and evaluates the primary theoretical and analytical arguments set forth in the book, I also evaluate the lessons of deutsche mark politics for international and European monetary governance.

Because the cases studied here were not chosen randomly, and because they are so atypical of normal monetary policy and monetary diplomacy, some researchers may contend that the arguments and predictions I put forth are not at all plausible or generalizable to other cases or countries. In response, I argue that case studies and a chronological approach, demonstrating the larger political, economic, and historical forces at work in the arena of deutsche mark politics, offer the detail and richness that pure econometric modeling cannot provide.

It will always be a problem in analyses such as these that the conclusions one draws from the lessons of the past may turn out to be irrelevant to today's world or tomorrow's. Given this concern, the time frame for my analysis (1985–1998) was chosen to cover periods before, during, and after reunification so as to more fully illustrate the changing conceptions, pressures, and interests of deutsche mark politics and whether these changes have had any significant impact on policy. This time frame also highlights, as I argue, the final breakdown of the post–Bretton Woods consensus on exchange rate management and the emergence of the German monetary norm of international monetary cooperation. More significant, the time period captures the Europeanization of German monetary policy. Upset with the continued international monetary instability generated by the United States, the Germans focused on developing a coordinated "European" response to influence international monetary governance. This response would manifest itself in the drive toward EMU and the ultimate decision to sacrifice the DM.

In the course of reconstructing the constellation of factors surrounding each case study and especially in evaluating the relationship between the Bundesbank and government and the emphasis they each place on domestic, regional, and international monetary policy, I interviewed more than forty of those elite state actors most involved in the kinds of monetary negotiation, bargaining, and decisionmaking investigated here. The interviews were conducted in an unstructured format in both English and German. Anonymity was given to those interviewed in order to encourage discussion and frankness. Although reliability remains a problem with any anonymous interview, the intent was not to pinpoint specific positions or catch an official slip-up, but rather to elicit open reflections on the role of the Bundesbank and the government in international monetary negotiations, the interaction of these two actors, and the interviewees' individual recollections and opinions of some significant monetary negotiations and issues. The official positions of the Bundesbank and government are readily available from other source material and published interviews in the press (see, for example, the excellent summaries in *Auszüge aus Presseartikeln,* published by the Bundesbank, or visit their Web site at www.bundesbank.de).

* * *

Among the faculty in the Department of Political Science at the University of California, Santa Barbara, I would like especially to acknowledge the support, guidance, and criticism of the late Wolfram Hanrieder—"Doktor Vater," critic, teacher, and friend. His influence on my intellectual and professional development is greater than perhaps he ever realized. His approach to the study of international relations will be sorely missed in the discipline. I thank Benjamin J. Cohen, whose commitment to detail and style enhanced not only my knowledge of monetary affairs but also my writing style, for his extraordinary time and effort in bringing this study to fruition. I am grateful to Peter Merkl for his guidance on all things relating to German politics, as well as his help in securing funding for my various research trips to Germany. I would also like to express appreciation for the encouragement and guidance of John T. Woolley and Stephen Weatherford during earlier stages of this manuscript. As for the editors at Lynne Rienner, especially Bridget Julian, their support and help in finalizing this project, were invaluable.

There are several universities, programs, and institutions that also deserve special acknowledgment. I greatly appreciate the generous institutional and staff support of the University of California, Santa Barbara, and West Chester University. I am particularly indebted to the Center for German and European Studies at the University of California, Berkeley, and the Institute on Global Conflict and Cooperation at the University of California, San Diego; without their support I could not have spent a year of study in Germany. I would also like to acknowledge Helga Haftendorn at the Free University of Berlin for welcoming me into her research seminars; Hans-Eckart Scharrer at the Hamburger Welt und Wirtschaft Archiv for taking the time to discuss my project in its initial stages; and the staff of the German Academic Exchange Service (DAAD) for their fellowship during a crucial period in the development of the project. Particular mention and thanks go to the employees and officials of the Bundesbank, all of whom made me feel welcome and maintained an open door and open mind during our discussions. The concrete facade on the outside masks the character of this truly unique institution.

Finally, this book is dedicated to my parents, William and Ingeborg, for their unceasing support; to my family in Germany, who repeatedly opened their doors for my visits; to my wife, Belinda, for her patience; and to my children, Christian and Katarina, for their motivation.

1

The Political Economy of Deutsche Mark Politics

Fundamentally, the Bundesbank can only use the instruments of monetary policy in an overall way, with a view to doing justice to the needs of the economy as a whole. A differentiation between individual groups of the economy is a matter for general political decisions and belongs to the tasks of the government and parliament. The Bundesbank would exceed its sphere of responsibility were it to take part in this political activity.

—Helmut Schlesinger, former Bundesbank president, quoted in *Monetary Policy and Economic Developments in West Germany*

Part 1: A Political History of Deutsche Mark Politics

During the carnival celebrations in 1992, one of the floats that passed by the onlookers provided a biting commentary to the recently completed negotiations on European Monetary Union (EMU). The float consisted of a large milk cow labeled "EG" feasting on a basket of German deutsche marks (DMs).[1] The audience could only speculate as to what the cow might manufacture from these DMs—namely, worthless European currency units (ECUs).[2] The people watching the parade laughed apprehensively. The Maastricht Treaty's stipulations that Germans might have to relinquish their treasured DM to the management of a potentially inflationary-prone European Central Bank (ECB) caused some uneasiness that day, as it still does today, among the German public. With the ECU, or euro, coming into circulation, Germans can no longer poke fun at the image of a feasting cow, for they are now an intricate part of it. The DM, as a symbol of the nation, would soon cease to exist.

Similar monetary images have often framed the political debate in Germany. The image of thousands of East Germans streaming across the border shortly after the Berlin Wall was pulled down in November 1989 and seeking their DM 100 visitation money revealed the inherent dangers to some German politicians, especially Chancellor Helmut Kohl, that a gradualist approach to reunification might hold. Shortly thereafter, tens of thousands of East Germans lined up at midnight on July 1, 1990, in front of hastily erected Deutsche Bank branches waiting impatiently for newly printed DMs. German Economic and Monetary Union (GEMU) undoubtedly generated inflationary nightmares for the Bundesbank and left budget gaps for the finance ministry. More recently, Chancellor Kohl's attempt to revalue gold reserves in order to achieve budgetary targets aimed at EMU also struck a forceful resistant chord among the German public, to say nothing of the Bundesbank. Under a wither of criticism and domestic political backlash, the Kohl government had to back down.

As these examples illustrate, Germany's engrossment with the DM (some would contend an obsession) is linked directly to Germany's foreign policy. Monetary policy is foreign policy to the Germans. The DM has become an instrument of wielding Germany's influence in European and global affairs, as the strength of the DM has become synonymous with the strength of the German state. For example, following the Black Wednesday European currency crisis of September 1992, some German newspapers proudly carried banner headlines such as "Starke Mark: Was jetzt alles billiger wird," translated roughly as "The Strong mark: Everything That Is Now Cheaper." Others commentated on the desirability of the Italian and British exit from the European Monetary System (EMS). Although perhaps not representative of elite German opinion, these instances struck a powerful chord with the general public's long-held concerns, fears, hopes, and pride, all centered on the revered DM. The DM had become a symbol of pride for the German people, both at home and abroad.

This characterization of the DM illustrates what I label deutsche mark politics; the role that money plays in society, the value of the currency, as well as the government's external monetary diplomacy, are all highly political and volatile issues in Germany. As part of the German national subconscious, monetary policy retains a prominent and consequential role in the political economy of Germany.[3] In fact, the writing of German history can be punctuated by monetary affairs. The social and political consequences, to say nothing of the financial and economic ruin, of the hyperinflationary period in 1923, for example, led to the undermining of the Weimar government's credibility and legitimacy, exacerbating the attacks of extremist movements on the left and right.[4] Following World War II, the historic currency reform of June 20, 1948, launched the German Wirtschaftswunder (Economic Miracle) that helped lay the foundations for the globally admired economic and political ascent of the Federal Republic of Germany (FRG) and its internal social stability and economic dynamism.

GEMU would also mark a new era in German politics, as will EMU when the euro replaces the DM in the year 2002.

These highly visible periods in German political and economic history illustrate the political nature of monetary policy and its importance as a fundamental socioeconomic and political foundation or pillar of the FRG. In fact, as these examples show, the stability and, in extreme cases, the very existence of the democratic order itself may depend on politically sensitive monetary decisions.[5] Hans Herbert von Arnim sets forth a theory of democracy that posits the primary importance of central bank independence to the stability and democratic order of the German political system. In other words, the Bundesbank has become the guarantor of German democracy by acting as a guide and protecting the German government from an irresponsible policy that could destabilize the democratic order. Arguably, then, monetary stability and social stability are one and the same. It is the confidence of the people in the large German middle class (to say nothing of the upper class) in the money they have earned after years of hard work that provides the building blocks of German democracy. German monetary policy should, therefore, be examined for the political and social character it represents rather than in strictly economic terms. This study thus incorporates both political and economic factors that shape deutsche mark politics.

To examine deutsche mark politics is to examine the quasi-independent Bundesbank, which commands a towering and lofty position within the political economy of Germany. For many Germans from all socioeconomic strata, the Bundesbank guarantees the soundness, stability, and foundations not only of the currency but also of the democratic and stable political order. Without a sound and stable DM, society could easily be buffeted by undemocratic forces bent on subverting the established political-economic order of which the Germans are so proud. The Germans learned their bitter lesson about defacing and devaluing a nation's currency and entrusted to the Bundesbank the task of defending the stability of the currency.

However, there are many Germans who strongly believe that a proper arranging of society and the political economic order also require an accountable, democratic, pluralistic, and representative federal republic—the concept of the *Rechtsstaat*. Political power and the decisions exercised by government authorities, including those decisions surrounding a nation's monetary policies, come from the consent of the people. This consent is granted through free, competitive, and democratic elections. In addition, the government must obtain the ongoing consent and legitimacy from the people and must be responsive to the people's will as expressed by a majority of its citizens. Hence, politically and socially sensitive monetary questions, such as those surrounding GEMU in 1990 or the decision to proceed with EMU, are decided by the people's representatives in the federal government. Only these sovereign elected officials, the chancellor and leaders in the finance and economics ministries, for example, can ultimately resolve the conflicting requirements and clashing demands that would surround such momentous monetary decisions. Those who would like to see the independence of central banks diminished can accurately point out how inflation is not merely a simple technical issue but a deeply political one. One can further argue that it is wrong that the unelected can overturn the desire of elected officials, as with Chancellor Helmut Kohl's desire to see European unity as a German overriding foreign policy goal undercut by Bundesbank policy. Finally, an independent central bank does not, in and of itself, guarantee price stability. In politics, nothing is guaranteed. Examining the role of the Bundesbank's relationship to the government is the first step in developing an analytical framework for understanding deutsche mark politics.

Not only does there exist a national struggle for monetary control between the Bundesbank and the government over the direction of Germany's monetary policy, but there also exists the pressures, demands, and forces that are foisted upon national actors by the international political economy. A well-functioning international monetary system is the crucial nexus of the international economy. Moreover, the international monetary system, with the norms, rules, and conventions that govern it, have important distributive effects upon the power of nations and on the welfare of groups within those states. As a result, the international monetary system cannot be a neutral mechanism, for every nation will seek to influence the system to meet its own objectives of national policy. And, as I argue, these objectives of national policy may at times differ between the two primary German monetary actors in the international monetary system: the Bundesbank and the federal government. Each actor tries to carve out its own policies that will accommodate its primary goals, objectives, or interests. These interests may converge, but they may also diverge.

Central to this international process is the issue of system governance. Governing the international or European monetary system entails four primary tasks: enforcement, provision of a system of arbitration, regulation and supervision, and macroeconomic stabilization. We take these tasks for granted at the domestic level, but we cannot take these for granted at the international level. Nonetheless, a system of governance within both the international and European monetary system has emerged in the form of monetary regimes. Whether within the more formally institutionalized forum and rules of the Bretton Woods fixed exchange rate system from 1944 to 1973, within the EMS since 1979, or within the more pluralistic and less supranational forum of the floating exchange rate system governed by the Group of 7 (G7) along with the International Monetary Fund

(IMF) (1975 to the present), these regimes have reduced monetary conflict, uncertainty, and have added a measure of stability and predictability to the system. To some degree, they have even facilitated cooperation among member nations. Such governance mechanisms, of course, are not without controversy, but they do provide the focus for external exchange rate management among the leading industrial nations.

Germany's influence over the process of international monetary governance and monetary cooperation is significant. One of this book's primary objectives is to trace Germany's influence, specifically the pattern of German-G7 monetary interaction and the German-EMS partnership within the framework of monetary governance. My preliminary proposition contends that German insistence upon strict anti-inflationary policies at home and minimal monetary and exchange rate coordination abroad has increasingly become the standard norm and guiding principle for international and regional monetary governance since the early 1980s. More important, German monetary authorities have carefully and skillfully nudged just such a standard onto the international and European monetary system. Indeed, the Germanization of the international and European monetary system has taken place.

This chapter proposes a model that places German state monetary authorities at the center of an analytical framework that underscores the tripartite (domestic, regional-European, and international-G7) dimension of German monetary policy. While emphasizing the importance of domestic political institutions and state actors in German monetary policy (the Bundesbank, the chancellor, and the finance ministry), this framework integrates the regional-European and international sources of influence upon German monetary policy within a theoretical model of negotiating. I argue that during the negotiating process, German monetary authorities will alter their bargaining strategies depending upon the regional-European or international level of the bargaining environment, resulting in differing configurations of cooperation and conflict. These varying strategies in negotiations with European and G7 counterparts depend on two critical factors: (1) the governance structures within which German monetary authorities bargain, specifically the particular formal institutional position and relationship of the Bundesbank to the federal government within European and G7 governance structures; and, (2) the dynamic political tension between the Bundesbank and government over the direction and control of German monetary policy.

A Model of Deutsche Mark Politics

We need to commence our investigation by identifying who or what is acting, making policy, and implementing German monetary policy—in other words, the strategic actors. A solid analytical and theoretical base must then be developed not only for understanding the domestic sources for examining monetary policy but also for investigating how the state balances internal-domestic demands with the pressures the state faces in the international policy arena.

With these caveats in mind, analyzing German monetary policy can best be achieved by an institutional-statist approach. This approach implies that our analysis will focus on the domestic-institutional structure of Germany's political economy and the central role that state actors—the Bundesbank and the federal government (chancellor's office and finance ministry[6])—perform in defining both the internal and external dimensions of German monetary policy. The Bundesbank and government are the "units of analysis," or decisionmaking state. The decisionmaking state is therefore defined as the central governmental actors (for example, Chancellor Helmut Kohl or former Bundesbank president Karl Otto Pöhl) and the institutions (the Bundesbank and government) in which they reside.[7] This definition of the state and its strategic actors allows analysis of who is actually negotiating on behalf of the state and crossing the contested boundary between state and society. Negotiating the proper path between the Scylla of the international monetary system and the Charybdis of the domestic political-economic system remains the overriding goal of the Bundesbank and government.

The focus on the decisionmaking state has theoretical implications as well. Scholars have argued persuasively that large theoretical gains can be made in understanding efforts at international cooperation, or the lack thereof, through the use of domestic-level theories of state behavior.[8] In contrast, I argue that system-level explanations of monetary policy fail to adequately capture the intricacy of state bargaining, where the bargainers and the ratifiers (the Bundesbank and government) to a particular international agreement interact and compete with one another, as is the case in Germany.[9] Each strategic actor, the Bundesbank and the government, often has differing objectives and alternative strategies of achieving those objectives. Such a complex process of policymaking certainly muddles the process of defining any straightforward conception of the national interest. In addition, approaches to international relations emphasizing structural realism are also unable to rigorously conceptualize the interactions among institutional actors such as the Bundesbank and government.[10] Structural realism fails to explain differing bargaining strategies and policies between nation-states, for example Germany and Great Britain, comparably located within the "structure" of economic power. In short, system-level studies do not satisfactorily account for decisions made within monetary policy where domestic interests and institutions play such a decisive role in determining the final outcome of any policy decision. In analyzing German monetary policy, the scholar first *must* discuss the Bundesbank-government political interaction in order to capture the meaning of deutsche mark politics. Reductionism is analytically necessary to the process of theory building and, as I shall argue, to understanding the processes surrounding international monetary cooperation.

Ultimately, the differing interpretations and perceptions as to the proper path of German monetary policy can pose significant policy dilemmas for German monetary authorities in the Bundesbank and government, the final arbiters of German monetary policy. German monetary authorities must find a position of equilibrium between domestic and international interests and/or economic and political pressures. They will, however, have a difficult time finding the right balance. German monetary authorities are not driven exclusively by domestic factors nor do they act solely in response to international actors and influences. They struggle with each other and with the powerful forces in the international political economy. In short, only by developing theoretical propositions and hypotheses of the negotiating and bargaining behavior of the Bundesbank and government in the European-regional and international monetary arenas can we build a truly comprehensive model of German monetary policy. This model can pinpoint specific instances that reflect the political compromises characteristic of deutsche mark politics. Such an approach also opens up the potentialities of theories of negotiation where "everybody's strategy depends on everybody else's," where "any belief in the autonomy of national foreign policy" can only spell disaster for policymakers.[11]

The Triangulation of Deutsche Mark Politics

The development and management of German monetary policy and the complex efforts of the Bundesbank and government to achieve internal and external political and monetary equilibrium can best be conceptualized and analyzed within a framework identifying a triangular,[12] or tripartite, relationship, a relationship that Hugo Kaufmann has termed the most interesting interaction of the international monetary system.[13] The use of the tripartite framework for this purpose is not new.[14] The triple dimension of German monetary policies and its interaction between internal and external preferences and interests is implicit, if not explicit, in most works addressing this issue area. In contrast to previous accounts, however, which tend to lack much formal conceptualization, the present study will be both systematic and rigorous, building on existing theory to develop a formal model of bargaining in the German context.

Kaufmann cites as the most important problem area in international monetary relations the "triangular interaction between the Deutsche Mark, the United States dollar, and the functioning of the European Monetary

System."[15] Symbiotic interactions of these three points on the policy axis of German monetary policy (Figure 1.1) indicate the potentially complex policy arena within which the German decisionmaking state must act.

As Figure 1.1 suggests, at the center of both my analysis and this triangulation are German monetary institutions—the Bundesbank and government. The basic monetary objectives of these monetary authorities must be balanced, however, with the monetary concerns of Germany's special European policies, especially continuing integration of the European Union (EU) and the functioning of the EMS. These domestic and European objectives must also be balanced with Germany's key role within the larger global monetary arena, especially G7 summitry and G7 attempts to govern the international monetary system.[16] It is interesting to note that when confronted with the concept of the tripartite framework, Bundesbank officials first claimed not to differentiate between European and international monetary influences. For them, external stability and imported inflation were one and the same, whether they came from Europe or the G7. However, when pressed and given an example of the entangled web of Germany's exchange rate policy, nearly every official commented that the tripartite framework did indeed reflect Germany's external monetary interactions. As one Bundesbank official reluctantly concluded, "Although it [the triangulation of German monetary policy] may not be explicit in our

Figure 1.1 The Triangulation of Deutsche Mark Politics

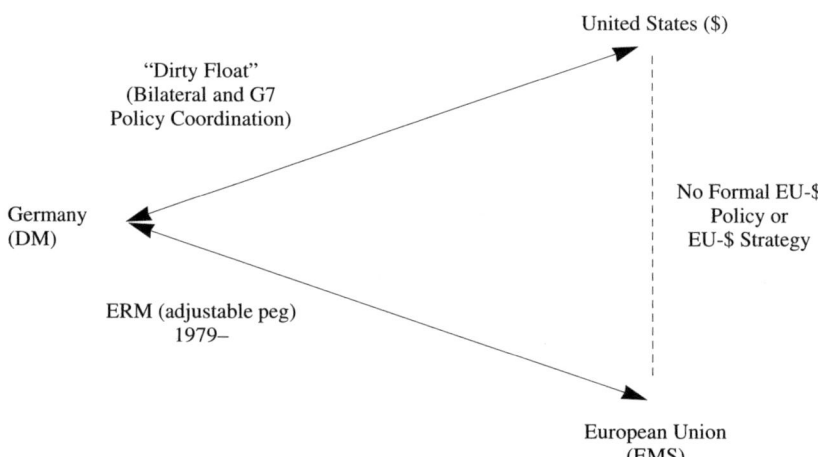

Source: Pierre-Henri Laurent and Marc Maresceau, eds., *The State of the European Union: Volume 4, Deepening and Widening.* Copyright © 1998 by Lynne Rienner Publishers, Inc. Used by permission of the publisher.

discussions, it certainly was implicit in how we responded to particular events."[17]

This triangular relationship of deutsche mark politics, then, leads one to ask some rather basic questions. What role does the DM play between the dollar and the EMS? What are the consequences of Germany's central role in this relationship to questions of monetary governance in Europe and the international monetary order? Finally, do the Bundesbank and government respond differently to pressures emanating from the EMS and the G7? The answers to these questions provide the insights into how tensions at home (within Germany), within the EU, and within the international monetary system are interrelated and how the triangulation of interests influences monetary policy within Germany and abroad.

The central link in this triangulation is the DM. The DM is the pivotal element between the U.S. dollar and other EMS currencies. As a result, from the perspective of European currencies, the G7 often becomes a forum for German-U.S. monetary interaction. The DM thus can play a crucial role as the transmission agent of dollar volatility and instability into the EMS. If, for example, the United States and the dollar were to exert strong pressure on Germany's monetary authorities to tighten their domestic monetary policy, such a policy decision would be quickly transmitted throughout the EMS as other EMS members adjust their policy to keep their currency pegged to the DM. Because of this role, Germany must consider how its own domestic monetary policy and its DM-dollar policy may impact its European partners. As another example, when the U.S. Federal Reserve focuses on the relationship between the dollar and the DM in its exchange rate and/or interest rate policy, European central bankers have to decide whether and how they intend to react to this policy. They cannot rely simply on the Bundesbank to pursue a policy course that is congruent with European interests. Their disparity in response can provide fertile soil for disagreement between the Bundesbank and the Federal Reserve, on the one hand, and the Bundesbank and EMS partner central banks, on the other.

A second important aspect to this tripartite arrangement is that there has never been a formal EMS-dollar exchange rate policy, either from the U.S. or German perspective.[18] Any reference to such a policy has usually pertained to the desirability of a DM-dollar policy. A joint European dollar float would be possible, however, only as long as the EMS partners accept, in the absence of a single EMS currency, one member currency that would function as the key currency. Under the operation of the EMS from 1979 through 1998, this scenario was impossible as long as member states, (in particular France), demanded formal symmetry within the system—despite the de facto hegemonic role of the DM—and maintained opposing domestic and external goals. Moreover, although the DM acts very much like a key currency in the EMS, Germany has often conducted its own DM-dollar exchange rate policy in order to defend its own currency. Finally, differing preferences on appreciation and depreciation among each European state and an unequal distribution of currency diversification (as short-term capital often moves first into Germany and not into other countries of the EU) complicate matters further.[19] In short, the triangulation of German monetary policy places immense demands, pressures, and responsibilities upon the Bundesbank and government.

German Monetary Objectives: Domestic, European, and International

Given the triangulation of German monetary policy, what then are the basic objectives of the Bundesbank and government in the domestic, regional-European, and international monetary arenas? Table 1.1 provides a summary of the basic monetary objectives of the Bundesbank and government.[20] Whereas Chapter 2 provides a highly detailed account of the Bundesbank-government interaction, a brief elaboration is needed here to understand the role of each strategic actor in the tripartite framework and bargaining games of German monetary policy.

First, for the Bundesbank, monetary policy is driven by the overriding imperative of maintaining price stability. The Bundesbank pursues traditional monetary objectives such as controlling the money supply, specifically M3,[21] which the Bundesbank identifies as a critical medium-term monetary target. The Bundesbank uses customary instruments such as controlling interest rates (Lombard and discount rate) and the repurchasing

Table 1.1 Bundesbank and Government Monetary Objectives: Domestic, European, and International

	Bundesbank	Government
Domestic	Price stability—as defined in Bundesbank Law	Monetary policy in support of price stability, full employment, and economic growth
European, EMS	Zone of monetary stability Export price stability through credible domestic monetary policy	Zone of monetary stability Export price stability and exchange rate stability through credible macroeconomic policy Monetary policy to promote European integration
International, G7	Export price stability through credible domestic monetary policy Limit G7 (and U.S.) pressure on exchange rate policy	Export price stability Limit G7 (and U.S.) pressure on exchange rate policy Play an integral role in global G7 governance

rate (or repo rate). The bank's vast research office and staff analyze data from all sectors of the economy and interpret such data within the framework of maintaining price stability, usually within a target annual inflation rate of 2 percent.[22] The Bundesbank also evaluates external forces such as currency flows, potential price shocks, and European or international monetary events. A narrow economic range of objectives dictated by legal mandate (the Bundesbank Gesetz, or Bundesbank Law[BBG]) to preserve price stability drives the Bundesbank's monetary calculus. The Bundesbank is not unaware of political constraints, but, as Schlesinger noted in the introductory quote, it seeks to avoid political complications in the pursuit of domestic price stability.

As for the government, monetary policy fits within larger macroeconomic objectives, such as full employment, sustained economic growth, and price stability. The government can claim that the Bundesbank's legal mandates are construed in such a way as to support the larger macroeconomic policy of the government, albeit without threatening price stability. Although not decisive in any policy determination, the government also remains sensitive to interests expressed through powerful labor and business associations (especially the large export-oriented corporations) as well as specialized associations with a strong interest in monetary policy, such as various financial, banking, and savings associations. More recently, the federal government may be becoming more responsive to public opinion, although such public pressure is not decisive in any final policy decision. More important, the federal government, specifically the finance ministry, is formally responsible for Germany's external monetary negotiations and policy. The Bundesbank has a large say in such negotiations, yet it is the government that will undertake the final agreement. As the Bundesbank often states, such agreements ultimately are political and not within the realm of Bundesbank responsibilities.

Given these domestic objectives, it should be noted that the *market* constrains the autonomous actions of the Bundesbank and government. In fact, this study could be considered an account of the process whereby German monetary authorities seek to retain as much domestic autonomy as they can in the face of unrelenting global market forces.[23] Many German politicians and central bankers, among them former chancellor Helmut Schmidt and former Bundesbank president Karl Otto Pöhl, counsel against massive, consistent intervention in foreign exchange markets because of its ineffectiveness in countering financial speculation.[24] Not only can these market forces significantly hinder autonomous action by politicians and central bankers, but intervention to counter market forces may even reduce the prestige and credibility of central banks that try it. What is more, the disruptive consequences of seemingly uncontrollable market forces on politicians and central bankers may alter their strategy toward long-stated goals such as EMU. The German decisionmaking state may retain a strong measure of domestic policy autonomy, but internationally driven market forces often impinge on the state's freedom to pursue domestic or foreign policy objectives.

To counter the market's potential for generating volatility, both the government's and Bundesbank's primary interest in the EU and its relatively strong support of the EMS has been to create an integrated regional "zone of monetary stability" in Europe. Efforts to form a truly integrated monetary system have been in the works for three decades, beginning with the publication of the Werner Report in 1969, and sped up by the breakdown of the Bretton Woods system in 1971–1973. Since the EMS's founding in 1979, the Germans have felt that they could use the EMS and the institutionalized arena of the EU as important political resources to ward off the direct monetary pressures of the United States.[25] Bundesbank officials never believed that the EMS would completely eliminate conflicts between German national autonomy and European cooperation nor the internal-external dilemma that existed under Bretton Woods. However, they did feel that a strong EMS, centered on the stabilizing influence of the DM, would promote European economic growth, political stability, and greater integration. Overall, and with a few notable exceptions, the EMS has been remarkably successful in providing a regional zone of monetary stability. With the DM at the center of this zone, many German monetary authorities consider exporting the stability of the DM to be a crucial factor in achieving Germany's European objectives.

Given the DM's preeminent position within the EMS and the anchor function it performs in stabilizing the system, Germany has not faced the same external pressure for adjustment that other EMS currencies have faced. In other words, the EMS is not symmetrical in its operation. This does not mean that Bundesbank officials have reacted without concern about possible transgressions upon the bank's autonomous decisionmaking, whether from the EMS's outset, through the Basel-Nyborg agreement of 1987, or more recently through the provisions of Maastricht. For example, former Bundesbank president Otmar Emminger secured a clause from Chancellor Schmidt in 1978 that the Bundesbank could opt out of EMS responsibilities.[26] The most worrisome responsibility from the perspective of the Bundesbank was an unconditional commitment to unlimited lending. For many years, this option—not to intervene if the bank believed it was unable to do so—was less than appreciated. Through the early years of the EMS, capital controls and realignments obviated the need for unlimited intervention. With the elimination of capital controls throughout Europe by the early 1990s and with the strong political commitment to EMU, the situation had become more complicated for the Bundesbank. As the EU's integrative financial and institutional net grew, the maneuverability of German monetary authorities inevitably narrowed.

It should not be forgotten, however, that German monetary authorities go to great lengths to assuage their European partners' fears about possible DM-dollar policies or the domestic-oriented German monetary policy priority of price stability. The Germans must account for their monetary actions on the European platform that, in turn, force them to consider special EMS policies in their strategic monetary calculations. Because Germany is a member of the EMS—in fact, the most important member—certain obligations are demanded of the Germans to make commitments to their fellow Europeans that might not normally exist in a Europe without the EMS. For example, the Bundesbank tolerated monetary growth levels in 1986 that exceeded its money supply target corridors, pointing to the complex triangular pressures it faced. The Bundesbank stated that "the powerful revaluation of the D-mark particularly against the US dollar—at times covered by D-mark interventions—and the tendency towards weakness of the currencies of some important partners in the EMS restricted the Bundesbank's room for maneuver."[27] In other words, as the French franc came under selling pressure and reached the lower intervention point in the EMS margins (while the DM reached the upper intervention point as a result of an appreciation against the dollar), the Bundesbank found itself heavily supporting the franc. Such interventions, even when "sterilized," cause disruptions in the ability of the Bundesbank to attain its domestic monetary targets.[28]

Importantly, though, at another level, this obligation to the EMS (especially the Franco-German partnership) depends on long-stated commitments to Western European integration and solidarity as part of Germany's foreign policy goal of becoming a responsible member of the European community of nations. These commitments and the role that Germans wish to play rest on Germany's credibility and reputation as a cooperative member of the EU and remain a pillar of Germany's foreign policy. For Chancellor Kohl, monetary union and political union are but two sides of the same European policy, whereby monetary union is used as a lever to force open the process of European political integration. This is an important source of differentiation in the political and monetary objectives of the federal government and the Bundesbank toward Europe. For many officials in the Bundesbank, the EMS operated effectively as it was structured. The crux of the disagreement in Europe between the Bundesbank and the government lies within the debate over whether some monetary autonomy should be sacrificed for political objectives like EU, to say nothing of exchange rate stability.

Within the international monetary system, both the German government and the Bundesbank share the overriding objectives of promoting global monetary stability; both actors seek to prevent currency instability. German monetary authorities must still contend with the possibility of imported inflation because of exaggerated exchange rate fluctuations (both an undervalued and overvalued DM) caused by fluctuations and volatility in the dollar that distort the Bundesbank's medium-term monetary growth targets. Furthermore, the United States has consistently placed great demands on German monetary authorities to take on a greater share of the burden as a locomotive of the world or regional economy (the two are interrelated, of course). This factor was a key issue in Helmut Schmidt's battles with the Bundesbank in 1981–1982 as a result of the agreements reached at the 1978 G7 Bonn summit. It was also an issue during the financial crash of October 1987, when the Germans stubbornly refused to accede to U.S. secretary of the treasury James Baker's charges that German monetary policy was undermining world growth and contradicting Group of Five (G5) agreements on currency levels, to say nothing of the international agreement for coordination developed at the Louvre in 1987. The ongoing pressure from the Bush administration through the U.S. recessionary period from 1990 to 1991 for lower German interest rates or the U.S. administration's dollar neglect under Bill Clinton fit this time-worn pattern of interaction with the United States.

Although such pressures are indeed forceful, the Bundesbank and government have effectively resisted efforts to actively pursue any G7 cooperative program that would significantly impact Germany's domestic monetary objectives. With few exceptions, the Bundesbank and government agree that Germany's role in the international monetary system should be one of inflationary watchdog. Both actors consistently stress the need for each G7 country to get their respective "economic house in order." Roughly translated, price stability and fiscal rectitude at home should come first before any grandiose plans for G7 cooperation. The Bundesbank, which maintains a more central and direct role within G7 forums for negotiation, most effectively puts this approach forth. Finance ministry officials who see the Bundesbank as a powerful advocate for global monetary stability based on a limited role for G7 cooperation acknowledge this role. While government officials recognize the need for Germany to play an integral role in international monetary governance, they argue that this role should be limited to such measures that encourage domestic monetary stability. Only when domestic price stability has been accomplished can international efforts at cooperation prove effective.

In sum, understanding Germany's monetary objectives requires examining two central state institutional actors—the Bundesbank and the government. Both actors often work together in setting the parameters of German monetary policy, but they also often work at cross-purposes. Both are in many ways dependent upon one another, and both face the pressures brought about by market-driven constraints. Both are concerned about independent room for political maneuvering, but both face intense political and economic pressures for adjustment and cooperation from European and G7 partners. As each actor seeks to decide the proper course of German monetary policy both at home and abroad, they realize that they must negotiate with one another to achieve particular objectives for German monetary policy. They are not united on all issues nor are they entirely insulated from domestic or foreign politics. It is to the issue of international monetary cooperation—the focus of much tension between the Bundesbank and government—that this chapter now turns.

Defining International Cooperation:
Autonomy Versus Exchange Rate Stability

As we have seen, at both the regional and international level, Germany's dominant economic position, exposure, and influence provide an easy target for external criticism and pressure. The desire to prevent any measure of imported inflation through intervention obligations, resisting pressure from other countries to see Germany stimulate domestic demand (either through fiscal or monetary policy), or engaging in other forms of exchange rate stabilization measures focuses in on the central dilemma in the international monetary system: the trade-off between national monetary autonomy and exchange rate stability.[29] As stated succinctly by Benjamin Cohen,

> In an environment of formally or informally pegged rates and effective integration of financial markets, any attempt to pursue independent monetary objectives is almost certain, sooner or later, to result in significant balance of payments disequilibrium, and hence provoke potentially destabilizing flows of speculative capital.[30]

For example, if Germany wishes to stabilize its exchange rate relationships within the European policy arena, the government will be compelled to restrict the ability of the Bundesbank to pursue its own autonomous policy objectives. These relationships exist as well in the international arena. Moreover, if the Bundesbank should resist such restriction—a strong likelihood given the bank's powerfully independent position within the political economy of Germany—the objective of exchange rate stability might have to be put on hold or compromised altogether. With the option of capital controls all but eliminated as a viable policy choice, German monetary authorities must weigh the political and economic trade-offs between monetary autonomy and exchange rate stability. The choice facing the Bundesbank and government is quite plain: Choose monetary autonomy and risk exchange rate instability or choose exchange rate stability and sacrifice some measure of control over the value of the DM.

One can conceptualize the relationship between monetary autonomy and exchange rate stability in terms of a continuum representing the varying degrees of monetary policy cooperation.[31] At one extreme lies the alternative of full monetary integration and a common currency, an extreme realized in the articles of the Maastricht Treaty of 1991. At the other extreme lies the alternative of absolute monetary autonomy where governments and central banks sacrifice exchange rate stability for the benefits of securing domestic macroeconomic objectives. German monetary policy, of course, lies somewhere in between the extremes of stability and autonomy. As an example, following the collapse of Bretton Woods, German monetary authorities finally felt free to autonomously secure domestic policy objectives. Cooperation toward the United States or the G7 were not among their highest priorities. Nevertheless, the Germans were called upon at the Plaza accord of 1985 to engage in exchange rate stabilization measures. Yet with Germany's participation in the adjustable fixed exchange rate EMS, with its primary goal of securing exchange rate stability, the Bundesbank often found itself in a position where cooperation on monetary policy was required for the system to function. Although painful for the Bundesbank, cooperation in the form of policy adjustment and a sacrifice in monetary autonomy were often the end result of negotiations.

It should be made clear that both the government and the Bundesbank prefer monetary autonomy. However, in the political world of monetary policy, sacrifices are and have been made for the goal of exchange rate stability. While a case can be made against such cooperation,[32] the case for policy cooperation remains persuasive and appealing. Such a case remains strong even for the Bundesbank, which has consistently faced negative repercussions on German monetary policy that have resulted from each G7 nation's uncoordinated pursuit of self-interest. Without cooperation, the ability of the Bundesbank to reach its chosen targets on its own is restricted. Cooperation can provide the bank with an additional instrument, albeit one to be used in a limited fashion, for securing monetary stability at home. Moreover, the federal government has seen its role as an important voice for global monetary stability enhanced by Germany's willingness at times to act as a leader in questions of global monetary governance. The politics of global interdependence necessitate that German monetary authorities remain fully involved in the global integration of markets for goods, services, and capital.

My interest is in accounting for the differences in the approach of German monetary authorities toward cooperation within the G7 and within the EMS. Is there a systematic difference in the approach of the Bundesbank and government toward monetary cooperation in Europe as compared to the G7? If so, why do German monetary authorities pursue varying bargaining strategies toward their European and international monetary partners? Has there been a systematic bias toward Europe in German monetary policy when it comes to cooperation? If so, why? These are fundamental questions that have been inadequately addressed in earlier analyses of German monetary policy. Part 2 of this chapter confronts these questions.

Part 2: Governance Structures and Bargaining Strategies

This study argues that the relationship between the Bundesbank and government and the formal link of these two actors to monetary governance structures (the EMS and the G7) determine German bargaining strategies (measured in terms of the autonomy–exchange rate continuum). In other words, the bargaining strategy of the government depends on the struggle for power between the Bundesbank and government and how each actor functions within the context of monetary governance structures that exist at both the European and international level.

We can define governance structures using two criteria: rules and institutions. The central component of any governance structure is its institutional design and the basic rules, both formal and informal, that govern the behavior of those actors participating in the designated policy arena.[33] The rules and institutions of the governance structures provide key functions such as the ability to enforce agreements, to arbitrate disputes among member states, and the degree of ongoing regulation and supervision of member state behavior. Another way of stating the functions of governance structures is to determine the ability of such structures to reduce the transaction costs of bargaining, to lower the uncertainty of the bargaining context, and to provide powerful incentives for decisionmakers to abide by agreements. For the Bundesbank and government, governance structures in the European and international monetary arena—the rules and institutions within the EMS and the G7—define each actor's roles and responsibilities toward each other as well as toward the other participating members of the governance structure.

A governance structure that entails a rules-based approach requires a responsible government agency (for example, a central bank) to stay on a predetermined path of external policy targets. Rules provide the guideposts, for example, of the Bundesbank's and government's responsibilities toward either the EMS or the G7. To illustrate, a fixed exchange rate system with designated currency trading margins, where a central bank is required to intervene to support the fixed rate, is a firm rule. In this sense, external policy targets take precedence over domestic policy targets. Rules also demand certain obligations on the part of the actor(s) participating in the governance structure. Rules provide a measure of ongoing regulation over participant behavior. Rules also act to deter certain types of behavior. For example, under Bretton Woods, the rule pertaining to a "fundamental disequilibrium" prevented participating members from competitively devaluing their currencies before an IMF decision could be made. Complexity at the international level has made rule-based governance mechanisms more difficult to sustain. Nevertheless, the history of post–World War II international monetary affairs has been one of the attempts by nation-states to create rules governing exchange rate and monetary interactions.

As this discussion might suggest, institutions play a crucial role in interpreting or enforcing rules. International institutions are instruments of organized cooperation.[34] An important distinction regarding such cooperation needs to be made, however, before we can assess whether institutions have some impact or not. Ad hoc cooperation exists when nations get together, negotiate, and if they agree, act together. If they do not agree, each nation goes home to pursue its own domestic-oriented policies. Institutionalized cooperation picks up where ad hoc cooperation ends. It ensures that decisions and actions are taken at the institutional, or system-governance, level, even when nations decide to disagree. For example, during the negotiations to expand the margins of the EMS to ±15 percent after August 1993, Germany and France disagreed as to what exactly should be done. Neither side wanted to budge, but a final decision—to preserve the EMS—was taken at the institutional, or system, level, specifically the Council of Finance Ministers. To be effective, institutions require transfers of some power and decisionmaking from the national to the international level. Nations do not necessarily surrender control of monetary policy to the institution, but they exercise that control formally at the system-governance level.

Governance Structures in Europe and the G7

Central to any governance structure is its relationship to the domestic political institutions of a member state. The link between a governance structure and domestic political institutions provides the foundation for bargaining to occur. The attempt to link foreign and domestic policies has, of course, a long and distinguished history in theoretical studies of international relations.[35] This study provides an additional conceptualization and clarification of this link between foreign and domestic politics. The link focuses upon the formal and informal role of domestic political actors within a particular governance structure. Specifically, I am interested in examining the interaction of the Bundesbank and government within the rule- and institutional-based governance structures of the European and international monetary system.

First in Europe, and more specifically the EMS, agreements trigger arrangements of the Exchange Rate Mechanism (ERM), and the rule-oriented bargaining environment provides a highly structured governance environment within which the Bundesbank and government must negotiate.

Although the EMS cannot enforce agreements, it arbitrates disagreements among members and provides an ongoing powerful forum of regulation of state behavior. Central rate decisions have become collective decisions at the level of ECOFIN (the European Council of Finance Ministers), rather than multilateral ratification of unilateral decisions. The EMS provides firm rules and distributes decisionmaking powers between national and supranational levels. Moreover, community institutions are equipped to take decisions and introduce important policy innovations. State actors do retain a large measure of discretion to negotiate within such institutions. Nevertheless, for such actors, the EU reduces the transaction costs of bargaining and lowers uncertainty going into any round of negotiation. Moreover, the rules and obligations for participating members are spelled out clearly before any round of negotiation. Each negotiator may not know exactly what the other side may want, yet they do know that common rules obligate members to participate in defined roles. Whereas the institutions and rules of the EMS or EU cannot prevent any one member from cheating or reneging on an agreement, by creating a common framework within which negotiations will take place, the rules and institutions do reduce the incentive of one actor to take advantage of the other. All actors will be held accountable at the system-level bargaining table.

Specifically, under the formal rules of the ERM, the Bundesbank has an unlimited obligation to intervene in the foreign exchange markets when the DM reaches the maximum permitted divergence from the central rate against the other currencies participating in the system. For most of the life of the EMS, the maximum divergence was ± 2.25 percent against most other currencies, with some exceptions. When intervening within the EMS framework, and assuming that the DM is in the strong position (the DM has never been devalued within the EMS), the Bundesbank can extend short-term credits to the central bank of the weak currency to sell on the open market. Under some circumstances as outlined under the Basel-Nyborg agreement of September 1987, the Bundesbank must lend DMs to its EMS partners even when their currencies have not yet reached the margins. Both measures, direct intervention and credit extension, affect the German money supply. Although the Bundesbank has extracted an "opt-out" arrangement should its obligations threaten domestic monetary stability, the ultimate decision as to whether an increase in the German money supply would threaten price stability lies with the German government.

Informally, the EMS has emerged as a deutsche mark zone as the Bundesbank's monetary policy has governed the operation of the ERM. Monetary policies of the other EMS members have converged toward the German monetary standard, rather than the European average as designed for the ECU. During the 1980s most European economies positioned their economies to accept the DM as the "nominal anchor" of the system. After

1983, with France making its commitment to the DM an explicit part of its foreign policy—the so-called *franc fort*—other countries soon followed in committing their currencies to existing ERM parities around the DM. In short, the informal rules of the EMS are as important as the formal rules. The central banks of the EMS manage the system primarily through the coordination of domestic monetary policies, a process that the Bundesbank dominates. Nevertheless, the responsibility of the DM as the informal anchor of the EMS places pressure on the Bundesbank and government to conduct domestic monetary policy, especially interest rates, with an eye toward European exchange rate stability. Moreover, the government remains sensitive to any claims that German monetary policy overtly dominates European macroeconomic policy.

Institutionally, political responsibility for the management of the EMS resides in ECOFIN, which consists of the member countries of the EU. As long as exchange rates remain stable, the finance ministry takes a generally hands-off approach to governance in ECOFIN. However, when exchange rates become unstable, the role of the finance minister becomes central to the process of negotiating possible new currency values. This formal rule has become powerfully institutionalized within the forum of ECOFIN. The most important aspect of the institutional setup of the EMS is that all decisions involving external monetary management are taken at the system level or at the level of ECOFIN. The Monetary Committee, a group that combines the deputies of the finance ministers and central bank governors in each country, assists ECOFIN. The Committee of Central Bank Governors of the European Community (EC) coordinated the central bank position and oversaw the EMS operationally between 1979–1993. Since 1994, the European Monetary Institute (EMI), based in Frankfurt, has replaced the Committee of Central Bank Governors. The EMI has a similar membership and acts to supervise the transition to monetary union before it assumes the role of the ECB. Although many analysts dismiss the significance of such institutions, all decisions surrounding exchange rate policy within, and the operation of, the EMS must be negotiated at the system-institutional level in the EU.

The link, therefore, between the EMS and the Bundesbank and government is quite explicit. Under the EMS, when the Bundesbank's exchange rate commitments conflict with its objective of restraining the growth of the domestic money supply, it will petition the finance ministry to initiate negotiations with the EMS partners for a realignment within the system. Partner governments might also initiate such negotiations at the European system level in the Monetary Committee and ECOFIN. The finance ministry formally conducts these negotiations for Germany, and the minister's approval is necessary for any decision. The Bundesbank can and does offer advice on the necessity, size, and timing of a realignment (among many other exchange rate management proposals) but is ultimately reliant on the finance ministry to act. The finance ministry works closely with the chancellor's office and foreign ministry (which may have other European foreign policy objectives to consider) to develop a coherent government position, although all such actors may at times disagree with one another. For its part, the finance ministry cannot ignore the requests of the Bundesbank, and consultation between the two actors is ongoing and intensive.

When the finance ministry refuses to grant a realignment, which did occur on occasion during the time frame under analysis here, the Bundesbank has no practical recourse for action.[36] The Bundesbank could theoretically renege by using its opt-out clause and refusing to honor its obligation to intervene at the margin of the ERM bands. Such a step would trigger a major political and monetary crisis both within Germany and within the EMS. The Bundesbank could consider such a move only if such intervention would dangerously affect the German money supply and if a realignment was vigorously opposed by domestic lobbying groups and the government. Even under such an opt-out scenario, which the Bundesbank has never used publicly, the Bundesbank must weigh larger foreign policy considerations of the government. Political support for the EMS and economic support for European integration are pillars of the German government's longstanding European policies.

Within the international monetary system, and more specifically, within the G7, similar EMS or EU rules and institutions do not exist. In other words, the governance structure in the international monetary arena differs systematically from the governance structure in Europe. In the international arena, the only basic rule is to meet once a year during the traditional G7 macroeconomic summits, although finance ministers do meet several times a year and consult even more frequently.[37] Since the breakdown of the Bretton Woods system, no formal, multilateral exchange rate regime exists. Those who negotiate such summits (sherpas) do meet regularly within other forums like the Organization for Economic Cooperation and Development (OECD), IMF, and the Bank of International Settlements (BIS), in terms of managing exchange rates, but no singular clearinghouse of decisionmaking exists. Variability of exchange rates has become the rule whereby the Bundesbank decides the extent of intervention (with few exceptions) with regard to non-EMS currencies. Although countries pledge to avoid exchange rate manipulation—through the use of interest rates, for example—for trade purposes, there are no formal, legal restrictions on state behavior. The Germans are under no obligation to peg or fix the value of the DM to the dollar. Some analysts have suggested that the Louvre accord instituted a mechanism of multilateral surveillance and a range or target zone for the DM and the dollar, but the strength of such a commitment by the Germans is difficult to evaluate. The contents of the agreement were never published officially or announced formally. My own interviews with Bundesbank and finance ministry officials suggest an interest in stability vis-à-vis the dollar, but both actors insist that no formal commitment exists.

In addition, decisionmaking and negotiating at the international level involve unilateral decisions taken by countries with institutions like the IMF or the G7 providing little more than formal post hoc ratification. Admittedly, at the international level, consultations exist in various forums like special IMF committees, conferences, councils, and summits. This gives the impression that management has become institutionalized. Moreover, given this impression, informal governance may be considered a part of the G7 governance process. Yet such management tends rather to be ad hoc, reactive, and crisis driven and not institutionalized in any systematic fashion around formal rules or decisionmaking procedures. Moreover, decisions made at Plaza or the Louvre, though perhaps politically binding, had no formal legal standing in Germany. No formal rule obligated Bundesbank intervention in the foreign exchange markets. Finally, despite the fact that additional informal norms of behavior (for example, the international reserve role for the dollar and the institution of the IMF) have persisted since the collapse of Bretton Woods, they do not provide any ongoing, systematic form of governance. In short, and on the insistence of the Germans, the convergence of each G7 nation's monetary policy (and macroeconomic policy in general) that can lead to exchange rate stability does not necessitate formal rules or institutions.

The link between the Bundesbank and government is not as explicit or formalized as within the international monetary system, with its particular rules and institutions. However, there are some definitive points of connection that can be stated. First, the Bundesbank plays a much stronger political and monetary role within G7 governance forums.[38] Under the flexible exchange rate regime, the Bundesbank retains a great deal of latitude in terms of interventions, realignments, and policy coordination. With the exception of the Plaza and Louvre accords within the G7, the Bundesbank alone, and not the government, has decided on an intervention policy vis-à-vis non-EMS currencies, especially the dollar and the yen. Even in such accords like the Louvre, which purportedly established confidential target ranges for currency fluctuations, the accord was not a legal codified document. The Bundesbank may have been constrained politically, but it was not legally bound. The Bundesbank's agreement to adhere to the measures discussed at the Louvre accord cannot be adequately assessed because components of the agreement were never published.

One interesting component of the bargaining context in Europe or the G7 is the possibility for conflict or turf-fighting between various institutions. In Europe, the relationship between ECOFIN and the Council of

Ministers is illustrative. Finance ministers were sometimes kept out of negotiations that led up to Maastricht. Key decisions were instead made by heads of state and foreign ministers at Hanover, Madrid, and Rome. At other times, central bankers, finance ministers, foreign ministers, and heads of state were all involved in the same bargaining over EMU but were proceeding on different tracks. This is in stark contrast to G7 international economic summits, where the central bankers and government officials operate at the same level. Here, such turf-fighting then manifests at the domestic level. Central bankers may use a sympathetic finance minister to pressure the head of state who may be receiving opposing advice from the foreign ministry. Or the head of state may use a sympathetic central banker to resist pressure from abroad. The Bundesbank, in particular, is very proactive in all forums of G7 negotiations. It is hard to imagine a scenario where the German foreign minister would preempt the finance ministry, let alone the Bundesbank, in G7 negotiations. The division of negotiating responsibility can serve the Germans well in negotiations or it can prove a liability.

The preceding analysis demonstrates that there exists a systematic difference in the degree of governance provided in the European monetary system as compared to the international monetary system. Within Europe, a *strong* form of monetary governance exists within which the Bundesbank and government must bargain. Such governance incorporates powerful formal and informal rules of engagement as well as an authoritative institutionalized forum for governance. A strong governance structure is therefore characterized as one with specific and definite rules of monetary obligation whereby decisions affecting monetary policy and exchange rate management are taken at the institutional level. In contrast, a much *weaker* form of governance exists at the international level. Whereas the G7 provides some measure of management and certain informal rules of interaction, few if any obligations exist for G7 members to orient their policy toward external goals. A weak governance structure can therefore be characterized by few, if any, formal or informal rules of obligation whereby decisions are more regularly taken at the state level.

In all necessary components of governance, from explicit rules of engagement to the provision of enforcement, arbitration, and regulation of state behavior, the EMS displays a significantly stronger form of governance than within the G7. Given such a contrast in the degree of governance, can we begin to identify a systematic difference in the impact of such governance upon the negotiating strategies of the Bundesbank and government? In other words, in terms of the willingness of German monetary authorities to sacrifice monetary autonomy for exchange rate stability—expressed in the negotiating strategies toward the EMS and G7—is there a systematic variation in terms of bargaining behavior? Scholars who discount the impact and significance of such governance structures on state behavior would argue no, but the following analysis demonstrates how governance structures do, in fact, shape the approach of the Bundesbank and government toward external monetary diplomacy and each other. Governance matters both for understanding monetary cooperation and deutsche mark politics.

A Model of Bargaining Strategies

I argue that by examining the bargaining strategies of German monetary authorities within the monetary governance structures in Europe (the EMS) and internationally (the G7), we can begin to identify the conditions under which the Bundesbank and government might choose to sacrifice monetary autonomy for exchange rate stability. The governance structure of the EMS and G7 provide the context within which the Bundesbank and government must bargain. The decision to cooperate (an autonomy versus exchange rate stability trade-off) emerges from the process of intergovernmental bargaining (the German government negotiating among other states within the EMS and the G7) and intrastate bargaining (between the Bundesbank and government). Bargaining strategies vary—from the pursuit of monetary autonomy at one extreme to the search for exchange rate stability at the other. We could look at the actual agreements made via the Plaza accord or the Maastricht Treaty, but my approach identifies patterns of bargaining strategies before the actual decisions were made.

The bargaining strategies of the Bundesbank and government focus on the extent to which German monetary authorities are willing to (1) adjust domestic monetary policy (interest rates, for example) to influence exchange rates; (2) engage in foreign exchange intervention to affect the value of the DM or other currencies in the exchange rate markets; (3) revalue or devalue the DM to secure exchange rate stability within a particular exchange rate system; and (4) strengthen institutional components of exchange rate systems that by definition might restrain domestic autonomy. These four dimensions incorporate the key elements of the bargaining strategies employed by the government in determining the extent of monetary cooperation. They also capture the domestic and foreign policy linkages of German monetary policy as well as the intent of the Bundesbank and government to cooperate with each other and their negotiating partners.

For further illustration, let us examine each of these four bargaining scenarios briefly. In the first situation, the government may enter into negotiations concerning instability within the EMS with the intention of not lowering interest rates. The government may be willing to pressure the Bundesbank to accept a small interest rate reduction in order to provide stability to the EMS. Regardless of the outcome of the final decision, the bargaining strategy of each actor is within the framework of the autonomy–exchange rate stability continuum. As an example of the second situation, both the Bundesbank and government may agree that foreign exchange intervention may be the most feasible option to reduce tension between the dollar and the DM. Although extensive intervention might affect the German money supply, whereby autonomy is reduced, the choice is made to pursue such a strategy to secure some measure of exchange rate stability. In the third scenario, German monetary authorities may face pressure to revalue the DM in order to reduce speculative pressure within the EMS, an option the Germans have pursued on occasion. In the fourth scenario, the negotiations surrounding the final decision reached in the Basel-Nyborg agreement, the Louvre accord, and EMU ultimately required sacrifices on monetary autonomy. In any one of the four situations, we can begin to identify the bargaining strategies of the Bundesbank and government in terms of the continuum of monetary autonomy and exchange rate stability and the trade-offs associated with each strategy.

The most recent attempts to more systematically develop our understanding of the process of negotiating include the works on the logic of two-level games.[39] Robert Putnam, in particular, argues cogently that older theories that tried to examine the link between domestic politics and international relations failed to adequately account for the processes or strategies of domestic ratification. National state leaders seek ratification, whether in the form of formal legislative approval, a referendum, or more informal mechanisms such as labor interests agreeing to reduced wage demands from their domestic-based constituents. The requirement is that any internationally negotiated agreement must in the end be ratified by domestic actors, in what Putnam argues is the "crucial theoretical link between the two levels,"—the domestic-internal level and the international-external level.[40] My interest in the use of Putnam's model comes in the form of investigating the formal connections, that is, the bargaining strategies between the international and the domestic level.

Hypotheses: Hard-Line Strategy Versus Compliant Strategy

I argue that the government must choose between two basic negotiating strategies, a hard-line strategy that preserves monetary autonomy or a compliant strategy that reveals a willingness by the government to offer some concessions in the form of sacrifices of monetary autonomy for exchange rate stability.[41] A hard-line strategy might also indicate a desire on the part of German negotiators to seek concessions from their negotiating partners. In other words, the government may come into the negotiating arena with very firm positions (resisting pressure to make concessions) as well as a desire to extract sacrifices from their negotiating partners. Furthermore, a compliant strategy merely indicates that the government is in a position where it *may* be willing to sacrifice or offer concessions in order to secure a final agreement. In fact, the government may come into negotiations with tough conditions often dictated by the Bundesbank. Nevertheless, the government may offer further concessions to move the negotiating process forward and secure a final agreement.

The choice of a hard-line or compliant strategy is the product of two key variables: (1) the level of disagreement between the two actors, and (2) the governance structure within which the two actors must negotiate.

With the first variable, the level of disagreement between the Bundesbank and government can set the tone for negotiations to come.[42] Earlier work on bargaining and negotiation has demonstrated that top decision-makers are often not unified in terms of negotiating.[43] And as noted, the Bundesbank and government are not always unified on what the government's negotiating strategy should be within the EMS or G7. Therefore, the Bundesbank and government will each stake out their respective positions, which may either differ considerably or converge. The further apart each minimally acceptable position is from the other, we can say that the level of disagreement is high. The closer the positions of the Bundesbank and government are together, we can say that the level of disagreement is low.

This dynamic of low or high levels of disagreement suggests various possible impacts on the government's negotiating strategy. A high level of disagreement between the government and the Bundesbank could lead to a hard-line strategy, for the government can argue that it is having difficulty securing Bundesbank support for any exchange rate agreement. Difficulty in assuring the Bundesbank's compliance is seen as a weakness in the government's ability to pressure the Bundesbank to comply with the government's objectives. In contrast, the lower the level of disagreement, it is likely that the government might find itself pressured by its negotiating counterparts to offer some concessions, that is, a compliant strategy. Because the Bundesbank is largely in agreement with the government, at least initially, the government may be willing in this scenario to exert further political leverage on the Bundesbank to accept an exchange rate agreement requiring some sacrifice of monetary autonomy.

The second variable focuses on the interplay of the bank and government within the European or G7 governance structures. In other words, the formal link between domestic political structures and international governance structures (defined as "strong" or "weak") can help us determine the degree of political leverage one actor might have over the other. Although I develop this conceptualization as a general rule applicable to any governance structure, I argue that the government has less political leverage over the Bundesbank in the international monetary arena than in the

European monetary arena.[44] Because of the strengthened institutional role of the Bundesbank in G7 negotiations and the absence of formal rules that might bind the Bundesbank to any government agreement, the Bundesbank retains a more forceful and independent role in negotiations. Here, a weak form of international monetary governance that strengthens the institutional and bargaining independence of the Bundesbank exists. The government may not seek to exert its political resources over the Bundesbank because of the lack of any formal obligations. In contrast, in Europe the government may seek to exert greater political leverage over the Bundesbank because of the formal rules that obligate the Bundesbank to assume certain responsibilities vis-à-vis the EMS as well as the formal rules that compel decision-making on European monetary affairs at the institutional-system level.

In examining these variables, which are presented Table 1.2, consider the following hypotheses (H):

H-1: If the initial positions of the government and Bundesbank are close together (*low* level of disagreement), and if the governance structure of the bargaining context is *strong*, then the government will pursue a more compliant strategy.

H-2: If the initial positions of the government and Bundesbank are close together (*low* level of disagreement), and if the governance structure of the bargaining context is *weak*, then the government will pursue a hard-line strategy.

Table 1.2 Final Bargaining Strategy of the Government

	Governance Structure Strong[a]	Governance Structure Weak[a]
Level of Bundesbank/ Government Disagreement Low	Compliant Strategy[b] H-1	Hard-Line Strategy[b] H-2
Level of Bundesbank/ Government Disagreement High	Mixed Compliant and Hard-Line Strategy H-3	Hard-Line Strategy H-4

Notes: a. Governance structure defined in terms of formal and informal rules and institutions. A strong governance structure is characterized by specific formal and informal rules and institutions that constrain the actions of the participants. A weak governance structure is characterized by few, if any, formal or informal rules or obligations on the part of participants.

b. Strategy defined in terms of the monetary autonomy versus exchange rate stability continuum. A hard-line strategy indicates the resistance to concessions on monetary autonomy. A compliant strategy indicates willingness to concede monetary autonomy for exchange rate stability.

H-1 and H-2 present two interesting versions of the model of bargaining strategies. Specifically, I seek to test the significance of governance structures upon the government's negotiating strategy. It has been argued here that a low level of disagreement between the Bundesbank and government should lead to a compliant strategy. Under the conditions of H-1, this strategy is likely because of the strong institutionalized governance structure that adds to the government's ability to pressure the Bundesbank to comply with the its objectives. What is more, the government's negotiating counterparts can use the strong governance structure as a source of leverage upon the government to seek concessions from the Bundesbank. However, under H-2, holding the level of disagreement constant (low), I argue that the government will pursue a hard-line strategy. This strategy is determined primarily by the weak governance structure that allows the Bundesbank a stronger direct voice in negotiations and reduces the government's political resources to pressure the Bundesbank to make concessions.

There are two other possibilities that reveal mixed bargaining strategies:

H-3: If the initial positions of the government and Bundesbank are wide apart (*high* level of disagreement), and the governance structure of the bargaining context is *strong*, then the government is likely to pursue a mixed hard-line and compliant strategy.

H-4: If the initial positions of the government and Bundesbank are wide apart (*high* level of disagreement), and the governance structure of the bargaining context is *weak,* then the government is likely to pursue a strong hard-line strategy.

Here, the degree of political leverage that the government will seek to exert over the Bundesbank is more difficult to assess. Moreover, under the conditions of H-3 and H-4, we should, in general, expect a more complex and fractious negotiation process between the Bundesbank and government and between the government and European or G7 negotiators. In addition, we know that a high level of disagreement between the government and Bundesbank will likely lead to a more recalcitrant bargaining strategy by the government as it finds it difficult to secure Bundesbank compliance. Therefore, under both H-3 and H-4, we would expect to see a hard-line strategy prevail. In fact, under H-4 we will definitely witness such a strategy. However, under H-3, even with high levels of disagreement between the Bundesbank and government, the government may try to force compliance upon the Bundesbank. The final negotiating strategy may not be that divergent from the Bundesbank's initial position (suggesting hard-line conditions), but some concession, however small, may be offered in the end to secure a final compromise agreement. As a result, a compliant strategy may best characterize the government's final negotiating strategy.

Finally, building on the propositions and hypotheses set forth above, we could also speculate on the dynamic interaction between international and European monetary negotiations in terms of a tripartite bargaining framework. In fact, German negotiators may play one bargaining arena off the other. Traditionally, Germany has often played Europe off the G7 by suggesting that a European zone of monetary stability could counterbalance instability generated from primarily U.S. pressure and dollar volatility. Therefore, while the government is pursuing a compliant strategy within the EMS (securing exchange rate stability), it might simultaneously pursue a hard-line strategy toward the G7 (strengthening monetary autonomy). Nevertheless, the reverse could occur as well. If the government is pursuing a more compliant strategy vis-à-vis its G7 partners, the Germans might then claim that such efforts are aimed at easing monetary tensions within Europe. As a result, the government may concurrently pursue a hard-line strategy in Europe, as stability between the dollar and the DM should translate into stability within Europe. With the triangulation of German monetary policy, a move in one arena can influence the position of German negotiators in another arena.

Conclusion

This chapter began with the proposition that deutsche mark politics can best be explained if we first focus our analytical eye inward and disaggregate the state into two primary actors: the Bundesbank and government. Broadly defined, deutsche mark politics includes the actions taken by the Bundesbank and government to affect monetary and other financial conditions both within Germany and abroad. The structure of the political economy of German monetary policy and the primary role that the Bundesbank and government play in the development, formulation, and execution of German monetary policy are central to the analytical and theoretical framework employed in this study.

The Bundesbank and federal government often disagree about their conception of German monetary policy, differ as to what is in the nation's best interest, and respond distinctively to disparate influences that ultimately shape German monetary policy. The Bundesbank and government balance their domestic political and economic objectives with regional and international monetary commitments within a triangular, or tripartite, framework of deutsche mark politics. European and international monetary governance structures do shape the outcome of the bargaining strategies pursued by the government. The following chapters elaborate upon both the bargaining strategies model and hypotheses set forth above.

Notes

1. EG stands for *Europäische Gemeinschaft* (European Community).

2. It should not be lost on the observer that ECU sounds like a *Küh,* or "cow," in German.

3. Monetary policy is defined broadly to include the actions taken by the Bundesbank and government to affect monetary and other financial conditions within Germany and abroad. Monetary policy is traditionally defined narrowly as the objectives of the central bank in exercising its control over money, interest rates, and credit conditions. In line with the subject of this book—deutsche mark politics—my definition seeks to capture both the internal and external (exchange rate management through currency intervention, mutual adjustment of interest rates, and so on) dimensions of German monetary policy.

4. See the work of Gerald Feldman, *The Great Disorder: Politics, Economics, and Society in the German Inflation, 1914–1924* (New York: Oxford University Press, 1993); and Gerald Feldman, ed., with contributions by Gerald Merkin et al., *The German Inflation Reconsidered: A Preliminary Balance* (New York: De Gruyter, 1982).

5. See Hans Herbert von Arnim, "Die Deutsche Bundesbank—Pfeiler der Demokratie," *Zeitschrift für Wirtschaftspolitik,* no. 37 (1988), pp. 51–63.

6. In German, *Kanzlersamt, Finanz-und Wirtschafts Ministerium.*

7. This study disaggregates the state into two primary institutions, the Bundesbank and federal government, and the officials who reside within them. Specifically, the federal government is defined here to include the important finance ministry and the chancellor's office. Although particular actors in the government do disagree on specific issues, there usually exists consensus as to the larger directions of monetary policy, and they seek to act in one voice. This point also applies to the Bundesbank where factions do exist within the Central Bank Council, especially between the Länder Bank presidents and the directorate. However, the Bundesbank, like the government, seeks to operate and voice its position with consensus.

8. See especially the plea of Helen Milner, "International Theories of Cooperation Among Nations: Strengths and Weaknesses," *World Politics* 44, no. 3 (April 1992), pp. 466–496.

9. See, for example, David Andrews, "Capital Mobility and State Autonomy: Toward Structural Theory of International Monetary Relations," *International Studies Quarterly,* no. 38 (June 1994), pp. 193–218.

10. Keneth Waltz, *Theories of International Politics* (New York: Random House, 1979); Andrew Moravscik, "Negotiating the Single European Act: National Interests and Conventional Statecraft in the European Community," *International Organization* 45, no. 1 (winter 1991), pp. 19–56.

11. The initial quote is from John McDonald, *Strategy in Poker, Business, and War* (New York, 1950), as noted in J. David Singer, "International Conflict: Three Levels of Analysis," *World Politics* 12, no. 3 (April 1960), p. 459.

12. The concept of the tripartite framework, or triangulation, of German monetary policy, has a long and distinguished history in analyses of German foreign policy and Germany in general. I am particularly indebted to the works of Wolfram Hanrieder, *Germany, America, and Europe* (New Haven, Conn.: Yale University Press, 1989); and James Sperling, *Three-Way Stretch: The Federal Republic of Germany in the Atlantic Economy, 1969–1976,* Ph.D. diss., University of California, Santa Barbara, 1986.

13. Hugo Kaufmann, "The Deutsche Mark Between the Dollar and the European Monetary System," *Kredit und Kapital,* no. 18 (1985), pp. 29–60; also Hugo

Kaufmann, *Germany's International Monetary Policy and the European Monetary System* (New York: Brooklyn College Press, 1985).

14. A partial, yet inevitably deficient, list would include the work of Hanrieder, *Germany, America, and Europe;* Otmar Emminger, *DM, Dollar, und Währungskrisen* (Stuttgart: Deutsche Verlags-Anstalt, 1986). More recent works include Ellen Kennedy, *The Bundesbank: Germany's Central Bank in the International Monetary System* (London: RIIA, 1991); David Marsh, *Die Bundesbank: Geschäfte mit der Macht* (Munich: Bertelsmann, 1992); and in comparative perspective, John Goodman, *Monetary Sovereignty: The Politics of Central Banking in Western Europe* (Ithaca: Cornell University Press, 1992). An excellent source is C. Randall Henning, *International Policymaking in the U.S., Japan, and Germany* (Washington, D.C.: Institute for International Economics, 1994).

15. Kaufmann, *Germany's International Monetary Policy,* p. 83.

16. I use the G7 to describe the governance structure of the international monetary system. Of course, the IMF also plays a central role on such questions as governance. But during the period of this study, the G7 was and remains the focal point and negotiating forum for questions of international monetary governance. From the German perspective, the United States and Japan (together often referred to as the Group of Three [G3]) are the critical G7 partners. Also, the G7 at times operated as the G5 (excluding Canada and Italy from the G7), for example, during the Plaza negotiations. I will at times use the G5 or G3 to indicate such specific rounds of negotiations, but use the G7 as the basic focus of international monetary governance.

17. Interview with the author, March 1992, Frankfurt.

18. Article 109 spells out the possible scenarios of a future exchange rate policy under EMU. These scenarios are examined in Chapter 8.

19. The most important issue is what happens when the dollar is in decline. The dollar is sold when the DM drives a wedge between itself and other EMS currencies and forces these other currencies to defend their link to the DM via tight monetary and fiscal policies. The burden of adjustment weighs heavily on other EMS members.

20. Objectives compiled from source data and interviews. See, especially, Deutsche Bundesbank, *The Deutsche Bundesbank: Its Monetary Policy Instruments and Functions,* Special Series, no. 7, 1989 (Frankfurt/Main).

21. M3 is an indicator of the money stock comprising currency in circulation and sight deposits, time deposits for less than four years, and savings deposits at statutory notice held by domestic nonbanks at domestic banks. The use of M3 is controversial but the Bundesbank defends the use of M3 by arguing that it is a weighted, broadly defined money stock concept and can function as an intermediate monetary target variable.

22. The Bundesbank does not publicly identify a target rate, but the author's conversations with Bundesbank officials indicates that 2 percent is often referred to as a rate around which monetary policy is aimed.

23. For a broad review of the role of global finance and its influence on the affairs of nations, see Benjamin J. Cohen, "Phoenix Risen: The Resurrection of Global Finance," *World Politics* 48 (January 1996), pp. 268–296.

24. See, for example, Karl Otto Pöhl, "Das Spannungsverhältnis zwischen nationaler und internationaler Währungspolitik aus der Sicht der Bundesbank," *Hamburger Jahrbuch für Wirtschaft und Gesellschaftspolitik,* no. 30 (1985), pp. 177–187.

25. For a view on the perception that the EMS would serve not only as a zone of monetary stability within Europe but also, implicitly, as a zone of monetary

stability vis-à-vis the benign neglect of Washington's dollar policy, see Hanrieder, *Germany, America, and Europe*, p. 304.

26. The debate over EMS is richly described in Emminger, *DM, Dollar, und Währungskrisen*, pp. 361–362. Emminger describes the essence of the agreement between the Bundesbank and federal government over EMS responsibilities as such: "The autonomy of the Bundesbank in monetary policy would particularly be put in jeopardy if strong imbalances with the future EMS resulted in extreme intervention obligations which would then threaten the value of the currency."

27. Deutsche Bundesbank, *Annual Report 1987* (Frankfurt/Main), p. 36.

28. Central banks sterilize intervention when they conduct open market operations to offset the effects of intervention on the domestic money supply. In terms of the effectiveness of exchange rate intervention, economists disagree. See Benjamin J. Cohen, "The Triad and the Unholy Trinity: Lessons for the Pacific Region," in Richard Higgot, Richard Leaver, and John Ravenhill, eds., *Pacific Economic Relations in the 1990s: Cooperation or Conflict?* (London: Allen and Unwin, 1993), pp. 133–158.

29. The trade-off between monetary policy autonomy and exchange rate stability is, of course, complicated by the third leg of the "unholy trinity," namely private capital mobility. Specifically, there exists an intrinsic incompatibility of these three key economic desiderata. I do not seek to underestimate or neglect the influence and power of the capital mobility; in fact, I incorporate its importance as a contextual variable into my analysis. However, in so far as the primary core of monetary debates in Germany focuses on the trade-offs between monetary stability and exchange rate stability, these two variables will be highlighted. The concept of the unholy trinity is from Benjamin J. Cohen, "The Triad and the Unholy Trinity." The classic formulation of this dilemma is Robert A. Mundell, *International Economics* (New York: Macmillan, 1968), pp. 233–271.

30. Cohen, "The Triad and the Unholy Trinity," p. 147. My examination draws heavily from this analysis and pp. 147–152.

31. Following the lead of standard scholarship of international political economy, cooperation is defined as mutual adjustment of national monetary policy through an implicit or explicit process of interstate bargaining.

32. Cohen, "The Triad and the Unholy Trinity."

33. See the useful summary and analytical distinctions made by Robert Keohane, "International Institutions: Two Approaches," *International Studies Quarterly*, no. 32 (1988), pp. 379–396.

34. This section borrows from Padoa-Schioppa's discussion of institutions in the management of multi-country economies. Tommasa Padoa-Schioppa, "Rules and Institutions in the Management of Multi-Country Economies," in Loukas Tsoukalis, ed., *The Political Economy of International Money* (London: RIIA, 1985), pp. 261–304.

35. See especially Hanrieder, *Germany, America, and Europe*.

36. This section draws closely on the discussion in Henning, *International Policymaking*, pp. 96–100.

37. See C. Fred Bergsten and C. Randall Henning, *Global Economic Leadership and the Group of Seven* (Washington, D.C.: Institute for International Economics, 1996), for their analysis of the role of the G7 in global finance.

38. Such a role was acknowledged repeatedly by both Bundesbank and finance ministry officials in interviews.

39. Robert Putnam, "Diplomacy and Domestic Politics: The Logic of Two-Level Games," *International Organization* 42, no. 3 (summer 1988), pp. 427–460.

40. Ibid., p. 436.

41. See the analysis of Lehman and McCoy for their elaboration and theoretical justification of the two-choice strategy model. Howard Lehman and Jennifer McCoy, "The Dynamics of the Two-Level Bargaining Game: The 1988 Brazilian Debt Negotiations," *World Politics* 44 (July 1992), pp. 600–644.

42. Creating a precise measurement to operationalize the intensity of internal conflict is difficult, and I recognize the limitations that this carries into the hypotheses to be set forth. However, a careful reading of the initial positions of each actor can reveal a qualitative judgment as to the level of disagreement between the two actors; hence, capturing the level of disagreement between them, whether high or low.

43. See Glenn Snyder and Paul Diesing, *Conflict Among Nations: Bargaining, Decision-Making, and System Structure in International Crises* (Princeton, N.J.: Princeton University Press, 1977), especially pp. 510–525.

44. This assertion does not rule out the possibility that the EMS governance structure may in the future be weaker than the G7 governance structure.

2

Bundesbank Preeminent, Not Predominant

> The independence of the Bundesbank is formal only through the Bundesbank law, then, a simple law, and not through the constitution. To be sure, this independence has obtained over the decades, through custom, a de facto quasi-legal and constitutional character.
>
> —Former Bundesbank president Otmar Emminger, *DM, Dollar, und Währungskrisen*

> The Bundesbank is a bit like whipped cream. The harder you beat it, the harder it becomes.
>
> —Bundesbank official, 1993

The preceding chapter outlined the importance of the Bundesbank and federal government in understanding deutsche mark politics. The tripartite framework firmly places the focus of German monetary policy on the interaction of these two institutional players. The nexus between the Bundesbank and government over the control and direction of monetary policy can often lead to differing perceptions as to what specific course German monetary policy should take as well as the direction of Germany's European and international currency diplomacy. Of course the Bundesbank attracts much of the spotlight in deutsche mark politics. The Bundesbank's quasi-constitutional independent position within Germany's political economy generates an unusual amount of attention and criticism due to its apparent intransigence in the face of domestic and foreign pressure. Most analyses of the Bundesbank argue that it is immune to or independent from the pressures of domestic, European, and international actors and institutions. This independence, in turn, makes Bundesbank cooperation highly unlikely. In fact, from the perspective of the Bundesbank, its job is not to cooperate; rather, its job is to act as a monetary gadfly.

However, the argument that will be advanced in this chapter contends that the Bundesbank is not as independent as most analyses suggest or as its detractors criticize. In fact, the Bundesbank lacks complete political, financial, or personal independence (the three key dimensions of central bank independence) from the federal government. German monetary policy, both in terms of domestic policy considerations and foreign monetary diplomacy, is necessarily a compromise of competing interests and pressures upon the Bundesbank and the government. To be sure, the Bundesbank may remain the preeminent state actor in German monetary policy, but it is not always predominant. As Chapter 1 emphasized, the government does have a measure of political leverage over the Bundesbank. The degree of leverage the government actually has over the Bundesbank is the focus of this chapter.

First, I will examine some underlying common Teutonic themes and threads that form the foundation for understanding the cultural context within which deutsche mark politics operates and the monetary objectives that flow from this framework. I then proceed to examine the concept of independence and the degree to which the Bundesbank is, in fact, independent. Although the Bundesbank remains one of the most independent central banks in the world, I argue that the bank's independence should not be construed to mean that it can pursue its objectives without compromise. The implications of this analysis for the ECB should not be lost on the observer. Finally, an abridged account of the past conflicts and dramatic interactions between the Bundesbank and the government will be undertaken.

Economic Culture in Deutsche Mark Politics

Before examining the Bundesbank and government, it would be useful to first describe the context within which these actors operate. This context, or, as I contend, economic culture, can set the basic parameters for certain types of behavior. Specifically, a nation's economic culture identifies the noninstitutional proscriptions and imperatives facing national authorities in the formulation and execution of economic policy; it defines the minimum tasks and responsibilities of the state and sets the boundaries of legitimate state activity based on distinctive national experiences.[1] In other words, historical experience can act as a brake and a source of divergence for the development of a nation's particular macroeconomic goals. Disparate national experiences hold not only for monetary policy but also for the division of labor between state and society; the mix of public, semipublic, and private structures; relationships between interest groups and bureaucracies; uses of taxation; sensitivity to unemployment and inflation; and attitudes toward economic growth. Policymakers and politicians, therefore, often work within a framework that can limit the potential for wide discretionary swings in policy.

We can also recognize economic culture as the social perceptions that structure macroeconomic policy. It is the confluence of cultural, historical, and circumstantial variables that creates the consensual knowledge of society and legitimizes policymaking behavior and mechanisms. This confluence of forces, in turn, allows a certain degree of freedom in the development and management of monetary policy, as long as the decisions conform to the predominant economic culture. Although always difficult to measure precisely, the German economic culture is said to demand fiscal rectitude and a deflationary macroeconomic policy targeting price stability. Two leading commentators on the international political economy, Susan Strange and David Calleo, state the German case more bluntly: "The German tribal memory heightens political awareness of the long-run penalties attached to inflation and, therefore, substantially assists inflation-resisting policies."[2] This economic culture gives German monetary policy a special quality, unique to the particular historical experience of the Germans.

Some may label this deeply ingrained attachment to currency frugality a peculiar Germanic monetary angst or paranoia, but it is a staple of deutsche mark politics and reflects the broader social and political context in Germany that has developed into a distinct monetary ideology. This ideology presents a fairly simple yet stark view and message to the masses of the dangers of currency instability. William Smyser characterizes the monetary tradition of Germany as one that recognizes the "fragility of value, the risk of total loss that can shatter lives and demolish families . . . [which] remain deeply ingrained in the Germany psyche even to this day."[3] A large cross section of German public opinion shares this broad conception. Perhaps more important, most leading political, financial, and economic elites within Germany share a similar view.[4] Certainly, those who lived through the hyperinflationary periods of 1923 and the period up to the Währungsreform of 1948 would share this feeling of monetary insecurity. Gordon Craig, a keen observer of the German experience, states that "the failure of the first German experiment with republican government was foreordained when the one commodity [money] that more than any other seemed to give people a means of rational assessment of their situation lost its power to do so any longer."[5] Unmistakably, social and economic conditions past, present, and future play a powerful role in German society and the course of monetary policy.

This monetary ideology, based on the fear of inflation and its sociopolitical consequences, manifests in the institutional structures of the German political economy, in particular through the creation of the powerful Bundesbank. Most analyses of the German political economy cite the foundations of the Bundesbank in the postwar German Constitution (Grundgesetz) that gives German monetary policy its special administrative and legal quality.[6] Monetary policy is also surrounded by traditional German political concerns with order and the rule of law (*Rechtsstaat*) and the proper role of civil servants in the administrative machinery. Legal precepts dictate a strong emphasis and respect for legal principles and details. At times, Germany's recourse to legal arguments in its foreign policy (especially during the period of nonrecognition of East Germany through the 1950s and early 1960s) often confounded its partners. In monetary policy, it is the Bundesbank's adherence to its strict legal and administrative duty to protect the currency that confounds its critics. As Bundesbank officials see it, it is their duty to administer legal precepts and not to engage in overt political tasks. They will use it as a shield in times of pressure or conflict and as a source of mass support.

The strength of public support for an independent central bank guaranteeing the value of their beloved DM adds to the resources of the Bundesbank in times of conflict. An attentive German public and a political, financial, and economic elite on monetary affairs help guard the independence of the Bundesbank. However, if the central bank is badly out of step with current economic conditions and misunderstands the cycles of history, the clashes with finance ministers and chancellors are less easily hidden from public debate, and no amount of independence can save the bank from strongly defending its position with the public. The Bundesbank thus goes to great lengths in maintaining a consistent and vocal public relations campaign.

As the former president of the Bundesbank, Helmut Schlesinger, has written, "The maintenance of monetary stability has been the highest goal" of German monetary policy over the past fifty years.[7] Although many economists and noneconomists have debated what exactly monetary stability means, what "safeguarding the currency" entails, or what methods are most appropriate for this task, the Bundesbank will continually return to this familiar German monetary leitmotif—a leitmotif surrounded by an aura of familiarity and respect to the public. One can argue that anyone who tries to understand the motivations of the Bundesbank—and German monetary policy, in general—should first base their analysis on Schlesinger's rather clear and forthright statement. The goals, objectives, and policies of German monetary policy, especially as espoused by Bundesbank officials, have remained remarkably consistent over the decades. They work within a narrow economic or monetary culture, a fear of the "psychology of inflation," as the respected scholar Elizabeth Noelle-Neumann has called it, that, as they see it, proscribes certain behavior.[8] These factors should not be lost on the Bundesbank's detractors and those who are astounded by the bank's concern with 2–3 percent inflation.

The Bundesbank's Goals and Objectives

Specifically, the primary function of the Bundesbank as defined in Paragraph 3 of the Bundesbank Law of 1957 is "regulating the amount of money in circulation and of credit supplied to the economy, using the monetary powers conferred on it by this Act, *with the aim of safeguarding the currency.*"[9] While the creators of the Bundesbank were clear about what the purpose of the bank should be, they were not clear as to how that purpose was to be implemented or achieved. This was to be left open for the officials of the Bundesbank and government to decide. Most analysts of Bundesbank policy do conclude that there are two overriding dimensions to the debate over how best to safeguard the currency. The first dimension centers on the proper relationship between monetary policy and the wider goals of the general economy as defined by the federal government. The second dimension focuses on whether the Bundesbank should aim for external currency stability (maintaining the level of the German exchange rate to other currencies) or internal currency stability (protecting against domestic inflation). Former Bundesbank president Otmar Emminger (1977–1979) has suggested that there is little disagreement between the government and the bank on the necessity of a stability-oriented monetary policy.[10] In other words, from the Bundesbank's perspective, safeguarding the value of the currency is a unifying goal for all political-economic actors in Germany, regardless of each actor's individual interests.

While most political-economic actors in Germany believe in price stability, the government, in particular, may have alternative goals to pursue. As in many other countries, the government is committed to simultaneously pursuing the macroeconomic goals of price stability, a high level of employment, and external economic equilibrium. The relevant legislation also mentions adequate economic growth, and limits the choice of instruments to those compatible within the framework of a market economy.[11] Most important, the power of exchange rate management lies with the government, not the Bundesbank. It is within this central nexus of competing internal and external demands and objectives that the basic disagreements and conflicts arise between the Bundesbank and government over the direction of monetary policy.[12]

It should be noted that most politicians and economists no longer fervently believe in the Keynesian-inspired philosophy of the Stability and Growth Pact of 1967.[13] However, fiscal debate within the government does still turn on interpreting the demands of monetary stability within the real world of the German political economy, pressured by vote-motivated chancellors, contentious allies, and demanding domestic pressure groups. From the perspective of the unions, the Bundesbank's emphasis on the goal of monetary stability ultimately impacts the ability of the government to achieve the other stability and growth objectives, specifically, labor's concern with full employment. The government may also see the external dimension of monetary policy (for example, making a political commitment to the viability of the EMS) as more important than Bundesbank preoccupations with inflation.

For its part, Bundesbank officials are keenly aware that the government operates under multiple political constraints. Government ministers face the electoral and political constraints of implementing ideological and party goals. These constraints are exacerbated by economic constraints, for example, the economic structure of the domestic political economy (which can determine the degree and effectiveness of various fiscal policy instruments), and by the effect of prices and wage rates, among many other factors. The government also faces financial constraints arising from the difficulty or ease at which it can secure credit to finance its expenditures. The period since German reunification should make clear how the pressures of financing reunification and restructuring and reintegrating the east German economy have constrained the policy latitude of the government to deal with other mounting pressures within the western half of Germany, namely structural unemployment, rising health costs, and social security.

Nevertheless, from the Bundesbank perspective, safeguarding the currency and maintaining price stability are the preconditions to a sound economy at home, within the EU, and in the global economy. This is the *German monetary norm* as dictated by the Bundesbank. In other words, full employment, adequate economic growth, and external equilibrium will follow from a Bundesbank policy that defends the value of the DM. Inflation, even a small amount, can destroy a country's currency in the medium term and can destroy the economy as a whole in the long term. The Bundesbank, therefore, regards its mandate to safeguard the currency as its principal objective, an objective that overrides its other task "to support the general economic policy of the federal government." As Bundesbank officials resolutely point out, this mandate is concretely supported by the ability of the Bundesbank's decisions to remain independent (*unabhängig* in German) of the advice of the government (as defined in the BBG, Paragraph 12). The Bundesbank bases its success on its credibility and predictability to institute its perceived mandate to make decisions independent of political influences. Independence from political-economic pressures has become the foundation of Bundesbank policy.

This discussion might lead one to conclude that the Bundesbank's strict monetary objectives that internally safeguard the value of the currency take precedence over other macroeconomic goals or externally oriented monetary policies of the federal government. However, in the realpolitik of domestic monetary policy and international monetary diplomacy—

the political arena of deutsche mark politics—this impression is somewhat misleading. Can the federal government, European actors, or international actors in turn alter or influence the behavior of the Bundesbank? In other words, in what ways is the ability of the Bundesbank to safeguard the currency limited by various domestic, regional, and international players? Is the Bundesbank as independent as most analyses suggest and the bank's supporters contend? It is to these questions that the analysis now turns.

The Concept of Independence

Let us first examine the conceptual problem of using the terms *independence* and *autonomy*. Although considerable literature exists that interchangeably employs both the concept of autonomy and independence to describe the "playing room" or "maneuverability" of a central bank, this study prefers to utilize the term *independence* to describe the political position of the Bundesbank vis-à-vis the government. As is especially true in the German case, the concept of independence carries with it a more substantive and definitive use in German and in the BBG (*unabhängig*).[14] Three distinct dimensions of independence will be defined further on in this chapter. The concept of autonomy will be employed in the larger framework of this study in accordance with the definitions and conceptualizations of the monetary autonomy versus exchange rate stability trade-off set forth in Chapter 1.

It would also be prudent at this juncture to discuss the arguments in favor of an independent central bank. Such a discussion is important not only in terms of the Bundesbank but also the future EC Bank that is modeled closely after the Bundesbank. Most empirical studies have shown that countries with independent central banks achieve substantially lower inflation rates than countries in which the central bank is controlled directly by the government.[15] Using an index compiled by the authors, Alberto Alesina and Lawrence Summers cite Switzerland and Germany as the two most independent central banks in the world with an average inflation rate over the period 1955 to 1988 of around 3.2 percent and 3 percent, respectively. No other comparable central bank comes close to either figure.[16] Others argue that independence is important due to technical factors; policymaking from an independent central bank can be more straightforward and responsive to short-term needs of the economy in order to avoid the inevitable delays or "decision lags" that exist in the normal political process. Whereas some can argue that central banks also suffer such time lags (for example, six to nine months or even much longer) and that their decisions have not always been accurate or timely in nature, proponents counter that an independent central bank will at a minimum remain consistent in its monetary policy orientation.

One can also see constitutional principles at work and envision an independent central bank as a separate branch of government that can check potentially damaging policies of other government branches. For example, Karl Otto Pöhl has stated that he felt that the Bundesbank acts as a state within a state, a coalition partner of the government.[17] In other words, the Bundesbank can act as a check upon the actions of the federal government. Furthermore, in view of the politicians' short-term motivation and propensity to spend in support of lobbies, interest groups, and other pressures, issuing credits should be limited or capped to some ceiling. As all Bundesbank presidents would contend, "Nur knappes Geld ist gutes Geld!" loosely translated as "Only tight money is good money!" And tight money can only be insured if the Bundesbank acts as an independent economic and political counterweight to the spending proclivities of the government. In short, the lessons of history have provided the Germans with the experience that a nation's currency should be protected by an independent central bank due to the government's inability to manage a nation's monetary stock.

Central bank independence and its corresponding impact on policy credibility have also been cited by many analysts as an important reason for freeing the hand of a central bank. Independence has a strong impact on policy credibility and vice versa.[18] A central bank with a strong reputation for credible anti-inflationary policies may be able to resist political pressures to reform the legal structures and statutes of the bank or give in to financial threats to price stability. More important, perhaps, the issue of credibility centers on whether and how policymakers can make credible commitments about their future conduct. As John T. Woolley notes, independence and the credibility that flows from it need to be understood in terms of actual behavior and not just institutions.[19] The structure of the economy and internal politics may present policymakers with difficult trade-offs between short-run policy benefits and long-run policy costs that may impact credibility. An institution such as a central bank can be considered credible if it is willing to let the government, the public, and the economy incur the costs of their decisions. For example, during the speculative crises within the EMS in 1992–1993, many observers puzzled over the fact that the French franc came under more pressure than the DM, despite the franc's underlying strength in terms of the economic fundamentals (primarily inflation) of the French economy. The answer to this puzzle is rather simple. It centers on monetary credibility: The markets trusted the Bundesbank to bring the inflationary pressures in Germany under control and turn them around; the markets did not believe the French government's ability in the face of elections and growing unemployment to withstand the pressure to reflate.

Credibility of monetary policy will also depend not just upon monetary policy alone but rather upon the perceived coherence of the overall macroeconomic program. This coherence, together with the intellectual and political consensus on the economic theory being used and the objectives and conduct of the economic policy, significantly influences credibility. Not surprisingly, the independent structure of institutions makes all promises about future behavior more believable. The Bundesbank uses this understanding of credibility in its decision to publish yearly quantitative targets of the money stock. Focusing on a medium-term monetary target like M3, the Bundesbank believes it can make credible commitments to ensuring a predetermined range of monetary growth. If the bank fails to meet such targets, which has been the case in the past, the credibility can be harmed.[20] Despite some problems with the M3 indicator, the markets still trust the Bundesbank to control monetary growth.

While these arguments carry with them considerable merit, they should not go unquestioned. Perhaps the strongest argument against central bank independence is based on legal, or democratic, theory. This theory would contend that an independent central bank cannot be held democratically accountable for its politically sensitive actions. One might ask who should be held responsible for the effects on employment created by the Bundesbank's monetary policy—the bank or the government? Central banks remain free from the task of legitimating their power via elections, unlike other representative institutions. In principle, one can argue that the final decisions and the priorities, which are given to monetary policy, must lie with a parliament or some other representative body. It follows that if necessary, monetary policy should be subordinated to fiscal policy or other objectives laid out by popularly elected officials. Only the democratically elected officials of the government have the respective legitimacy and authority to proceed with the negotiations and reach an agreed-upon solution. Should the Bundesbank have the power to derail the government's plans for European union? In this view, the answer is no.

From an economic policy perspective, one can further argue that monetary policy be considered an integral part of the government's overall economic policy. The government's ability to successfully deal with economic difficulties would be strengthened if fiscal and monetary policies were coordinated. Although most governments now accept that low inflation is essential for sustainable growth, the trade-off between a bit more inflation and a bit more unemployment can still be made in the short term, especially with elections looming on the horizon. As a result of this short-term motivation, an independent central bank and monetary policy could very well lead to government frustration, friction, and conflict. As we shall see, government frustration, friction, and conflict have characterized deutsche mark politics. In short, monetary policy and the central bank should be considered one important part of Germany's arsenal in dealing with weighty economic problems.

It is clear that both sides of this argument carry with them considerable merit. Within a democratic order, there must remain some mechanism of accountability to all governmental and administrative institutions and agencies. Only with some mechanism of accountability can the state gain and retain the legitimacy and credibility of its constituents. At the same time, in recognition that the decisions surrounding monetary policy in Germany carry with them an almost extragovernmental aura, limits of some degree to the role that citizens, the government, and interest groups should have in monetary decisions must be accepted. History provides a painful reminder to many Germans of the dangers to the state if there exists too much political involvement in monetary policy. The Bundesbank, for its part, attempts to walk a very fine tightrope between complete institutional independence and direct political accountability. When the bank pushes toward either end of the independence-accountability spectrum, conflict within Germany and even abroad can erupt. Restoring a careful equilibrium between absolute independence and close cooperation with the government remains a central task of the Bundesbank. Such a task will be required of the ECB as well.

Bundesbank Independence: Three Dimensions

There exists considerable literature in German that examines the Bundesbank, its powers and processes, and its political independence.[21] The literature in English has been more sporadic, with discussions on the econometric studies of monetary policy,[22] the Bundesbank's role in the social-market economy in Germany, or its role in the international monetary system.[23] Not surprisingly, as the Bundesbank's role has become more pronounced, there has been an increase in English evaluations of this institution. This chapter attempts to update and synthesize both English and German analyses in order to provide a definitive account of the concept of independence in the context of Bundesbank-government interaction.

Specifically, there are three distinctive contexts that have been identified within which the influence of the government, societal interests, and international actors must be excluded or greatly curtailed for a central bank to be considered independent. These three contexts are political independence, personal independence, and financial independence.[24] Within each one of these contexts, the regional and international dimensions that may limit Bundesbank independence will be analyzed. Moreover, the constitutional, economic, and political experiences and preferences that have operated within each of these three contexts in Germany will be examined.

Political Independence

Perhaps the pivotal concept in the study of central bank independence is its functional or political independence. For the purpose of definition, Woolley distinguishes two types of independence that prove useful.[25] Political independence refers to the ability of a central bank to choose a course of action independently without yielding to the pressures of others as to what that action should be. Functional independence refers to the central bank's ability to achieve its objectives without being affected by the actions of others. Functional independence, as Woolley argues, is generally not characteristic of monetary policy.[26] For my purposes, I will focus on political independence.

Political independence refers to the formal legal competence of the Bundesbank to choose a course of action independently and without yielding to the overt or covert pressures of other political actors. By almost all accounts and universal consensus among analysts, political independence has best characterized the monetary policy of the Bundesbank. Elke Thiel sets the tone for this monetary independence by arguing that "the German Bundesbank is committed to defend price stability by constitution and its status of autonomy provides the political independence to enforce this goal. All German governments have been very cautious to avoid any open conflict with the Bundesbank on monetary policy issues."[27] John Goodman supports Thiel's contention by arguing that, in particular, institutional independence gives German monetary policy its special independent character.[28] Institutional independence can act as an intermediate variable that determines whether monetary policy is influenced by domestic or foreign politics. From the Bundesbank's perspective, it is clear that institutional independence helps to dampen the effects of political parties, electoral pressures, business and labor interests, and European and G7 pressures.

As discussed earlier, monetary policy is entrusted to an independent central bank, and a policy rule is specified by law that precludes inflating. The BBG specifically states that the central bank shall "safeguard the value of the currency" (Article 3); and, according to Article 12, it is also required "to support the general economic policy of the federal government" but only in so far as this support does not undermine its task of preserving monetary stability. The Bundesbank remains "independent" of governmental direction (Article 12). This legal independence leads Goodman to conclude that the Bundesbank was often able to impose its own view. This ability results, at least in the short run, from the laws that define the central bank's independence. Goodman's study also accurately assesses the considerable political and public support of Bundesbank independence, which would suggest that it fulfills the requirements of political independence.

This independence provides the mechanism with which the Bundesbank can effectively counter efforts to influence its political-independent decisionmaking ability.

Absolute independence is not likely for a central bank, however, as with any other important federal institution or governmental agency.[29] No one believes in absolute independence just as no one demands that the Bundesbank be absolutely subjected to the government's discretion on monetary policy. But what is central to this analysis are the methods in which the balance of power and jurisdiction between the federal government and the important economic interest groups are played out in the political playing field. In other words, to what degree is the Bundesbank bound to the advice and direction of the government? This question is often very difficult to quantify and therefore requires analysis of the structures, patterns, and institutional behavior surrounding this relationship. Moreover, the relationship between the bank and government remains one of discretion and limited public visibility. Most major controversies or discussions are held behind closed doors, out of the view of the public; although, as we shall see in the following analysis, this has not always been the case.

Mention is made in the German Constitution, Article 88, that "the Government shall create a central bank," yet the actual piece of legislation that created the Bundesbank, the BBG, originated through a simple majority act of the legislative process.[30] The hotly debated and controversial parliamentary discussions in 1955–1956 over the BBG centered mainly on the degree to which the Bundesbank would have political independence. The debate sharpened when, during the debates leading up to the passage of the BBG, the first chancellor of the FRG, Konrad Adenauer, first suggested that the seat of the new Bundesbank remain within "the political sphere of Bonn."[31] Still upset from his early confrontations with the Bank der deutschen Länder (BdL), the predecessor to the Bundesbank from 1948 to 1957, Adenauer anticipated the inevitable conflicts that would emerge between the government and the still-to-be-created central bank over economic goals and objectives. Considerations were also given at the time to the creation of a secondary institution, or advisory council, that could arbitrate between the Bundesbank and the government in cases of "dramatic" confrontation.[32]

Despite some of Adenauer's concerns, the BBG was passed on July 26, 1957, with its aforementioned tasks and guarantees, giving the Bundesbank a significant amount of political independence. The strong support that the Bundesbank retains in the minds of politicians and the public alike does give it the quasi-constitutional character that Emminger mentions in the opening quote to this chapter.[33] However, the fact that many commentators argue that the Bundesbank has constitutional standing in the federal government of Germany and, hence, constitutional guarantees of independence, often leads to a confused analysis of whether the Bundesbank and its structure can in fact be altered.

Specifically, the contention that the Bundesbank has distinct constitutional guarantees, which would require a two-thirds majority vote to change the BBG, are, as one scholar has noted, "untenable."[34] According to Rolf Kaiser and Konrad von Bonin, the Bundesbank fails to meet the characteristics and qualities of a constitutional body because its duties and rights are not stated in the constitution itself. What is more, according to rulings and interpretations of the Federal Constitutional Court (Bundesverfassungsgericht), the Bundesbank fails to embody the "highest authority" and the "legitimization of the people" through proper electoral representation of its board members.[35] Moreover, if the Bundesbank and the BBG can be amended through a simple majority act of the parliament, then one can argue that independence of the bank is more limited and circumscribed than previously thought. For example, the threat to rewrite the BBG during the debate over gold revaluation in spring 1997 was very real and could have been pushed through the Bundestag by the Kohl government. Moreover, the BBG has now been fundamentally revised in preparation for EMU. Although some have argued that the entire process of rewriting the BBG was unconstitutional (see Chapter 7), it demonstrated the lack of constitutional protections centering on Bundesbank independence.

Paradoxically, the Bundesbank may well give up its particular independence on a contentious issue at any one time, choosing to follow the wishes of the government, in order to preserve its long-term independence. This point is made succinctly by A. Poullian.

> If the government . . . mainly fights against unemployment and, therefore, pursues an expansionary economic policy, the central bank must accept this goal preference order. . . . If the central bank were to refuse its support, it would run the danger of losing its independence through a corresponding change in the central bank law. . . . The end result of fundamental political conflicts would necessarily be the loss of central bank autonomy.[36]

A similar view is presented in Goodman's analysis in which he suggests that the Bundesbank will, at times, strategically retreat on specific policy initiatives in order to avoid uniting too many powerful opposing interests. These strategic retreats provide a glimpse of cooperative Bundesbank policy—which is the focus of deutsche mark politics—and they also demonstrate that the government does have political leverage over the Bundesbank.

The parliament can also question the Bundesbank about its relationship to the federal government and basic monetary policy questions. The responsible parliamentary committees (money and credit) can discuss and debate certain critical economic and monetary issues and can call on members of the Bundesbank to come before the committees. The full parliament can discuss any monetary issues as well as establish special investigative committees. However, it must be said that such cases are exceptional. One cannot compare the German case to that of the U.S. or British standing committees with oversight on these matters.

Finally, the government can attempt to personally lobby or persuade Bundesbank officials to pursue a particular policy. The minister of economics and finance as well as other invited members of the federal government are allowed to participate in the Central Bank Council (Zentralbankrat) deliberations. Such visits by the chancellor have been rare occasions of monetary importance. No government official has voting rights in the council. Normally, a leading assistant (*Staatssekretär*) from the economics or finance ministry will attend the meeting. Therefore, the weighty decisions of the central council are immediately heard by the government, and the government representatives can make a case for a particular course of action. A press conference with the president of the Bundesbank and representatives of the government then follows. An official written statement of the Bundesbank regarding its relationship to the federal government—which indicates that both sides have always been very open and that information shared and participation by the government have been useful for making decisions—indicates the lengths to which both sides seek to avoid disagreement.[37] Because of this close council consultation, no government has used its two-week veto power to delay central council decisions, although the central council has on occasion delayed a decision for two weeks in deference to the wish of the chancellor.

Most of the contact between the bank and government takes place in informal talks, personal consultations, and telephone conversations. Both actors consider cooperation in such day-to-day contacts excellent. In fact, members of the chancellor's office, finance ministry, and the Bundesbank's administrative machinery often have shared similar government positions with their current counterparts in their respective departments. There also exist nongovernmental interactions such as those that occur in private societal and business gatherings. Based on my own interviews, the Bundesbank and finance ministry have declared their various positions on the type of contact, mode of communication, arena for consultation and agreement, and mode of operation should disagreement occur. In cases of some conflict, both actors tend to solve the disagreement through low-level intrabureaucratic modes of consultation. However, in most of the cases of high levels of disagreement illustrated in this book, conflict escalated quickly to the upper levels of monetary decisionmaking. Consequently, it is interesting to note that only the Bundesbank has officially declared that it would take any serious disagreement over the course of German monetary policy immediately to the chancellor or finance minister. We should interpret this to mean that any disagreement would be assured of becoming public at which time the Bundesbank could mobilize the public to its advantage. As the debate over gold revaluation demonstrated, a heated battle of testaments will result.

As a result of the continuous consultation, governmental constraints, and legislative power, the German government does have, in theory, numerous formal political resources available to it in confronting the Bundesbank's vaunted constitutional safeguards. Admittedly, the Bundesbank does retain a notable amount of political independence, but the almost mythic level of political independence that so often characterizes German monetary policy and the Bundesbank, in particular, is somewhat overdramatized in public accounts. Moreover, the claim that the Bundesbank is a constitutional entity cannot be sustained. Although no government seeks confrontation and conflict with the Bundesbank, political resources do exist that the government could use to circumscribe Bundesbank independence.

Personal Independence

The issue of personal independence is closely related to political independence. The Central Bank Council is the supreme policymaking body of the Bundesbank. Up until 1992, the council consisted of a vice president, president, up to eight members of the directorate, and the eleven *Land* (state) central bank presidents of the former West Germany. Following the sometimes acrimonious and controversial discussions in the Bundestag and Bundesrat centering on the revisions to the Bundesbank Law during the reunification debates of 1992, the current number of Central Bank Council members can be at most seventeen: eight members of the directorate (reduced from ten) and nine *Land* central bank presidents (reduced from eleven as several *Land* central banks were combined).[38] The reduction in central council members was seen as a victory for the directorate, which often argued that there were too many members on the council already, resulting in inefficient and unwieldy discussions. Although the presidents of the *Land* central banks can and do outnumber the directorate appointees to the council, the recent changes have strengthened the hand of the "professionals" in Frankfurt, something that was already feared by the *Land* when the Bundesbank was created in 1957.

As the potential strength of the *Land* central bank presidents suggests, federalism plays an important conceptual role in organizing the Bundesbank. Early debate on its creation had examined whether to centralize the powers of the new Bundesbank or decentralize authority to the *Land*.[39] The federalist pattern chosen fit the traditional federalist structure of pre-Nazi

Germany as well as the concerns by the Bundesbank's creators to avoid centralizing control by the federal government. While the federalist structure can impinge on the personal independence of the Bundesbank, more important, it prevents the federal government from dominating or dictating policy. This system of shared power was a practical compromise between those who wanted government power to stay with each state (to provide a listening post for assessing public, labor, banking, farming, and business opinions and concerns) and those who wanted a national sovereign in control of monetary policy. The concern with a federalist structure has also found its way into the European System of Central Banks (ESCB).

Despite the federalist nature of the personal setup of the Bundesbank, the Bundesbank president and vice president play an extra special role in explaining and defining German monetary policy. More often than not, it is the president of the Bundesbank who takes a critical role in the policy interaction with the government over European monetary policy or international G7 negotiations. As heads of the directorate, the president and vice president oversee a huge administrative and bureaucratic organization that develops policy papers and drafts position papers and consultative documents for internal bank usage or interaction with the federal ministries. Of particular importance for this study is the international and foreign division, which up until 1991 was headed by Hans Tietmeyer, currently the president of the Bundesbank, having succeeded Helmut Schlesinger on October 1, 1993.

Specifically, then, the appointment process of the leading personalities of the Bundesbank both at the directorate level and at the *Land* central bank president level must be accepted as a given in a democratic society. There are, however, some clear criteria that curb governmental influence in the appointment process. First, the Bundesbank has the right to express its views on the appointees nominated by the government, although it has no veto right. The Bundesbank has on occasion raised some objections to various nominees.[40] No single candidate, however, has been turned away from a Bundesbank position by objections from Frankfurt.[41] A second important criteria is the length of the term of office. This standard is substantially more important than the first criteria because the longer the term of office the less likely the chance of electoral manipulation. Finally, the method of actually selecting nominees, either by the head of a *Land* government, the head of government, or some bipartisan committee, can have some impact on the personal independence of the Bundesbank.

How are the members selected for Germany? The strong personal independence of the Bundesbank results from the fact that less than half of the members of the central council are appointed at the suggestion of the federal government. The others are, of course, suggested by the *Land* governments. This decentralization of power through the appointment process limits any one interest or faction, whether regional or partisan, from attaining a practical majority on the council. Moreover, the terms of office are relatively long, normally eight years. The Bundesbank act decouples the "timing of the selection of top officials of the Bundesbank from the calendar of parliamentary elections," thus denying a new government "the chance to hand the bank over to their supporters to secure obedience."[42] Analytically, there thus exists a strong correlation between the length of the term of office and the degree of political influence. The more indefinite and the shorter the term of office is, the greater the opportunities are for politicians to interfere.

Moreover, new members to the Bundesbank are quickly acculturated into the dominant norms of behavior. A strong sense of community within the bank helps to ensure a code of independence. As David Marsh cogently argues, outsiders brought into the bank conform to the *Stabilitätspolitik* (stability-oriented policy) of the Bundesbank, known as the Becket Effect.[43] Tradition and operations of the Central Bank Council quickly integrate new members to Bundesbank culture that requires members to appear, at least, above party politics and factions. Once former party functionaries, for example Pöhl and Tietmeyer, new employees become apolitical and nonpartisan. As a result, one-time party allies (for example, Pöhl and Schmidt) may find themselves locked in intense political struggles. In addition, while there exist considerable differences of background and opinion on many policy decisions, the council works hard to display a united front on key decisions. This helps to strengthen the external public support that the Bundesbank values. This united front projects the image of a technical council concerned strictly with the economic situation, the exchange markets, and the capital markets. However, as EMU has revealed, the united front can be cracked and internal divisions displayed.

In terms of international influences, it is clear that there can be no direct international personal circumscribing of Bundesbank influence. However, interestingly, there does exist some tension among those members of the council who are more internationalist in orientation (primarily members of the directorate) and those with a stronger domestic orientation (the *Land* bank presidents). Considering that the number of voices of the *Land* bank presidents have been reduced, one can argue that there will be a corresponding shift toward a concern with external/international monetary relations.[44] However, this shift, if at all, should not be overemphasized.

Can particular interest groups seek singular influence with members of the council, and can they manipulate the appointment process to their favor? The answer is an unequivocal no. In terms of outside interests, organizations, and associations, all have consistently supported the Bundesbank's independence and do not seek to alter the process of appointment or actively manipulate appointments to a particular interest.[45] There have been demands made, however, especially by the unions, for a Bundesbank advisory council in which nonstate or societal interests would be represented and for the bank to hold more closely to the Stability and Growth Law. Along this line of reasoning, the unions argue that this would in fact strengthen the independence of the Bundesbank, because the Bundesbank could legitimize and add to its credibility by providing a direct voice to these groups.[46] But no such organ exists. However, according to Paragraph 9 of the BBG, there exists at the *Land* level such advisory councils to the *Land* banks. These advisory councils have representatives from a broad orientation of societal interests including labor, business, farming, and banking. In fact, during the debates and discussions leading up to the BBG in 1956–1957, one of the first government plans was to eliminate these advisory councils that existed already within the structure of the Bank der deutschen Länder. However, the members of the committee argued that it was important for the *Land* banks to remain close to "all groups in the market economy."[47]

Overall, through the decentralized selection process of members of the directorate and the *Land* presidents and the eight-year term of office, the Bundesbank maintains a significant level of personal independence. Moreover, government officials have gone to great lengths to avoid politicizing the selection process, in stark contrast with the selection of the first president of the ECB. If politicization should occur, it could only damage the standing of the government in the eyes of many in the public who see the Bundesbank as standing above the political fray. This does not mean that the *Land* governments or the chancellor do not try to fill spots with people who share a similar ideological or philosophical orientation.[48] However, efforts have been made to achieve a modicum of philosophical and partisan balance on the council.

Financial Independence

The third and final important aspect determining the level and degree of central bank independence is its financial independence from either the obligatory financing of government debts or obligatory external monetary arrangements such as those that existed under Bretton Woods and more recently within the EMS.[49] First, a government can exercise influence over and limit the discretion of central bankers if there exists the possibility that the government can finance its expenditures either directly or indirectly via central bank credits. Access to central bank credits, especially direct access, can result in an overlapping or fiscal circular flow of money into the money supply. If such financing mechanisms exist, monetary policy is by necessity subordinated to the diktat of fiscal policy.[50] In Germany, however, there are restrictions to this access. This restriction is given some teeth by Article 20 of the BBG, which prohibits the Bundesbank from granting the federal government more than a previously prescribed amount in short-term credit. It is also generally understood by the finance ministry that it cannot rely on the Bundesbank to bail the government out in times of irresponsible policy. However, the Bundesbank's dramatic refusal of the government's attempts to revalue the nation's gold reserves in order to provide the finance minister with the necessary budgetary leeway to attain Maastricht criteria does reveal that the government may still try to circumvent Bundesbank control. Overall, though, the Bundesbank has a significant amount of independence in this regard.

One should also consider the monetary instruments at the disposal of the Bundesbank and how they might be narrowed or restricted by the federal government. The Bundesbank has at its disposal the normal array of central bank powers and functions.[51] It issues currency, decides upon discount and other interest rates, conducts open market transactions, and establishes minimum reserve requirements. It can also carry out policies regarding government deposits, currency exchange, currency market interventions, and the sale or purchase of certain securities. Its principal instruments are the discount rate for loans to other banks, the Lombard rate for short-term funding requirements of banks, open market operations, and minimum requirement policies. Its use of the discount rate is generally aimed at long-term market adjustment. These internal and domestic levers all rest strongly under the control of the Bundesbank, and again, the federal government has little or no influence over the direct monetary levers of the Bundesbank.

The DM also plays a large role in terms of international reserves, especially in European foreign exchange reserve accounts. The Bundesbank reported in 1997 that about 15 percent of world reserves were denominated in DMs.[52] In comparison to the dollar, the DM is clearly not as widely used in global transactions (most commodities trade is denominated in dollars, for example), which is fine with the Bundesbank. Still, 15 percent of world trade is conducted in the DM, centered, of course, on Germany's deutsche mark zone in Europe. In addition, although not widespread, some major banks in the United States offer deutsche mark accounts for Americans who want to hedge some of their assets against a fall in the dollar.[53] In short, the DM is notably exposed internationally both in terms of financial markets and the trade of international goods and services. The DM, whether fixed or floating, is subject to the vagaries and volatility of the international market-based system of finance.

Most important and as noted in Chapter 1, the Bundesbank faces the financial constraints associated with the intervention requirements, institutional commitments, and interest rate pressures associated with exchange rate mechanisms. Changes in the rate of exchange are the prerogative of the federal government (as stated in Article 73 of the constitution), with the Bundesbank serving an advisory function (Article 13 of the BBG). If the central bank is bound to keep exchange rates stable (a political decision made by the government), the Bundesbank may be forced to automatically intervene in foreign exchange markets or may be pressured to pursue an interest rate policy so as to ensure the proper exchange rate levels. In a system of freely fluctuating exchange rates, this constraint no longer holds, and the central bank can pursue a policy solely concerned with domestic affairs. This has been the case at the international level since 1973 when German monetary authorities finally found themselves unbound by automatic interventions in the foreign exchange market.

However, in a system of dirty floating in the international monetary system or in a system of adjustable peg rates, such as exists in the ERM of the EMS, the central bank must buy and sell foreign currency in order to meet commitments built into the ERM's various trading bands.[54] The Bundesbank may also face pressure from the United States and Japan or other G7 members to intervene in the currency markets in order to achieve a prearranged DM-dollar rate, for example. As the Bundesbank itself admits, the external scope of its policy range has narrowed within the EMS, with increasing integration in financial markets and with greater global interdependence. Such international agreements made either under the institutionalized rules and binding conditions of the EMS or the less binding conditions of the G7 can limit the policy action and hence independence of the central bank, a fundamental point of contention that will be further explored in the following case studies. The finance ministry's monetary diplomacy, based at times on the foreign policy considerations of the government, can compromise the Bundesbank's mandated mission of price stability. As a result, external exchange rate commitments may severely circumscribe the Bundesbank's financial independence.

* * *

Compared to most central banks and in terms of all three dimensions of central bank independence, the German Bundesbank retains a significant measure of independence. The Bundesbank also has the most clearly defined political, personal, and financial independence than any of its European counterparts. The Bundesbank remains a model of central bank independence, price stability, and policy credibility throughout Europe and in the developing world.[55] However, there are limits and constraints on Bundesbank independence. While the Bundesbank remains the preeminent monetary actor in German monetary policy, it is not predominant. Despite a significant level of political, personal, and financial independence, the Bundesbank has had to consistently defend its independent status within the political economy and defend its mandate to safeguard the value of the DM. As the brief history examined in the next section indicates, the Bundesbank's independence has been leveraged on account of political imperatives imposed by the government.

The Limits to Central Bank Independence: A Brief History

Today's Bundesbank bears some resemblance to its predecessors, and several important lessons drawn from history are noteworthy.[56] Between 1875 and World War I, the Reichsbank's room for maneuver was greatly hampered, both politically and financially. When the Reichsbank was founded in 1875, its board was subordinated to the prime minister, limiting its political independence considerably. Although the board members were appointed for their lifetime (giving the Reichsbank, in principle, a substantial degree of personal independence), more important was the existence of considerable financial dependence due to the gold standard, which, although operating far from perfectly, governed the course of monetary policy in Germany until 1914.

The period of World War I and its aftermath, including the hyperinflationary period of 1923, provided strong arguments in favor of central bank independence. The primary objective of monetary policy from 1914 to 1918 was the inflationary financing of the war effort.[57] Following the end of the war, the monetary situation worsened to such an extent that the allied countries urged the newly established Weimar government to establish the autonomous status of the bank in order to pursue a more stability-oriented policy. The government did respond with legislation establishing the independence of the bank in 1922, but this did nothing to hinder the bank from continuing to finance government expenditures. Interestingly, legal and political independence did not prevent the government from influencing the bank or monetary policy. The infamous hyperinflationary period of 1923 came about under the tenure of a formally independent central bank.

Nonetheless, important lessons were learned. The culmination of a printing-press economy and the hyperinflationary period of 1923 forced the government to reform the monetary system. The government's steps included the successful issue of the rentenmark in November 1923, the drastic restriction on central bank credits to the government, and a fixing of the exchange rate to the dollar. These steps helped stabilize the German currency, both internally and externally. These reforms ultimately found their way into the Bank Act of 1924 that preserved and extended the political and personal independence of the Reichsbank under its powerful new president, Hjalmar Schacht. Financial independence was also strengthened mainly through the limitation of the volume of bank credits to the government, clearly the main source of the inflation through 1923. A semblance of monetary order thus re-emerged within Weimar Germany.

This considerable theoretical independence could not, however, hold off the political and economic onslaughts of the upcoming decade. During the late 1920s and early 1930s, the problems in the international monetary system and the resulting monetary mismanagement both within Germany and abroad cannot be blamed on the relative independence of the Reichsbank but rather on the deflationary impact of the resurrected gold standard and the linkage of the German economy to the U.S. economy.[58] And by 1933, no central bank survived intact the impact of the Great Depression and, in the case of Germany, Hitler's *Gleichschaltung,* or coordination of all important institutions of society under Nazi control.[59] The attempt by the Nazi government to finance its expansive policies led to a rewriting of the 1924 Bank Act in 1933 and again in 1937 after some members of the Reichsbank quietly objected to what they felt were Hitler's irresponsible financial policies. The 1937 revision removed any semblance of personal independence from the bank and directly subordinated it to the Nazi government. Up until 1939, however, most members of the Reichsbank were proud of their accomplishments, that is, re-establishing the value of the reichsmark and protecting the economy from macroeconomic monetary shocks from above (through autarkic fiscal, monetary, and trading policies). By 1939 the honeymoon between the bank and Hitler ended. The president of the Reichsbank, Schacht, and other leading members of the board were replaced because of a letter they had written in protest to the inflationary spending of the government.

The basic foundation of the personal and political independence in the 1924 Bank Act ultimately was resurrected in the post-1948 central bank in Germany. The currency reform of June 20, 1948, replaced the worthless reichsmark with the DM. The new currency was issued first by the BdL and, as we have seen, in 1957 was transformed into the Deutsche Bundesbank. In 1958 the full convertibility of the DM, which had been abolished in 1931, was restored. By the late 1950s, however, on the external front the financial independence was being undermined due to the system of fixed exchange rates under the dollar-dominated Bretton Woods system. Like the period during the gold standard between 1875 and 1914 or during Weimar, the exchange rate system led to severe conflicts between maintaining external and internal equilibrium. Whereas the earlier problem had primarily been imported *deflation*, the problem during the period 1948–1973 was imported *inflation*. Germany, a surplus country, experienced large capital inflows in anticipation of a revaluation of its currency.

Specifically, repeated confrontations between Germany and the United States over the operation of the Bretton Woods system demonstrated markedly the limitations on Bundesbank independence. In the period 1960–1961, the Bundesbank found itself under immense political pressure to agree, which it ultimately did, to a 5 percent revaluation of the DM. The period from early 1968 through 1969 posed further problems for the Bundesbank's stability-oriented policies and its independence. Constant pressure on the DM to revalue, coupled with occasional crises over the French franc, led to a series of movements on the exchange rate front (including, from the Bundesbank's perspective, exchange rate "gimmickry"[60]) that forced the bank into repeated confrontation with the government. While the Bundesbank emerged in some cases stronger, the external flank of German monetary policy remained exposed. The last stages of Bretton Woods placed further pressure on the Bundesbank as it faced off with the popular and knowledgeable "super minister" Karl Schiller. However, the Bundesbank, with support from Willy Brandt, saw its policies prevail over those of Schiller, leading to the infamous Schiller Sturz. Despite occasionally emerging on the victorious end of many debates, the Bundesbank found itself constantly under direct political and financial limits to its independence.

Dramatic conflicts between the government and the Bundesbank over domestic monetary politics were also notable. In most cases, the Bundesbank emerged politically on top, but not without great controversy. The first significant conflict between the BdL and the government occurred in 1955–1956 as the bank raised interest rates from 3 percent to 5 percent. Adenauer was greatly "distressed" that the rise in interest rates would cut off growth at a crucial period in the early stages of the Wirtschaftswunder.[61] Despite a public attack on the Bundesbank by Adenauer (the "Fallbeil" speech), the BdL set a powerful precedent for central bank independence by resisting pressure from Adenauer. By early 1966, tensions rose as Chancellor Erhard faced rising unemployment and the first sputtering of the German economic miracle. The Bundesbank effectively resisted pressure from Erhard to ease the rates at the time, leading in some part to the weakening of the Erhard government. New elections in 1966 brought into government a Grand Coalition of Christian Democratic Union (CDU)/Christian Social Union (CSU)–Social Democratic Party (SPD) under the leadership of Chancellor Kurt George Kiesinger (CDU). Even in the face of electoral pressure, the Bundesbank continued to reinforce its political independence at home.

The period of the 1970s and early 1980s saw increased pressures placed upon the Bundesbank by the government headed by the SPD and Chancellor Helmut Schmidt (1974–1982). With Schmidt at the lead, European officials recognized the need for a united European dollar policy.[62] First, using the Werner Report as its basis, the Europeans embarked on a European joint float (commonly known as the "snake") in April 1972 against the dollar.[63] The lack of a formal institutionalized mechanism for currency support, however, weakened the potential for monetary cooperation. The snake, with the DM as the anchor, eventually fragmented. Especially in regard to its external monetary flank, the Bundesbank felt a tremendous burden lifted with the disintegration of Bretton Woods and the snake. The bank felt it could now pursue a narrower "monetarist" policy focusing on monetary targets and corridors for domestic monetary policy.

However, Schmidt's concern with U.S. interest rates, the dollar's exchange rate against the mark, a sluggish German economy, and the energy crisis culminated in a four-year period (1978–1982) of ongoing tension, acrimony, and conflict with the Bundesbank over the objectives and goals of monetary policy.[64] The end result of this confrontation was the collapse of the Schmidt government in 1982 and a period of heightened monetary turmoil within Europe and between Germany and the United States. Much to the Bundesbank's dismay, the first G7 summits from 1975 to 1978 were aimed at stabilizing the international economy from the effects of the first oil crisis and the collapse of Bretton Woods and were guided by a shared economic philosophy of demand management.[65] The culmination of this new international constraint was the 1978 G7 Bonn summit that required Germany to pursue a fiscal stimulus package in return for U.S. commitments on inflation reduction.

On the European front, the tension between Schmidt and the Bundesbank sharpened over the implementation of the EMS in 1979, as the Bundesbank was not eager to surrender its formal exchange rate freedom to a European venture that would mire the Germans in an *Inflationsgemeinschaft*. As indicated earlier, the Bundesbank was initially outright skeptical if not hostile to the whole arrangement and would only agree to the EMS if the bank had written assurances from the government that it would not have to intervene in the markets if such intervention limited its financial independence. Despite assurances by Schmidt that the EMS would not impinge upon the financial independence of the Bundesbank, the fact that the political independence had been questioned in Schmidt's bold move to create the EMS signaled to many Bundesbank officials that the EMS would indeed curtail the bank's independent financial latitude. Moreover, the Bundesbank now found itself in the formal position of balancing not only domestic monetary concerns but also European and international (dollar) pressures as well.[66] With the United States experiencing renewed inflationary pressures, which only further sharpened the internal-external policy debate, the triangulation of German monetary policy had become institutionalized.

In response to the tensions surrounding the creation of the EMS and exacerbated by the weakening dollar and inflationary pressures within

Germany, the Bundesbank—by 1979 now under the direction of its new Schmidt-appointed president, Karl Otto Pöhl—began to slowly hike up the discount rate from 3 percent to 7 percent with the Lombard rate rising to 9 percent. The rate hikes were justified in the view of the Bundesbank due to the very un-German inflation rate that reached 5.5 percent by 1980. For Schmidt the problems of the German economy, a trade deficit of DM 25 billion, and a record budget deficit of DM 28 billion, or 1.82 percent of gross domestic product (GDP), were straightforward: high U.S. interest rates, relatively high German interest rates, and the second oil shock of 1979. Internal dissatisfaction within the SPD, which saw heavy pressure from the trade unions to stimulate domestic demand, and coalition problems with the Free Democratic Party (FDP), especially the economics minister, Otto Graf Lambsdorff, who was pushing for further budget cuts, further exacerbated Schmidt's problems.

Complicated by a weak mark and the familiar concern about imported inflation, the Bundesbank dramatically raised the basic rate in February 1981 by a maximum of three full points, from 9 percent to 12 percent, suspended commercial bank access to overnight funds through the Lombard rate, and instituted a special Lombard rate that would vary daily, a rate that shot up to 28 percent one week after the bank's announcement. Pöhl, in defending the move, shifted the blame onto the government's deficit policies and the wage demands of the unions. Although Schmidt directly pressured the Bundesbank to lower rates, the Bundesbank refused, even after the unions had lowered their wage demands and the DM strengthened in international markets and stabilized in the EMS. Both sides sought publicly to outflank the other. Both Schmidt and the Bundesbank sought to directly influence each other in order to secure victory. Although such influence was not unheard of, the level and degree of open confrontation was certainly unprecedented. One might argue that the Bundesbank emerged dominant as the Schmidt government collapsed in the fall of 1982. Nevertheless, the Bundesbank also found that a determined chancellor could constrain the vaunted independence of the Bundesbank.

Conclusion

This chapter has demonstrated that the Bundesbank has a large measure of political, personal, and financial independence and remains the preeminent state actor in monetary policy. But as these dimensions of independence are in some ways noticeably limited and as the historical record has illustrated, the Bundesbank is not always the predominant actor in deutsche mark politics. Disagreement over policy has been at times quite intense, and the Bundesbank has had to retreat on occasion in the face of sustained political pressure. The ongoing conflict over monetary influence is the essence of deutsche mark politics and the subject of the remaining chapters.

Notes

1. For a conceptual analysis, see Paul Egon Rohrlich, "Economic Culture and Foreign Economic Policy: The Cognitive Analysis of Economic Policy Making," *International Organization* 41, no. 1 (1987), pp. 61–92. The concept has also been used in the German context by James Sperling, "The BRD, the United States, and the Atlantic Community," in Peter Merkl, ed., *The Federal Republic at Forty* (New York: New York University Press, 1989), pp. 367–390.

2. Susan Strange and David Calleo, *Paths to International Political Economy* (London: George, Allen, and Unwin, 1984), p. 111.

3. W. R. Smyser, *The Economy of United Germany: Colossus at the Crossroads* (New York: St. Martin's Press, 1992), p. 138.

4. Such a view was confirmed repeatedly in interviews with public and private officials. In almost every interview conducted, the interviewee mentioned the broad public consensus and support that the Bundesbank receives.

5. Gordon Craig, "Money," in *The Germans* (New York: Meridian, 1982), p. 121.

6. The German Constitution tends to be very precise in its dispersal of responsibilities and duties in order to strengthen state authority.

7. Helmut Schlesinger, "Kontinuität in den Zielen, Wandel in den Methoden," in Wolfgang Filc, Lothar Hübl, and Rüdiger Pohl, eds., *Herausforderungen der Wirtshaftspolitik: Festschrift zum 60. Geburtstag von Claus Köhler* (Berlin: Duncker and Humblot, 1988), p. 197.

8. Elizabeth Noelle-Neumann, "Geldwert und öffentliche Meinung: Anmerkungen zur 'Psychologie der Inflation,'" in C. A. Andreae, K. H. Hansmeyer, and G. Scherhorn, *Geldtheorie und Geldpolitik: Zum Gustav Schmölders 65 Geburtstag* (Berlin: Duncker and Humblot, 1968).

9. Emphasis added by author.

10. Otmar Emminger, *Verteidigung der DM: Pladöyers für stabiles Geld* (Frankfurt/Main: Fritz Knapp, 1980), p. 10.

11. See *Gesetz über die Bildung eines Sachverstandigenrates zur Begutachtung der gesamtwirtschaftlichen Entwicklung* (August 14, 1963) and *Gesetz zur Förderung der Stabilität und des Wachstums der Wirtschaft* (June 8, 1967), better known and hereafter referred to as the Stability and Growth Law.

12. Frey and Schneider in their study of German central bank behavior define *conflict* as the result of opposing fiscal and monetary policies pursued by the government and the central bank. A state of conflict exists when, for example, the Bundesbank pursues a deflationary monetary policy and the government pursues an inflationary fiscal policy. Bruno Frey and Friedrich Schneider, "Central Bank Behavior: A Positive Empirical Analysis," *Journal of Monetary Economics* 7 (1981), pp. 291–315. Their definition is contested by Thomas Baum in "Empirische Analysen der Bundesbankautonomie," *Konjunkturpolitik* 29, no. 3 (1983), pp. 163–185. Baum's alternate definition of conflict (less of a concern with opposing policies and more of a concern with the rate or pace of divergence) leads to different conclusions vis-à-vis Bundesbank independence (greater independence than Frey and Schneider conclude). Neither analysis provides for an adequate understanding of the external exchange rate management dimension of conflict.

13. For an excellent account of the weakness of Keynesian ideas in Germany, see Christopher Allen, "The Underdevelopment of Keynesianism in the Federal Republic of Germany," in Peter A. Hall, ed., *The Power of Economic Ideas* (Princeton, N.J.: Princeton University Press, 1989).

14. See the conceptual discussion in Rolf Caesar, *Der Handlungsspielraum von Notenbanken* (Baden-Baden: Nomos, 1981), pp. 56–62. An example of the complexity and conceptual difficulty of these terms arose during my discussions with German political and economic scholars who, when asked by me how they defined either term, answered that they hoped I could shed further light on the debate.

15. In particular, see the work of Alberto Alesina and Lawrence Summers, "Central Bank Independence and Macroeconomic Performance: Some Comparative Evidence," *Journal of Money and Credit* 25 (1992). See also Richard Burdekin and Thomas Willett, "Central Bank Reform: The Federal Reserve in International Perspective," *Public Budgeting and Financial Management* 3, no. 3 (1991), pp. 619–650; "Central Banks: America v. Japan—The Rewards of Independence," *The Economist*, January 25, 1992.

16. As a comparison, the United States managed to secure an average inflation rate for the period 1955 to 1988 of 4.1 percent.

17. See Karl Otto Pöhl's comments in David Marsh, *The Germans: Rich, Divided and Bothered* (London: Century, 1989), p. 150.

18. Keith Blackburn and Michael Christensen, "Monetary Policy and Policy Credibility," *Journal of Economic Literature* 27 (March 1989), pp. 1–45. The authors cogently summarize the contending views on credibility.

19. See the analysis in John T. Woolley, *Monetary Politics: The Federal Reserve and the Politics of Monetary Policy* (Cambridge, UK: Cambridge University Press, 1984). This is especially true as more and more nations loosen the political ties of their respective central banks. However, it is one thing to proclaim the bank independent. It is another thing to consistently, over time, maintain price stability. See Blackburn and Christensen's discussion, pp. 32–35, on whether institutional independence alone can insure policy credibility.

20. There exists debate over the usefulness of using monetary aggregates such as M2 or M3. Alan Greenspan, the current chairman of the Federal Reserve, admits that monetary aggregates are no longer a reliable guide for policy. The Bundesbank is one of the last central banks to focus exclusively on the M3 money target. Some economists prefer to target nominal GDP (broadly speaking, the sum of inflation and real growth in output), although the problem with GDP is that it is always out of date. See "Central Bankers All at Sea," *The Economist*, July 31, 1993; see also "Auf Wiedersehen M3," *The Economist*, May 5, 1994.

21. Older treatments include the authoritative analysis of Joachim Spindler, Willy Becker, and Ernest Starke, *Die Deutsche Bundesbank* (Stuttgart: Verlag W. Kohlhammer, 1967); and Dieter Duwendag, ed., *Macht und Ohnmacht der Bundesbank* (Frankfurt/Main: Athenauem, 1973). Several books appeared in the middle 1970s and early 1980s that examined the increasing visibility and conflict surrounding Bundesbank independence. These include Rudiger Robert, *Die Unabhängigkeit der Bundesbank* (Regensburg: Athenauem, 1978); Rolf Kaiser, *Bundesbankautonomie—Möglichkeiten und Grenzen einer unabhängigen Politik* (Frankfurt/Main: Rita G. Fischer, 1980); Caesar, *Handlungsspielraum;* and Konrad von Bonin, *Zentralbanken zwischen funktioneller Unabhängigkeit und politischer Autonomie* (Baden-Baden: Nomos, 1979). This list is, of course, not comprehensive but does provide a broad sketch of the literature on this subject.

22. Gerald Epstein and Juliet Schor, *The Political Economy of Central Banking*, discussion paper, no. 1281, Harvard Institute of Economic Research, Cambridge,

Mass., 1986; Richard Burdekin, "Cross-Country Evidence on the Relationship Between Central Banks and Governments," *Journal of Macroeconomics* 9 (summer 1987), pp. 391–405; Donald Hodgman and Geoffrey Wood, *Macroeconomic Policy and Economic Interdependence* (London: Macmillan Press, 1988).

23. Peter Katzenstein, *Policy and Politics in West Germany* (Philadelphia: Temple University Press, 1987); Ronald Sturm, "The Role of the Bundesbank in German Politics," *West European Politics* 12, no. 2 (1989), pp. 33–50; Ellen Kennedy, *The Bundesbank: Germany's Central Bank in the International Monetary System* (London: RIIA and Pinter Publishers, 1991); John Goodman, *Monetary Sovereignty: The Politics of Central Banking in Western Europe* (Ithaca: Cornell University Press, 1992); David Marsh, *The Bank That Rules Europe* (London: William Heinemann, 1992) (in German, *Die Bundesbank: Geschäfte mit der Macht* [Munich: Bertelsmann, 1992]). See also C. Randall Henning, *Currencies and Politics in the United States, Germany, and Japan* (Washington, D.C.: Institute for International Economics, 1994).

24. Alesina and Summers use an index that measures two components of independence—political and economic—that correspond to the use of political and financial independence in my model. However, I use one more index, that of personal independence (although closely intertwined with political independence), for it provides an additional concrete measure of independence and is used more often in the German literature. See also von Bonin, *Zentralbanken,* and Caesar, *Handlungsspielraum.* I also expand on the concept of external financial independence.

25. John T. Woolley, *Monetary Policy,* pp. 10–14.

26. Woolley, p. 13. As Woolley argues, typically, no actor controls all of the instruments relevant to achieving particular goals. Thus, any actor's ability to reach his or her objectives depends to some degree on the actions of others, even if the actor's own choice of action is completely free. The effects of monetary policy actions are dependent, in part, on fiscal policy, bank regulatory policy, and events in the private sector, among other factors.

27. Elke Thiel, "Macroeconomic Policy Preferences and Co-ordination: A View from Germany," in Paolo Guerriri and Pier Carlo Padoan, eds., *The Political Economy of Monetary Integration: States, Markets, and Institutions* (Savage, Md.: Barnes and Noble Books, 1990), p. 203.

28. Goodman, *Monetary Sovereignty,* chapter 4.

29. This belief was expressed by all Bundesbank officials the author interviewed. When pressed to indicate at what theoretical point the Bundesbank's independence might be circumscribed by the government, every official answered similarly by suggesting that such a theoretical point has never been reached. In other words, the Bundesbank continually seeks to avoid escalating conflict to such a point.

30. See the analysis and discussion of the surrounding events in Deutsche Bundesbank, *30 Jahre Deutsche Bundesbank: Die Entstehung des Bundesbankgesetzes,* vom 26. Juli 1957 (Frankfurt/Main, 1988).

31. "Adenauer will grösseren Einfluss," *Hamburger Anzeiger,* September 13, 1956. Adenauer was criticized for this suggestion by the press. Specific references were cited by the press of past inflationary periods that resulted from central bank dependence. See "Die Notenbank nach Köln," *Frankfurter Allgemeine Zeitung,* September 14, 1956.

32. See Deutsche Bundesbank, *Abschlussbericht des Vorsitzenden des Bundestagsausschusses Geld und Kredit,* vom 28. Juni 1957 (Frankfurt/Main), in Deutsche Bundesbank, *30 Jahre Deutsche Bundesbank,* p. 74.

33. Former Bundesbank president Pöhl states this point another way: "The independence of the Bundesbank has, I'm convinced, won the level of a constitutional norm, and would, therefore, be difficult to do away with through a simple majority." Interview in *Wirtschaftswoche*, July 30, 1982.

34. Arthur Woll, "Zur Unabhängingkeit der Deutschen Bundesbank," in Volker Nienhaus and Ulrich van Suntum, eds., *Grundlagen und Erneurung der Markwirtschaft* (Baden-Baden: Nomos, 1988), p. 189. For a more conservative interpretation of this debate, see Otmar Issing, "Die Unabhängigkeit der Bundesbank," in W. Ehrlicher and D. Simmert, *Geld-und Währungspolitik in der Bundesrepublik Deutschland* (Berlin: Duncker and Humblot, 1982), pp. 50–51.

35. See the excellent summary and discussion of the constitutional debate in Caesar, *Handlungsspielraum*, pp. 5–20. Caesar presents a long supporting list of documentation and legal interpretation to this debate.

36. See quote by A. Poullain, in Bruno Frey and Friedrich Schneider, "Central Bank Behavior," p. 295, footnote 4.

37. Deutsche Bundesbank, "Bundesregierung und Bundesbank," in *Monthly Report of the Deutsche Bundesbank*, August 1972, (Frankfurt/Main), p. 15ff. This view was confirmed in my own interview of Bundesbank officials.

38. The nine new Landeszentralbanks are located in Bavaria, Baden-Württemberg, Rheinland-Pfalz/Saarland, Hessen/Thüringen, Saxony, Brandenburg/Berlin, Nordrhein-Westfalen, Bremen/Lower Saxony/Saxony-Anhalt, and Hamburg/Schleswig-Holstein/Mecklenburg-Vorpommern.

39. See the discussion in "Zentrale oder föderlistische Bundesnotenbank," *Frankfurter Neue Presse*, April 10, 1957.

40. It should be noted that the Central Bank Council reserves the right to recommend against any candidate it deems inappropriate. This recommendation is nonbinding and can be overridden by government. Several nominees from the *Land* banks were voted down by the council, only to have them appointed anyway by the *Land* minister. One of the most recent examples was the appointment of the radio talk show host Julia Dingwort-Nusseck, who was rewarded for her service to the Christian Democratic Union (CDU) in Lower Saxony. The fact that the council has recommended against a candidate indicates a level of politicization, especially at the *Land* levels.

41. This does not mean that the appointment process has not been used to influence policymaking in more partisan-friendly terms. Controversies arose over the appointments of Hans Hermsdorff, the former *Land* president of Hamburg, Claus Köhler, as a member of the directorate, and even for Pöhl as vice president and eventually president of the Bundesbank. In all these cases, many observers (the CDU in particular) saw an attempt by the Schmidt government to push the Bundesbank toward a more expansionary monetary policy. The two candidates also had close ties with the SPD. More recently, controversy erupted over Helmut Kohl's appointments of members of the directorate that more closely shared the chancellor's views on EMU. However, most appointments are made with the idea of balancing diverse views and opinions on the council.

42. Sturm, "The Role of the Bundesbank," p. 232.

43. Marsh, *Die Bundesbank*. See also Karl Kaltenthaler, "Central Bank Independence and the Commitment to Monetary Stability: The Case of the German Bundesbank" (paper delivered at the annual meeting of the American Political Science Association, Washington, D.C. 1997).

44. There do exist, for instance, differences over the importance placed on external monetary stability. Stricter monetarists in the Bundesbank adhere to the

internal stability standard and urge other nations to pursue a similar hard-line anti-inflationary standard. However, unless all countries pursue such a policy, which, of course, does not happen, the Bundesbank's ability to achieve internal price stability at a constant DM exchange rate is impossible.

45. Based on the author's own interviews and compilations from source information. See also Rolf Haase, *The European Central Bank* (Gütersloh: Bertelsmann Stiftung, 1989).

46. See the arguments made by Roland Kneiper, "Bundesbank Autonomie?" *Gewerkschafltiche Monatshefte* (August 1975), pp. 791–799.

47. See the analysis in Deutsche Bundesbank, *30 Jahre Deutsche Bundesbank*. See also von Bonin, *Zentralbanken*, p. 190.

48. For an interesting account of Kohl's attempts to leave a pro-Maastricht, pro-European monetary union contingent in influential monetary positions both in the Bundesbank and the administration, see "Dann ist Maastricht erledigt," *Der Spiegel*, April 5, 1993.

49. One can argue that budgetary independence (that is, freedom from the need to get legislative approval of the central bank's operating budget) should also be considered. Although it may be important in some countries, the issue of operating budgets has never been a source of contention between the bank and government.

50. In the last analysis the bank must be ready to cover the financial requirements of the government that cannot be met from other sources. Interestingly, the Bundesbank is required by law to turn over a percentage of its "profits" earned from its operations during the preceding year to the federal government. The amounts are not inconsequential and can hover in the range of DM 10 billion to DM 20 billion a year.

51. See the Bundesbank's own discussion of its functions in Deutsche Bundesbank, *The Deutsche Bundesbank: Its Monetary Policy Instruments and Functions,* 1989, Special Series, no. 7 (Frankfurt/Main), chapter 3.

52. Deutsche Bundesbank, *Monthly Report of the Deutsche Bundesbank,* April 1997 (Frankfurt/Main).

53. Cited from *International Capital Markets: Developments and Prospects* (Washington, D.C.: International Monetary Fund, 1986), p. 29.

54. Such a point was made by Bundesbank officials during the negotiations surrounding the creation of the EMS. Bundesbank president at the time Otmar Emminger secured an agreement from the federal government limiting the intervention requirements of the Bundesbank should these requirements threaten the bank's ability to maintain the value of the currency.

55. Chile, for example, has patterned the legislation creating the Chilean Central Bank on the Bundesbank model.

56. I cannot here do adequate justice to the entire history of German central banking. For a more detailed analysis, see Knut Borchart, "Währung und Wirtschaft," in *Währung und Wirtschaft in Deutschland, 1876–1975,* ed. Deutsche Bundesbank (Frankfurt/Main: Deutsche Bundesbank, 1976), pp. 3–55; Herbert Giersch and Harmen Lehment, "Monetary Policy: Does Independence Make a Difference?—The German Experience," *Kieler Sonderdrück 100*, (Kiel: Institute für Weltwirtschaft Kiel, 1981); Marsh, *Die Bundesbank*.

57. Geirsch and Lehmet, "Monetary Policy," p. 9.

58. See the discussion of this complex period in international monetary history in Charles Kindleberger's authoritative version, *The World in Depression, 1929–1939* (Berkeley: University of California Press, 1973).

59. For a fascinating account of the Hitler-era relations to the Reichsbank, see Borchart, *Währung und Wirtschaft in Deutschland,* pp. 305–307. See also Marsh, *Die Bundesbank,* pp. 28–32, 64–76.

60. Instead of a revaluation of the DM as the Bundesbank insisted, the government decided in favor of an "Ersatz-revaluation" in the form of an import-easing and export-encumbrance tax. The Bundesbank felt that this was not a powerful-enough measure to achieve external equilibrium. The SPD reacted sharply to the Bundesbank's public position on this offer, which led other nations to demand a massive revaluation of the DM. "A stab in the back," as an official SPD pronouncement claimed, led to some of the first serious discussions about limiting the Bundesbank's independence. Others applauded the Bundesbank for its openness. The whole issue came to the fore when Germany's finance minister, Franz Joseph Strauss, forced the issue by leaking a report that the French were about to devalue the franc, to which Charles DeGaulle replied that this was "the worst form of absurdity." See Hugo Kaufmann, *Germany's International Monetary Policy and the European Monetary System* (New York: Brooklyn College Press, 1985), p. 26; Caesar, *Handlungsspielraum,* p. 180.

61. See Otmar Emminger's account in *DM, Dollar, und Währungskrisen* (Stuttgart: Deutsche Verlags-Anstalt, 1986), p. 77. Also *Der Speigel,* June 6, 1956. Although the conflicts between the Bundesbank and Bundesregierung have at times been quite sharp, as this case demonstrates, several Bundesbank presidents have claimed that there have never been conflicts between the two. Instead, "disagreements" have emerged among various personalities in the government. Klasen in a radio interview in 1976, quoted in Rolf Caesar, *Handlungsspielraum,* p. 192, footnote 150.

62. On the connection between monetary and trade matters and the difficulties faced by European officials in the transatlantic relationship in the late 1960s and early 1970s, see Thomas L. Ilgen, *Autonomy and Interdependence: U.S.–Western European Monetary and Trade Relations, 1958–1984* (Totowa, N.J.: Rowman and Allanheld, 1985), especially chapter 4.

63. See the analysis in Kaufmann, *Germany's International Monetary Policy,* pp. 34–40.

64. This period is artfully explained in great detail in Kennedy, *Die Bundesbank,* pp. 40–55. I seek here only to briefly summarize this time frame in order to further illustrate questions of independence. It should be stressed that even though the ending of Bretton Woods alleviated a great deal of pressure on the Bundesbank, both Schmidt and the Bundesbank still found themselves buffeted by Washington's benign neglect of the dollar.

65. Such is the conclusion of Robert D. Putnam and Nicholas Bayne, *Hanging Together: Cooperation and Conflict in the Seven-Power Summits* (London: RIIA, 1987), p. 92.

66. The Bundesbank, of course, faced similar "three-way" pressures before, including the period of the snake, but now these pressures had become formally institutionalized with the EMS.

3

From Plaza to Black October: The Europeanization of Deutsche Mark Politics, 1985–1987

> Stable, credible monetary policies are the necessary foundation for continued economic growth. Artificial demand stimulation would be the first step in the direction of another stability crisis. . . . Exchange rate adjustments cannot replace political adjustment.
>
> —German finance minister Gerhard Stoltenberg, 1986
>
> A milestone for cooperation in the monetary field.
>
> —Danish finance minister Palle Simonsen, on the Basel-Nyborg agreement, 1987

The period from 1985 to 1987 illustrates dramatically the negotiating strategies pursued by the Bundesbank and government when confronted by the choice between maintaining national autonomy or enhancing exchange rate stability. The period can best be summarized by the general reluctance, with a few exceptions, of the government or the Bundesbank to place too great an emphasis upon "artificial" methods of enhancing exchange rate stability at the expense of domestic monetary autonomy. The mood of German monetary authorities at the time is best captured by the former head of the Bundesbank, Karl Otto Pöhl.

> Huge trade imbalances and strong divergences in . . . economic, fiscal, and monetary policy still exist. In these circumstances, overambitious commitments to peg certain exchange rate levels or target zones run the risk not only of clashing with domestic monetary objectives but of collapsing when the markets test them. Central banks and governments can easily lose their credibility in such a process. Therefore, it is less ambitious but more realistic to concentrate on managing the existing system pragmatically and flexibly.[1]

Interestingly, Pöhl holds out the possibility for "pragmatic" and "flexible" efforts at stabilizing exchange rates. Would such cooperative efforts be forthcoming from Germany?

In the G7 monetary arena, the record of cooperation would be mixed. The German government's resistance to U.S. pressure throughout the 1985–1987 period was based on the Bundesbank's concern that the over-reliance on intervention in the foreign exchange market would damage the credibility of the central bank. Moreover, pressure by the United States on the Bundesbank to reflate the German economy through monetary stimulus ran counter to the Bundesbank's primary interest of safeguarding the value of the domestic currency. Specifically, on the international front, after the U.S. dollar neglect of Ronald Reagan's administration, international monetary cooperation and multilateral surveillance reached a zenith with the agreement in September 1985 at the Plaza Hotel in New York. The agreement pledged the G5 members to actively pursue a policy of realigning currencies, in particular, depreciating the value of the dollar. However, by October 1987, even after the conclusion of the February 1987 Louvre accord, which aimed to stabilize exchange rates, U.S. treasury secretary James Baker was publicly criticizing the lack of German monetary cooperation, helping to trigger the Black October market crash. Baker would go on to describe German monetary policy as significantly undermining international monetary cooperation, a policy engineered by the "little clique of rigid monetarists" in the Bundesbank.[2] International monetary cooperation would fluctuate widely along with the value of the dollar.

On the European front, the Bundesbank and federal government also faced serious tensions and pressure brought on by the Plaza agreement. Secretary Baker's promotion of a weaker dollar from Plaza up through Louvre led to tensions within the EMS by attracting funds to the DM, thus driving up the DM relative to weaker EMS currencies. Based on the adjustable fixed exchange rate system of the ERM, EMS currencies were obliged, usually through intervention or an appropriate interest rate policy, to maintain their par value with the appreciating DM.[3] If the speculative pressures on the various EMS currencies became too intense, as was the case at differing points during 1985–1987, some countries would inevitably face the prospect of a realignment of the EMS, implying a revaluation of the DM and a devaluation of other EMS currencies. Although beset by periodic crises and two realignments brought on in large part by the subsequent depreciation of the dollar following Plaza, both the Bundesbank and government actively pursued a monetary course that indicated their increased willingness to work together and accommodate their policies to their European partners all in the name of promoting regional monetary stability.

This chapter proceeds chronologically with a brief account of the mid-1980s period leading up to the Plaza agreement reached in September

1985, an agreement that marked an important high in the annals of international monetary coordination and diplomacy. The Plaza agreement also marks an important demarcation in terms of shifting international and regional monetary power and indicates the elevation of Germany to one of the most powerful monetary actors in the global community. Moreover, the signing of the Plaza accord marked the slow Europeanization, or shift of emphasis of monetary interests and priorities, of the Germans to the European arena, culminating in early 1988 with the Germans' decision to strongly push for a single currency for Europe.[4] Although this time frame has been dealt with by other scholars in great detail, my analysis synthesizes many aspects of these accounts and concludes with a more pessimistic account of the degree of German monetary cooperation within the G7.

The Plaza Accord

The Reagan administration entered office in January 1981 with the belief that U.S. power could be reaffirmed and that President Reagan could restore the twin pillars (U.S. global preeminence and economic power, both domestic and foreign) of U.S. foreign policy autonomously and without government intervention or adjustment. The administration's approach to international economic policy and monetary diplomacy in particular reflected such thinking. The superiority of market solutions to economic problems and an emphasis on private economic activity would provide the global economy with the engine of noninflationary growth required to shake the fetters of stagnation and talk of decline. In other words, international monetary coordination took on a distinctly laissez-faire orientation during the first five years of the Reagan administration. Reagan's macroeconomic policies had the impact of attracting huge amounts of foreign capital that drove up the value of the dollar to heights not seen since the end of the floating exchange rate system of Bretton Woods in 1973. From mid-1980 to mid-1985 the dollar appreciated 53 percent against the deutsche mark.[5] As Cohen has described it, "what was most striking during this period was the way in which policy was determined in almost total disregard for the outside world."[6]

By 1985 the Reagan administration conceded that its policies had neither promoted sustained economic growth nor appeased resentful allies and that the sources of monetary tensions needed to be dealt with seriously. In other words, the inability of the United States to reassert unilaterally the twin pillars of U.S. policy was a confirmation of the extent of limited U.S. power. Mutual accommodation, a recognition of U.S. constraints, and an increased willingness to cooperate were soon identified by the new treasury secretary, James Baker (who replaced Donald Regan in

January 1985), as the most effective means of achieving U.S. and allied interests in economic growth. Baker's motives for accommodation were also heavily driven by his desire to curb protectionist tendencies in Congress. Such accommodation would have had to include concrete measures on reducing the U.S. budget deficit and easing monetary policy (neither of which happened) in order to bring about a gradual reduction in U.S. interest rates and the dollar. On the international front, accommodation would also have had to include a resumption of coordinated currency interventions to achieve an alignment of exchange rates more consistent with internal and external monetary balance and economic fundamentals. From the standpoint of the Germans, such a turnaround in U.S. policy and attitudes was a long time in coming. In particular, the new U.S. orientation toward adjustment and accommodation was eagerly encouraged by the Bundesbank as it sought to regain some measure of control over German monetary targets and the money supply, which, in turn, would enhance the stability of the EMS.

Movement on the international front came by April of 1985 at a meeting of the OECD in Paris as Baker raised the possibility of hosting an international conference to review the functioning of the floating exchange rate system. The new Treasury team also considered an overall coordinated package that would include U.S. action on the budget deficit matched by fiscal and monetary stimulus in Europe, especially from the Germans, in the form of interest rate and tax reductions. The United States believed that the dangers of corrective action (recession from tight fiscal policy or inflation through higher import costs) at home could be offset by faster growth abroad. With an enviable 2.5 percent inflation rate in Germany (although, from the Bundesbank perspective, too high[7]) and a government plan to implement a tax cut of DM 20 billion by 1986, the German government became an obvious target for U.S. pressure. However, Kohl and Gerhard Stoltenberg refused to accelerate the government's carefully planned tax cuts. Furthermore, the Bundesbank argued that accelerating the tax cuts could not be financed by reviving inflation.[8] This resistant attitude for domestic fiscal or monetary adjustment became the standard line of argument by the Germans over the next several years.

At a minimum, the Germans—in particular the Bundesbank—indicated some willingness to discuss how exchange rate stabilization could be achieved, and urged the United States at the Bonn summit in May to make a formal commitment to exchange rate stabilization.[9] The Bundesbank had been involved during the spring months in substantial foreign exchange market intervention in the sum of U.S.$11 billion to level off and steady the value of the dollar. As a result, the bank was interested in reaching an accord that would bring some semblance of stability to the dollar. In actuality, the Bonn summit reached little in terms of monetary coordination.

The United States did pledge to reduce its budgetary deficits, but Kohl made no promise to accelerate tax cuts. More important, the summit exerted no influence upon the G-10's upcoming report on improving the monetary system that was to be approved by finance ministers in June of that year. Finally, action on the monetary front at the Bonn summit became entangled with the French desire to prevent movement on the trade front.[10] François Mitterand's concern about the farm vote in the pre-electoral period of 1985, protecting the EC's Common Agricultural Policy (CAP), and the general debate over the launching of a new General Agreement on Tariffs and Trade (GATT) round ultimately limited the potential for reaching some form of international monetary accord. Given the minimum level of agreement on monetary and trade matters at Bonn, further significant movement on the international monetary front appeared, at least in public, unlikely.[11]

The United States, however, had been advancing bilateral overtures to Japan and individual European G5 members. Building upon the G-10 study that advocated stabilizing the international monetary system, on September 22 the finance ministers of the G5 secretly arrived at the Plaza Hotel in New York. The ministers released a communiqué declaring that the dollar was too strong and no longer reflected fundamental economic conditions. They called for an orderly appreciation of other currencies relative to the dollar and for the United States to participate, in full, in coordinated exchange market intervention. Central bank intervention over the following months totaled U.S.$10 billion with a substantial amount of that intervention coming from the United States. The dollar depreciated accordingly, up to 4 percent on the day after the communiqué. For most analysts, the Plaza accord marked an important milestone in international monetary cooperation and collective adjustment.

For the Kohl government and the Bundesbank, Plaza represented a minimum measure of accommodation, as the Germans offered few, if any, significant concessions. Instead, the Bundesbank and government sought concessions from the United States. Baker wanted the G5 to focus on broad-based economic policy coordination and not solely on exchange rate stabilization. The Germans were not buying. Kohl and Stoltenberg, under pressure from the Bundesbank, resisted any pressure to expand their 1986 tax cuts or reduce interest rates. It was not Germany that was making the compromises but rather the United States that had committed itself to almost unilateral adjustment—primarily in terms of commitments to bring down the budget deficit but also in the amount of exchange market intervention—to meet the standards of Plaza. Entering into negotiations from a position of strength, the German economic house was in order, and the G7 institutional arena appeared more concerned with lowering expectations and encouraging informal exchanges than achieving formal reciprocal commitments or decisions. The Plaza accord from both the Bundesbank and government perspective was more a signal of intentions rather than an ironclad agreement to intervene endlessly in the currency markets. It was the United States, not Germany, that now abandoned its laissez-faire attitude and committed to domestic macroeconomic adjustment.

While concerned with the Bundesbank's mounting interventions on the exchange market and the inflationary impact of a weak DM, Pöhl was driven at Plaza, in large part, to minimize the impact of any exchange rate program upon the EMS. Essential to understanding the German's Plaza strategy is to appreciate the German position within the context of the EMS. A "hard landing," or rapid depreciation of the dollar, would have caused serious difficulties in the EMS, as pressure on the DM to revalue would have exacerbated tensions between German exporters and European governments obliged to peg their currency to the DM.[12] In other words, most German monetary authorities felt that an orderly and slow realignment of the dollar was needed in order to maintain currency stability and strength of the EMS.[13] For both Stoltenberg and Pöhl, movement on securing a slow depreciation of the dollar was in the primary interest of all EMS members and the maintenance of the region's zone of monetary stability. The costs associated with dollar volatility and with disruption within the EMS would be great and demanded a careful German response to action on the international G7 front. In many respects, movement on the international front in terms of securing a slow depreciation of the dollar coincided with action on the European front to secure an orderly adjustment of the EMS, all in the name of exchange rate stability.

Despite a parallel or an overlapping interest in seeing exchange rate stability in Europe and between the dollar and the DM, a key difference remained in the Germans' negotiating position vis-à-vis the United States and vis-à-vis its European monetary partners. Both Pöhl and Stoltenberg felt that the markets should determine the relationship between the DM and both the yen and the dollar. However, the Plaza accord was a recognition by both the Bundesbank and government that some form of minimum level of foreign exchange rate intervention was necessary to restore the dollar value to levels more in accordance with market fundamentals. On the European front, the Germans (more the government, less so the Bundesbank) preferred a more government-supported and central bank–regulated, adjustable fixed exchange rate system for the EMS. However, following the Plaza accord, the Bundesbank was increasingly more willing to support the EMS through intervention, interest rate policy or realignments, and more likely to resist U.S. pressure to do more on the domestic front. During the period 1985–1987, as one Bundesbank official maintained, the bank preferred two separate and distinct monetary regimes: an adjustable fixed exchange rate system for Europe and floating rates outside Europe.[14]

The costs associated with diminishing European monetary stability, both in terms of German industrial competitiveness and Kohl's prominent European foreign policy agenda, were noticeably greater than in the international arena. It is to this story that we now turn.

Stabilizing the Appreciating DM in Europe

By the end of 1985, the DM had appreciated from DM 2.85 to DM 2.65 against the dollar. For Pöhl, the slide of the dollar had reached a point in December 1985 that was acceptable to the Germans. He also faced intense domestic pressure by many leading German industrial exporters, especially in the auto and machinery industry, concerned about their competitiveness on world markets. They argued that the threshold for further action on the exchange rate had been or would soon be reached. Moreover, even though the Germans had, at least initially through the fall of 1985, actively pursued policies in accordance with Plaza, the United States, particularly articulated through the testimony of Under Secretary of the Treasury David Mulford, was still pressing the Germans to do more on the exchange rate front. Not long after the ink had dried on the Plaza accord, Bundesbank resistance to a further drop in the dollar indicated the Germans' weakening commitment to further G5 efforts to cooperate on currency levels.

Although the Bundesbank could not unilaterally halt the continuing slide of the dollar into the spring of 1986, the Bundesbank and government recognized that they could return some of the pressure to adjust back on the United States. Baker's credibility to deliver on U.S. promises to reduce the budget deficit was markedly weak. Given the deadlock between Reagan's commitment not to raise taxes any further and Congress's insistence that no more budget reductions would be forthcoming unless a corresponding revenue generator existed, it was clear that Baker had less room to maneuver in his own bargaining game back home. Moreover, developing internal Federal Reserve divisions during the spring of 1986 over an appropriate monetary policy further weakened the bargaining position of the United States.

Taking advantage of this weakness, both the Bundesbank and the finance ministry sought to consolidate advancements on the European front and within the EMS by seeking to reduce the tensions that had increasingly been developing with the strengthening DM.[15] Both Pöhl and Stoltenberg were cognizant of the pressure the French were facing with an upcoming parliamentary election on March 16. On March 6, the Bundesbank lowered the discount rate from 4 percent to 3.5 percent. The French immediately responded with a corresponding reduction from 8.5 percent to 8.25 percent. After the election in early April, to further ease pressure on the French, the currencies of the EMS were realigned with a 3 percent revaluation of the DM and a 3 percent devaluation of the French franc.[16] Stoltenberg declared the purpose of the recent German monetary moves as "a major step in strengthening cooperation and coordination within the EMS" and a signal to European partners for them to lower their interest rates.[17] Importantly, the decision to realign was a political decision reached by the government in response to European concerns. The Bundesbank recognized that a further drop in the discount rate would be seen as acquiescing to U.S. pressure, so it instead pushed for a corresponding realignment within the EMS in order to signify the commitment of the German government and the Bundesbank to Europe.

The significant policy actions taken by the Germans through March and April of 1986 did indicate a willingness by the Bundesbank and the finance ministry to accommodate the Europeans. In contrast, the Germans, especially the Bundesbank, increasingly tried to distance themselves from the Plaza accord through the spring of 1986. Although the Federal Reserve, the Bank of Japan, and the Bundesbank—through Federal Reserve chairman Paul Volcker's insistence—jointly lowered their discount rates in March, the move to lower rates in Germany had already been expected.[18] The Bundesbank's decision to lower its discount rate originated primarily as a result of the tensions in the EMS and not as a result of U.S. insistence, although U.S. pressure undoubtedly may have had some bearing on the decision.[19] Moreover, the Federal Reserve had already voted in February to unilaterally lower its rates, a move that Volcker opposed.[20] As a result, it was Pöhl and the Bundesbank who exercised dominant influence over the situation when the United States followed the Germans on March 7 to lower rates.

**The Road to Louvre:
Strengthening the German-European Monetary Position**

Shortly after the European realignment in April, in an interview in the German *Handelsblatt*, President Reagan continued the policy of talking down the dollar.[21] Reagan stated that a continued weakening of the dollar, with a corresponding improvement in the U.S. trade balance, would reduce protectionist tendencies in Congress. Although the comment was aimed largely at the Japanese, German exporters were also targeted. German exporters were not amused and voiced their displeasure to the German government and the Bundesbank. As a result, both the Bundesbank and government were not as willing to jump on the stronger DM bandwagon. Throughout the period of May 1986 to January 1987, Baker, in the face of Bundesbank resistance, ceaselessly proclaimed that unless the Germans took measures to raise domestic demand, the dollar would have to drop further. Such comments were reiterated by Volcker. In short, this entire period can be characterized with one scenario: Pöhl and Stoltenberg voicing their opposition to U.S. pressure with Baker describing such German resistance as "regrettable."[22]

Specifically, to try and rein in the recalcitrant Germans at the Tokyo G7 summit in May, the United States proposed and initiated a far-reaching framework for macroeconomic coordination. At the summit, the communiqué announced the creation of a new forum for G7 finance ministers, which would use economic indicators to guide policy adjustments in the interest of noninflationary growth.[23] Although Baker and others in the U.S. contingent felt such a forum could provide greater influence over foreign macroeconomic policies, the new forum never amounted to anything significant. From the Bundesbank's perspective, any forum that coincided with its own calls for the United States to lower its deficits and converge or harmonize its policies more in line with Germany's noninflationary policies would be welcome. Although the federal government was not as wary as the Bundesbank of an international macroeconomic forum with the intent of coordinating policies, such a forum could prove useful to enhance the Bundesbank's influence within the G7. In addition, such a platform could provide the Germans with another mechanism for exporting its own policy of emphasizing fiscal responsibility and monetary stability.[24] In fact, Bonn had been pushing for such an arrangement since early 1986.[25]

Through the summer and autumn of 1986, the United States began to slowly de-emphasize a strategy of talking down the dollar further in order to achieve the stabilization of exchange rates. With the Federal Reserve and Volcker urging Baker to slow down the depreciation rhetoric and the Federal Reserve's own concern with the inflationary impacts of depreciation and the potential for an overheating U.S. economy, the United States sought to stabilize exchange rates with the Japanese and the Germans. The Germans, however, were hesitant to join any further arrangements that might identify ranges or "target" zones for exchange rates and/or intervention or consultation responsibilities. In addition, German monetary authorities were noticeably absent from the Baker-Miyazawa accord announced at the end of October.[26] As Cohen contends, toward the end of 1986, "it was already evident that the interests of the major players were beginning to diverge again as the dollar's depreciation carried beyond what many regarded as desirable."[27] In fact, the fall of 1986 marked an important turning point in the German negotiating position vis-à-vis European partners and the United States.

To solidify their bargaining position in the European arena vis-à-vis the United States, the Bundesbank and government requested a meeting among the finance ministers of the EMS on September 21, 1986, in Gleneagles,

Scotland.[28] This meeting, I argue, marked a pivotal shift toward "Europeanizing" Germany's monetary policies and signaling Germany's intention to accord EMS policies a higher national priority. At the meeting, the European finance ministers endorsed a strong German bargaining position vis-à-vis the Americans. With Germany at the head, the Europeans would continue to resist U.S. calls to further stimulate domestic demand and central banks would pursue a joint effort to buttress the value of the dollar against the DM.[29] In return, the Bundesbank would be more agreeable to intramarginal interventions to support EMS parities, a move that soon demanded the Bundesbank to fulfill its promise. Although Bundesbank officials were less vocal, Luxembourg's finance minister, Jacques Poos, summed up the European position by arguing that the Europeans wanted "to stop the fall of the dollar by all means possible," while adding that the Europeans wanted "to speak with one voice toward the U.S."[30]

The meeting at Gleneagles could not have been more important or symbolic. One year after the Plaza accord had been signed, currency issues remained divisive, and international economic policy coordination remained elusive. With the DM falling below an important psychological threshold of DM 1.98 to the dollar shortly before the meeting at Gleneagles, the German government and Bundesbank were less willing to offer any more concessions to the United States. In fact, the day after the Gleneagles meeting, the dollar rose 4 percent on currency markets. Some analysts wondered if the European decision questioned the viability of the Plaza accord. Moreover, the Germans could point to solid economic growth for the year 1986, which picked up after a sluggish start and low inflation rates.[31] As Stoltenberg contended, "The artificial fueling of demand would lead to another cycle of inflation" and jeopardize the painful progress in combating inflation and solidifying public finances.[32] What is more, for some German monetary authorities, U.S. pressure and the constraints they felt reminded many of them of the 1960s Bretton Woods period when chronic U.S. trade-payment deficits forced the Bundesbank to accommodate the U.S. deficits by revaluing the DM. Although the formal governance structure was far different in September 1986 than it was under Bretton Woods in the late 1960s, the fact that some German monetary authorities drew such an analogy indicated the extent of their displeasure with the United States.

Following the ECOFIN meeting, a great deal of speculation was present at the Thursday meeting of the Bundesbank, regularly scheduled shortly before the IMF meeting. The Bundesbank held firm to its position by refusing to reduce the discount rate. As a result, Stoltenberg and Bundesbank officials were awaiting a public assault from Baker at the upcoming G5 meeting. However, secret G5 meetings did manage to paper over any open public recriminations between the Germans and the United

States. Instead, G5 officials discussed the stabilization of exchange rates at current levels and various "zones" or "ranges."[33] Foreshadowing their position at the Louvre, the Germans were especially hesitant to announce any specific commitments. Instead, the final communiqué read that the G5 ministers could make no decision on either currency or interest rate policies but that they did pledge to work more closely together.[34] In fact, given the rift between Volcker and Baker and Baker's own inability to realistically control the levers of fiscal or monetary policy, the Germans had little incentive to commit to any more formal agreement.[35] Finally, political realities, namely Bundesbank independence, prevented Stoltenberg from committing to the U.S. position. As the finance minister summed up, "The basic limit [to commit to international agreements] is based on the fact that we are political democracies."[36] The reality, of course, was that the powerfully independent Bundesbank could "check" the minister's ability to reach any agreement within the G5.

Although not formally institutionalized or articulated, the German commitment to support EMS currencies was soon tested. Tensions within the EMS persisted throughout the rest of 1986 as the DM continued to strengthen, despite the attempts at the September IMF/World Bank meeting to stabilize exchange rates at roughly the current levels.[37] In August the Irish punt was devalued. Toward the end of 1986 the French franc along with the Danish krone continued their drop toward the lower trading margins of the ERM. In response to the continuing turmoil in the exchange rate markets and within the EMS and the noticeable weakness of the franc, on January 6, 1987, the French government under Jacques Chirac acrimoniously demanded changes in how the EMS operated. Claiming that there existed a DM crisis, the French pushed for a meeting of the European Monetary Committee on January 10. Up to this point, the Bundesbank had been purchasing record amounts of dollars (more DMs were sold than in the immediate aftermath of Plaza) in order to keep the EMS currencies within their ERM margins.[38] German government officials stated that a realignment was unlikely because economic fundamentals did not warrant a change. The more likely reason was that a general election was to be held in Germany in several weeks.

The developing turmoil highlighted the increasing tensions between Stoltenberg and Pöhl. Bundesbank intervention in the exchange markets (DM 5 billion on January 6 alone) presented serious risks to the bank's attempts to control German money supply growth after extensively overshooting its targets throughout 1986. Because of the Central Bank Council's concerns with the money supply, it was highly unlikely at this time that the Bundesbank would lower interest rates that were already considerably low, as the French were demanding. With this option not forthcoming, a realignment of the EMS appeared the most likely outcome of negotiations.

Stoltenberg, however, ruled out any such move, as a DM revaluation would have added to the competitive problems already felt by West German exporters as a result of the DM's sharp rise against the dollar. After the Bundesbank's tough line vis-à-vis the United States in September of 1986, Stoltenberg's position was strongly supported by Kohl and the rest of the cabinet ministers.[39]

Facing increased speculation and unrest within the EMS, a decision to realign the major currencies was reached during the weekend of January 10–11.[40] Pressure from the Bundesbank and a realization that the situation within Europe required the German government to offer some form of concession to its European partners eventually overcame Stoltenberg's and Kohl's resistance to the realignment. Pöhl openly welcomed the realignment, with Stoltenberg ultimately offering his public support as well. Stoltenberg reiterated that the Germans were responding to the needs of their European partners, especially the French, even in the face of domestic pressure from industrial exporters.[41] Stoltenberg recognized the political nature of the final decision but stated bluntly to reporters that the EMS did not in any way equate with the problems that had existed under Bretton Woods. Finally, as a result of the turmoil and realignment, both Stoltenberg and the EC Commission president, Jacques Delors, indicated that the turmoil in the EMS was a wake-up call to strengthen the EC and speed up the processes of integration.[42]

The realignment, however, did not ease the pressure within the EMS. Financial markets in Europe, the United States, and Japan were skeptical that the realignment had significantly altered the fundamental relationship between the DM and the dollar. The Germans, in particular the Bundesbank, were called upon to make further concessions to the Europeans. With Stoltenberg, the German government, and German industry bowing to Bundesbank pressure to push through a realignment earlier, it was now the Bundesbank's turn to make room for accommodation. The Bundesbank responded with an interest rate cut of another 0.5 percent, from 3.5 percent to 3 percent, on January 23 to head off any further tension. The bank's response was an indication of its willingness to ease pressure in the EMS and explicitly stated that its decisions were in no way in response to U.S. pressure.[43] Stoltenberg reinforced the Bundesbank line by continuing to urge the United States to get its economic house in order. Although such public statements must be interpreted with some measure of skepticism, this view is corroborated by the United States' quick, negative response to the German moves.[44] Moreover, the Bundesbank could have lowered its rates earlier to ease the pressure within the EMS. Instead, trying to avoid looking as if it was bowing to U.S. pressure, the Bundesbank again sought first to realign currencies within the EMS.

Interestingly, the Bundesbank's reduction in the discount rate was offset by a corresponding increase in its reserve requirement to 10 percent.[45]

The United States stated that the Bundesbank rate cut was not enough to stimulate the German economy and to stabilize currency markets. The counterbalancing move by the Bundesbank was their method of "sterilizing" the impact of the lowering of its discount rate. Although concerned about the potential politicization of monetary policy (the cut came just two days before the January 25 federal election, which returned Kohl's CDU-CSU/FDP coalition to power), the Bundesbank rate cut prior to the election was a response to the continuing massive pressure within the EMS.

In sum, the Bundesbank stuck as closely as possible to its preferred option of allowing the DM to appreciate vis-à-vis the dollar or to revalue within the EMS when market pressure forced it in an upward direction instead of adjusting its domestic monetary policy. With the exception of the January 23 rate cut, this pattern was firmly held by the bank. As Yoichi Funabashi writes, "Especially on the EMS matter, German central bankers tried to shift the decision-making burden from the central bank to the ministry of finance," the agent responsible for any such decision.[46] Stoltenberg and the Kohl government would have to make the politically painful decision to revalue—a decision, however, that was palatable to the Bundesbank and, eventually, the leading industrial and trading associations in Germany, the BDI and the DIHT.[47] Moreover, the realignment thus provided the necessary room for a relatively small interest rate reduction that was required to further stabilize the EMS. In short, the Bundesbank's and government's bargaining positions vis-à-vis the United States converged and hardened throughout this time period. In the European monetary arena, while the Bundesbank and government at times disagreed on the proper method of stabilizing the EMS, both eventually offered some concessions—a realignment and an interest rate reduction—to their European currency partners. Both the Bundesbank and government were intent on solidifying European monetary cooperation and regional monetary stability.

The Europeanization of the DM

With discord developing within the U.S. financial community and between the United States and Japan over yen-dollar exchange rates, in February of 1987, the G5 met at the Louvre to try and ease the macroeconomic conflict and stabilize exchange rates. The Louvre accord, an accord that Baker had joined somewhat reluctantly, asserted that currency values were now "broadly consistent with underlying economic fundamentals" and that the G7 governments "agreed to cooperate closely to foster stability of exchange rates around current levels." The agreement was hailed as another significant step in policy cooperation, but the Bundesbank saw it as nothing more than an affirmation of its own interest in attaining stable exchange rates based on economic fundamentals and not on intervention in the currency markets. Specifically, the German pledge in the communiqué was that "monetary policy will be directed at improving the condition for sustained economic growth while maintaining price stability." Nowhere was it stated that the Kohl government or the Bundesbank would coordinate monetary policy or be obliged to intervene to maintain the range or reference zones discussed at the Louvre.[48] Although the Germans did agree to move up a planned tax cut, such a move easily proved consistent with Kohl's policies and would not seriously threaten the Bundesbank's money targets.[49] Moreover, the Louvre accord was seen by the Bundesbank as strengthening its ability to enhance the stability of the EMS. On the European front, exchange rate stability became, after the all-important objective of domestic price stability, a noted priority for the Bundesbank. This stability generated on the international front by Louvre could be transmitted to the European arena.

The Louvre accord did appear to bring a certain level of currency stability back to the international monetary system, but the pressure on the Bundesbank and government continued. The attainment of a modicum of exchange rate stability was not a result of internal German fiscal or monetary adjustment but the result of massive exchange rate interventions. The Bundesbank, however, was not as active a partner as were other countries.[50] In addition, through the spring and the Venice G7 summit, the United States was again calling on the Germans to lower interest rates and, now, prevent a further depreciation of the dollar. Baker needed to secure further concrete measures (German intervention or economic stimulus to support the dollar) that addressed persistent trade imbalances.[51] At the April G7 meeting, Baker was again blaming the Germans for their lack of intervention or domestic economic stimulus. The Germans resisted such pressures. Pöhl openly repudiated the U.S. methods by insisting "that prevention of inflation should be priority over the achievement of exchange rate stability." Stoltenberg reaffirmed Pöhl's position by asserting that Germany had reached "the limit of its growth potential."[52] The Venice summit in May 1987 continued this increasingly worn-out and antagonistic pattern of interaction between the United States and the Germans.

While international policy coordination continued to suffer, European efforts to deal with persistent monetary tensions increased. Specifically, the turmoil in the earlier part of the year within the EMS and the displeasure among the various EMS members (again, primarily the French but also smaller EMS countries like Ireland) over the financing and intervention mechanisms of the ERM led to the finance ministers' meeting in Nyborg on September 11–13. At Nyborg, the finance ministers announced a plan for EMS intramarginal interventions to accommodate the position of weak-currency countries.[53] Although borrowing mechanisms had always been possible under the EMS, the agreement specifically identified a renewed commitment to a financing system that allowed central banks whose currency came under pressure to borrow a strong currency from another central bank. In due time, this meant borrowing DMs from the Bundesbank. In addition, short-term loans could be repaid in ECUs, which allowed the borrower the privilege of not having to come up with hard currency to repay the loans.[54]

The Bundesbank was at first skeptical of any "automatic" or "obligatory" financing mechanisms and intramarginal interventions, although it appears Pöhl was initially in favor. In general, the bank felt that it was seldom useful to shore up a currency under severe market pressure and found the binding requirements of intramarginal interventions a limitation to the bank's ability to pursue an autonomous monetary policy. Interventions would require the Bundesbank to buy up foreign currencies that then would be converted into DMs thereby increasing the domestic money supply.[55] Moreover, the Bundesbank consistently maintained that such interventions would only add to the speculative turbulence. The credibility of the central bank would be damaged by unlimited intervention or financing mechanisms. For a majority of the Central Bank Council, increasing the convergence of its European partner's macroeconomic policies toward the Bundesbank price-stability standard was the only true method for dealing with market pressure. More important for the Bundesbank, the Nyborg arrangement could lead to a greater degree of automaticity and supranationality in European monetary relations that, for some Bundesbank officials, would mean an abdication of its responsibilities to the Bundesbank Law.[56]

In the end, the Bundesbank agreed to the proposal as long as the main precondition for intervention would be that it would not threaten price stability.[57] Furthermore, the Bundesbank felt that giving in to the government on this issue would protect the long-term independence of the Bundesbank, as negotiations would soon be under way on full monetary integration.[58] The Bundesbank also acceded to the concerns of industry as well as its own belief that the EMS continued to serve the important function of stabilizing payment relations between European nations and solidifying the regional zone of monetary stability, which had been one of the primary reasons for establishing the EMS in the first place. At this time, fluctuations of currencies within the EMS were due mainly to the large volume of trade and service transactions, unlike the capital flows between the dollar and the DM, which were more affected by political and psychological factors.[59] With exports to the EC accounting for more than 50 percent of Germany's total exports (in addition to almost 70 percent if one includes the European Free Trade Area [EFTA] nations, many of which pegged their currencies to the DM), the Bundesbank accepted exchange rate stability in the EMS, even with the potential that the intramarginal interventions would compel the bank to cede a measured amount of policy autonomy.

Moreover, defending the integrity of the EMS and enhancing the measures of inter-Community coordination could only strengthen the insulating effects of the EMS to the volatility of the dollar.[60]

The significance of the Nyborg agreement should not be underestimated. The Germans, especially the Bundesbank, were willing to go to great lengths to offer concessions on intervention and financing mechanisms within the EMS in return for enhanced European exchange rate stability.[61] The gentlemen's agreement at Nyborg indicated a significant amount of flexibility on the part of the Bundesbank and the Kohl government at a time when both were increasingly inflexible toward the United States. The agreement implied at least a minor loss of the DM's traditional dominance over the EMS. Moreover, the decision to adhere closely to the Nyborg agreement can be seen as the price Bonn and Frankfurt were willing to pay and the concessions they were willing to offer for ensuring that other EC states abolish capital controls, further proceed toward the goals outlined in the Single European Act (SEA) of 1986, and converge their macroeconomic policies more in line with the German monetary norm.[62] Most important, such movements on the SEA were major prerequisites to the support from banking and business associations. These issues were crucial elements in the support of the Bundesbank and would prove an important link to the general support of the Bundesbank and government heading into the first stage of negotiations over EMU set to begin in the spring of 1988. The agreement also demonstrated that the Bundesbank's vaunted independence could be constrained by external financial considerations, namely, commitments to intramarginal interventions to stabilize EMS currencies, given the proper constellation of political and economic factors.

As compared to the fairly detailed provisions of the Nyborg agreement, the Louvre accord provided signatories with a good deal of ambiguity on how they would actually implement the decision.[63] There existed no formal institutional obligations or enforcement mechanisms that could have changed the perceptions and preferences of the Germans that they would have to adjust their policies to meet the requirements of fostering stability of exchange rates. A trade-off between autonomy and exchange rate stability had not been made at the Louvre. When confronted over the degree of cooperation the German government or the Bundesbank should give to the Louvre accord, it was the Germans who first demanded concessions on the part of the United States in terms of constraining budget deficits and relinquishing the alternative of further talking down the dollar. When it came to cooperation at Louvre, the most the Germans could offer was a commitment to improving the condition for sustained economic growth while maintaining price stability, a statement that no Bundesbank official could disagree with. Given the time frame from February to September 1987—a period of general economic stability—the German government definitively differentiated its bargaining behavior based on strategic calculations of what was acceptable for the Bundesbank in Europe as compared to the global monetary system.

The October Crash

After Nyborg and by the time of the October market crash,[64] Baker's demands that the Germans, through a reflationary fiscal and monetary policy, play a larger role in shouldering the burden of providing liquidity and stability to the international monetary system, could be more easily resisted. Stoltenberg and Pöhl each realized that domestic and EMS stability had, for the time being, been achieved.[65] Moreover, the Bundesbank had already begun to tighten monetary policy,[66] a path that was heavily criticized by Baker and one that would continue onward through 1992. Specifically, the stock market crash on October 19 was precipitated by Baker's public criticism of a modest Bundesbank tightening of monetary policy that apparently, in his mind, violated the spirit of G7 consultations and the Louvre accord. Moreover, Baker's comments concerning the unwillingness of the United States to support (in the form of raising interest rates) the falling dollar merely exacerbated a market anxious over inflation, exchange rate stabilization, interest rate volatility, and disruptions within the G7. Although exchange rate markets remained remarkably stable, the Dow dropped 508 points in one day.

Baker immediately met with Stoltenberg and Pöhl in Frankfurt to issue a public statement to calm the markets and ease the tension between the Germans and the United States. The three reaffirmed their agreement to the "flexible" application of the Louvre accord with the aim of cooperating "on exchange rate stability."[67] Even after the markets calmed several weeks later, Baker continued to issue statements suggesting that preventing a further depreciation of the dollar had now received a low priority in the Reagan administration. Calls for further international economic policy coordination, which were now coming under heavy domestic opposition within the United States,[68] and foreign demand stimulus fell on increasingly deaf ears in Germany. Baker's leadership had come under question not only for his role in the market crash but also for his involvement in international discussions concerning U.S. domestic monetary policy, a policy domain that many in the Federal Reserve felt belonged firmly under its control. Although the Germans were just as concerned about market instability, from the Bundesbank perspective there existed few politically feasible options that they could offer to the United States.

The situation stabilized toward the end of 1987 as talks in the United States on reducing persistent budget deficits concluded with a modest two-year bipartisan package that appeared to address some of the problems that had plagued earlier efforts at budget reduction. With some measure of trust having returned to Baker and the United States, the Germans were more willing to enter into a December 22 agreement, the so-called Telephone accord, directed at stabilizing exchange rates at around the DM 1.65–1.70 range. One might argue that this accord was the last hurrah of international exchange rate coordination in the 1980s. The finance ministers reaffirmed their commitment to the "basic objectives and economic policy directions agreed in the Louvre Accord."[69] The G7 also orchestrated a January 1, 1988, attempt to support the dollar and stabilize its relationship to the DM. Concerted G7 intervention, primarily on the shoulders of the United States, helped stabilize exchange rates and displayed the commitment of the United States to prevent further depreciation. It was the United States, however, that was exchanging some measure of domestic autonomy for exchange rate stability. Furthermore, despite efforts on the part of the United States and Germany within the G5 to intensify international monetary cooperation, the Europeanization of German monetary policy, symbolized by the Basel-Nyborg agreement, had become by the end of 1987 the dominant mode of Germany's external monetary interaction.

Conclusion

As Funabashi writes, Germany's "compliance under EMS pressure—mainly from the French—to revalue the deutsche mark and its subsequent willingness to subordinate the goals of domestic policy for harmony among the EMS countries demonstrate a priority given to maintenance of EMS arrangements."[70] For Europe, a significant degree of monetary cooperation would characterize German policy. Within the G7, cooperation would mark the beginning of the period but would cease toward the end, culminating in the most significant financial shock of the 1980s. The relative success in enhancing the exchange rate stability of the EMS was due in large part to the Bonn government's agreement to revalue the DM at crucial EMS realignment negotiations, despite political problems on the domestic front and some resistance from the Bundesbank. Furthermore, at critical junctures in the negotiating process, both the Bundesbank and government were willing to cooperate with their European partners, which in turn created greater opportunities for achieving cooperative solutions. As Peter Katzenstein suggests, the EMS was political because from a domestic standpoint the EMS offered something for everyone: The EMS "seemed to meet long-standing demands of the dissatisfied unions for monetary expansion, curbed slightly the power of the central bank, and promised to slow down the general upward drift of the Deutsche Mark, which had become a major problem for West Germany's export industry."[71]

Overall, in Europe, the government pursued a more compliant bargaining strategy. The governance structure remained strong and, one can argue, was strengthened by the Nyborg agreement. The government consistently *offered* concessions (the Gleneagles ECOFIN meeting, the EMS realignment, and the Nyborg agreement) to their EMS partners. Even the Bundesbank contributed to the monetary détente of 1987 by lowering a key interest rate in January to defuse a potentially explosive situation. German monetary authorities were by the beginning of 1988 now ready to make the biggest sacrifice in terms of domestic monetary autonomy for the purpose of European monetary stability, namely a single European currency and central bank.

The more hard-line G7 bargaining strategy used by German authorities toward the end of 1987 reflected the difficulty they would have in convincing German domestic actors that further policy cooperation—for the good of the United States—would also be good for them. Rather, the government and Bundesbank consistently *sought* concessions from their G7 partners. The level of disagreement between the Bundesbank and government remained generally low, although there was some broader disagreement over the extent of commitment made by the Germans at the G5 agreements at Plaza and Louvre. Moreover, although the basic governance structure remained weak, attempts were made to strengthen some of the informal commitments to cooperation. As a result, a mixed bargaining strategy would characterize the German bargaining strategy from 1985 to 1987.

Notes

1. *First Annual Arthur F. Burns Memorial Lecture* (New York: American Council on Germany, 1987), cited in Wolfram Hanrieder, *Germany, America, and Europe* (New Haven, Conn.: Yale University Press, 1989), p. 316.

2. Baker's quote cited in "Helmut Schlesinger: Bank Chief Makes His Mark," *Los Angeles Times*, September 22, 1992.

3. For example, participating EMS central banks would intervene to support their currencies should they run up against the lower end of the trading margins of the ERM. The burden of adjustment weighed heavily on the weakening currency.

4. Accounts of this period in international monetary politics are dealt with in I. M. Destler and C. Randall Henning, *Dollar Politics: Exchange Rate Policymaking in the United States* (Washington, D.C.: Institute for International Economics, 1989). Another excellent source is Yoichi Funabashi, *Managing the Dollar: From the Plaza to the Louvre* (Washington, D.C.: Institute for International Economics, 1988). Partial coverage of this period is dealt with in Robert D. Putnam and Nicholas Bayne, *Hanging Together: Cooperation and Conflict in the Seven-Power Summits* (Cambridge: Harvard University Press, 1987); Michael Webb, *The Political Economy of Policy Coordination: International Adjustment Since 1945* (Ithaca, N.Y.: Cornell University Press). For a more condensed version, see Benjamin J. Cohen, "The Triad and the Unholy Trinity: Lessons for the Pacific Region," in Richard Higgott, Richard Leaver, and John Ravenhill, eds., *Pacific Economic*

Relations in the 1990's: Cooperation or Conflict? (London: Allen and Unwin, 1993), pp. 133–158.

5. Statistics drawn from the U.S. Department of Commerce, *U.S. Trade Performance in 1985 and Outlook* (Washington, D.C.: U.S. Government Printing Office, 1986), pp. 105–106.

6. Benjamin J. Cohen, "An Explosion in the Kitchen?: Economic Relations with Other Advanced Industrial States," in Kenneth Oye, Robert Lieber, and Donald Rothchild, eds., *Eagle Resurgent?: The Reagan Era in American Foreign Policy* (Boston: Little, Brown and Company, 1987), p. 126.

7. See Deutsche Bundesbank, *Monthly Report of the Deutsche Bundesbank*, March 1985 (Frankfurt/Main), for an early concern of the potential for inflationary pressures in the German economy.

8. For a good summarization of the German view, see Helmut Schmidt, "Währungs Politik," *Die Zeit*, February 15, 1985.

9. Kohl sought to keep the Bonn G7 summit low-key. Kohl also sought to enhance his standing for domestic consumption, given the upcoming provincial elections that followed closely after the summit. The summit was largely overshadowed by the controversy surrounding Reagan's trip to Bitburg, and little if anything substantial on monetary or trade matters was achieved.

10. Interestingly, efforts at international monetary coordination were seen by the French as a unique opportunity for developing alternative means of putting international pressure on the Bundesbank to be more accommodating in its policies. The process of international monetary coordination at the G7 level was a politically less costly form of focusing attention on the impact of German monetary policy on regional (EC) growth. A reverse form of behavior exists on trade matters, for the Germans see international trade negotiations as the opportunity to place greater pressure on the French.

11. One reason for the overall less than enthusiastic German attitude toward government intervention in the exchange markets was the strong opposition of Stoltenberg. Although he acknowledged the importance of reducing volatility and enhancing some elements of surveillance, Stoltenberg argued that there was no alternative to the flexible exchange rate system at the international level.

12. Paraphrased from an interview with a German official. Cited in Funabashi, *Managing the Dollar*, p. 109.

13. With the exception of the devaluation of the Italian lira in January 1985, the EMS had experienced a relatively harmonious two years (1983–1985) of currency interaction.

14. Interview with the author in Frankfurt, September 1993.

15. An important side note was the agreement in February 1986 by the European Council to the Single European Act (SEA) that committed the Europeans to eliminate capital controls and the removal of all barriers to financial flows throughout the EC. The commitment of the Europeans to capital flow liberalization was deemed very important by the Germans because the Bundesbank and federal government were both opposed to further monetary integration unless such steps were taken. The Bundesbank strongly believed that freedom of capital markets and coordinated economic policy must precede the consideration of further monetary coordination. Reference to eventual monetary union was included in the preamble of the SEA, although references that might have limited the scope of a future union were also included. See Andrew Moravscik, "Negotiating the Single European Act: National Interests and Conventional Statecraft in the European Community," *International Organization* 45, no. 1 (winter 1991), pp. 42–43.

16. Up until the realignment, the Bundesbank and the Bank of France had been making sizable purchases of DMs to further ease pressure within the EMS. The realignment essentially switched positions between the franc and the DM as the DM fell to the bottom of the trading bands. This reversal of currency roles increased the room for further interest rate reductions among other EMS currencies.

17. "West Germany Can Take Revaluation 'in Its Stride,'" *Financial Times*, April 7, 1986. At the press conference following the EC finance ministers' meeting, Stoltenberg went even further in stating Germany's intention of discussing a "new international monetary order" built on Germany's monetary stability. Such a statement was clearly aimed at the United States.

18. Many analysts cite the lowest inflation figures in Germany and the stubborn level of unemployment of around 10 percent as the prime reasons why the Bundesbank lowered the discount rate.

19. At a press conference at the time of the rate cut, Pöhl indicated that the move came as a result of close consultation with European central bankers.

20. The Federal Reserve officially proclaimed that there was no relationship between any G5 discussion in January 1986 and Germany's decision to lower its discount rate. The decision to jointly lower rates was reportedly made at the insistence of Volcker in a private meeting with Pöhl at the Bank for International Settlement meetings in Basel in February of 1986. Volcker had sought to delay U.S. action until after the March 6 Bundesbank meeting.

21. "Weitere DM Aufwertung ist sehr Willkommen," *Handelsblatt*, April 23, 1986.

22. Funabashi, *Managing the Dollar*, p. 52. Stoltenberg and the vice secretary in finance at the time, Hans Tietmeyer, were at first more willing than the Bundesbank to be more accommodating toward the United States. However, they placed no serious direct pressure on the Bundesbank and soon joined the Bundesbank in unified opposition to the United States. The Bundesbank's resistant position was bolstered by the continuing concerns of the export industry.

23. The economic indicators included gross national product (GNP) growth rates, inflation rates, interest rates, unemployment, fiscal deficit ratios, current account and trade balances, monetary growth rates, reserves, and currency rates. As one Bundesbank official I interviewed stated, "The decision to examine these indicators was nothing new from our perspective. We have been doing this for years. Including them within the G7 forum did not in any way alter our view on coordination."

24. For the Germans, especially the Bundesbank, the emphasis on convergence (a passive notion) over coordination/cooperation (an active notion) should not be underestimated. Coordination/cooperation and convergence are neither synonymous nor do they necessarily coincide.

25. "Stoltenberg: Währungsbeschlüsse fördern Stabilität," *Süddeutsche Zeitung*, April 7, 1986.

26. The Baker-Miyazawa accord committed the Japanese to action in "promoting world economic growth" while also stating that "exchange rate instability could jeopardize stable economic growth." The communiqué was followed by a Japanese interest rate reduction from 3.5 percent to 3 percent. Baker felt that he could use the Japanese to pressure the Germans to also go along with the agreement. After he announced the U.S.-Japanese agreement, Baker publicly cited the "uncooperative behavior" of the Germans, which would lead to the failure of global policy accommodation.

27. Cohen, "Explosion in the Kitchen," p. 141.

28. The meeting was called one week before a pivotal IMF/World Bank meeting in Washington, D.C. Baker had been increasing the pressure on the Germans to do more to stimulate domestic demand in order to address the trade imbalance between Germany and the United States or else the Germans would see the dollar drop further. Bundesbank officials countered with statistics supporting their view that imports were up 7.5 percent for the first half of 1986 while exports were up only 2 percent. Less known, yet critically important, was Germany's DM 43.5 billion current account surplus with the United States.

29. *New York Times*, "Europeans May Prop the Dollar," September 22, 1986, pp. D1. The German economics minister, Martin Bangemann (FDP), stated that the Germans were doing about as much as can be expected to sustain world growth. "In so far as we can act as a locomotive for the rest of the world, we already are." Bangemann, a strong proponent of European policies and a leading critic of U.S. policy, became an important ally of the Bundesbank.

30. Ibid.

31. Bangemann stated bluntly that "it is an illusion to assume that German growth can cure the world or the U.S. balance of payments," and that currency questions were too often "conducted in a spirit of confrontation." *New York Times*, "Europeans May Prop the Dollar," September 22, 1986, p. D10.

32. "A Year After Plaza Accord, Currency Issues Remain Divisive," *New York Times*, September 22, 1986.

33. It should also be noted that no participant knew what the "right" value of the dollar should be. The markets were still somewhat uncertain at this point where the dollar should "stabilize." See the discussion in *The Economist*, "The Fall of the Dollar Is Smaller Than It Seems," October 11, 1986.

34. *New York Times*, "Baker Bids to Lower U.S. Dollar," September 29, 1986.

35. It was increasingly known that Volcker, concerned about potential inflationary pressures at home, did not want to see the dollar drop any further.

36. *New York Times*, "Baker Bids to Lower U.S. Dollar," September 29, 1986, p. A1.

37. As an indication of the Bundesbank's commitment to stabilize the dollar, the bank intervened in the amount of U.S.$100 million on September 29. Despite a concerted, yet ultimately ineffectual effort by the Bundesbank and Europe to prop up the dollar, it should not have been surprising to see the dollar continue to drop as Baker continued to make threats against the Germans and Japanese.

38. In the week preceding the realignment on January 12, DM 16 billion were spent in intermarginal interventions to support weak currencies. Institutional arrangements, however, limited European Monetary Cooperation Fund (EMCF) operations, as no short-term loans of the intervention currency were available. The problems of financing the interventions pointed toward the increasing dissatisfaction among all EMS actors with the financing mechanism of the ERM.

39. "Central Banks Mount DM5bn Operation to Calm Money Markets," *Financial Times*, March 7, 1987.

40. The DM was revalued 3 percent with the French franc remaining unchanged. The Irish finance minister, John Bruton, termed the entire realignment decision as "symbolic and political." In particular, the French did not want to see the Danish krone or Belgian franc revalued even as low as 1 percent. In the view of the Chirac government, such a move would have indicated that the French franc was the "sick currency" of the EMS, a position that could not be tolerated.

41. The industrial associations had a tough choice to make between re-evaluation and the potential damage to their competitiveness or continuing instability

in the European markets. Recognizing the danger of the latter, the industrial associations offered their tentative support for the deal, solidifying the ratification consensus needed for the agreement. See their response in "Eine Aufwertung ist zum jetzigen Zeitpunkt besonders ungünstig," *Handelsblatt*, January 11, 1987.

42. "Die Mark um drei Prozent aufgewertet: Paris zufrieden—Stoltenberg: Stabilisierung," *Frankfuter Allgemeine Zeitung*, January 13, 1987.

43. In fact, the move came as quite a surprise to most observers. Concurrently, the United States and Japan were engaged in heavy discussions over the rising yen. The Japanese were especially placed under the gun to stimulate their economy. Baker went even so far as to call the German move "largely cosmetic." Pöhl angrily shot back that Baker's methods were "dangerous" to global stability and that Baker was "playing with fire" by continuing to talk down the dollar. *New York Times*, "U.S. Reticence on Dollar Seen as Part of Plan," January 23, 1987, p. A1.

44. "Reagan-Administration will den Dollarkurs noch tiefer sehen," *Handelsblatt*, December 14, 1987.

45. The reserve requirement is the portion of deposits that a bank must set aside in the form of cash, or, in this case, non-interest-earning deposits with the central bank. Such a move may have been in response to the criticism that the Bundesbank faced from the German Savings Association, in particular, its director, Helmut Geiger. Geiger felt that any further reductions in interest rates or other monetary levers would spark inflationary tendencies in the German economy.

46. Funabashi, *Managing the Dollar*, p. 61.

47. Bundesverband der Deutschen Industrie and the Deutscher Industrie- und Handelstag, respectively.

48. Although discussion centered on whether explicit ranges or zones had been set, there was no public acknowledgment at the time that any zones or ranges had been agreed to.

49. The tax cut was in fact just a slight increase in what would have been expected from the Kohl government and would not go into effect until 1988, as originally planned.

50. The Bundesbank had intervened even less than France, Great Britain, and Italy, only U.S. $750 million during the three-month period following the Louvre. Funabashi, *Managing the Dollar*, p. 191.

51. The pressure on the administration to appease protectionist forces increased as the Democrats regained control of the Senate following the elections in November of 1986.

52. *Wall Street Journal*, "U.S. and Allies Reaffirm Pact on Currencies," April 9, 1987, p. 3.

53. As compared to the earlier form of intervention "at the margins," intramarginal interventions meant that central banks would intervene *before* a currency reached the upper or lower margins of the ERM. This important correction was seen as easing some of the strains that would develop when a currency had already reached the limits of the margins by intervening before there was no room for maneuver.

54. Earlier in the year, the Bundesbank eased restrictions on the use of ECUs in private investment in Germany. The Bundesbank had long held that an "artificial" currency such as the ECU violated the bank's constitutional duty to safeguard the value of the currency. Under pressure from the German economics minister, Martin Bangemann, a leading proponent of European monetary integration, the Bundesbank relented in its opposition to a larger role of the ECU in Germany. See the discussion in "Segen aus Frankfurt: ECU," *Wirtschaftswoche*, May 28, 1987.

55. Since Basel-Nyborg, in practical terms, the Bundesbank has maintained its preeminent position in the EMS without undermining its policy autonomy, even after accepting all financing requests for intramarginal interventions.

56. The Bundesbank's views on Nyborg are well summarized in "Im Zeichen von Nyborg," *Frankfurter Allgemeine Zeitung*, August 27, 1987.

57. Pöhl went to great lengths at the press conference following the Nyborg announcement to reassure all participants that the agreement would in no way impinge upon the autonomy of the Bundesbank. He indicated that the bank found it very difficult to accept all aspects of the provisions. Moreover, in the face of domestic criticism, Pöhl went on the public relations offensive to detail how the bank had not transferred any monetary authority. The French, of course, had deemed the provisions of Nyborg as "presumably automatic." See "Leichterer Griff zum Geldhahn," *Süddeutsche Zeitung*, September 15, 1987.

58. Pöhl also stated that the decision to support the accord did not "fall easy" for the Central Bank Council. However, the bank did not have any control over institutional changes of the EMS, which were solely under the discretion of "political decisionmakers" and not the competencies of the bank. "Bundesbank verteidigt Autonomie durch Kompromiss," *Süddeutsche Zeitung*, September 14, 1987.

59. Such was the contention of many analysts as the dollar appreciated to record levels through 1985. Although difficult to prove empirically, political and/or psychological expectations surrounding currency speculation should not be underestimated for their impact. See the discussion on the dollar's rise in "Dollar's Strength Persists: Expectations Bolster Value, Analysts Say," *New York Times*, February 19, 1985.

60. Such was the case at the end of October following the market crash as the tumbling dollar precipitated renewed turmoil in the EMS. The French were quick to skillfully exploit the recent changes in the EMS in their defense of the franc. The French were able to prevent their currency, under speculative attack, from being forced to devalue by flexibly using intervention techniques and through support from the Bundesbank. The French franc and the EMS survived this round of turbulence in large part due to the changes agreed upon in Nyborg. "EMS Takes Up the Strain of Falling Dollar," *International Herald Tribune*, October 30, 1987.

61. It was also clear to many observers that the incompatibility of free-flowing capital, generally fixed exchange rates, and domestic monetary sovereignty would continue to sharpen as a result of the SEA and Basel-Nyborg agreement. Some commentators warned of the limits that were increasing upon the Bundesbank's freedom to pursue its domestic-oriented monetary targets. See, for example, "EG-Fesseln für die Bundesbank?" *Wirtschaftsdienst*, no. 9, 1987. Other commentators urged moving the EMS more quickly along toward a joint monetary policy if they were going to cope with the free movement of capital among them as outlined in the SEA. This position was supported by a working group of the EC Commission led by Tommaso Padoa-Schioppa, which issued a strong position paper in mid-1987 outlining such a strategy for the EMS.

62. The decision to shift some of the burden of adjustment away from weaker currencies to the DM would also make full EMS membership more palatable to the British government.

63. Many of the provisions of the Louvre accord were never stated publicly, which only increased the likelihood that each nation could interpret their responsibilities differently than the others. The insistence of the Germans, the Bundesbank in particular, that no public declarations in terms of target zones, exchange rate ranges, or specific provisions be issued weakened the incentives of all actors to unqualified support for the Louvre accord.

64. See the discussion in Destler and Henning, *Dollar Politics*, for a more comprehensive treatment, pp. 62–67.

65. When confronted with the fact that German inflation rates of 1 percent, sluggish growth rate, and 8.4 percent unemployment were sufficient for stimulating the economy, Bangemann responded by stating, "We cannot accept it when someone tells us we have done things wrong when quite clearly we have achieved things." *New York Times*, October 30, 1987.

66. The Bundesbank modestly raised interest rates after the Federal Reserve, now in August under the new chairman, Alan Greenspan, who had decided to raise the discount rate, in large part to establish his noninflationary credibility. At the late September IMF–World Bank meeting, there was a conspicuous omission of interest rates and monetary policy from the G7 communiqué.

67. "G-7 Efforts to Stabilize Markets," *New York Times*, October 20, 1987. The full communiqué read,

> Today, Secretary of the Treasury, James A. Baker III, Finance Minister Gerhard Stoltenberg and Bundesbank President Karl Otto Pöhl, had a very positive, private meeting in Frankfurt, Germany which had been agreed upon early last week. The parties agreed to continue economic cooperation under the Louvre Agreement and its flexible application including cooperation on exchange rate stability and monetary policies. They are consulting with their G-7 colleagues and are confident that this will enable them to foster exchange rate stability around current levels.

68. See the comments of William A. Niskanen, "A Lower Dollar vs. Recession," *New York Times*, October 27, 1987. The former chair of the Council of Economic Advisors, Martin Feldstein, testified as a private citizen in public hearings in Congress that the United States abandon efforts at international macroeconomic coordination. See the analysis in Destler and Henning, *Dollar Politics*, p. 65.

69. *The New York Times*, "OECD Prods U.S. and Bonn," December 23, 1987, p. D1. The operative section on exchange rate policy was quite explicit, stating that the ministers of the G7 would monitor and implement policies to strengthen "underlying economic fundamentals" and would seek to prevent a further rise or decline of the dollar to the extent to which it would be "destabilizing to the adjustment process" or world economic growth.

70. Funabashi, *Managing the Dollar*, p. 58.

71. Peter Katzentsein, *Policy and Politics in West Germany* (Philadelphia: Temple University Press, 1987), p. 95.

4

Exporting the Deutsche Mark to Europe, 1989–1991

> Germany is our fatherland, Europe is our future.
>
> —Chancellor Helmut Kohl, 1990

> If there is agreement that inflation is democracy's enemy number one, success in ensuring price stability should be taken as adequate testimony to the (European) central bank's accountability.
>
> —Former Bundesbank president Karl Otto Pöhl, 1990

The period 1988–1991 marks an unusually intense period in German monetary history and monetary diplomacy.[1] Of course the monumental undertakings associated with GEMU in 1990 overshadowed in many respects the transformations within the regional and global economy. This chapter, however, examines only how GEMU affected the internal power struggle of the Bundesbank and government and how this struggle manifested itself in the bargaining strategies of each actor in the negotiations surrounding the Maastricht Treaty and the waning interests of Germany toward G7 international monetary cooperation.

The primary focus of this chapter is on the question of why German negotiators did not dismiss the idea of EMU out of hand (given the implications of the prospective treaty) but instead were willing to offer the DM as the sacrificial lamb in return for EMU. Despite some of the efficiency gains from a single currency, Germany would not expect to benefit a great deal from the reduction in transaction costs (primarily on the export side than on imports) because a sizable proportion of German trade within Europe was already denominated in the DM. Nor would Germany immediately benefit from the anti-inflationary credibility of the future ECB. Indeed, the reverse could happen. Even if the ECB's independence from political control was more formally guaranteed than the Bundesbank's, it was arguable that the ECB would find it hard to inherit the Bundesbank's reputation and credibility. Moreover, the Bundesbank was not altogether convinced that other European central banks could deliver the same level of price stability. In sum, the persuasiveness of the economic motivations should not be stressed in understanding the German approach to EMU.

Instead, a political explanation is required. Internally, the political will of Germany's leading politicians led to a great deal of overt and tacit pressure placed on the Bundesbank not to derail the negotiations on EMU. The key government players, Chancellor Kohl and his foreign minister, Hans-Dietrich Genscher, had a singular interest in EMU, which reflected long-standing foreign policy goals and ideas built on the Treaty of Rome and the Franco-German axis. The more conservative finance minister, soon to be Theo Waigel, was less influential in deciding the government's strategy heading into Maastricht. Moreover, the political importance for both politicians of European integration expanded as Germany slowly reasserted its dominant political and economic position in Europe during the late 1980s. German reassertion of power and influence could best be expressed within the comforting and binding constraints of the EC and an overall strengthened European identity. Finally, with the seeming month-by-month collapse and disintegration of the Eastern Bloc through 1989 and with the looming prospect of German reunification into 1990, the political (or foreign policy) salience of EMU moved to the foreground for German and European politicians. As the historic "German problem"—the long-held political, economic, and military-strategic concerns of Germany's geopolitical position in the heart of Europe—came to the forefront of debate, irrevocably binding Germany to the EC, monetary union became the negotiating mantra of German politicians and their European partners.

The Bundesbank's distinctive position on EMU and the Maastricht Treaty negotiations is best summarized in its "Statement on the Establishment of an Economic and Monetary Union in Europe," *Monthly Report of the Deutsche Bundesbank,* September 1990. The bank's views should not have been surprising to anyone and reflected longstanding principles associated with earlier European discussions on EMU, beginning with the Werner Report in 1970. The bank's cautious approach toward EMU centered on its belief in the coronation theory (*Krönungstheorie*), the view that EMU must result only as the final stage of a prolonged period of convergence of key economic variables (notably inflation, but also budget deficits and public debt) and institutional safeguards (political independence of a European central bank). Apparently, the Bundesbank believed that convergence in line with the Bundesbank model would greatly slow down the process of EMU such that monetary union might never arrive. The bank also argued that "substantial transitional problems as a result of the intra-German unification process" and the uncertainties in Eastern Europe justified postponement of any further steps on EMU until the economic situation in Germany as a whole and in the EC could be regarded as sufficiently consolidated. The Bundesbank accurately and justifiably feared being pressed to support EMU because other countries had supported Chancellor Kohl's rapid movement on GEMU. In sum, would the Bundesbank's EMU concerns be adequately addressed? Or would the government seek to compromise on crucial issues, in other words use its political leverage over the bank to secure some kind of agreement on EMU?

Some analysts also argue that the Bundesbank's own domestic monetary policy was increasingly uncooperative during this period (steadily rising interest rates furthering tensions within the EMS and the G7). In some respect, this is true, but such a view looks solely at the domestic monetary policy of the Bundesbank and not the external monetary diplomacy of the federal government. Therefore, one singular overriding fact cannot be disputed: The German government secured the approval and consent of the Bundesbank to the Maastricht Treaty, a treaty that would effectively do away with the Bundesbank's sovereign control over German monetary policy. The Bundesbank did not grant its approval without hesitation or preconditions. In fact, the Maastricht Treaty reflects a number of the Bundesbank's key concerns, including guarantees of a European central bank's political independence, its clearly specified objective of ensuring price stability, strict EMU entry requirements, as well as movement on political union. However, the Bundesbank had essentially consented to an agreement that no one thought possible—a single European currency regulated by a supranational European central bank that would do away with the DM in Germany. In terms of the objectives of exchange rate stability and monetary autonomy, the Germans had *offered* the greatest concession of all to Europe: the DM.

Within the G7, exchange rate stability, though important to the Germans, would not come at the cost of major concessions to the United States. While simultaneously negotiating the demise of the Bundesbank and the sacrifice of the DM to Europe, German monetary authorities continued to pursue a tough bargaining position vis-à-vis the United States. The Germans *demanded* increased concessions from the United States over continued exchange rate stabilization and domestic adjustment. In return, the Germans *offered* little in the way of concrete proposals, concessions, or action on international cooperation. German monetary authorities saw few political or economic incentives and benefits associated with G7 policy coordination. The pattern of G7 interaction and the lack of an institutional focus for developing the kind of intra-G7 monetary linkages and tradeoffs, as compared to the European bargaining arena, limited the opportunities and increased the constraints for the G7 members to reach accommodation. Moreover, the political capital, in the form of political influence that the government had over the Bundesbank, was increasingly being expended on the negotiations over EMU and GEMU. It should not have been expected, therefore, that the Bundesbank or government would be willing to adjust their policies for the G7, at least to the same degree as in the European arena. The international monetary regime that focused on the interaction of the G7 came under repeated attack and criticism as an ill-defined and frail international institution for policy coordination.

Part 1:
Moving Forward on EMU and Away from G7 Coordination

The Delors Plan

Beginning in 1988, there was a strong push by the French and West German governments to see the EMS strengthened and movement initiated toward EMU. The Germans had assumed the presidency of the EC at the beginning of 1988, and Kohl and Genscher were intent on stamping a German imprint on the processes of European integration. As a result of some of the tensions within the EMS during 1987, the French were no longer willing to accept that Bonn and the Bundesbank so completely dominated the EMS. An initiative for a single European currency and central bank to relieve the EMS of the asymmetry that existed—despite the provisions of the Nyborg agreement that sought to shift some of the burden of adjustment off weaker currencies—would be the only recourse for addressing monetary and political imbalances in the EC. Moreover, the confusion and ultimate conclusion of a treaty on the Franco-German Economic Council, initially proposed by Kohl in November 1987 and finally ratified in November 1988, exacerbated the calls by the French for EMS reform.[2] The Bundesbank's sharp reaction and criticism of the council, which aimed for new legal and formal policy-coordination mechanisms, and the negotiation process between the French and Germans (which the Bundesbank was not part of) forced the chancellor to amend the treaty to meet the Bundesbank's strict interpretations and standards. The German and French governments recognized the need for a broader approach toward European monetary coordination and integration.

At the end of February of 1988, Genscher called for a group of economic, political, and monetary experts to be set up at the Hanover summit in June of that year to discuss the long-held European objective of a single currency. Genscher recognized the necessity of closer cooperation in the monetary field brought on by the SEA and the push toward implementing the internal market by the end of 1992. The Bundesbank was certainly aware of these long-held German objectives as well as European pressures to proceed, but given the fallout from the fiasco over the Franco-German Economic Council, the political push in Bonn and within the EC strengthened.

Through the first half of 1988, the Bundesbank argued that the monetary strategy of Germany had successfully served as a nominal anchor for the policy of other European central banks and that it had accepted, de facto, the underlying philosophy of the German Central Bank. Bundesbank officials argued that greater symmetry in the EMS might actually prove detrimental to the real anchor of the system if it would impair the ability of the Bundesbank to pursue an effective monetary policy.[3] Norbert Kloten, a member of the Central Bank Council, gave voice to such concerns by stating that the boundary conditions already connected with the Louvre accord and the tensions within the EMS as well as the common interests on both sides of the Atlantic in holding interest rates down had immobilized the Bundesbank.[4] Moreover, with Genscher taking the lead on monetary issues over the finance minister, the Bundesbank was concerned that the foreign minister might be more easily satisfied with monetary agreements that did not strictly meet the Bundesbank standard.

The Bundesbank felt at first that the weight of the discussions surrounding EMU would eventually disappear. The same debates for and against EMU were well known to all participants. The push for monetary integration often sprang from cyclical periods of "Europhoria," only to be replaced by a round of "Europessimism." Moreover, the Bundesbank had gone through the same process before in the context of the Werner Report (1969–1970) and the founding of the EMS in 1978. But throughout 1988–1989 and as Pöhl became one of the leading figures on the Delors Committee, more resistant members of the Bundesbank council realized that outright resistance to the idea of EMU would not work. Instead, the Bundesbank switched to a more subtle strategy. Although not formal policy, the Bundesbank decided that it should be in the forefront of the debate, defining the agenda and the key principles of the debate, and generating negotiating conditions so unacceptable and unbearable for most EMS partners that EMU would never prove feasible or acceptable to EC members.[5] The Bundesbank's position on the conditions, likelihood, and feasibility of EMU was paralleled in large part by the Kohl government, although Kohl and Genscher both realized that some form of compromise would in the end be necessary to achieve a truly comprehensive framework for EMU. Nonetheless, Kohl stuck closely with the Bundesbank position throughout the Delors Committee period. As an example of the tough position Kohl would take, when Jacques Chirac, the French prime minister, insisted on a quick move toward a European central bank at the Hanover summit, Kohl publicly rebuked Chirac in blunt terms, stating that Germany would move at its own pace toward EMU.[6]

The summons by Genscher in February for movement on EMU finally came together at the EC heads of government meeting in Hanover in June of 1988. The general discussion of monetary politics at the summit centered on the composition, institutional setup, and charge of the committee to review and suggest an approach to EMU. Preliminary discussions also focused on the debate over how best to proceed toward monetary union. Importantly, in a critical concession to the Germans, it was decided that the monetary committee would be independent not only of national governments but also of the Council of Ministers and the European Commission, although Jacques Delors chaired the committee. The seventeen-member committee comprised the EC's central bankers including Pöhl and Tommaso Padoa-Schioppa and leading academics like Niel Thygessen.[7] Not surprisingly, the Delors Committee decided to look closely at the Werner Report, as many of the same arguments both in favor and against the report had already been debated in its formulation—including the need for the free flow of capital, the absolute "irrevocable" fixing of exchange rates and/or a single currency for Europe, and the free convertibility of all currencies in the system. This time around, however, most participants were intent on seeing the process completed.

From the start, a number of groups and individuals attempted to influence the outcome of the Delors Committee in a direction not completely parallel to Frankfurt. Perhaps the most influential commentator on European monetary politics both within Germany and Europe remained the former chancellor of Germany, Helmut Schmidt.[8] For Schmidt, the culmination of the single market required a single European currency. What is more, the creation of a single currency would provide the optimal international monetary balance to the dollar, which was one of the primary reasons for the EMS's creation in the first place. Schmidt would almost single-handedly continue to push for EMU from his influential post on *Die Zeit*. Schmidt also had his European allies, especially among the influential business leaders in leading European transnational corporations—such as Cor van der Klust, president of Phillips, and Giovanni Agnelli, the Fiat chief—who had formed the Association for the Monetary Union of Europe. The Association pushed for a monetary union with an independent central bank, a single currency, and a union committed to price stability but not necessarily through the coronation theory approach of the Bundesbank.[9] The single market would demand a single European currency, and the creation of European institutions to set this process in motion would be erected to speed the process along. Most German industrial leaders supported the idea of a single European currency as well. The weekly magazine *Wirtschaftswoche* published its own survey of more than 500 leaders of German corporations indicating that about 60 percent of those businesses surveyed found reason to support EMU.[10] Even labor unions were in general support of the idea of European integration and EMU, if various social and work-related initiatives and safeguards were included in the final agreement.[11]

A number of other interested actors, however, expressed a good deal of skepticism and concern on the feasibility of EMU. The Scientific Council to the German Economics Ministry warned in early 1988 that a monetary union was still risky and that the EMS should be strengthened first through more coordination and through the building of a *Stabilitätsgemeinschaft* (community of stability).[12] The Association for the Protection of German Savers, a close ally of the Bundesbank on almost all issues, saw monetary union as a great threat to the ability of the Bundesbank to pursue its price stability goal.[13] Others feared the "salami tactics" of the European Commission that were being used to wrest away piecemeal the monetary control of the Bundesbank. In January of 1989, a survey of the Institute for Demoskopie, Allensbach, found only 20 percent of West German citizens supportive of the replacement of the DM by a single European currency, with 57 percent against the idea.[14] More than 90 percent of the respondents placed great trust in the DM, and only 20 percent of those surveyed felt "positive" toward the ECU. Members of Kohl's own coalition sounded their concern with the creation of a European central bank or single currency.[15] There were also members of the Bundesbank council who were publicly stating their reservations about any EMU concept based on "empty formulas" and any loss of domestic autonomy.[16]

Pöhl attempted to reassure his colleagues in the Bundesbank as well as businesses and the public that the Bundesbank would remain true to its price-stability standard. Nonetheless, he sharply criticized those who maintained that the Bundesbank was impeding talks on EMU.[17] By binding the Bundesbank to one nonnegotiable position, Pöhl argued that such an approach actually weakened the bargaining influence of the Bundesbank by placing it under greater pressure from the government to compromise. Furthermore, the fact that the DM had become the anchor of the EMS—not through the wishes of the Bundesbank but more through the currency's strength, convertibility, and international usage—remained the biggest obstacle to moving more quickly toward EMU. Pöhl doubted whether all of the EMS nations were in fact ready to relinquish the DM's anchor role. "It would be fateful," he asserted, "if one were to try and loosen the anchor. No one would be served by such an action."[18] Despite such concern, Pöhl remained a strong supporter of the EMU ideal as long as it was based on certain institutional provisions such as political, personal, and functional independence, strict convergence criteria, and on the association of other EC nations, in particular, Great Britain, to the EMS. Perhaps a bit cynically, yet publicly, Pöhl maintained that in principle, he was a convinced supporter of a European central bank.[19]

Although Pöhl felt that EMU was a long way off, it would ultimately be up to future intergovernmental conferences and the participating governments to decide how exactly to proceed. He also felt assured that the

Bundesbank and federal government could push a similar negotiating hand in any future negotiations. Hans Tietmeyer, the state secretary in the finance ministry at the time, extended the government's support for the Bundesbank's priorities. "There is a high degree of agreement between Frankfurt and Bonn," Tietmeyer indicated.[20] For example, the finance ministry issued a position paper on EMU that outlined most of the same strict requirements of the Bundesbank. Yet Pöhl acknowledged that any decision on EMU would ultimately be a political decision by the government.[21] He also felt that the government would likely diverge from the Bundesbank, however slightly, in order to secure an agreement. The Bundesbank's role in the following debate over EMU would thus be to act as a political and institutional check on any governmental decision. To have the EMU negotiations succeed, the government would have to secure the support of the Bundesbank. What role the Bundesbank would play and the stakes involved were now clear.

In December of 1988, the Delors Committee issued a preliminary report suggesting that convergence toward economic integration in the EC should take precedence over major monetary or institutional initiatives such as the creation of a European central bank or common currency.[22] The report, which was circulated among central bankers shortly before an ECOFIN meeting, argued that forcing the pace of monetary union could cause deindustrialization and forced emigration in less advantaged areas of the EC. In addition, the report implied that monetary union was a long-term goal, but it did set out in some detail the principles that would apply to the creation of a European central bank. The Delors working group also suggested that a European central bank should be a federal structure, modeled on the Bundesbank, and that it should have as much independence as possible (still undefined) and would set as its primary goal the fight against inflation. Finally, the report also pointed strongly to the costs associated with movement on EMU without parallel movement on steps to coordinate fiscal and budgetary policies and what impact that would have on "periphery" regions in Europe. In sum, the Delors Plan paralleled many of the points initially argued by the Bundesbank.

It should be noted that the relative stability of the EMS provided a supportive economic and political context from which the Delors Committee could focus on the provisions of EMU. Since the January 1987 realignment, exchange rate instability had considerably lessened due to the institutional changes brought on by Nyborg and by the relative stability in the dollar-DM relationship. As a result, during the period from early 1988 through mid-1989, EMS participants did not have to seriously consider realignments or undertake major concerted efforts to support or defend particular currencies, at least at the level seen in 1987 or later in 1992 or 1993. Moreover, the monthly meetings of the Delors working group had increased consultation and information sharing among leading financial circles and strengthened the interaction and discussion among ECOFIN members. A supportive structural and contextual environment had developed within which EMU negotiations were occurring.

Despite the positive developments, Bundesbank vice president Helmut Schlesinger warned against optimism or limiting the ability of members of the EMS to change their exchange rates in the run-up to the 1992 deadline for creating the single internal market. Schlesinger predicted that exchange rate adjustment would be an important way for weaker EMS currencies to adjust to the economic pressures of 1992.[23] With the Bundesbank raising the Lombard rate another half point to 5.5 percent in December of 1988, the bank's M3 targets overshooting for the third straight year, and with an indirect tax to come into effect on January 1 (which potentially would feed through into wages and thus inflation), the Bundesbank was intent on preserving its anchor and leading position within the EMS. Other Bundesbank officials indicated their interest in seeing a Europe of two speeds (*Europa der zwei Geschwindigkeiten*), for some members of the EC and the EMS would not likely soon meet the strict requirements of the current ERM or a future EMU.[24] Although the concept of a two-speed Europe would play into the debates on EMU in the later stages of the negotiations over Maastricht, the tone of the Bundesbank position hardened.

In addition to the traditional cautious conservatism of the Bundesbank, the British remained the most vocal and outspoken critics of EMU.[25] The British, through the Atlanticist orientation of Prime Minister Margaret Thatcher, made it abundantly clear that EMU was a divisive issue and not on the British agenda (or ever would be).[26] Even the governor of the Bank of England, Robin-Leigh Pemberton, a member of the Delors Committee, suggested that there was no consensus among European governments that a structure going beyond the first stages of policy coordination through existing institutions should be put in place at all.[27] The British were intent on watering down any proposals emanating from the Delors Committee and limiting any suggestions that might restrict the sovereignty of British policy. Some analysts even suggested that the Bundesbank tacitly supported the British. In the sense of slowing the entire debate over EMU, such a suggestion was true. However, the Bundesbank, as articulated by Pöhl, had committed to the idea of a European central bank and a single currency. With the EMS celebrating ten years of its existence, with Delors supported by France, Spain, Portugal, and Italy, and with Germany continuing to play a leading political role in the debate over European integration, the British would increasingly be isolated from the EMU debates.

The Delors Plan, published in April of 1989, envisioned the achievement of monetary union via three successive stages.[28] More important, the plan, in most of its elements, represented the German government and

Bundesbank view on union. It stressed the enormous difficulties in the way of a single currency and the importance of ensuring that the performance of the European economies be much more similar before member governments abandon the ability to use their own exchange rates to correct balance of payments problems. Moreover, several intergovernmental conferences would be required to revise the original Treaty on Europe and to implement Stages 2 and 3 of the report. Stage 1, to begin on July 1, 1990 (and agreed to at the Madrid summit of the Council of Ministers in June 1989), involved a single financial area with a free market in financial services and free circulation of capital, the inclusion of all member states' currencies in the ERM, the removal of impediments to the private use of the ECU, and the substantially greater and more public role for the existing Committee of Central Bank Governors.

Stage 2 would require amending the Rome Treaty to establish the ESCB. The ESCB would absorb the EC's existing institutional arrangements and begin the transition from coordination of national monetary policies to formulation and implementation of a Community monetary policy. The ESCB would be independent of national governments and other community institutions. During this phase, the margins of fluctuation in the ERM would be narrowed, in preparation for moving to zero in the final stage. Stage 3, or the final stage, of the process would see the irrevocable fixing of exchange rates and the assumption by a European central bank of full responsibility for monetary policy and exchange market intervention in third currencies. Importantly, the report did not see the adoption of a single currency as conceptually necessary, but that it would be convenient, reduce transaction costs, and might be practically necessary if markets did not otherwise find the irrevocable fixing of exchange rates credible. Stage 3 would also require "binding rules" imposing upper limits on budget deficits of member states. The financing of government debt by monetary means (monetization of debt) would be prohibited.

On the whole, and with the exception of the British, who rejected the plan outright,[29] the plan was greeted positively in the capitals of Europe. Lutz Stavenhagen, a senior aide to Kohl, stated that the German government, as a whole, welcomed it.[30] Pöhl warned about too much euphoria but stated (with a touch of pride) that the Delors document was "realistic and full of good judgment."[31] Pöhl also indicated that the plan was a preliminary outline with recommendations and implications of policies and that it was in no way binding for anyone. Nevertheless, in Pöhl's view, the politicians that would have to make such a decision would have a hard time denying the validity of the arguments, logic, and the policy recommendations. Pöhl was especially pleased that the plan emphasized the independence of the future European central bank, the goal of price stability, and, through implication of support for the *Krönungstheorie,* rejected the concept of a parallel currency. In response to commentary in support of setting a date for EMU, the central bank president also was careful to warn negotiators not to be in any hurry to achieve EMU.[32]

Securing the agreement of the EC heads of state at the Madrid summit would prove the last step in the Delors process. To encourage compromises, Spanish prime minister Felipe Gonzales indicated that the Spanish peseta and the Portuguese escudo were set to join the EMS, albeit with wider trading bands. Genscher and Kohl were ready to push for the acceptance of the plan because it encapsulated most, if not all, of the Germans' concerns.[33] Despite British objections, the heads of state agreed to the outline of the Delors Plan, including implementing Stage 1 on July 1, 1990, and to the institution of an intergovernmental conference to work on the details of the revisions to the Treaty of Rome required to implement the other aspects of Stages 2 and 3. As one senior European Commission official stated, "Madrid got us off the drawing board and on to the building site."[34] The German government had agreed upon the first significant step in the transfer of German monetary autonomy. More important, perhaps, the Madrid summit provided a stable foundation for the EC, as the tremors that would develop with the collapse of the Berlin Wall and the reunification of Germany would make further movement on EMU difficult.

Preserving the G7 International Monetary Regime

The primary goal of the G7 following the October 1987 crash and the conclusion of the December 1987 Telephone accord was clearly "regime preserving."[35] The strengthening of the dollar through the first six months of 1988 eased some of the earlier pressures that had built up within the international monetary system and, with an election year in the United States under way, the G7 members shifted their attention further inward and on resurgent inflationary pressures. The renewed strength of the dollar brought on by economic growth in the United States, a tightening U.S. monetary policy, and a moderate shrinking of the U.S. trade deficit for the first quarter of 1988 were met with support in German and U.S. monetary circles. Throughout the early months of 1988, Treasury Secretary Baker declared the United States' satisfaction with German fiscal and monetary policy, despite the lack of demand stimulus in Bonn. At the February G7 ministerial meeting, Baker and Stoltenberg indicated in a joint statement their satisfaction with the current value of the dollar. As an indication of the shared perceptions of the United States and Germany at the annual OECD meeting in May in Paris, the Germans rejected and the United States viewed skeptically a French idea of a modified plan of returning to an international monetary system of fixed rules.[36] The close consensus on currency values or on maintaining current policy objectives between the

United States and Germany indicated the extent to which the United States was willing to ease pressure on the Germans following the turmoil of the fall of 1987. Indeed, regime preservation was the dominant mode of U.S.-German macroeconomic interaction through the first six months of 1988.

At the G7 Toronto summit in June, the debate among heads of state and ministers further revealed a general consensus among G7 members as each reflected on the final presidential participation of Ronald Reagan and the sustained world economic growth over the prior five years. On Canada's behalf, the summit focused on longer-term "structural" issues such as education, bureaucratic overregulation, and agriculture. The section of the final nonbinding communiqué on monetary issues and exchange rates was a verbatim reissue of an earlier April G7 IMF statement on exchange rate stability. Economics Minister Martin Bangemann (FDP) had already declared before the summit that he did not expect much pressure on the Germans on the fiscal and monetary front. In fact, Bangemann declared the "locomotive theory" dead, although this was not entirely the perspective from U.S. officials.[37] One analyst described the mood leading up to the summit as such: "On the surface, the G7 seemed to maintain their appearances by reaffirming their commitment to international economic policy coordination," but if push came to shove, each nation would proceed down their own path.[38] To highlight this point and the bank's independence, the Bundesbank raised the rate on repurchase agreements from 3.25 percent to 3.5 percent on June 21, just before the seven nations issued their joint declaration. Consensus among the G7 remained only skin deep.

The strength of the dollar through the election year of 1988 led some analysts to conclude that an international financial conspiracy was under way to support the Bush campaign.[39] While German, Japanese, and U.S. officials all denied any "orchestration" of a strong dollar, the G3 members all had an incentive to see the dollar stabilized, indeed moderately strengthened. For the United States, the strengthening of the dollar, although somewhat damaging to trade balances, provided an element of stability following the October 1987 crash. For Baker and Bush, a strong dollar reassured stocks and bond markets in an election year.[40] A strengthening dollar would also not be seen as counterproductive (in the sense of the sharp rise in the dollar before Plaza) but reflected an informal agreement on a softer range of G3 currencies, where the value of the dollar and DM could fluctuate more broadly. The Germans were also content to see the DM weaken. In addition to the German interest in stabilizing the global monetary system, the weaker DM enhanced the competitiveness of German industry and, with oil prices relatively low, imported inflation remained of little concern for the Bundesbank. Through the summer of 1988, the dollar continued to gain strength following a Federal Reserve raise in the discount rate to 6.5 percent; the dollar stood at DM 1.92. Despite the relative stability of the DM-dollar relationship (which, as we have seen, eased tensions within EMS, allowing for progress on EMU), with the election of George Bush to the presidency in November 1988, many analysts pointed to the possibility of a renewed bout of global monetary instability. With Bush suggesting no new taxes to deal with the budget deficit and the U.S. trade deficits remaining steady, it would be only a matter of time before the deviating interests of the G7 members resurfaced.

During 1989, divergent opinions among the G7 members, particularly among the G3 leading nations, slowly began to escalate. A more comprehensive form of policy coordination appeared doomed because of inherent discrepancies between international and domestic policy goals.[41] Short-term interest rates in both Germany and the United States had risen almost a full percentage point since the fall of 1988. Germany and the United States were both simultaneously trying to fight inflation by raising interest rates. With the Federal Reserve tightening its own grip on the money supply, driving up the value of the dollar and further weakening the DM, the Bundesbank raised its discount rate a half point to 4 percent on January 19 in order to head off higher import prices. The Bundesbank pointed to a 2.5 percent (annual rate) rise in consumer prices in January to justify its move and retorted that a weakening mark did not favor the adjustment process in terms of bringing down the trade deficit in the United States.[42] Despite a U.S.-inspired policy proposed at recent G7 ministerial meetings of tracking G7 economic developments by using mutually acceptable economic indicators provided by the IMF, the idea could not move beyond peer pressure into a formal agreement on institutionalizing a rule-regulated monetary system.

Following Bush's inauguration, there was further disagreement over whether finance ministers and central bankers should even meet to discuss the value of the dollar, the U.S. budget situation, and the further course of G7 cooperation. At the first G7 ministerial meeting of 1989 in February, it was clear that domestic priorities of fighting inflation would still take precedence in all countries, as the ministers could only pledge separately their commitment to policy coordination. For the G7 members, such an approach to international cooperation was fine as long as there existed a convergence of domestic policy objectives and exchange rate management (eased at the time with a strong dollar). Moreover, the focus shifted upon the United States for leadership and upon George Bush to come up with a "total concept" (*Gesamptkonzept*) for dealing with the U.S. deficit in public and private savings.[43] As if to test G7 resolve, the foreign exchange markets launched new speculative pressures on all G7 currencies. As one analyst suggested, "the politics and the economics are not just in conflict . . . they are in increasing conflict."[44] As long as there existed no agreed-upon plan for addressing the U.S. budget, one could not expect any bold measures to eliminate threats to exchange rate stability.

By the April IMF/World Bank G7 meeting, the negotiating situation among the G7 had again sharpened after a surprise (at least from the U.S. perspective) Bundesbank interest rate rise of the discount rate by a full percentage point from 3.5 percent to 4.5 percent and the Lombard rate from 5.5 percent to 6.5 percent. Not surprisingly, no agreement was reached at the meeting in terms of Germany joining Japan and the United States in a joint coordinated adjustment of interest rates to help stem a rising dollar, although the Bundesbank rate hike helped briefly stem the dollar's rise. In fact, the ministers agreed that no major coordinated economic changes were needed to cope with resurgent global inflation. The Bundesbank and the Federal Reserve could more easily pursue their goal of price stability unilaterally. Finance Minister Gerhard Stoltenberg did suggest that he hoped interest rates would fall, although such a move was doubtful given a rising M3 indicator in Germany and Bundesbank concern with wage and price increases in the early months of 1989.[45] The G7 communiqué noted that inflationary pressures had recently appeared in a number of countries, and that sustained noninflationary growth was essential in dealing with global economic problems. The G7 also pointed to the rise in the dollar that undermined "adjustment efforts," yet no specific course of action was suggested for easing these efforts. The situation was summed up cogently by the *New York Times,* which commented that "there appears to be a breakdown in collaboration on interest rates."[46] Moreover, as one private commentator stated, "They have a common preoccupation with inflation, and they can dress that up as a common international concern and say they're fighting inflation together. But they're not. They're fighting it separately."[47]

Despite emerging differences between the Germans and the United States on the overall process of policy coordination, exchange rate instability had remained mild through the first half of 1989 due to the moderate strength of the dollar. The period of mild exchange rate instability would not last long, however. The strength of the dollar confounded market analysts and the markets themselves, although some analysts pointed to the political weakness of the German chancellor and poor economic indicators in Germany in explaining the weak DM. The dollar-DM relationship, which in May now stood at DM 2 to the dollar, soon posed problems for the United States' trade position. By mid-May, concern over the value of the dollar prompted intervention by the Federal Reserve. The Bundesbank remained conspicuously absent from concerted intervention operations.[48] Pöhl stated publicly that the weak DM posed no difficulties for the German economy as a whole. In fact, the weak DM was adding to the strength of German exporters—overwhelming other currencies within the EMS and feeding a growing German surplus against its trading partners.[49] Despite Pöhl's confident proclamations, the international monetary system was again coming under strain due to the dollar's appreciation, although moderate, and diverging conceptions among the G7 as to what they could do, if anything.

At the Paris G7 summit in July, an attempt was made to restore some credibility to the coordination process as ministers pointed optimistically at their efforts "under the Plaza and Louvre agreements" aimed "at fostering stability of exchange rates consistent with . . . economic fundamentals."[50] Supported by the recently published reports of the Delors Committee, Mitterand was interested in pursuing an explicit international monetary agreement based on "clear principles and procedures," and the French finance minister, Pierre Bérégovoy, indicated that these principles should be similar to the EMS.[51] The French proposal was quickly rebuffed by both the United States and Germany as too all-encompassing and ambitious. In addition to French attempts to bind German monetary policy at the international level, the United States was expecting Germany to stimulate demand through monetary policy so that G7 growth rates would remain steady.

Despite such pressure, central bankers, including Pöhl, were not interested in emphasizing a coordinated approach to exchange rates, a process that had increasingly lost credibility on the international front.[52] The Bundesbank had just raised the discount rate on June 29, thereby eliminating any possibility that the bank would respond with a rate cut just three weeks later. The lack of coordination to stem the rising dollar indicated a weakening of the minimal efforts of Plaza and Louvre to maintain exchange rate levels and the exchange rate regime itself. Returning to a familiar German concern on managing exchange rates or currency levels, Pöhl stated emphatically before the G7 summit: "We can't intervene at all costs."[53] The Bundesbank, supported by the federal government, was intent on setting strict limitations toward G7 policy coordination, whether on the exchange rate front or on Germany playing the role of locomotive.

The dollar's unchecked rise through the summer of 1989 appeared to re-create some of the trade and monetary strains of the mid-1980s. With improvement in the U.S. trade deficit slowing and no movement on the U.S. budget deficit, the likelihood that a concerted G7 effort to reduce global trade or financial imbalances would be forthcoming still remained minimal. Many analysts began to question the ability of the G7 or G3 to coordinate and manage a stable international monetary system. Diverging national interests indicated the weakness of the leading G7 members to achieve consensus or pursue accommodating policies. Other analysts pointed to the continued weakening of U.S. power and influence.[54] Only with the imposition of a new international institution with formal rules and obligations or with the willingness and interest of a dominant power to guarantee the underlying stability and strength of the system could full policy coordination re-emerge. The lack of a dominant economic power that could enforce the rules of the monetary regime that had increasingly become trilateral in nature—the United States, Japan, and the EC, built on the foundation of the DM—demonstrated that each G3 member could influence the other to a significant degree. In pursuit of domestic macroeconomic objectives, each G3 member remained to a certain degree dependent upon the actions of the others, yet the lack of formal institutions or hegemony prevented any overarching form of policy coordination. In contrast to Germany actively pursuing efforts to more formally institutionalize and advance the functioning of the EMS, the significant lack of international monetary coordination pursued through 1988 and into 1989 reflected an ad hoc, nonsystematic approach to coordination and policy accommodation.[55] The lack of global monetary leadership from the G3 or any one member and the lack of any agreed-upon formal, regular system of management foreshadowed more difficulties to come. Regime preserving came to mean autonomy preserving for Germany and the United States.

Part 2: The Impact of German Reunification

The Road Through Dublin

After the Madrid summit, the debate centered on which, if any, specific course of action would be taken to implement the Delors Committee's recommendations. In effect, the Madrid communiqué represented only one way toward the goal of EMU. The British had their own view and countered the Delors Plan with their publication of *An Evolutionary Approach to Economic and Monetary Union,* which envisioned "competition" between Community currencies.[56] This approach, and its entrance (to the Bundesbank's irritation) into the negotiations over the details of a new treaty on EMU, centered on the "hard ECU," or parallel currency, and a reliance on market forces to bring about economic and monetary convergence.[57] The removal of restrictions on the use of currencies of other member states would enable individuals and firms to choose which currency to use both for transactions and for savings. This, it was claimed, would lead to low-inflation currencies displacing high-inflation ones, with the consequent incentives for all national authorities to pursue anti-inflationary policies. In essence, monetary union and the relinquishing of domestic monetary autonomy were not necessary, as national currencies could be adjusted through continued revaluation and devaluation of currencies around the hard ECU. The hard ECU approach was also politically appealing for some EC countries because it implied the possible removal of the DM as the leading anchor currency of the EMS.

The Bundesbank saw some benefits to this approach, for example, the fact that other competing currencies might ease some of the burden on the DM as a reserve currency, but the bank rejected the British approach. In particular, Pöhl argued that there were no significant advantages in having, in addition to the twelve national currencies, a thirteenth EC currency that had no quality standard of its own.[58] On the contrary, the road to completely fixed exchange rates, namely, to EMU, was likely to be somewhat longer and more difficult if a parallel currency was introduced. It would not lead to the desired objective: an internationally recognized hard currency zone. The necessary uniform replacement of all EC currencies, including the DM, by the parallel currency could only come about if the currency had the same standing internally as each national EC currency and could compete even with the strongest EC currency as an investment currency, after taking due account of interest and exchange rate risks. Finally the currency had to be associated with the lowest possible costs as a transaction currency, which, in effect, would only be the case if it was safeguarded by sufficiently fixed exchange rates vis-à-vis the national currencies. Because such conditions were unlikely, the Bundesbank saw little value in a hard ECU.

Academic opinion in Germany was less favorable toward the hard ECU or even the need for EMU. The Council of Academic Advisors (Sachverständigenrat) as well as the Board of Academic Advisors, a group of thirty academics that advises the economics ministry, both sounded numerous objections to the EMU process. Although the council, in its annual report released in November 1989, stated that the Delors Plan provided a good basis for further examination and debate, it argued that there were some serious problems with the plan. The council's concerns echoed the Bundesbank's apprehension over convergence criteria and the transitional phase. The German Board of Academic Advisors was more sharply critical of EMU. It rejected the coronation theory as unworkable, for there existed the danger that the transitional arrangements would become permanent without the proper establishment of a fully independent central bank. Moreover, the economic and financial affairs council, envisioned by the Delors Committee to be responsible for coordinating the transitional phase, would acquire a political weight incompatible with the autonomy of national central banks. The board also doubted the assumption within the Delors Plan about the ability for formal coordination among member states and the binding rules for fiscal policy. Finally, while some points did make economic sense, they were politically unfeasible.

Chancellor Kohl was caught between the skeptical and cautious approach of the Bundesbank and academia and the more pressing attitude of Genscher and his French colleagues. Genscher continued to push for a rapid process of Western European integration as a means of furthering his own overall vision of bringing together Eastern and Western Europe.[59] While sharing the generalities of the Genscherite vision of Europe as well as the real concerns of the Bundesbank, Kohl saw the creation of a European central bank as partly a means of completing Franco-German rapprochement, which Kohl saw as postwar Europe's main success story. With the French pressing for an early convening of the intergovernmental conference to discuss Stages 2 and 3 of EMU, the Kohl government saw little likelihood of a conference occurring before the end of 1990 at the earliest, and more probably occurring after the 1990 federal elections. With the German public not overly anxious to see the DM replaced by any artificial currency unit and both the business and labor association urging caution as well,[60] Kohl found the more cautious approach of the Bundesbank, at least for the next year or two, to be initially the favorable course of action leading up to the Strasbourg summit in December. At that point, Kohl would be more ready to discuss the full implications and details of EMU.

The Bundesbank's full percentage-point increase in both the Lombard (7–8 percent) and discount rates (5–6 percent) on October 6, largely as a result of Bundesbank concern with domestic inflation and the rising dollar, did much to change a few minds in Europe on the need for EMU.[61] Many EMS partners felt trapped into supporting what seemed a fruitless DM-dollar policy. The usually restrained Danes reacted to the Bundesbank move, done without any consultation of EMS partners, by issuing statements in support of limiting Bundesbank dominance over the EMS and speeding up EMU. In the Netherlands, with inflation running at around 1 percent, the rate hike by the Bundesbank was also met with regret. Even in Britain, pro-EMS Tories found more support in their calls for EMS membership to counteract German dominance. To strengthen the falling pound, the British had to follow the move like everyone else by bringing up UK interest rates to 15 percent. Britain, it appeared, had all of the constraints associated with EMS membership but none of the advantages. The only way to counterbalance Germany's growing power, both political and financial, would be, as Mitterand argued, to "build Europe."

Kohl's more cautious approach and the Bundesbank's freedom, albeit limited, would soon be overtaken by the historic and monumental transformations occurring in the east. The first impact of the collapse of the Berlin Wall on November 9, 1989, on the Germans' position toward EMU came as Kohl and Mitterand agreed to an outline of a plan that would have fixed a final date for the EC to move to full monetary union, including a supranational central banking system, to June 1994.[62] The proposal also included ideas on strengthening the hand of the European Parliament, which was a key condition of the Kohl government. Despite the agreement on a tentative date (a timetable that the Bundesbank rejected outright) for EMU, Kohl did not accede to Mitterand's request to decide at the December

1989 Strasbourg summit on a date when EC governments would begin negotiating the new treaty for monetary union—in other words, turning Stages 2 and 3 of the Delors Plan into a formalized EC treaty.

Nonetheless, at Strasbourg, it was decided that the European Commission would prepare a document for the Dublin conference in June of 1990, highlighting how exactly the second and third stages of EMU could be implemented. No decision was made on exact timetables for an intergovernmental conference, although the ministers did agree, against British objections, to discuss possible treaty revisions required for EMU at the Rome summit in December 1990. What were initially scheduled to be low-key EC summits in Dublin and Rome for 1990 suddenly took on historic importance and significance both for Germany and the EC. Ministers would not only have to address EMU but also the transformations in the east and how they affected the plans for European integration.

The impact of the collapse of the wall (and the potential for German reunification) weighed heaviest on the Franco-German partnership. It was evident from the French perspective that reunification would create a more inward-looking Germany, more preoccupied with the economic and social problems of its new eastern *Land* than with the political future of the EC. As a result, the Franco-German alliance took on a renewed importance for the success of EMU. Kohl's 10-Point Plan of November 28 outlining West German efforts at increasing the ties between East and West Germany had been greeted initially with caution and some mistrust in many European capitals, including Paris. The Strasbourg EC summit in early December became the first test of Kohl's Europeanist credentials and indicated a renewed willingness of the Kohl government to offer significant concessions (outlining the future of a European central bank by 1994) to their European partners in return for support of Kohl and his initial tentative steps toward German reunification. The support by Kohl for some of the French requests reflected German efforts to reassure French sensitivities over the rapidly transforming German question. The DM would, as it turned out, become the victim of European, in particular, French, support for German reunification.

The Bundesbank's own policies were not easing relations among the EMS members. By the beginning of 1990, the Bundesbank was calling for a realignment of the EMS. With the DM beginning to strengthen again after a period of weakness (vis-à-vis the dollar) through 1989, with the uncertainty developing over the situation in the east, and with the implementation of the full liberalization of capital markets in July of 1990 (Germany, France, the Netherlands, and Belgium already had fully liberalized their markets, and other EMS nations were on the way), the only avenue to ease the pressure building up over the prior three years would be through a realignment.[63] Since November 10, one day after the wall fell in Berlin, the surge of the DM of around 10.7 percent against the dollar and 7.4 percent against the sterling placed renewed strains on the EMS just as the members were intensifying their negotiations on EMU.[64] The move by the Italian Central Bank in January to devalue the lira by 3.7 percent as a prelude to a jump into the more narrow band of the ERM, at roughly 2.25 percent, helped ease some of the immediate pressure but foreshadowed future difficulties for the EMS. The complications associated with the unholy trinity were becoming more pronounced to many central bankers but remained almost invisible to the politicians responsible for realignments.

The surge in the value of the DM would continue, brought on by expectations that the German economy would obtain a supply-side boost from the recent inflow of Eastern European immigrants, profits from the opening and liberalization of East Germany and Eastern Europe, and the fact that the Bundesbank would be expected to keep any potential inflationary pressures under control. This prospect raised considerable concerns within the European Community and especially among Germany's EMS partners.[65] In the Netherlands, concern was raised about the prospect of sacrificing the traditional German standard of price stability and the value of the DM to German reunification and how that might destabilize the EMS. The Italians, who were about to take over the presidency of the EC leading up to the Rome summit in December, favored speeding up European integration as a way of restoring some measure of "European" control over the EMS. With the potential that German power and influence would increase following reunification, the Italians were intent on ensuring an Italian-influenced road to EMU. Reflecting these and other European cross-national concerns, the multinational Giscard-Schmidt committee for the monetary union of Europe issued their final report stating the importance of speeding up the process of EMU and that German reunification should proceed parallel to European unification.[66]

Pöhl, caught off guard by Kohl's February 6 announcement on currency negotiations with East Germany and sensing the impact that such a move might have on the EMU negotiations, sought to formulate both debates in a Bundesbank-friendly direction (see Table 4.1 for a chronology of GEMU).[67] Intent on preventing the political surprises from occurring in the European arena that were occurring at home, the Bundesbank president articulated his vision of EMU more forcefully. Pöhl envisioned EMU taking place many years in the future after a prolonged period of experience with an era of complete market liberalization and the internal market of 1992. This period of time would allow participating members of the EMS to coordinate policies more closely together, build on the institutional foundations of the EMS already in place, and allow nonparticipating members to join the EMS. Convergence continued to be the Bundesbank's EMU leitmotif. The Bundesbank position was largely supported by Kohl,

Table 4.1 Chronology of German Economic and Monetary Union (GEMU), November 1989–July 1990

November 9, 1989	Borders with the FRG open for all German Democratic Republic (GDR) citizens.
November 28, 1989	Chancellor Helmut Kohl proposes 10-Point Plan on enhancing ties between the FRG and GDR.
December 8–9, 1989	European Council meeting in Strasbourg indicates European support for German unification within the context of European integration.
February 2, 1990	Kohl's cabinet begins first serious discussions on monetary union. Two models are envisioned. One model sees a quick transition to unification. A second model views unification as a gradual process.
February 6, 1990	Kohl offers negotiations on currency union. Bundesbank president Karl Otto Pöhl, who is in Berlin for discussions with his GDR counterpart, is surprised by the offer.
February 7, 1990	Pöhl attends cabinet meeting where discussions on monetary union are first seriously reviewed.
February 12, 1990	Mikhail Gorbachev signals support for German unification within framework of two-plus-four talks.
March 14, 1990	Cabinet endorses Kohl's plan to convert *Kleinsparer* at 1:1 exchange rate—ostmarks for DMs.
March 18, 1990	CDU–allied Conservative Alliance wins first democratic East German election.
April 2, 1990	Bundesbank publishes its proposal on GEMU that largely argues for a 2:1 exchange rate—ostmarks for DMs.
April 23, 1990	Kohl publishes his own formal proposal on GEMU that differs noticeably from the Bundesbank proposal. Most conversions of ostmarks to DMs would be exchanged at 1:1.
May 2, 1990	Kohl government and GDR government agree on larger outlines of GEMU.
May 18, 1990	Finance ministers of GDR and FRG sign the State Treaty on Unification. GEMU largely conforms to Kohl's plan.
June 22, 1990	State Treaty ratified by both parliaments.
July 1, 1990	GEMU takes effect.

who would not agree on any intergovernmental conference until after national elections in the late fall of 1990, but which could be postponed even further due to the complications brought on by the negotiations surrounding GEMU.

More important, perhaps, extra time would allow the Bundesbank to shape the embryonic European central bank to its liking.[68] Recognizing that the institutional make-up of the future ECB would be of critical importance, the Bundesbank began to formulate more concretely its proposals for the ECB. Specifically, national governments would appoint members to long terms (eight years) to the bank's council (in charge of broad policymaking), and the EC Council of Finance Ministers would choose the board responsible for day-to-day operations. The president of the European Commission and the chairman of ECOFIN could attend the bank's council meetings, but without voting privileges. Most important, the bank would be politically independent of the guidelines of the European Commission or member governments. Finally, the bank would be legally committed to the sole goal of ensuring price stability. Although the remaining negotiations over the ECB would at times examine the Dutch model,[69] and other EMS members (the Italians and the French) would suggest alternative models, including voting rights based on the IMF model—the Bundesbank's position became a minimum acceptable condition for the government in the EMU negotiations. In fact, as the debate moved forward, Delors and the EC Commission's position on the future ECB came to parallel and encompass most of the Bundesbank's views on the ECB.

By the April meeting of European finance ministers in Ashford Castle near Galway, Ireland, Germany's position on the nature of the European central bank and over what form of budgetary discipline should accompany EMU indicated that a lot of work would still need to be done before an intergovernmental conference could hammer out treaty details.[70] The finance ministers had reached some consensus on the stricter version of a European central bank as the process leading toward EMU became more focused. The French supported the Bundesbank's tough line on the ECB and indicated their willingness to examine closely the importance of securing the political independence of the Bank of France.[71] In anticipation of the implementation of Stage 1 of EMU on July 1, 1990, Italy agreed to eliminate all capital controls. At the international level, EMU received a boost when the G7 ministers' meeting for their April conference signaled its formal support for European monetary union. As a result, a good measure of optimism prevailed in many European capitals heading into Dublin. At Dublin, the summit participants agreed on pursuing the treaty revisions necessary for economic and political union through a series of intergovernmental conferences aimed for December 1990.

The idea of a political union resurfaced in response to concerns expressed by various EC members, including the Germans, over the need for European-level forums of political and economic accountability. Both Kohl and the Bundesbank attached great weight to political union. For Kohl, the reasoning was clear. Political union was part and parcel of a larger federal Europe.[72] For Kohl (and the French), a federal Europe was an acceptable framework for German power. Germany could continue to find its own national identity—now under further strain due to reunification—through the successful experience of European integration. For the Bundesbank, their support for a political union was somewhat less clear. The primary reason behind the bank's push for political union was based on the bank's fundamental belief that only an accountable, fully empowered European Parliament could responsibly pursue a centralized European-wide budgetary policy to deal with tax issues and intergovernmental transfers.[73] Perhaps the Bundesbank felt that negotiations on political union would slow down the entire negotiating process, including EMU. Whatever the reasons, the negotiations on political union clogged the European agenda by linking political and monetary union. The remaining timetable for completing EMU negotiations would almost prove impossible to preserve.

Losing Credibility: The G7 and Reactive Macroeconomic Coordination

Following the Paris G7 summit in July 1989, the dollar had been largely untamable, roaming outside its informal Louvre ceilings and undermining the credibility of the G7's policy of stabilizing the dollar and the effectiveness of economic policy coordination. That the dollar's fluctuations, albeit not large, undermined efforts at policy coordination should not have been a surprise to analysts. Not only had the Paris communiqué failed to mention the value of the dollar or any efforts to correct the instability, but G7 members were openly declaring their intent on pursuing their own domestic macroeconomic objectives. At the September G7 ministers' meeting of the IMF/World Bank summit, the Federal Reserve was primarily worried about inflation and fears of an unexpected, stronger showing in U.S. economic growth. The Bundesbank, however, was straddling the fence between not wanting to dampen economic growth and keeping a lid on rising inflationary pressures in the German economy. The Kohl government was not so concerned with the high value of the dollar either, as low oil import prices and competitive German exports kept domestic concerns satisfied. Despite the diverging nature of domestic concerns and priorities, the ministers did manage to agree that the dollar was slightly too high, which endangered efforts to adjust trade imbalances.[74] A coordinated effort at market intervention (with the Germans again noticeably absent) proved ineffective. With no movement on any significant level of G7 interest rate coordination or significant exchange rate intervention, one noted analyst of international economic affairs labeled the G7 coordination process in "shambles."[75]

At the beginning of January 1990, *The Economist* called for a renewed effort to develop a global monetary regime.[76] The time to tether currencies together was now proclaimed by the magazine. *The Economist* argued that the 1980s era of floating had actually increased economic volatility. Floating exchange rates, it was earlier believed, would offset international differences in inflation rates. High-inflation countries would see their currencies depreciate; their firms would thereby stay competitive in international markets without the awkwardness of having to lower wages. In addition, floating would be the most appropriate mechanism of dealing with the U.S. trade imbalance (all trade imbalances, in general). But the dollar's extraordinary rise and fall in the mid-1980s had little to do with inflation and had everything to do with short-term interest rates and financial market speculation about government policy. As a result, far from narrowing the gaps between international costs, the dollar's fluctuations widened them. The dollar's 40 percent drop between 1985 and 1988 did little to reduce the United States' trade imbalance. In sum, and even with the Plaza and Louvre accords to look back on, the 1980s provided little if any redeeming and permanent elements of a model of international monetary policy cooperation or governance structure.

But would a more fixed international monetary system, in fact, be feasible? A system of pegged currencies must entail two bottom-line requirements if it is to function properly. First, to succeed, a system of fixed exchange rates must be credible. If financial markets expect an exchange rate to be changed, the attempt to keep the system fixed is almost already lost. Second, the system should have price stability built securely into it. Under a fixed exchange rate system, every country must accept the group's joint inflation rate if the system is to develop any amount of credibility. At the European level through the adjustable but increasingly fixed ERM, the DM anchored the EMS. Germany had been increasingly willing to sacrifice some measure of monetary autonomy for exchange rate stability. As a result, a generally credible system of exchange rate relationships had developed. As the earlier examination in this chapter on G7 policy coordination demonstrated, the problem at the international G7 monetary arena was that neither Germany nor any other G7 member was willing to provide monetary or political leadership necessary to develop a more stable system of exchange rate relationships. In fact, Germany appeared firm in its belief that by enhancing the institutional foundations of the EMS and possibly permanently tethering EMS currencies together, Europe could strengthen its zone of monetary stability vis-à-vis the international monetary arena. EMU would have to come first—along with a successful completion of the process of GEMU, which had preoccupied German monetary officials through most of the early months of 1990—before movement could take place on the G7 front.[77]

Following the statement of the G7 ministers in Washington in February, which again rhetorically reaffirmed their commitment to coordinate economic policy and stabilize exchange rates, other analysts questioned the whole process of policy coordination.[78] Many questioned whether coordination could be sustained over time and that half-hearted efforts at stabilizing exchange rates actually did more damage than good, a point that the Bundesbank strongly supported. The U.S. Treasury could not make any credible commitments to G7 coordination, and the likelihood of sovereign democratic governments subordinating some national economic concern to improve the economic welfare of the group remained small, if not improbable. Policy coordination would not lead to expected outcomes or achieve most policy goals. Instead, each government would put its own domestic house in order first, the German monetary norm. If the G7 governments wanted to reduce the U.S. current account deficit without a decline in the dollar exchange rate, the United States would have to reduce the growth of domestic demand (at a risk of recession) and other governments would have to increase their domestic demand at a substantially higher rate of risk of inflation. Given the contention between these competing objectives and the lack of formal institutional constraints at the G7 level, it could not be expected that any G7 member would accommodate its policy for the others. The recent record of G7 coordination supported this view.

At the April 1990 G7 meeting in Paris, the United States and Germany lined up together in their refusal of a Japanese proposal for a concerted rate cut to help alleviate speculative pressure of the yen. From the German perspective, the preoccupation with fighting inflation overrode any considerations for a G3 attempt to ease pressure on the yen. Specifically, the Germans took the view that Japan was largely the author of its own misfortunes. The Japanese would have to resolve for themselves the differences between the Bank of Japan and the government and raise interest rates to curb inflationary pressures and possibly strengthen the yen.[79] The unstirring communiqué released at the end of the meeting stated the G7 commitment to keep the yen "under review." The Japanese responded by keeping their monetary representatives away from the next ministerial meeting in May. As before, many analysts and policymakers were questioning the whole concept of a collective commitment to multilateral surveillance. Whatever form of G7 coordination that existed tended to be quite reactive rather than proactive. One analyst described active macroeconomic policy coordination to be "in abeyance."[80] On a positive note, the G7 did state that German unification could lead to a betterment of world economic growth and the reduction in imbalances in Europe. If the United States could not pressure the Germans to take on the global locomotive role, then the collapse of the Berlin Wall might provide the impetus.

Whereas the G7 initially greeted GEMU, the focus of currency and monetary coordination among the G7 countries through the summer months of 1990 shifted from the adjustment of the dollar/yen value to the impact of German currency union on the world's financial markets. Despite the assurance of Kohl and Theo Waigel (the Bundesbank did not offer similar statements) at the April G7 summit meeting that they would be able to contain any inflation that might result from GEMU, other G7 countries remained concerned.[81] Although not taking a specific position on the controversial GEMU exchange rate issue or trying to influence the domestic debate,[82] the G7 feared inflation might result from the plan and the increased spending of the German government, which could possibly lead to higher interest rates. These higher interest rates might also result in a shortage of savings due to the investment demand in a unified Germany and Eastern Europe. Such a shortage could also lead to higher worldwide interest rates at a time when the United States appeared to be heading into an economic slowdown. A global "crowding out" might result from GEMU as well as a G7 battle in the capital markets.[83] Ironically, it might be the Germans who would now have to finance their domestic agenda through high interest rates.

Despite such concerns, the annual G7 Houston summit of July 1990 demonstrated to the global community the political support of the G7 for German reunification. What is more, Houston marked the renewed determination and emergence of the leadership of Chancellor Kohl in G7 negotiations.[84] On almost every issue discussed at the summit—from European farm subsidies to environmental issues to aid to the Soviet Union—the German chancellor emerged as a new leader in identifying German and European interests that would take, in some instances, precedence over U.S. concerns. For example, on aid to the Soviet Union, the Germans wanted to secure more direct aid to the Soviets to ease Soviet qualms about GEMU. The United States was opposed to this idea until genuinely irreversible political and economic changes had occurred in the Soviet Union. In the end, the final communiqué reflected the German position on support of Soviet aid. Currency questions were not even seriously addressed. Concerned with the possible inflationary impacts of the recent GEMU process, avoiding monetary issues suited the Germans just fine. What emerged was a new leader, albeit tentatively, in global economic and political affairs. British prime minister Margaret Thatcher acknowledged that "there are three regional groups at the summit, one based on the dollar, one based on the yen, and one based on the deutsche mark."[85] Houston signaled to many participants in the G7 arena that a shift in the global geopolitical and geoeconomic distribution of power and an emergence of zones of interest had taken place. The Germans' G7 bargaining position had toughened.

* * *

The period from August 1989 to July 1990 should be noted not for the monumental steps forward on EMU (although there was some progress on the issue of the independence of the future European central bank) or G7 policy coordination but rather for the changing shape of the negotiating arena. In August 1989, the Berlin Wall stood strong and the likelihood of reunification remained as distant as it had during the height of the Cold

War. By July 1, 1990, East Germans were swapping their worthless "alumichips" for hard DMs and experiencing their first trips to supermarkets and department stores to buy goods previously unseen to most East German citizens. The full merging of the two states stood only months away. The reunification of Germany had radically transformed the inner-German political economy, the European political landscape, and global power relations. The Bundesbank and government would both be tested in their ability to respond institutionally to unification and the pressures from European and global partners. Despite the bank's and government's Europeanist and G7 commitments, their attention would inevitably shift inward. More important, following the conflict between the Bundesbank and government over GEMU, the internal struggle for power and balance between the two institutions had shifted, albeit narrowly, in favor of the government.[86]

Part 3: Maastricht

The European Arena: Through Rome and On to Maastricht

In the annals of German monetary policy, July 1, 1990, marked a historic political, economic, and psychological point of transition. With GEMU occurring simultaneously to the implementation of Stage 1 of EMU, the implications of both actions on the role and value of the DM should not have been lost on any German citizen, let alone the Bundesbank.[87] Given the inevitable complications to German monetary policy brought on by GEMU and EMU, Pöhl, along with the Bundesbank vice president, Helmut Schlesinger, increasingly raised louder doubts about rushing headlong toward a single currency.[88] The Bundesbank would resist any pressure for a quickened pace of monetary integration until convergence had, in fact, been met. For many analysts, the Bundesbank's concerns were well founded. The credibility that the Bundesbank had built up over forty years contributed significantly to EMS credibility.[89] The EMS acted as a political and economic discipline. When a currency of a small and relatively poor country such as Ireland, Spain, or Portugal is in the EMS, its internal economic policies inevitably were influenced by German policies. Thus, EMS members generally secured lower inflation rates during the 1980s that encouraged business investment attractive in today's global markets. According to F. Giavazzi and A. Pagano, the German anti-inflationary attitude lent credibility to the anti-inflationary policies of other countries in the EMS that had experienced higher inflation in the past.[90] In sum, being in the EMS gave governments credibility they might not have had otherwise.

Following the Dublin summit, the debate over a two-speed Europe resurfaced. Although Delors rejected the idea as politically unacceptable to the southern tier of EC states, the concept of a hard core of EC members pushing ahead with EMU had a lot of supporters. According to the French and Germans, both of whom had been suggesting such an approach through the summer of 1990, not all the EC countries would be ready to assume the full discipline of economic and monetary union or relinquish the requisite monetary sovereignty at the same time.[91] Even with a report of ECOFIN issued in July 1990 supporting the idea of a longer period of convergence in Stage 2 of EMU, it had become apparent to the central bank and finance ministers that only a few countries would ultimately, if ever, attain the convergence criteria. The core group of "ripe" currencies would provide a point of focus for the remaining EC members seeking to join the initial group of EMU members. In fact, Pöhl suggested that most European governments, not just the British government, were not really prepared to accept the consequences of a transfer of far-reaching powers over monetary policy to a supranational institution.[92] But if the politicians were ready for such a decision, then a two-speed model would prove a useful mechanism for regulating entry into EMU.

The likelihood that the Rome summit would conclusively resolve all the treaty details declined in September, as a meeting of ECOFIN broke down into various competing groups.[93] The French, Italians, Belgians, and Danes—supported by Delors—sought to ensure a January 1, 1993, move to EMU; the Germans and the British sought to slow down the process either through a long period of convergence for both or a resurrected hard ECU that Britain advocated. The EC members also were split along the two-speed approach supported by the French and Germans and the "institutionalist" approach of Spain and Italy that envisioned the setting of monetary goals, dates, and institutional constraints that would force all EMS members to converge together. With the prospect of higher inflation brought on by the Gulf crisis, the distraction to Germany of putting its newly unified house in order, and with the all-German elections set for early December (Kohl was not intent on bringing up the idea of losing the DM to the ECU so shortly after GEMU), it appeared unrealistic to believe that the Rome summit could resolve such pressures and the persistent divisions among the EC states.

Many contend that German reunification sped up the process of European integration and EMU, yet reunification appeared to in fact slow down the entire negotiating process and provide the Germans (as well as the British who had recently joined the EMS in October) the time to analyze the implications of convergence and the potential loss of monetary autonomy. According to the Bundesbank, the impact of GEMU, namely, the high unemployment in the east and the lack of industrial competitiveness among most east German firms, should have been a lesson to those countries that would give up control over national exchange rates too quickly.[94]

Kohl also rebuffed efforts to set any firm timetables for the final move toward EMU, as many of the particulars had yet to be decided.[95] However, an important communiqué issued on October 27 at a special Rome summit indicated the support of Kohl for opening some form of a monetary institute on January 1, 1994, whose primary task would be to maintain price stability. The communiqué did reflect the Germans' and Pöhl's influence on monetary matters by delaying the establishment of some form of a European central bank to 1994, a year later than had been proposed by EC president Jacques Delors.

Pöhl, however, was not entirely satisfied and criticized the notion that a European central bank would be needed by 1994. Pöhl warned that a common monetary policy should not be imposed on nations with very different economic conditions.[96] A single currency, according to Pöhl, could proceed only after the twelve nations achieved a substantial degree of economic convergence.[97] Indeed, the European Community economies at the time ranged from healthy to endangered. Inflation ranged from 1 percent in the Netherlands and 3 percent in Germany to 13 percent in Portugal and 16 percent in Greece while unemployment ranged from 8 percent in Germany to the high teens in Greece. Greece's budget deficit as a share of its economy was seven times that of Germany's in 1990.[98]

The persuasion and cajoling among the key actors leading up to the Rome summit reached a sharp tempo in the month before the December 14 meeting. Reasserting its preeminent position in the EMS by raising the Lombard rate a half percentage point in November to 8.5 percent, the Bundesbank issued a position paper on Stage 2 of EMU listing a score of stringent requirements.[99] These conditions included the total completion of the single market, the banning of monetary or compulsory financing for public deficits, the securing of central bank independence in other EMS states, two years of exchange rate stability with all EMS states participating in the narrow band of the ERM, inflationary convergence, and the final ratification of the treaty by all EC members. As Pöhl suggested, "This is a bargaining process . . . and you cannot start the negotiations of a treaty without making your position very clear."[100] The Bundesbank's position rang clearly through the EC. For its part, the European Commission issued its own report listing the numerous advantages associated with EMU, the most important of which were increased price stability and a reduction in transaction costs.[101] The report also echoed some of the analyses within Germany that suggested that EMU would facilitate international policy coordination and give more weight to the community in encouraging global cooperation, a point that is often underestimated in understanding the German push for EMU.[102] It would also ease pressure on the DM as an alternative reserve currency in international financial circles. Besides, at a time when a slowdown was taking place among many industrialized countries, united Germany's economic dynamism was acting as a locomotive for the European and world economy. EMU would merely enhance such a process.

The Rome summit in December 1990 laid on the table various versions and plans for completion of economic and monetary union. An agreement was reached on the timing of the final set of negotiations and the goal of securing one year later at Maastricht a full treaty revision. Specifically, the EC members committed themselves to meet bimonthly to discuss the set of treaty proposals on political union and economic and monetary union as well as redesigning the EC's basic institutional structure. With the Rome summit complete, the primary question surrounding the EMU negotiations was whether Helmut Kohl could finally convince the last holdouts in the Bundesbank to accept his vision of a united Europe based on Germany playing a leading role in the EU. Could the resistance so displayed by Pöhl at the October Rome conference be overcome? Pöhl stated that he could not think of any circumstance in which the federal government agreed to any compromises that the Bundesbank had already turned down.[103] With quite a few compromises already rejected by the Bundesbank, there was not much room for Kohl to maneuver. In addition, the Bundesbank had also signaled its intent on restricting monetary growth for 1991 within a narrow 4–6 percent monetary target corridor. "Excessive wage demands" and public debt remained a cause for concern and restricted the Bundesbank's policy freedom.

But for Kohl, the economic welfare for Germans was inextricably tied to European welfare and, hence, European integration and unity. Recently emboldened by the overwhelming success of the electoral victory in the first all-German elections in December 1990, Kohl would put the Bundesbank on the defensive by pressuring the bank to accept a minimal set of agreements on EMU and European union. Moreover, with the conservative-liberal electoral coalition secure, Kohl could have his finance minister Waigel and foreign minister Genscher work closely together to push a united government front vis-à-vis the Bundesbank.[104] The stage was set for the drama of Maastricht.

Heading Toward Maastricht

The supportive political and economic context within which the EC had operated was by early 1991 now weakening. The February 1 Bundesbank discount rate increase to 6.5 percent from 6 percent and Lombard hike from 8.5 percent to 9 percent demonstrated once again that the bank was taking steps contradictory to the proclaimed aims of European cooperation. *Le Monde* characterized German behavior as such: "Germany reminds one, that in economic and monetary terms, Germany's individualism remains stronger than its desire to further international cooperation."[105] Germany's growth in GDP, which had been expanding at a 4.6 percent annual rate for 1990 and was strengthened by the voracious appetite for imports, had saved Europe from tumbling into recession. But the situation was now changing as the German economy slowly began to stutter and the full weight of the economic collapse in east Germany was realized. Higher interest rates, tax increases, and spiraling wage demands, many forecasters suggested, could shrink real growth in western Germany to 2 percent for the year. Pöhl's mid-March comment to an economic and monetary committee of the European Parliament that the impacts of GEMU were a "disaster" added further uncertainty to financial markets and the operation of the EMS. Moreover, confusion on the foreign policy and security front over contributions to the Gulf War and the emerging Bosnia crisis heightened the uncertainty within the EC on whether the Community could develop a coherent and unified political union.

As a result of Pöhl's comments before the committee and his increasingly strong attacks on the likelihood of EMU, the Kohl government stepped up its support for the negotiations under way. Kohl supported the Bundesbank's position on the ECB. The ECB, it was argued, "should be created only if and when it has been decided which countries are ready, and able, to set up a monetary union, to fix exchange rates irrevocably and to transfer sovereignty to the bank to decide on interest rates and liquidity."[106] More subtle differences remained, however, between Bonn and Frankfurt over how far to go in compromising on such details as foreign exchange rate intervention and the degree to which the new ECB should be even more insulated from political oversight than the Bundesbank. As one Kohl adviser stated, "We are going to be very tough, but we've made clear that our position is not set in concrete. Maybe that isn't good enough for the Bundesbank."[107]

For some, the Bundesbank's actions seemed aimed at mobilizing public opinion against EMU. Given the strong attachment of the German citizenry to the DM, such apprehensions were warranted. In addition, the Bundesbank feared Kohl would compromise on monetary union in return for concessions from the French on strengthening the European Parliament and political union. According to the bank, politicians would use the still vaguely defined Stage 2 and the ECB as a back door toward influencing Bundesbank policy and that other EMS members would be tempted to postpone indefinitely the hard choices involved in the transition to Stage 3. While recognizing these and other points, Kohl would not be dissuaded from seeing the process of European integration or union completed.

The Luxembourg summit of June 1991 made some progress on the draft treaty on EMU, but many detailed provisions of EMU still to be resolved demonstrated that there remained a considerable amount of tough negotiations to work through.[108] The most central difference between the Germans and their European partners centered on formalizing a detailed timetable for EMU. France pushed for 1994, but the Kohl government could not envision any final movement on EMU coming until 1997 at the earliest. The Bundesbank was opposed to the setting of any firm timetable. Moreover, although Delors and other southern tier nations had rejected the two-speed Europe approach as politically unacceptable, the final draft document appeared to incorporate many elements, namely, the convergence criteria, that suggested an EMU with a two-speed formula built into it. Finally, how exactly the limits on fiscal policy and the government's freedom to borrow would be imposed also remained a difficult issue to resolve. The issue of debt financing was often tied to the negotiations surrounding political union, which were themselves bogged down over a host of issues including immigration, social policy, agriculture subsidies, and defense and security policy. The December timetable for completing the negotiations looked less believable.

The assumption of Helmut Schlesinger, who often was described as a "rigid monetarist" by critics, to the presidency of the Bundesbank in August only exacerbated fears in some European and German circles that the Bundesbank would stiffen its resistance to EMU. What is more, analysts had come to question the bank's credibility given the weakening of the DM over the prior months and the impact of GEMU on the Bundesbank's independence. A sudden jump in inflation in July to 4.5 percent, the highest in Germany since 1982, proved the first test for the new Bundesbank president. The Bundesbank responded in August with a full percentage point increase in the discount rate from 6.5 percent to 7.5 percent and the Lombard rate a quarter of a point from 9 percent to 9.25 percent. Ironically, just as the EC was getting closer to European economic and monetary union, European monetary policy was becoming more divergent. Given a marked slowdown in the German economy into the third quarter of 1991 (as compared to the earlier part of the year), the interest rate increase could only have exacerbated the growing recession throughout Europe. If there existed any greater incentives for the other EMS members to irrevocably lock the Bundesbank and German monetary policy to a European standard more reflective of the differing economic levels of Europe, they would be hard to find.

It should be noted that for the United States, the meaning of European political and economic union and the whole Maastricht process to U.S. interests remained hazy, and U.S. politicians expressed few, if any, fears about the summit.[109] The United States and the Bush administration were preoccupied with domestic economic and political concerns brought on by a fear of sliding further into a deepening recession and the prospects for the upcoming electoral year. The European common market had not proved to be as impregnable a structure as some U.S. business leaders feared; "fortress Europe" had proven a misnomer since many of the divisive trade issues between Europe and the United States (outside of agriculture and Airbus) had been resolved. Moreover, the United States had long supported a strong, unified, and cohesive Europe and perceived the realization of EU in its own economic and security interests. The EU could act as an anchor of stability in an increasingly unstable Europe. Finally, given the ongoing problems in securing a GATT agreement, if trade protectionism were to re-emerge as a hot political issue in the United States, it would be with Japan not Europe. In sum, the United Sates took a generally hands-off approach to Maastricht.

The negotiations in the fall picked up speed as urgency of completing drafts for the Maastricht Treaty in December heightened. Further turmoil in the Soviet Union (the August coup attempt) and a belief that now could be the last opportunity to take advantage of the German support for the EC helped stimulate interest in finding compromises. The Dutch, who took over the EC presidency and closely aligned with Germany on most monetary issues, proved themselves efficient draftsmen and proposed some concrete treaty revisions. In particular, the Dutch draft incorporated the strict convergence criteria for EMU and developed the idea of a European Monetary Institute for 1994 and a European central bank only for Stage 3. Many countries in the southern tier of possible EMU candidates, including Italy, argued that the plan would lead to a two-speed Europe. However, with the possibility that the convergence criteria might be loosely interpreted so as to allow candidates entry into Stage 3, Italy eventually came to support the draft document. The Maastricht compromise was beginning to take shape.

In Germany, the Dutch proposals were greeted with a general sense of enthusiasm, except from within some circles in the Bundesbank. What is important to note is that Horst Köhler, Kohl's personal G7 and EC "sherpa," assumed a leading position in the negotiations. Finance Minister Waigel, who was busy with domestic financial issues tied to GEMU, remained absent from many of the critical sessions leading up to the Dutch proposals in September. Köhler, a close CDU ally of Kohl, shared the same larger political vision of the chancellor and his desire to see some sort of treaty signed at Maastricht. In the finance minister's absence, the Bundesbank voiced the tough position by calling for much greater progress toward economic convergence, specific regulations backed by sanctions to control deficit spending, and absolute political independence for the ECB, even from "guidelines" by government ministers.[110] Tietmeyer also focused comment on the EMI and warned that the institute could not have any supranational elements whatsoever. The Bundesbank warned that there could not exist any "gray zone" between national monetary autonomy and a European central bank until that point where the final jump to EMU would take place. Compromise on any one of these issues could not be accepted.

The final elements of the Maastricht bargain came into shape in the last hectic days of bargaining before the actual summit.[111] First, the idea of a full-fledged political union would have to be set aside, and a more modest set of supposedly "irreversible" policy and institutional mechanisms would be accepted for the time being.[112] Although a political union of the ideal form that Kohl had envisioned remained an elusive goal, it was enough to secure his support for EMU, where the details fit closely to many of the stricter requirements outlined by the Bundesbank. Instead of creating a powerful European central bank on January 1, 1994, the EMI would have the task in Stage 2 of EMU of guiding member states toward convergence in inflation, interest rates, and budget deficits. The treaty specifically outlined the economic preconditions, or convergence criteria, for EMU membership (which Germany, ironically, at the time did not fulfill):

- For one year prior to membership, an inflation rate that is less than 1.5 percentage points higher than that of the three lowest national inflation rates in the Community.
- For one year prior to membership, an inflation rate that is less than 2 percentage points higher than those of the three countries with the lowest inflation rates.
- For two years prior to membership, no devaluations from within the narrow band of the ERM.
- A national budget deficit of less than 3 percent of GDP.
- A public debt of less than 60 percent of GDP.

The treaty also enshrined the idea of an independent European central bank guided by the price stability standard. Moreover, other EC members would have to seek their own central bank independence as a precondition to EMU.

The key component of the Maastricht deal was the trade-off between the strict requirements for entry that France and Italy agreed to in return for the timetable that was agreed to by the Germans. The timetable concept recognized in part the idea of a two-speed Europe, for some members of the EC would undoubtedly not be able to meet the standards of entry and, thus, would probably be left behind by those countries able to meet the requirements. The key concession by the Germans was the agreement on the ultimate end date for starting EMU, 1997 at the earliest and 1999 at the latest. The transition to EMU would begin at the beginning of 1997 when the finance ministers would decide, by qualified majority, which members met the convergence criteria. A summit would then decide, again by qualified majority, whether at least seven countries were ready for EMU, and if so, whether and when it should start. If no date was set, another summit would meet before July 1998 to decide which members were now ready. Those countries would then choose whether to adopt the ECU as their single currency on January 1, 1999, with a European central bank responsible for monetary policy.

There were, however, a number of other potentially significant concessions made by Kohl that implied that the Bundesbank model had not, in fact, been exported to the EC. First, the convergence criteria were not hard and fast rules for admission. Waigel had stated that the criteria should not be applied "mechanically."[113] All decisions on membership in the union would ultimately be made using the qualified majority-voting rule established in the SEA. Moreover, the treaty explicitly directs governments to base their decision only on whether members have made good-faith efforts to meet the criteria. In other words, should a qualified majority of EC governments vote to include less well-performing members, then those countries would be able to join EMU. The conflict between political expediency and economic prudence would undoubtedly come to the fore, especially in the case of Italy. Would a majority of members be prepared to exclude a founding and central member of the EC from probably the most important development in Europe since the creation of the Community? A difficult question to answer, indeed.

Second, the provision on exchange rate management remained ambiguous. Article 109 of the treaty does not accurately clarify which institutions—the ECB, the Council of Ministers—will manage external exchange rates. Paragraph 1, Article 109 declares that the Council of Ministers may "conclude formal arrangements for an exchange rate system for the ECU with respect to non-Community currencies," including primarily the dollar. Paragraph 2, Article 109 also states that the Council, by qualified voting, may "formulate general guidelines for exchange rate policy vis-à-vis these currencies." Yet it was assumed that the ECB would have a central role in any exchange rate policy that would require its consent. It is unclear how the issue will be resolved. Would the ECB be bound to the political decisions of an as yet ill-defined body?[114] The resultant situation could possibly approximate the German case whereby the government has responsibility for external monetary diplomacy and exchange rate realignments and the Bundesbank has control over the domestic monetary instruments. Given the many illustrations of the conflict in this study between the Bundesbank and government over this very issue, the potential for disagreements within the new EMU/EU configuration on exchange rate policy would likely remain high.

Third, ECB decisions would be by a simple majority of the governing council (made up of an executive board and the heads of member central banks), where a majority of members could vote for "loose money" and outvote the technocrats on the executive board. There was no guarantee that the other central bank governors would share the same stability consensus as the Bundesbank. Finally, the sanctions upon member states that pursue "excessively" loose fiscal policies (fines or requirements to make non-interest-bearing deposits in the ECB, Article 104c) lacked strong enforcement mechanisms. The decision to take action against a high deficit or debt government would also lie with a qualified majority in the Council of Ministers and not with the ECB. If a blocking coalition in the Council existed, it would be impossible to sanction EMU members. Moreover, if governments believed that others would view their national economy as too big to fail, and hence cover their debts rather than to allow the country to default, the temptation to pursue expansionary fiscal policies would increase. The lack of movement on strengthening some of the budgetary and fiscal components of the political union is significant in this respect.

Such interpretations of the treaty were summarily criticized by a number of politicians, scholars, and Bundesbankers.[115] Perhaps understating the point somewhat, Bundesbank president Schlesinger admitted in a speech in Paris shortly after agreement on Maastricht that there were a "few details that were not wished by the Bundesbank."[116] Lothar Müller, the president of the Bavarian Landeszentralbank, saw more than a few ill-advised aspects of the treaty and called for a referendum. Müller and others in the CSU described Maastricht as a one-sided treaty that did not take into account the Bundesbank's concerns with price stability or political union. Müller wanted to renegotiate the entire treaty. SPD members of the Central Bank Council Wilhelm Nölling and Reimut Jochamsin openly criticized Kohl for agreeing to the 1999 timetable and the near "automaticity" of the arrangement. Such points, they argued, were intolerable. Moreover, while efforts were made to include and strengthen the provisions of the treaty dealing with political union, the actual treaty failed to deal comprehensively with the strengthening of the European Parliament. The former economics and finance minister Karl Schiller (SPD) also questioned the treaty provisions and timetable.[117] In the rush of post-Maastricht public commentary, public opinion turned even more decidedly against the idea of relinquishing the DM to any European currency.[118]

Despite the protestations and concerns raised, the decision to secure a treaty on EMU was a political calculation reached by the chancellor. The Bundesbank could only stand by and advise the chancellor as to what the bank saw was the best path to take. Many of the preferred provisions of the Bundesbank for EMU had, in fact, been met in the negotiations. Strict convergence criteria as suggested by the *Krönungstheorie*, the independence of the ECB, and the price-stability goal characterized the overall EMU arrangements. Yet a form of automatic timetable, an ill-defined exchange rate policy, and a weak enforcement mechanism for fiscal policy were also terms of the agreement. Maastricht was a political document, not an economic theory; a compliant strategy was needed in order to launch EMU. Whatever the interpretation, the formal, legally binding Maastricht document had committed Germany to full monetary cooperation in Europe, the full and irrevocable fixing of exchange rates and a single currency.

Should the International Monetary Regime Be Preserved?

Instability on global financial markets sharpened as pressure was exerted on the G7 to stabilize the markets following the invasion of Kuwait by Saddam Hussein in August of 1990. The resultant rise in oil prices, the fear of a new global economic crisis, and a recession in the United States seemed to demand concerted action to stabilize the global economy and the dollar, which was facing a renewed round of speculative attacks. In September 1990 at the IMF/World Bank meeting, the G7 ministers did manage to reaffirm the members' mutual commitment to exchange rate stability, declaring that "exchange rates were now broadly in line with continued adjustment of external balances," although the term *broadly* indicated that the G7 left it up to individual nations to define what that meant. The ministers also asserted, as usual, that they would "continue to cooperate closely on exchange markets in the context of the economic policy coordination process." At a minimum, the meeting helped stabilize worried financial markets. Nonetheless, diverging interests expressed at the meeting between Germany, the UK, and Canada on controlling inflation and the United States in stimulating growth revealed the facade of G7 unity.[119] In addition to the Gulf crisis, rapid changes in the Soviet Union and Eastern Europe heightened uncertainties and the political instability surrounding the G7 members' efforts to provide a united economic front.

As if to demonstrate this point, through the rest of 1990, there were few if any concerted actions taken to coordinate the economic policy process, which reflected upon the value of the dollar as it began to weaken considerably on financial markets.[120] In late October, the U.S. dollar stood at near record lows vis-à-vis the DM at DM 1.49. The drop of the dollar paralleled the Bush administration's own declining rating in public opinion polls. The Bush administration was intent on seeing the dollar weaker because the only source of strength in the economy, according to some administration officials, was in exports.[121] Treasury Secretary Brady stated his view that the decline in the dollar was "orderly." In addition to the Germans, the Bush administration did not appear interested in a coordinated, activist effort to re-establish target zones for exchange rates, even though foreign investment in U.S. government bonds, which might have been needed to finance the war effort in the Gulf, had sharply decreased in

1990. The IMF's annual report for 1990 reflected the overall attitude of G7 coordination. The IMF characterized G7 interaction as having "a preference" among G7 members for "exchange rate stability" but that, "on the other hand, the extent to which this preference affected policy actions may at times have seemed unclear; the decline in the dollar . . . encountered virtually no resistance from official operations in foreign exchange markets . . . and the objective of exchange stability may have appeared not to have had a major influence on policy actions."[122] Supporting the IMF view, one scholar characterized G7 efforts at cooperation and policy accommodation at the end of 1990 as strained and lacking credibility.[123]

The process of policy coordination actually worsened into 1991. The entire period of G7 monetary cooperation was dominated by conflicts over interest rates differentials, the impact of GEMU on G7 cooperation, and a renewed U.S. global locomotive strategy of pressuring the Germans to lower interest rates. At the January G7 ministerial meeting, the discussions were dominated by questions of burden sharing and how much the other G7 members (besides the United States) would contribute to the costs of the Gulf War. Germany agreed to pay U.S.$2.2 billion, but Waigel let it be known that U.S.$2.2 billion would be the maximum the Germans could contribute given the costs of reunification and the DM 13 billion already granted to the Soviet Union in return for their support of reunification. The ministers also discussed the role of central bank intervention should the dollar drop dramatically because of the length and costs of the war. Fortunately, the war's quick end prevented a testing of the central bank's resolve in backing up its verbal commitment.

Furthermore, both Pöhl and Waigel were not impressed with U.S. or French complaints at the meeting about international capital flows into Germany to finance reunification. It was clear that along with the crisis in the Gulf, the reunification of Germany would further burden the limited efforts at G7. Despite a weakening U.S. dollar, the Bundesbank raised interest rates by a half of a percentage point on both the Lombard and discount rates on the last day of January 1991.[124] The move came just two weeks after the January G7 meeting at which the Bundesbank had "promised" that no rate increase would be forthcoming.[125] The Bundesbank was concerned with inflationary pressures in Germany as early 1991 statistics indicated that the bank's monetary growth target corridor of 4–6 percent for 1991 was already being overshot. Moreover, January 1991 also revealed Germany's first current account deficit (DM 1.2 billion) since 1981.

It was becoming clear that for 1991 the Bundesbank had shifted German monetary policy inward upon domestic-level concerns while external monetary diplomacy increasingly focused upon European-level matters. The differentiation in Germany's monetary policy became ever more apparent as the German government and the Bundesbank increasingly felt squeezed between the triple pressure points of domestic concerns, European monetary integration, and the developing global recession. Given such a constellation of pressures, it should not have been surprising to see a continued retrenchment on global monetary cooperation as German monetary authorities sought to secure agreement on more demanding domestic and European policy questions. Moreover, as the January decision to raise interest rates suggested, the Bundesbank had apparently reneged on a commitment at the G7 level to stabilize its interest rate policy vis-à-vis U.S. policy. The Bundesbank ultimately found it unacceptable to accede to the agreement reached at the January G7 ministers' meeting.

Continued tensions at the February G7 ministerial meeting and the weakening dollar hinted at the conspicuous diverging interests of Germany and the United States. For example, the German rate move at the end of January was followed by an interest rate reduction by the Federal Reserve. From the German point of view, higher domestic interest rates were needed to offset the inflationary pressure brought on by reunification. The weak dollar and lowering of U.S. interest rates were, from the U.S. point of view, appropriate means to combat the U.S. economy sliding into recession and persistent trade deficits. Some analysts suggested, however, that the weakening dollar could also, in the future, bring on inflation in the United States and that the value of the dollar relative to the DM should be prevented from dropping below DM 1.40. One noted monetary specialist suggested that the Japanese and Germans peg their currencies at DM 1.45 and 120 yen to the dollar.[126] Another leading economist suggested that the United States continue its policy of benign monetary neglect in order to stimulate the economy and concentrate on getting the United States out of recession.[127] With German and U.S. monetary policy moving in two different directions, the February G7 ministerial meeting demonstrated all too clearly the difficulties surrounding efforts to secure a binding G7 agreement on policy coordination.

By April of 1991, the DM-dollar relationship had again altered as the dollar strengthened noticeably. The DM-dollar rate had stood at 1.45 DM to the dollar in February but now stood at DM 1.75 to the dollar, a roughly 21 percent increase.[128] Such currency movements illustrated the volatility of exchange rates and the inability of the G7 nations to work together to offset such instability. At the April G7 meeting, Germany managed to secure the understanding and support of the Japanese on the outlines of Germany's interest rate policy as the two jointly rejected a proposal by Brady for a coordinated easing of interest rates, despite last-minute personal appeals by Bush. Bush's renewed interest in G7 coordination came on the heels of a report from the National Bureau of Economic Research that showed the U.S. economy slipping deeper into recession.

At home, Pöhl remained preoccupied by the restructuring of the Bundesbank council and the accommodation of new representatives from eastern

Germany into the Zentralbankrat. Specifically, interest rate reductions were, according to Pöhl, "not on the agenda" at the G7 meeting. Pöhl in customary style suggested that the Germans were not against lower rates, but that they must be earned.[129] Waigel also suggested that the United States cut its own rates.[130] Overall, the Germans could point to fairly optimistic economic growth projections of the five leading economic institutes that suggested growth at an annual rate 2.5 percent for the year 1991. With solid growth and continued inflationary fears, the Bundesbank was not intent on lowering interest rates.

The reasoning behind the United States' pressure on Germany to lower interest rates indicated some divisions within U.S. monetary policymaking circles. Lower interest rates in Germany at that time would have virtually obliged the Federal Reserve to cut U.S. rates in order to brake the dollar's further rise, which seemed to be exactly what Brady wanted. Despite the rejection of the plan, Brady anticipated the possibility of a further strengthening of the dollar (and U.S. interest rate drop) given the post–Gulf War confidence in the U.S. economy, a fundamentally undervalued (as measured by purchasing power parity) dollar, and the belief that the German economy would soon weaken or even collapse. Moreover, a weak DM also implied for some analysts that the bargaining strength of the Germans within the G7 would be undermined.[131]

However, it was U.S. monetary policy that came under increasing scrutiny.[132] In particular, the independent position of the Federal Reserve and its anti-inflationary credentials had come under question. Several days after the conflict-ridden April G7 meeting,[133] the Federal Reserve cut interest rates, with Brady suggesting that with 5 percent inflation, the United States had achieved "relative price stability." Such comments were incomprehensible in the German view. Moreover, the leader of the international monetary system was failing to live up to its responsibilities. With monetary policy in both Germany and the United States on divergent paths, G7 coordination was all but nonexistent; fears over another October 1987 crash heightened.

Through the summer of 1991, the disagreements continued. At a meeting of the G7 in London in June, the ministers agreed that monetary policy should be left to individual countries according to their particular economic conditions.[134] In July at the G7 annual summit in London, the heads of state and finance ministers could only agree, in effect, to disagree over the proper path toward achieving price stability, economic growth, and exchange rate stability. The communiqué issued at the end of the summit reflected the different economic situations among the G7 countries as well as continued disagreements over Soviet aid. The London summit was perhaps more important for the political issues discussed and less for the monetary or financial issues. With Soviet president Gorbachev joining the G7 heads of state throughout most of the summit, the emphasis of G7 summitry shifted clearly from its original purpose of macroeconomic policy coordination in the mid-1970s to more of a global clearinghouse for political debate and ensuring political stability. The G7's most important statement from the summit was its support for Gorbachev's reform efforts and the Soviet associate status in the IMF. What might have been an opportune time for the G7 members to seriously rethink strategies to address global economic governance, the summit instead was overshadowed by the looming economic and political crisis in the Soviet Union.

With an election year coming up in the United States in 1992 and Germany becoming overly preoccupied with the negotiations over EMU and the problems associated with reunification, it was doubtful that G7 coordination would increase or emerge from a year of instability and confusing rhetoric. The United States, it appeared, had given up by the fall of 1991 on its policy of publicly and actively seeking an interest rate reduction from the Germans. Such a strategy had clearly failed and possibly added to the volatility of both the DM and the dollar. German monetary policy focused increasingly inward as the Bundesbank raised the discount rate to 7.5 percent and the Lombard rate to 9.25 percent in August.[135] The dollar had weakened again, dropping to around 1.65 by the fall. At the October G7 meeting in Bangkok, Helmut Schlesinger could argue that the IMF member countries now understood where German monetary policy was coming from; there was little discussion of German monetary policy. Instead, the focus of the G7 and IMF criticism was on Kohl's and Waigel's fiscal policies.[136]

Although the G7 members could still reaffirm their continued support for economic policy coordination at ministerial meetings in September and October, by December the Bundesbank had continued to raise interest rates to record levels with the Lombard rate standing at 9.75 percent and the discount rate at 8 percent. More important, the Bundesbank did not consult with or inform the United States or Japan of its interest rate hike. The *New York Times* labeled G7 monetary interaction as "economic warfare," as the United States was intent on lowering interest rates to offset a demonstratively slowing U.S. economy.[137] If there were such a thing as an international monetary regime, it would have been very hard to identify at the end of 1991. Although outright economic gunboat diplomacy might not have characterized German-U.S. monetary interaction, it was clear that each country was intent on guiding their economic ship of state down a separate path. The dominant question for students of the international monetary system was whether there existed a meaningful monetary regime within which the G7 operated. Competing interpretations of the norms, principles, and decisionmaking procedures of G7 monetary interaction undermined the remaining credibility of the governance structure.

* * *

On EMU, the German government's bargaining strategy was quite clear and consistent. More important, the government's strategy largely paralleled the Bundesbank's many concerns, and disagreement between the bank and government was low. As a result, the government ultimately overwhelmed Bundesbank resistance to the very nature of EMU. Chancellor Kohl and his foreign minister, Hans-Dietrich Genscher, came to view EMU as a necessary step in the overall process of European integration to which the Federal Republic had long been committed. EU, built on the foundation of EMU, would form the nucleus for future peaceful cooperation and coexistence within Europe. The continued success of the EMS and movement toward EMU were perceived to be necessary conditions for progress on European integration. The status quo was not an option for the Kohl government, especially after German reunification in 1990 and the disintegration of Eastern Europe and the Soviet Union. If the European Community was not to develop into a new system, then its very viability, as well as the other Community objectives, like completing the internal market of 1992 and EMU, would be placed in jeopardy.

Moreover, German unification altered the negotiating calculus of both the Europeans and Germans, including the Bundesbank. The constraints that the Bundesbank confronted with a Kohl government deeply committed to Europe and Maastricht and high on the success of reunification shifted the intra-German bargaining political balance in favor of the government. The greater leverage that the government had over the Bundesbank in the final stages of EMU negotiations provided the necessary mix to secure an agreement between the two institutions. The government and Bundesbank did push a set of rigid conditions on EMU. The final agreement incorporated strict Bundesbank objectives. Yet the final compromise reflected a compliant strategy, where the Bundesbank and government agreed in the end that a conclusive agreement at Maastricht would be needed.

Notes

1. A sizable amount of literature exists that covers this time period. I do not presume to have read all of it or suggest that I can integrate all the analyses into this volume. However, most of the literature covers the interaction between European and German monetary politics and thus fails to integrate the international dimension into their accounts. This chapter seeks to again synthesize and integrate the international dimension into a broader and comprehensive treatment of German monetary policy. I am particularly indebted to the work of Barry Eichengreen and Jeffry Frieden, *The Political Economy of European Monetary Unification* (Boulder,

Colo.: Westview Press, 1994); J. M. Artis, "The Maastricht Road to Monetary Union," *Journal of Common Market Studies* 30 (1992); P. DeGrauwe and L. Papademos, *The European Monetary System in the 1990s* (London: Longman, 1990); and Wayne Sandholtz, "Choosing Union: Monetary Politics and Maastricht," *International Organization* 47, no. 1 (winter 1993), pp. 1–39.

2. See the account in Ellen Kennedy, *The Bundesbank: Germany's Central Bank in the International Monetary System* (London: RIIA, 1991), pp. 94–97.

3. During the first half of 1988, the EMS continued to be quite stable, which only provided further proof for some European partners that movement on EMU could proceed promptly. Pöhl countered such statements by suggesting that the EMS stability resulted from the Bundesbank's independent ability to ensure DM stability. See Pöhl's statements in "Die Mark hat den Standard gesetzt," *Süddeutsche Zeitung*, February 2, 1988.

4. Norbert Kloten, *Auszüge aus Pressartikeln*, January 20, 1988.

5. When pressed in interviews, Bundesbank officials admitted only that their position was the minimum they could accept. If those conditions were unacceptable or unbearable to other EMS members, it could be implied that the Bundesbank would have been happy to accept the possibility that no agreement would be reached.

6. See the analysis in "Ein Privatissme für Kohl zur Währungsautonomie," *Handelsblatt*, June 15, 1988.

7. Padoa-Schioppa had recently argued that EMU was not possible given the "inconsistent quartet" of EC objectives (free internal trade, full capital mobility, fixed exchange rates, and national autonomy in monetary policy). The inconsistent quartet's blockage of movement on EMU could best be resolved with the elimination of national monetary autonomy. See the analysis in Tommaso Padoa-Schioppa, "The EMS: A Long-Term View," in F. Giavazzi, S. Micossa, and M. Miller, eds., *The European Monetary System* (Cambridge, UK: Cambridge University Press, 1988).

8. Helmut Schmidt, "Blockiert von Kleinmütigen," *Die Zeit*, April 21, 1988.

9. The Association published its concept of EMU shortly before the Hanover summit in order to maximize the influence of the group on the future Delors Committee. The Association envisioned the establishment of a European central bank and the use of the ECU as a parallel currency by 1992. Member central banks would be bound formally to strict monetary standards. A single European currency, probably the ECU, would come into usage at some later date. See "Europäische Zentralbank muss nicht der Endpunkt sein," *Frankfurter Allgemeine Zeitung*, June 26, 1988.

10. *Wirtschaftswoche*, March 31, 1989.

11. See the analysis of Andrie Markovits and Alexander Otto, "German Labor and 1992," *Comparative Politics* 24, no 5 (January 1992), pp. 163–180.

12. See the analysis in "Währungsunion zu riskant," *Süddeutsche Zeitung*, February 21, 1989.

13. "Zweifel am EWS," *Frankfurter Allgemeine Zeitung*, March 29, 1989.

14. "Blick durch die Wirtschaft," *Frankfurter Allgemeine Zeitung*, January 31, 1989.

15. See the view of Kurt Falthhauser, CSU member of parliament and head of the CSU working group on the budget and finances, "Schädliche Hektik um Europa," *Die Welt*, April 10, 1988.

16. Otmar Issing, "Europaische Notenbank—ein Phantom," *Frankfurter Allgemeine Zeitung*, March 11, 1988.

17. See the interview with Pöhl, conducted by Franz Thoma and Otto Schwarzer, in "Europa braucht eine Stabilitätsunion," *Süddeutsche Zeitung*, March 2, 1988. See also "A European Central Bank and a European Currency Could Be the Crowing Achievement of the Long and Difficult Process to Monetary Union in Europe," *Auszüge aus Pressartikeln*, April 6, 1988.

18. Interview with Pöhl, conducted by Franz Thoma and Otto Schwarzer, in "Europa braucht." Such a view was supported by the work of Niels Thygesen and Daniel Gros in *The EMS: Achievements, Current Issues and Directions for the Future* (Brussels: Center for European Policy Studies, 1988).

19. "A European Central Bank," *Auszüge aus Pressartikeln*, April 6, 1988.

20. "Pöhl Doubts European Unit Likely Soon," *Wall Street Journal Europe*, May 5, 1988.

21. "Pressegespräch nach der Zentralbankratsitzung am 5. Mai 1988 in Frankfurt am Main," *Auszüge aus Presseartikeln*, May 6, 1988. The Bundesbank never completely accepted the usage of the ECU as a "real currency" and argued that the ECU had no "backing" from a national authority.

22. "Delors Team Opts for Economic Unity," *Financial Times*, December 9, 1988.

23. Ibid.

24. "Köhler's Pariser Alleingang," *Handelsblatt*, October 6, 1988.

25. See, for example, "Monetary Union for EC Fades Toward Oblivion," *International Herald Tribune*, February 9, 1989

26. There existed, of course, internal opposition to Thatcher's policies.

27. Robin Leigh-Pemberton, "The Future of Monetary Arrangements in Europe," occasional paper, no. 82, Institute of Economic Affairs, London, 1989.

28. See the analysis in the Committee for the Study of Economic and Monetary Union, *Report on Economic and Monetary Union in the European Community* [Delors Plan] (Luxembourg, 1990).

29. The plan was agreed upon unanimously by the Delors Committee including the British Central Bank governor, Leigh-Pemberton.

30. "Britain Rejects EC Plan for Economic Union," *International Herald Tribune*, April 17, 1989.

31. "Pöhl ermahnt zur Realismus und Augenmass," *Börsen Zeitung*, April 19, 1989.

32. "Pöhl warnte vor Übereile bei der Währungsunion," *Süddeutsche Zeitung*, June 8, 1989. See the ideas of Helmut Haussmann and Hans-Dietrich Genscher who supported setting an immediate timetable for EMU, "Genscher fordert Termin für eine Währungsunion," *Frankfurter Allgemeine Zeitung*, May 7, 1989; and the arguments in favor of EMU in Helmut Schmidt, "Eine Währung für Europa," *Die Zeit*, June 22, 1989. See also the criticisms of the Delors Committee by the Scientific Advisory Council to the Economics Ministry, "Kritik am vorgeschalgenen Weg zur Währungsunion," *Frankfurter Rundschau*, June 20, 1989.

33. For a comprehensive and balanced analysis of the strengths and weaknesses of the Delors Plan and what it might mean for the various EMS members, see "From A to EMU," *The Economist*, June 23, 1989. The plan still failed to reconcile, at least for period of years, the problem of the unholy trinity.

34. "Building from a Disputed Blueprint," *Financial Times*, July 9, 1989. The summit almost broke down when Mitterand suggested completing the entire intergovernmental and treaty revision process by 1992 (the first opportunity for a meeting would be after the July 1, 1990, implementation of Stage 1) in order to complement the single market of 1992.

35. Benjamin J. Cohen, "The Triad and the Unholy Trinity: Lessons for the Pacific Region," in Richard Higgot, Richard Leaver, and John Ravenhill, eds., *Pacific Economic Relations in the 1990s* (London: Allen and Unwin, 1993), p. 143. This account and others in this chapter draw, in part, on the work of Cohen as well as I. M. Destler and C. Randall Henning, *Dollar Politics: Exchange Rate Policymaking in the United States* (Washington, D.C.: Institute for International Economics, 1989).

36. At the time, the Germans were in the midst of celebrating forty years of the founding of the DM and the stability that the DM had brought to the German economy and political system. If there is such a thing as poor timing for re-establishing an international monetary system on a par with Bretton Woods, now was such a time. For a powerful restatement at the time of the role of the DM for Germany, Europe, and the G7, see Karl Otto Pöhl, "Eine konsequente Stabilitätspolitik hat uns das Vertrauen des Auslands erhalten," *Die Welt*, June 19, 1988.

37. "Gipfel in Toronto soll Wachstum sichern," *Die Welt*, June 15, 1988.

38. "Inflation Fears Could Weaken G7 Resolve," *The Japan Economic Journal*, July 1, 1988.

39. See, for example, Jeffrey E. Garten, "How Bonn, Tokyo Slyly Help Bush," *New York Times*, July 21, 1988; Irwin Seltzer, "The Election Dollar," *The American Spectator*, September 1988, pp. 28–33.

40. Baker was replaced by Nicholas Brady in the Treasury in September 1988.

41. A slightly more optimistic view at the prospects of G7 cooperation can be found in Peter Norman, "Central Bankers Look to the U.S.," *Financial Times*, January 9, 1989. The optimism was predicated on the likelihood of budget reductions in the United States.

42. "Is the G7 on the Road to Splitsville?" *Business Week*, February 12, 1989.

43. "Internationale Verflechtung schränkt den Aktionsradius der Bundesbank ein," *Handelsblatt*, January 31, 1989.

44. Christopher Huhne, "After G7: Hold On for the Roller Coaster," *The Guardian*, February 7, 1989.

45. "G7 Nations Emphasize Trade and Debt Woes Over Inflation," *International Herald Tribune*, April 3, 1989. See also, "Bundesbank Medicine Fails to Cure," *Financial Times*, May 23, 1989.

46. *New York Times*, May, 12, 1989, cited in Cohen, "The Triad and the Unholy Trinity," p. 144.

47. Cohen, "The Triad and the Unholy Trinity," p. 144.

48. Destler and Henning, *Dollar Politics*, p. 72.

49. "The G7 Is Acting More Like the Seven Dwarfs," *Business Week*, June 4, 1989.

50. *New York Times*, July 7, 1989. In a postsummit interview, Secretary Brady declared that the value of the dollar had not even been discussed at the summit. Brady did not see the need for the heads of government to address exchange rates or coordination issues, although the summits were designed and intended as a permanent institutional forum for such discussions. See the analysis in Destler and Henning, *Dollar Politics*, p. 72.

51. See the analysis of the Paris summit in Samuel Brittan, "Time to End the Summits," *Financial Times*, July 12, 1989.

52. "The G7 Won't Be Singing Harmony," *Business Week*, July 16, 1989.

53. Ibid.

54. See the analysis of two German scholars, Bernhard Herz and Joachim Starbatty, "Ende der Hegemonie," *Wirtschaftswoche*, June 22, 1989. The authors surveyed

thirty-one German experts to determine the ability of the United States, Japan, and the Federal Republic of Germany to independently pursue their own national macroeconomic objectives. The survey indicated the increasingly "balanced" nature of G3 influence and the dependent nature of the G3 relationships.

55. A study by the Group of 30 published in 1988 pointed toward the use of exchange rates as the best way to coordinate international macroeconomic policy, not because exchange rates were considered all important, but because the attempt to manage them inevitably brought up most other issues (all components of fiscal and monetary policy). With Germany already working within an adjustable "managed" exchange rate system in Europe, German monetary authorities were not interested in entering another formal arrangement on exchange rates. Interview with a Bundesbank official, September 1993. See also the study, "International Macroeconomic Policy" (Washington D.C.: Group of 30, 1988).

56. The British Treasury, *An Evolutionary Approach to Economic and Monetary Union*, November 1989.

57. See the analysis of Ian Harden, "Sovereignty and the Eurofed," *Political Quarterly*, no. 4, (October/December 1990).

58. See Pöhl's analysis in Karl Otto Pöhl, "Two Monetary Unions—The Bundesbank View," in *Europe's Constitutional Future* (London: Institute of Economic Affairs, 1990), pp. 21–52.

59. Within Genscher's own FDP, divisions arose over which was the proper course on EMU. The party leader, Otto Graf Lambsdorff, largely supported the position of the Bundesbank. See Lambsdorff's remarks in "Europa ist noch nicht reif genug für die Gründung der gemeinsamen Zentralbank," *Handelsblatt*, October 12, 1989.

60. A survey conducted by the Emnid Institute in the late summer of 1989 indicated that 56 percent of German respondents trusted the DM over any future European currency. See "Zukunft eines Europäische Währungs System," *Aussenwirtschaftsbrief*, no. 4 (July/August 1989). For a view of the BDI and Deutsche Gewerkschaft Bund (DGB), see their copublished position paper on 1992, "Die Chancen des Europäischen Binnenmarktes nutzen," summarized in "BDI and DGB: Währungsunion braucht Zeit," *Börsen Zeitung*, July 31, 1989.

61. "Why Should Europe Dance to Germany's Economic Tune?" *Business Week*, October 23, 1989.

62. "Bonn Sets New Deadline for Full Monetary Union," *The Guardian*, December 6, 1989.

63. "Das nächste Realignment rückt näher," *Börsen Zeitung*, December 12, 1989.

64. "Adjustment in the EMS," *Financial Times*, January 8, 1990.

65. See the commentary in "Schrille Signale von der Themse," "Holland setzt auf Tradition der Stabilität," and "Brüssel reagiert mit Task Force," *Die Welt*, February 9, 1989.

66. "Giscard and Schmidt: Rasche Währungsunion," *Auszüge aus Presseartikeln*, February 19, 1990. The committee also stated their support for institutionalizing and operating a functioning European central bank by the beginning of 1993.

67. See the interview with Pöhl, "Das muss doch die DDR entscheiden," *Die Zeit*, February 2, 1990. For an excellent summary of the entire GEMU process, see Jonathon Zatlin, "Hard Marks and Soft Revolutionaries," *German Politics and Society*, issue 33 (fall 1994), pp. 57–84.

68. See the excellent analysis and discussion of this topic in "What Kind of EMU?" *The Economist*, February 10, 1990.

69. The Dutch Central Bank, the second-most independent central bank in Europe, remains—in theory—subject to parliamentary control.
70. "Tiny Steps Toward Agreement on EMU," *Financial Times*, April 1, 1990. Waigel stated bluntly that "budgetary discipline is for me a central element for the success of EMU." Delors complained about the German position and that he was being "badly repaid" for support of Germany unity.
71. "Neues Selbstbewusstsein," *Die Zeit*, April 20, 1990.
72. "A German Idea of Europe," *The Economist*, July 27, 1991.
73. My own interviews with Bundesbank officials confirm this view.
74. "Financial Officials Seek Better Global Harmony," *New York Times*, September 25, 1989.
75. "Stabilizing the Dollar," *New York Times*, September 22, 1989, p. D2.
76. "Time to Tether Currencies," *The Economist*, January 6, 1990.
77. Interview with Bundesbank official, September 1993.
78. See the comments and analysis of William A. Niskanen, "Policy Coordination by G7 Is an Illusion," *The Japan Economic Journal*, March 3, 1990.
79. See the presummit analysis in "Japan Moves to Centre Stage," *Financial Times*, April 5, 1990; and "Brady lässt sich Solidarität bezahlen," *Handelsblatt*, April 5, 1990.
80. Michael Webb, "International Economic Structures," *International Organization*, no. 45 (summer 1991), p. 334.
81. "Waigel Confident on Unity," *Financial Times*, April 8, 1990.
82. See "Zurückhaltende Kommentare Greenspans zur deutschen Währungsunion," *Neue Zürcher Zeitung*, June 8, 1990.
83. See the analysis "Ronald Reagan lässt sich schön grüssen," *Süddeutsche Zeitung*, February 13, 1990.
84. The G7 summit was overshadowed in part by the NATO summit in London one week earlier. At the NATO summit, the members agreed on the inclusion of a reunited Germany into the NATO structure and secured, in part, initial Soviet support for the vague outlines of the plan.
85. "A New Balance of Power," *New York Times*, July 12, 1990.
86. Although the actual terms of GEMU reflected many of the Bundesbank's own concerns, the bank's reputation suffered over its inability to resolutely counter all the government's objectives. Many analysts questioned the policy credibility of the bank. See Jonathan R. Zatlin, "Hard Mark and Soft Revolutionaries," *German Politics and Society*, no. 3 (fall 1994), pp. 57–84.
87. See an analysis of the implications for both actions in "Die D-Mark wird abgeschafft," *Der Spiegel*, June 25, 1990.
88. See the official comments of the Bundesbank on Stage 1 of EMU, Deutsche Bundesbank, "The First Stage of EMU," *Monthly Report of the Bundesbank*, July 1990 (Frankfurt/Main).
89. F. Giavazzi and A. Giovanni, *Limiting Exchange Rate Stability: The European Monetary System* (Cambridge, Mass.: MIT Press, 1989). See also the review by David Cobham, "European Monetary Integration: A Survey of Recent Literature," *Journal of Common Market Studies* 29, no. 4 (1991), pp. 363–383.
90. See the analysis of F. Giavazzi and M. Pagano, "The Advantage of Tying One's Hand: EMS Discipline and Central Bank Credibility," *Discussion Paper*, no. 135 (London: Centre for Economic Policy Research, 1986). See also the analysis of Frank McDonald and George Zis, "The European Monetary System: Towards 1992 and Beyond," *Journal of Common Market Studies* 27, no. 3 (March 1989), pp. 185–202.

91. Thomas Hanke, "Ein ECU neuer Prägung," *Die Zeit*, July 13, 1990.
92. "The Demon Banker," *The Guardian*, September 6, 1990.
93. "EC Ministers Fall Out Over Speed of Monetary Union," *Financial Times*, September 9, 1990.
94. "Bundesbank Adds a Voice to Bonn's Go-Slow Chorus on EMU," *Financial Times*, September 21, 1990.
95. "Kohl: 'Zweite Stufe' 1994, wenn . . . " *Börsen Zeitung*, October 19, 1990.
96. "Europe Wonders: Buddy, Can You Spare an ECU?" *Los Angeles Times*, November 13, 1990.
97. Ibid.
98. *Organization for Economic Cooperation and Development* (Paris: Eurostat, 1990).
99. "Stiff Conditions for Next Move to Monetary Union," *Financial Times*, October 8, 1990.
100. "Bundesbank's Pöhl Fashions German Position in Europe's Drive for Unified Monetary System," *Wall Street Journal*, October 15, 1990.
101. European Commission, *One Market, One Economy,* no. 44, 1990. See also Commission of the European Communities, *The ECU Report,* prepared by Michael Emerson and Christopher Huhne, 1991.
102. Roger de Weck, "Vom Unfug des DM-Nationalismus," *Die Zeit,* October 19, 1990.
103. Ibid.
104. Waigel, as a member of the right-conservative CSU of Bavaria, often found himself playing a more resistant role in the EMU debates in order to retain potential voters who were attracted to the far-right Republikaner, which had campaigned on an anti-Europe platform. Specifically, the Republikaner appealed to those voters concerned with losing the DM to some "foreign" money.
105. Cited in Thomas Hanke, "Ein Streit um des Kaisers Bart," *Die Zeit,* March 7, 1991.
106. "Pöhl Says Germany and Its Neighbours Could Create Monetary Union Now," *Financial Times,* March 19, 1991.
107. "Few Expect Pöhl's Attack to Slow Monetary Union," *International Herald Tribune,* March 21, 1991. See also the analysis by Thomas Hanke and Wilfried Herz, "Rebellion im Nebensatz," *Die Zeit,* April 5, 1991.
108. "Hatching Out," *The Economist,* May 18, 1991.
109. "Die USA shauen gelassen auf den EG-Gipfel," *Der Tagesspiegel,* December 11, 1991.
110. "Bundesbank Deputy Calls for Tough Line on EMU," *Financial Times,* September 18, 1991. See also, "Bonn vor dem Konflikt mit der Bundesbank," *Frankfurter Allgemeine Zeitung,* September 20, 1991.
111. That some agreement would be reached still remained in doubt in the weeks before Maastricht. See the analysis in "Eine Schicksalgemeinschaft—verstrickt im Grabenkampf," *Berliner Zeitung,* November 29, 1991.
112. See Helmut Schmidt's analysis in "Europa muss die Weichen stellen," *Die Zeit,* December 6, 1991.
113. "The End Is Nigh," *The Economist,* September 28, 1991.
114. See the work of C. Randall Henning, *Cooperating with Europe's Monetary Union* (Washington, D.C.: Institute for International Economics, 1997). See also the analysis on exchange rate policymaking in the future EMU in Chapter 8, this volume.

115. The Bundesbank did release a statement pledging their unanimous support for EMU. Individual statements by Bundesbank council members reflected, as Schlesinger termed it, "personal opinions." See the interview with the Bundesbank president, "Technische Probleme," *Wirtschaftswoche*, March 20, 1992. See also the analysis of the Bundesbank's criticisms in David Marsh, *Die Bundesbank: Geschäfte mit der Macht* (Munich: Bertelsmann, 1992), chapter 9.

116. See the analysis in "Eine Mark für Zwölf," *Die Zeit,* December 20, 1991, p. 7.

117. "Deutschland ohne DM?" *Der Spiegel,* December 9, 1991.

118. See the issue of *Der Spiegel,* "Angst um die Mark," December 9, 1991. The mass-circulation *Bild Zeitung* launched repeated attacks on the plan. The author's own interviews with Germans during the Maastricht signing indicated the true lack of knowledge over the exact meaning of the treaty. Many could not fully comprehend that the Bundesbank would no longer set monetary policy or that the DM would no longer be the currency of Germany.

119. See the comments of Japanese ministers in "Even Facade of G7 Unity Shows Cracks," *The Japan Economic Journal*, October 6, 1990; and Beate Reszat, "Noch nicht begonnen: Währungskooperation am Ende?" *Wirtschaftswoche*, September 6, 1990.

120. The fact that the value of the dollar continued to weaken even during the heightened state of the international crisis in the Gulf indicated the belief in the markets that the economic negatives in the United States outweighed political considerations. The dollar normally had been a safe haven for international investments during international crises.

121. "Dollar's Plunge May Keep Rates Up, Economists Warn," *Los Angeles Times*, October 20, 1990.

122. International Monetary Fund, *Annual Report of the International Monetary Fund for 1990*, Washington, D.C, 1991, pp. 91–95.

123. Cohen, "The Triad and the Unholy Trinity," p. 145.

124. The Bundesbank move was met with heavy criticism from abroad. See the analysis in "U.S., Germany on Divergent Monetary Paths,*"* *Los Angeles Times*, February 11, 1991.

125. Ibid. The use of the term *promised* came from a senior U.S. Treasury official. The Bundesbank had suggested that no further rate increases were likely.

126. See the interview with Paul Krugman, Richard Rosecrance, John Rutledge, and Robert A. Mundell, "Must Americans Decline Along with the Dollar?" *Los Angeles Times*, February 10, 1991. The suggestion comes from Mundell.

127. Ibid. See especially the comments of Paul Krugman.

128. "Talking About the Dollar, Worrying About the Economy," *The Economist*, April 27, 1991.

129. "U.S.' Bid for Global Interest Rate Cut Fails," *Los Angeles Times*, April 29, 1991.

130. "U.S. Failure at G7 Reveals the Limits of Policy Making," *International Herald Tribune*, April 29, 1991.

131. See the analysis of Roger de Weck, "Mark und Macht," *Die Zeit*, May 2, 1991.

132. "The Diminished Fed," *The Economist*, May 4, 1991.

133. The meeting did manage to produce a vague written pledge to maintain growth-oriented policies and a close "monitoring of the situation."

134. "Talking Down the Dollar," *The Economist*, June 29, 1991. There was some speculation that central bankers had agreed to limit the rise of the dollar

through coordinated market intervention. A coordinated move on July 12 brought the dollar down 4 percent against the DM. However, the dollar strengthened somewhat thereafter, and no public comments could confirm or deny the move.

135. The Bundesbank had in July already lowered its monetary target corridors for 1991 from 4–6 percent to 3–5 percent, indicating the bank's intent on circumscribing the limits for the growth of M3. See Deutsche Bundesbank, *Monthly Report of the Deutsche Bundesbank,* July 1991 (Frankfurt/Main), p. 14. The Bundesbank was increasingly under domestic pressure to, at a maximum, ease monetary policy, and, at a minimum, stabilize rates at current levels. See also the analysis in "Ist die Geldpolitik zu restriktiv? Zeitgespräch mit Rüdiger Pohl, Manfred J. M. Neumann and Franco Reither," *Wirtschaftsdienst* 9 (1991), pp. 12–20.

136. "Schlesinger: Verständnis für deutsche Geldpolitik," *Frankfurter Allegemeine Zeitung*, October 16, 1991. See also "Tadel für den Musterschüler," *Die Zeit,* October 18, 1991.

137. "Economic Warfare, 1991 Style," *New York Times*, December 22, 1991.

5

Bundesbank Under Pressure, 1992–1993

> Foreign exchange markets are inhabited by nervous, myopic, private-sector herd animals, economically illiterate politicians and wide-eyed innocents masquerading as central bankers and monetary technocrats. How these players are driven matters little if no two experts agree on what the fundamentals are or how they affect exchange rates.
>
> —William Buiter, August 1993

Up until December 1991, the full economic and political impacts of GEMU and unification had not entirely been felt in Germany. A certain postunification optimism still prevailed in both the east and west as citizens and politicians alike looked toward a future of economic prosperity and continued political stability. Despite some dislocations and disruptions within eastern Germany and the application of a solidarity tax on western Germans to help pay for the massive transfer program under way, 1991 had brought a mini demand-push economic boom to the German economy. Chancellor Kohl continued to ride the crest of his all-German election victory in December 1990, firm in his belief that the costs (in terms of unemployment, budget deficits, and "temporary taxes") of unification could be kept within reason and limited to a short duration.

Responding to the inflationary pressures brought on by GEMU, the Bundesbank was not so optimistic or confident that it could remain within its stated monetary targets or restrain inflation to below 4 percent. In reaction to the perception that the Bundesbank had lost some of its policy credibility as a result of the GEMU decision, the bank was intent on re-establishing its credibility and leading position as the preeminent inflation-fighting central bank in Europe. Importantly, the Bundesbank sought to reassert autonomy over German monetary policy. The end result of the Bundesbank's concern was a highly restrictive monetary path from 1992 to 1993 that was determined to wring inflation out of the unified German economy.

On the European front, the signing of the Maastricht Treaty appeared to eliminate, at least formally, the future dilemma of trade-offs involving exchange rate stability and national monetary autonomy. German monetary authorities, including the Bundesbank, had negotiated strict entry requirements for future EMU. Nonetheless, the Bundesbank's singular influence over European monetary policy would eventually come to an end January 1, 1999, at the latest. Despite the well-designed plans for EMU, in September 1992, the EMS underwent a major transformation, culminating in the significant widening of the trading margins of the ERM of the EMS in August 1993. During the year-long monetary crisis, the complications of the unholy trinity presented tough choices to the Bundesbank and government. For many observers, Bundesbank intransigence put an end to further European monetary integration and the objectives of the Maastricht Treaty that were so painstakingly negotiated. Although an institutionalized forum of monetary interaction still existed, central banks of the EMS and Europe retained more potential policy latitude to pursue domestic monetary objectives. The year-long monetary crisis swept two members of the system (Italy and the UK) off the ship of monetary integration and ran the EMU ship aground on the banks of national interest, forcing member nations to again re-evaluate the trade-offs between exchange rate stability and national monetary autonomy. For the time being, autonomy appeared to be the prevailing policy option.

On the international front, the United States and the Bush administration were confronted by the effects of the recession and the rhetoric of an election year. These two facts should have indicated the less than favorable conditions for international monetary stability or international cooperation. First, as a result of the recession, the Bush administration was not interested in offering any concessions on the altar of international cooperation that might further weaken the economic position of the United States or the electoral position of the president. Second, the 1992 election indicated that American minds had focused inward to reorient government and public awareness on domestic issues. In one sense, the combination of these two factors resulted in a renewed bout of external benign neglect. In another sense, it could be expected that the United States would continue to pressure the Germans to play a more active role in stimulating global demand through a combination of fiscal and monetary policy. Finally, despite incoming president Clinton's attempt to reinvigorate G7 cooperation in 1993, the Sinatra doctrine of doing it "my way" continued to dominate G7 policy coordination.[1] The end result of German-U.S. monetary interaction was predictable, namely, tensions and little, if any, movement of international monetary cooperation.

What Happened to the Spirit of Maastricht?

The primary issue addressed in this chapter is how the well-designed plans of European Union,[2] built upon the solid foundations of the EMS, could almost collapse. In particular, what role did German monetary policy and the Bundesbank play in the year-long crisis? Did the underlying structural changes in the international environment—including instability generated from the United States on the monetary front—contribute to the instability and insecurity that Germany and the EU experienced through the period 1992–1993? Given the traditional dilemma faced by German monetary authorities over the trade-off between exchange rate stability and domestic monetary sovereignty and the extraordinary changes occurring in Germany and Europe, did the government pursue fundamentally different strategies than in years' prior? Or did the government remain firm to its European commitments? The following analysis suggests some possible answers to these questions.

The impact of the "asymmetric" shock of German reunification on the Bundesbank, German monetary policy, the EMS, and the international monetary system provides the central thematic thread to this chapter. The underlying domestic and international milieu within which the Bundesbank operated changed significantly. Most important, perhaps, the world changing beyond the borders of the EU, from the collapse of communism and the reunification of Germany, drastically altered the external dimension within which the EU operated. The EU, it should not be forgotten, was in part a creation of the Cold War. In fact, one can convincingly argue that the economic (and by the 1970s, monetary) integration pursued by the Europeans was the product of an interstate bargain driven by the imperatives of European political, economic, and military integration in the face of the overwhelming Soviet threat to their independence (as well as by the avoidance of war among European nations). Moreover, in the 1970s and 1980s, as some West Europeans sought to assert their independence militarily-strategically, diplomatically, and economically from the United States, it should not have been surprising to see efforts by the French and Germans to create a zone of monetary stability in order to shield themselves from international monetary (U.S. dollar) turbulence. The impact of the early 1990s recession in the United States and the inward-looking nature of an election year exacerbated fears of declining U.S. leadership and a further weakening of G7 cooperation. The United States was in the process, as it is today, of re-evaluating its position and redefining a new military-strategic and political-economic role in the world. In essence, the tensions that developed in the period 1992–1993 should be placed within the transforming context of the global distribution of power.

Second, the EU and the ERM of the EMS became a club that others wanted to join. In this regard, the institutional context of the EU maintained its powerful hold over nation-states. The "Europessimism" of the early 1980s gave way to "Europhoria" as the success of the ERM countries in achieving steady growth, and more important, low inflation, prompted Spain to join the EMS in June 1989, followed by Britain in October 1990 and finally the Portuguese in April of 1992. No longer was the EMS centered primarily and exclusively upon the Franco-German economic and monetary alliance. Moreover, the transitioning economies of the east, in particular, Poland, Hungary, and the Czech Republic, sought to join the EU within the next decade. Second, beginning with the Hanover summit of 1988, in which the EU decided to push ahead strongly with economic and monetary union, a strong consensus emerged around the belief that there was only one credible path toward promoting European integration. As a result, alternative proposals and concepts that did not meet the intellectual designs of the EU Commission and its president, Jacques Delors, may have been disregarded prematurely. Thus, as the tensions developed through 1992–1993, there was little room for discussion about pursing an alternative track toward European monetary integration. As one German finance ministry official stated, "Once the monetary train toward EMU started, there was little if any chance of stopping, turning around, or getting off."[3]

Finally, the hegemonic leader of the EMS, the Germans, through the credible anti-inflationary policies of the Bundesbank, experienced an unanticipated shock to the political and economic foundations of their stability-oriented social-market economy and leadership role in the EMS. The way in which the Germans politically and economically handled the shock of reunification, together with the worsening economic developments within EU countries, placed the stability consensus both within Germany and Europe in question. As a result, from 1992 onward, it became clear that there was no longer one single course that all EU countries were pursuing in terms of macroeconomic policy. In Germany, the inflationary pressures of unification led to the restrictive monetary policy path implemented through the Bundesbank's high nominal interest rates. The developing economic downturn in France with high unemployment (a downturn that was delayed in western Germany due to the postreunification boom) was sharpened by the high real interest rate, or *franc fort* (strong franc), policy that sought to align the franc tightly to the DM and uphold the quasi-fixed EMS, at least since 1987. The British sought largely to "free ride" their way to monetary stability. The inescapable contradiction in diverging policies spelled disaster for the EMS.

As a result of Germany's diverging national objectives and earlier experiences with the quasi-fixed ERM of the EMS and the Bretton Woods system, it should have become clear to all that nominally fixed monetary relations between nations in addition to independent autonomous monetary policies and a generally free flow of capital were not compatible—the unholy trinity.[4] However, up until September 1992, the conflict among these three objectives appeared for many European monetary politicians to be firmly resolved. With the dissolution of the last capital controls in 1990, most EU members adhered closely to the belief that if each country pursued convergent macroeconomic policies centered on the Bundesbank's hard anti-inflationary doctrine, nothing could derail monetary stability and the eventual goal of EMU. Since 1987, the ERM had become rigid in its application and thus was unable to adjust to economic shocks and dislocation. It worked well while Germany remained a strong and credible anchor of monetary equilibrium, yet this singular factor no longer held true.[5] Furthermore, the shock of reunification and the United States' own preoccupation with defining a new global role, whether military-strategic or economic, reinforced diverging national interests in the international monetary arena. In sum, the overarching bargaining context of deutsche mark politics had been notably transformed.

Bundesbank Policy

The objectives of the Bundesbank must be accurately characterized to understand fully the political economy of the prolonged monetary crisis in Europe and the lack of international monetary cooperation in this period. Due to the public and political backlash surrounding Maastricht and the GEMU decision, the Bundesbank, under the leadership of Helmut Schlesinger, sought to re-establish and reinvigorate its political position within Germany, Europe, and the G7. Bolstered by its primary institutional source of power, that is, interest rates, the Bundesbank pursued a strongly independent domestic monetary policy course. The Kohl government, in contrast, was increasingly put on the defensive for its plans for financing reunification and its 1990 election-year promises of a "second German economic miracle" in the east. As a result, the intra-German power-political landscape had shifted back in the direction of the Bundesbank. Although the Bundesbank would, in short, be criticized in some circles for its high interest rate policy, the bank, supported by the public's own concern over inflation and the potential loss of the DM to Europe, saw its bargaining leverage vis-à-vis the government strengthened.

In terms of specific policy, for those who claim that there was no indication of what was developing within Germany and what impact German monetary policy might have on Europe or the global economy, one need only point to the numerous statements made by Bundesbank officials or to the bank's published reports articulating its objectives. As early as 1990, the Bundesbank was of the view that,

> To the extent that the stability of exchange rates or even the pronounced strength of a number of partner currencies that do not belong to the "hard core" of the EMS can be explained essentially by inflation-induced higher rates of interest,[6] it can basically be justified only if it is consolidated by domestic economic policy durably geared to stability. If success is not achieved in coping with the structural causes of inflation within a reasonable period of time, it will probably become increasingly difficult over the long term to avoid having recourse to exchange rate adjustments.[7]

When German economic and monetary unification brought the internal monetary objective of price stability into conflict with Germany's external commitments to the EMS, the Bundesbank, as codified in the Bundesbank Law, responsibly requested that the federal government pursue a general realignment of the EMS and a DM revaluation. Due largely to the euphoria surrounding the monumental steps being advanced in anticipation of the Maastricht Treaty and the belief among the EMS participants and, in particular, the German government that a realignment—specifically, a revaluation of the DM coupled with a devaluation of the pound and other currencies—would be "inappropriate and bad timing," the Bundesbank plea was repeatedly disregarded.[8] The Bundesbank saw a realignment, however, as a necessary adjustment process required between the economies of the EU.

True to its strict monetary doctrine, the Bundesbank steadfastly held to its monetary targets and its primary monetary indicator, the broad-based medium-term M3, throughout the period 1990–1992, leading up to September 1992. The Bundesbank's monetary target corridors, however, were thrown off by the sharp asymmetric shock of GEMU and the strong demand push in western Germany caused by the postreunification boom. The result of these shocks was a steady rise in German interest rates as the Bundesbank sought to rein in the M3. The Bundesbank also cited the wage policies both in the east (the pace at which wages are to be equalized) and the west (unwarranted wage demands double the rate of inflation) as well as postunity financing and the deficit-creating fiscal policy of the government as the key factors in driving the potential inflationary spiral.[9] According to the Bundesbank, the bank might have even delayed a tighter monetary policy back in 1991 and into 1992 because of its concern with the effects that such a tightening would have on Europe.[10] Although such statements must be taken with a measure of skepticism, they do reflect the thinking among some members of the Bundesbank, even those with a more Europeanist orientation. Such thinking does suggest, however, that the

Bundesbank may have been willing to alter its policy to secure European exchange rate stability and cooperation.

Finally, an important factor that is often disregarded in analyses of this period of heightened European monetary tension was the dollar neglect of the Bush administration. During the summer, the dollar sank to historic lows (DM 1.40 to U.S.$1.00). As the primary transmitting agent of the dollar's influence in the EMS, the Bundesbank came under tremendous U.S. and European pressure to lower rates. Finding a policy equilibrium between maintaining monetary autonomy and exchange rate stability would prove difficult for the Bundesbank under these conditions. The Bundesbank's monetary policy was thus caught in a triple bind: (1) confronting the government's ill-defined financing plans for reunification and the developing economic slowdown in Germany on the domestic front; (2) confronting its EMS intervention commitments as well as the powerful driving forces of monetary integration surrounding Maastricht; and (3) confronting an indifferent U.S. dollar policy caught up in election-year imperatives and U.S. disinterest in the weakening dollar as many Bush administration officials saw a weak dollar as an effective means of fighting mounting trade deficits with Japan. Not surprisingly, when caught in this triple squeeze, the Bundesbank turned to its most potent political resource to ward off such pressure: its legally mandated duty to "safeguard the value of the currency." Without the option to pursue a realignment within the EMS and little if any control over the United States' dollar policy, the Bundesbank had only one course of action—raising interest rates. Given the rigidity of the ERM and divergent national interests and priorities, it was only a matter of time before market speculation, political indecisiveness, and the not-so-subtle monetary diplomacy of some EMS members triggered the crisis.

The Election-Year Neglect of the Dollar

Compelled by election-year motives and persistent trade imbalances, the Bush administration launched 1992 with "A Strategy for World Growth" that would include economy-boosting measures at home along with similar measures among the G7 members. Announced at a special Tokyo summit meeting between Bush and the Japanese prime minister, Kiichi Miyazawa, the initiative was aimed particularly at Germany. With the Japanese responding to U.S pressure by reducing the discount rate from 5 percent to 4.5 percent on December 30, 1991, and the dollar weakening slowly against the yen (a weakening supported by U.S. officials), the Germans now remained the focus for U.S., indeed G7, pressure. The statement and planning initiative announced by the United States and Japan was met, however, with skepticism and outright contempt by Germany. Bundesbank officials labeled the entire meeting an "exercise in rhetoric" that would have little, if any, impact on persuading the bank to lower interest rates. In fact, the Bundesbank had just recently raised interest rates in December of 1991. German monetary authorities in the finance ministry repeatedly pointed toward the increasing difficulties facing the reunified German economy, including inflation, and that Germany deserved some more understanding from its G3 partners. Already by the beginning of 1992, the tone and pattern of U.S.-German monetary interaction had been set.

The situation eased somewhat by the end of January at a G7 ministers' meeting in Garden City, New Jersey. The obligatory communiqué from the meeting explicitly recognized the German position on a medium-term course for growth and price stability. Interestingly, the communiqué also noted the G7's concern with high wage demands in Germany, especially as the new round of wage negotiations were about to begin in Germany. Reduced wage demands could ease the pressure on the Bundesbank to pursue lower interest rates. Bundesbank president Schlesinger noted specifically that only when "monetary growth slows and wage pressures ease, can we have room to lower interest rates."[11] No specific strategies, however, for coordinating world growth were discussed. Despite the lack of consensus on specific coordinated growth strategies, Treasury Secretary Brady optimistically labeled the meeting a "great success."[12] For the Bundesbank and Finance Minister Waigel, the meeting appeared to confirm Germany's "special" situation and position toward international monetary cooperation.

Surprisingly, the German position was substantially strengthened by support from an unlikely source, Britain. Robin Leigh-Pemberton, the governor of the Bank of England, stated his support for and full "faith" in the underlying strategy that the EMS had pursued since the late 1980s.[13] Sounding every bit the Bundesbank official, the governor supported the recipe for durable recovery based on the restoration of price stability and the pursuit of stable budgetary policies as the preconditions for sustainable growth. Moreover, from the German perspective, the governor expressed his explicit support (a view not necessarily shared by John Major) for the Bundesbank's counterinflationary policy. Leigh-Pemberton argued that "the importance of stability as the basis for sustainable growth is the reason I have considerable sympathy with the priority the Bundesbank gives to the fight against inflation."[14] With such strong support from some British officials, German monetary authorities could proceed with a stronger measure of confidence and bargaining strength heading into any European or G7 negotiations.

By April, the differences in fiscal, monetary, and overall economic policies could no longer be ignored by the G7. Global economic negotiations surrounding the oft-delayed GATT talks, diverging national macroeconomic policies, and the ongoing debates over financial support for the former Soviet republics and Russia, in particular, demanded that a concerted effort be undertaken by the G7 to develop a coordinated plan of action. Despite such imperatives, the April IMF/World Bank meeting indicated the marked differences in German, European, and U.S. interests. In response and before the meeting was even under way, Waigel said he was "not going to be put in the dock" over Germany's high public borrowing requirements and rejected U.S. and IMF protestations that Germany's overall fiscal deficit (at 6 percent of GDP) was too high.[15] Sensing the increased pressure on the Germans, Waigel stated forcefully that the demands and "accusations" would not serve anybody's interest in seeing the world economy grow. Schlesinger reinforced Waigel's and Germany's hard bargaining position by stating that the Bundesbank saw no room to lower interest rates in view of the rapid growth in Germany's monetary aggregates and inflationary pressure on the wage front.[16] The Bundesbank and federal government were pushing a united negotiating front.

The April IMF/World Bank meeting marked another significant low point in international economic cooperation. For the United States, the issues were clear: After three years of subpar growth, progress in the industrialized economies needed to be cranked up in order to end the recession. Addressing the G7, Brady said: "The time for concerted action to promote recovery and boost its strength is now. World growth is not like a light switch that can be turned on and off. It must be tended closely to be sure its flame does not flicker out."[17] From the German perspective and some European supporters, the issues were also clear. The flame should not flicker out, but it also should not be sparked up too quickly. International economic cooperation could only be expected when there was a convergence of underlying conditions among the major industrial countries. Moreover, the Germans resented what they considered the transparent use of the international financial arena to help get George Bush re-elected.[18] Horst Köhler, the German government's chief G7 trade and monetary negotiator, bristled at U.S. criticism, stating forcefully that "it was not acceptable that the deliberation of the G7 ministers should be burdened by one-sided and partly false public comments" by U.S. officials.[19] The diverging perspectives among many G7 members pointed toward a less than successful Munich G7 summit in July and increasing exchange rate pressures on the international and European monetary front.

Setting the Stage for Exchange Rate Instability

By the summer of 1992, the world's currencies stood suspended on financial markets as the markets attempted to interpret the G7's ongoing lack of coordination and the perception that German interest rates were exacerbating a weak European economic recovery. Despite diverging national economic priorities, exchange rate volatility had actually declined through the first months of 1992.[20] As an example, the dollar's fluctuation range against the DM in the first four months of 1992 was DM 0.50 to DM 0.68. In 1991, the range was 39 pfennigs and in 1985, the range was a staggering 105 pfennigs. The relative stability of the exchange rate range was attributed to the high priority given by all industrialized nations on combating inflation, the regional integration and stability of the EMS, and the greater skill of central bank intervention, as they did not have to defend specific currency rates. Nonetheless, these underlying structural factors should have suggested that the assumption of calm markets would be false. In addition, perhaps the biggest unknown on the horizon was the election in the United States. Consequently, with financial markets fearing the policies of potential "tax and spend" Democrats in the White House and as the Bush campaign headed into troubled waters through the summer of 1992, the potential for dollar instability increased. As the summer of 1992 heated up, the possibility that foreign exchange markets might test the ability of governments and central banks to defend particular rates also increased.

One of the first significant signs of trouble came from one of the smallest participants in European monetary affairs, the Danes. The Danish rejection of the Maastricht Treaty through a referendum in June unleashed the stored-up speculative pressures in the EMS. The impact of the referendum was an attack on the Danish krone and the Italian lira and increased instability within the EMS and foreign exchange markets in general. With uncertainty facing the upcoming G7 summit in July due to weak leaders presiding over feeble economies, foreign exchange markets quickly sensed the potential to secure short-term profits by attacking frail currencies. Despite intervention in the exchange markets to secure EMS parities, Bundesbank officials shrugged off any concern about what impact the Danish referendum might have on the EMS, monetary union, or Germany's monetary supply.[21] The smooth road toward monetary union or relative exchange rate stability remained clear for many analysts. Although the Danish vote did not fundamentally alter perceptions among leading monetary actors, the trouble that lay ahead was foreshadowed by the public backlash in Europe and foreign exchange market instability brought on by the referendum.

The diverging national interests and priorities characterizing the negotiating approach of the leaders of the G7 at the July summit in Munich were to be expected.[22] Facing a difficult election battle and unemployment figures for June 1992 in the United States reaching 7.8 percent, Bush had to hope that the Federal Reserve's 0.5 percent cut in interest rates would make a timely difference, for many Bush officials felt that little would be forthcoming from the G7.[23] The Japanese economy had slowed sharply, and sluggish growth rates indicated that large positive trade balances and current account surpluses for the Japanese would continue. The German government announced shortly before the G7 summit a tight budget for 1993 along with a plan for limiting the increase in its spending over the next four years to 2.5 percent a year. Kohl had hoped that movement on the budget deficit and government spending might ease the pressure on the Bundesbank to lower interest rates. Despite Kohl's efforts, the Bundesbank pointed discouragingly at excessive wage demands and increases in the M3. Otmar Issing, the Bundesbank's chief economist, indicated that monetary growth would have to fall before interest rates could be cut.[24] In fact, just two weeks after the Munich summit, on July 17, the Bundesbank raised its discount rate by a half percentage point to 8.75 percent, a postwar high.[25] The move only heightened the uncertainty and pressure within the EMS and on the dollar-DM rate.

Although some movement on aid to Russia was completed in Munich, there was little, if any, fundamental change in terms of converging increasingly divergent national economies. In fact, the lack of any significant movement at the Munich summit on G7 cooperation indicated that each participant country was unwilling to sacrifice domestic autonomy in return for a collective effort at global coordination of macroeconomic policies. Many commentators saw a lost opportunity at Munich to develop the G7 into an "economic security council" for the increasingly unstable world. For many, the credibility of the entire G7 process and leadership had been damaged. Despite some of the problems resulting from failed efforts at international coordination, as in trade talks, for example, from the German perspective, greater efforts at cooperation could not and should not have been expected. Following the Munich summit Köhler articulated the German position toward G7 cooperation:

> If individual countries fail to put their own house in order, the aggregate strategy pursued by G7 countries as a group will also fail. Successful coordination in the sense of a common policy to strengthen global economic growth can be achieved only if each country's own national problems are resolutely tackled. In other words, coordination will not make sense if national problems remain unresolved. . . . Economic policy coordination, with an orientation towards the medium term and agreement on the basic principles, is still the right approach.[26]

While recognizing the importance of international economic coordination, Köhler's approach, indeed the whole German approach toward coordination, appeared to preclude any joint effort to attack the similar domestic economic problems facing many G7 nations.

Given Germany's own problems in resolutely tackling the budget deficit or the financing of reunification and the United States being engaged in an electoral year fit of monetary neglect, the stage was set for the August crisis of the dollar. Following the less than successful Munich summit and the July 17 rise in the discount rate, the dollar slipped into near record-low territory. By the end of July the dollar bought 1.45 DMs. In order to stem the fall of the dollar further, central banks from Europe, including the Bundesbank, followed the Federal Reserve's lead in buying dollars on the open market. Most analysts expected the instability to continue and predicted that the central banks would not be able to stop the decline of the dollar, an indication of the power of financial flows overwhelming central bank willingness to expend reserves on a futile effort to support a weakening currency. The Bundesbank was, as it often is in terms of dollar interventions, hesitant in its foreign exchange market operations. Although the Germans could accurately maintain that long-term interest rates were not that far apart, short-term rates differed substantially, from 9 percent in Germany to 3–4 percent in the United States. On August 28, the differential between U.S. and German short-term rates stood at 6.5 percent.[27] Seeking a higher return, dollars continued to flow into DM accounts.

Bush's acceptance speech at the Republican convention in August further led to speculative pressures against the dollar. His speech, in which he proposed a vague plan of federal tax cuts and spending cuts for 1993, was not well received in financial circles and pointed to the lack of confidence in the ability of the United States to reduce its deficit and get the economy moving again. Concern spread in financial markets that the Federal Reserve would have to raise interest rates in order to stem the outflow of dollars, further unnerving U.S. stock markets. On Friday, August 21, the dollar, which had stood at DM 1.65 in April of 1992, now bought only DM 1.42, a new postwar record low. Although the weak dollar benefited U.S. competitiveness abroad, the sharp decline of the dollar and the inability of central banks to stem that fall raised the possibility of a dollar free fall. Based on the belief in foreign exchange markets that the Bush administration was solely interested in seeing the trade deficit dealt with through a weak dollar policy, it would remain easy for currency traders to speculate against the dollar. Reflecting on the instability and the 75-point two-day drop (August 20–21) in the Dow Jones, some commentators pointed to a similar set of factors—rising interest rates, a sinking dollar—back in October of 1987. On Monday, August 24, the dollar stood at another postwar low of 1.40, having briefly dropped to 1.39 in early trading on Asian markets.

The inability of the G7 to act concertedly either through central bank intervention, G7 summitry, or through other official institutional avenues hinted at the problem countries had in managing the massive financial flows that elusively remained beyond the domestic controls of nations. Moreover, the rather sharp drop in the dollar over the period of four months further exacerbated tensions that had been developing within the

EMS. Specifically, with the DM gaining in strength and with interest rates high in Germany, other EMS central banks had to either face a realignment within the ERM (meaning a devaluation of their currencies vis-à-vis the DM) or raise their interest rates (furthering dampening economic activity at home) to keep their currencies on par with the strengthening DM within the narrow trading margins of the ERM. In my opinion, it is, therefore, important to note that external or global monetary disturbances brought on by the election-year benign neglect in the United States helped precipitate the September 1992 crisis within the EMS. In fact, Germany's and other G7 members' lack of collective commitment at the international level to stabilize exchange rates merely exacerbated the underlying pressures of the EMS. This point is often forgotten in many analyses of the EMS crises of September 1992 and August 1993.

**Turmoil on the European Front:
The British and Italian Exit from the EMS**

The primary "fault line" within the EMS through the summer of 1992 and up until the British exit from the EMS developed between Frankfurt and London, although, as I have suggested, the line extended across the Atlantic to Washington, D.C.[28] The British, for their part, increasingly aimed their interest rate policy at domestic goals with complete disregard for external monetary implications, lowering their base interest rate from 15 percent in October 1990, the date they entered the EMS, to 10 percent in May 1992.[29] As a result of the less than credible British commitment to the EMS, the sterling rate came under extreme pressure in the context of doubts surrounding the Maastricht Treaty and the British government's reluctance to raise interest rates to support the pound in the ERM.[30] In response, the British chancellor of the Exchequer, Norman Lamont, called for an ECOFIN meeting on September 4–5 to pressure the Germans to lower interest rates and to discuss how much more of the hard pounding the ERM currencies could sustain. British prime minister John Major asserted British confidence that the ERM would continue to be successful regardless of what happened to the Maastricht Treaty.

What might have been a promising and unique opportunity to discuss the central mechanical and technical problems of the ERM, the Bath summit merely underlined Germany's dominant economic and political role in the EU and Germany's sensitivity to inflation. The Bundesbank was asked at the meeting, even pleaded with, to promise it would not raise interest rates in the near future.[31] The Bundesbank did make a vague promise not to raise rates in the "near future," but the lack of specified conditions detailing how or why the Bundesbank would not raise rates further fueled the speculation. The EU ministers reaffirmed their commitment to fixed exchange rates, but Bundesbank president Helmut Schlesinger declined to give his full support to the communiqué. Schlesinger instead insisted that the German position not to raise interest rates in the near future was consistent with what the Bundesbank council had agreed upon at their regular Thursday meeting on September 3.

Both the British and the Germans realized that the credibility of the ERM and the future operation of the EMS were at stake. The problem was that the more doubtful the political commitment to EMS became, the more it should have been reasserted. But the costlier the commitment became, politically and financially, the more it had to be doubted by the markets. What is ironic is that the German delegation appeared to be willing to negotiate going into the meeting at Bath. Köhler and Schlesinger both pleaded with Lamont to place the idea of an interest rate cut as part of a general realignment of the entire system on the agenda.[32] The British, however, were unwilling to accept the trade-off of a German interest rate cut for a possible devaluation of the pound.

As a result of the inability to reach a satisfactory conclusion at Bath, tensions in the EMS quickly resurfaced as the markets launched renewed speculative attacks against the Italian lira. With the Bundesbank intervening massively to support the lira and other EMS currencies, the Germans, including Kohl, again demanded an ECOFIN meeting to suggest a general realignment in return for a German interest rate cut.[33] Following the ECOFIN announcement of September 13 of a lira devaluation of 3 percent (the British again refused to consider a devaluation of the pound) and an unusual Bundesbank promise to move on interest rates, Schlesinger convened the Bundesbank council on September 14 in an unprecedented Monday meeting to push through an interest rate cut of 0.25 percent in the Lombard rate and a 0.5 percent cut in the discount rate, the first rate cut since 1987. It appeared to many observers that the crisis had been resolved, that the Bundesbank had finally placed European interests ahead of domestic interests, and that the British had secured a minor diplomatic victory.[34]

Once the markets reacted to the less than expected size of rate cut, the British and Italian currencies came under renewed pressure—the British pound closing the September 15 day's trading only two pfennig away from its ERM-defined floor of DM 2.778.[35] The subsequent interview with Schlesinger in the German *Handelsblatt* on September 15, which implied that the system could have been further eased if there had been a more comprehensive realignment—which was interpreted by many as a signal to the markets that the pound should have been included—helped trigger renewed pressures. When the markets opened on September 16, there was massive selling of the pound. At various points through the day the British raised interest rates, first to 12 percent then to 15 percent. At this point, the

British essentially had three options: (1) continue to raise interest rates as had the Swedes; (2) temporarily suspend the pound from the ERM; or (3) announce an indefinite suspension of the pound.[36] Option one was rejected on the grounds that it was not clear whether it would have been effective, and option two was rejected because the pound would have had to re-enter the ERM at a devalued parity. Although the other ERM countries pleaded with the British to choose option two, Lamont announced at the end of the day that the UK, in its "best interests," was suspending membership in the ERM indefinitely. At the emergency Monetary Committee meeting that evening, called for by Lamont, the British urged a suspension of the entire ERM and a general float of all currencies. The Monetary Committee rejected the British proposal, briefly noting in its communiqué that it "took note" of the British decision to suspend.[37] According to *Financial Times*, the ERM members saw the UK proposal as an attempt to save political face at home, and as a threat to the future of the EMS.[38]

The disarray in the ERM would at best delay and at worst destroy the EU's hopes for economic and monetary union by the end of the century. The troubles and tensions within the EMS might have been avoided and the EMS strengthened, however, if the central banks involved had, at a minimum, cooperated more intensively on intervention strategies and, at a maximum, coordinated their monetary policies through 1992. Central banks could have consulted more closely with one another in assessing the impact of increasingly divergent monetary policies and whether German interest rates should have been lowered earlier. A critical failure was that the remaining EMS countries in September 1992 did not seek to stabilize the system. A realignment may have gradually eased the market pressures. Moreover, to re-establish the credibility of the system after the lira was first devalued, the new parity of the lira had to be defended. The Italian Central Bank had few reserves left; it could only have survived with massive support from the Bundesbank and the Bank of France. With all central banks making a firm commitment at that point through intervention to support the lira and through a coordinated monetary strategy on the ERM in general, the future of the EMS and EMU could possibly have been rescued.

Adding to the triangular pressure on German monetary authorities, at the IMF/World Bank meetings in late September, U.S. undersecretary of the treasury David Mulford stated that the United States was always of the opinion that it would be useful for Germany to lower its interest rates. Schlesinger, having resisted European pressure for so long, was in no mood to hear the United States talk of Germany's monetary unilateralism and rebuffed Mulford's pressure by insisting that the Germans had even less room for maneuvering than before the September crisis. Waigel stated bluntly that "Germany is not responsible for the currency turmoil."[39]

Nonetheless, the G7 ritualistically called for further monetary coordination, forgetting that each nation had unilaterally pursued its own national monetary objectives autonomously, with little regard for external exchange rate stability.[40] The G7 only had itself to blame for the crisis as monetary cooperation lay in near ruins.[41]

Bundesbank As Scapegoat?

The Black September crisis in the EMS and the ongoing lack of collective G7 policy coordination seem to suggest that German monetary policy had entered a new phase of noncooperation. In response to inflationary pressures within Germany, the Bundesbank appeared intent on going its own way, with complete disregard for the externalities associated with its policies. In some sense this was in fact true, and in this section I critique whether the Bundesbank policies were indeed appropriate for internal and external conditions. The picture, however, is not so clear, and blame can be given equally to the German government and other EU governments. More important, I believe, the Bundesbank decision to respond with a cut in interest rates on September 14, albeit small, under intense governmental pressure and external pressure within the ECOFIN meetings did indicate an unusual willingness to adjust its policies to external circumstances. Cooperation accurately characterizes the Bundesbank's decision to lower rates. Moreover, the decision to lower rates came about as a direct result of the institutionalized bargaining forum of ECOFIN (or in Schlesinger's terms, "external factors") and would not have come about had not the institutional and organizational elements of the EU existed. The Bundesbank had initially agreed not to *raise* rates in the near future. They had not promised to lower rates in the near future, but this is exactly what they ended up doing.

The problem that developed during the heated negotiations in September, over the period 1990–1992, was not primarily with the Bundesbank but rather with the participating governments in the EMS. One of the most frequently asked questions surrounding the September tensions was why there was no early realignment of currencies that, after all, had in the past been a practical and useful mechanism to ease pressure within the EMS. The EMS, it should be remembered, was never a fixed exchange rate mechanism but instead a semi-fixed adjustable mechanism of monetary interaction among member countries (the EMS had not experienced a realignment since January 1987). Foreseeing the tensions that were developing, an editorial in *The Economist* stated in 1992 that had the DM been revalued in 1990, it would have been helpful in dampening the economic boom in Germany and the inflationary pressures that developed because of reunification. As a result, the inflation that developed could have been kept in check with lower interest rates.[42] Other ERM countries might, in turn, have lowered their interest rates, which, in addition to possibly spurring investment and easing unemployment, could have spurred the export sector as well.

Two actors in this drama realized early on that a realignment could possibly diffuse the tensions that had been generated within the EMS by the diverging policies of the EMS members. First, the Bundesbank at the time of German monetary unification saw a realignment of the EMS as a necessary step in the adjustment processes required between the economies of the EU.[43] Interestingly, however, although the Bundesbank received a lot of external (European and U.S.) and internal (labor unions, Social Democratic Party) criticism over its interest rate policy, lower inflation brought on by a realignment might not have spurred the Bundesbank to lower interest rates further or quicker. The Bundesbank's policy was also a signal to Bonn to tighten its fiscal policy and to discourage wage unions from seeking wage parity in the east and west. Second, the exchange markets also realized that a realignment was necessary. As long as the governments of Germany and France held fast to the *franc fort* policy and with the lukewarm British commitment to the EMS, the markets could continue to test the foreign exchange markets.

Therefore, short of a significantly softer line by the Bundesbank on interest rates and the reimposition of capital controls on the foreign exchange markets,[44] there are several interrelated answers to the question of why there was no movement for a realignment. First, the outright refusal of the British to devalue and accept certain minimum standards of ERM membership (closer consultation among central banks and government officials on the course of future monetary policy), and the refusal of the French to back down from their *franc fort* policy, a problem that would resurface through 1993, indicated an increasingly inflexible negotiating environment. As the British entered the ERM in October 1990, the Bank of England indicated that it would follow strict guidelines for membership, including the use of realignments as a last resort. There also existed considerable resentment both in France and Germany over the conditions of British entry, including the pound's central rate in the ERM (DM 2.95) and the political timing of the final announcement coming on the last day of Labor's annual party conference.[45] In addition, French finance minister Pierre Bérégovoy repeatedly pledged that if a realignment within the ERM were to occur, the French franc would be revalued upward in the same proportion as the DM.

Closely related, the second answer to "why no realignment?" was the rapid push toward EMU. The quickness with which the complex details of the Maastricht Treaty were negotiated made a realignment during 1990–1992 politically awkward. In theory, successive realignments would have helped overcome the developing monetary frictions, leading to a gradual adjustment and economic convergence that, in the long term, would have enabled the return to more stable exchange rates. Gradual adjustments were the way the EMS worked in the beginning. But with the emerging plans for EMU, the political context of the system changed significantly. Adjustment through realignment was practically ruled out as a policy option. Even at the time of the collapse of the Berlin Wall and with the Bundesbank already beginning its tight monetary policy, former Bundesbank president Karl Otto Pöhl commented that "the political will" was "lacking" for an ERM realignment.[46] As one German finance ministry official bluntly stated, "the timing of Maastricht made a realignment impossible."[47] Moreover, exchange rate stability over a period of two years had been a key convergence condition required to qualify for EMU under the Maastricht provisions.

On both counts, the situation was further complicated by the lack of political leadership by the German government within Europe. In January 1990, Pöhl indicated that a realignment of the EMS was not on the agenda of most EMS member states, making it clear that it was not only the French who were opposed to a DM revaluation but also the German government that did not want to push for a politically awkward realignment.[48] Such a public statement from the Bundesbank president could only have strengthened the bargaining hand of France and Britain and their refusal to consider a realignment. In fact, one of the primary reasons for rapidly pushing forward with the Maastricht plan was to cope with the perceived newfound strength of a reunited Germany. Ironically, what had become obvious was that the more immediate threat was Germany's newfound political and economic weakness. That the Bundesbank was unable to pressure the federal government to more vigorously push through a realignment should not have been surprising. The domestic political problems over immigration, financing reunification, and devising a coherent security policy paralyzed German leadership in the EMS at a time it was most needed.

By 1992, the benefits of a revaluation of the DM were less than clear. A sizable revaluation of the DM on the scale of around 10 percent would have helped ease inflationary pressures in Germany and perhaps allowed the Bundesbank to lower interest rates. However, a revaluation of the DM of such a magnitude might have resulted in a corresponding large devaluation of other ERM currencies. A devaluation might have helped the export trade balance but it also might have damaged the hard-won anti-inflationary credibility many EMS countries had built up over the prior five years. Moreover, any realignment after a long period of stability, by 1992 close to five years, could possibly have increased the perceived risk of future devaluation on non-German currencies. Such speculation about realignments had already occurred from the autumn of 1991 through 1992. Moreover, a revaluation of the DM might have made exports of other ERM countries more attractive, but they would have had to be large to actually make a significant difference.

As a comparison, under the Bretton Woods monetary system, realignments were permitted when a currency was in "fundamental disequilibrium," which was never clearly defined, and exchange rates could only be supported at the cost of undesirable distortions in domestic economic policy, for example, for the West Germans, imported inflation. That system broke down when disagreements between the United States and Europe over underlying macroeconomic policy became irreconcilable. In the case of the EMS, a more painful policy conflict existed where the combination of loose fiscal policy and tight money in Germany had the effect of exporting deflation to the rest of the ERM. As with Bretton Woods, the changes in the EMS in September 1992 were merely a temporary solution to the fundamental policy differences that could only be solved by a major agreement encompassing realignment, a Bundesbank interest rate cut, and a possible widening of the trading bands for some EMS currencies.

In a sense, the bargaining framework within Germany and Europe had been reversed: It was the Bundesbank that was interested in seeing a realignment of the EMS currencies, but it was the German government, along with the governments in other EMS countries, that would not initialize the process. From 1990 through September 1992, the Bundesbank could not convince the governmental participants of the benefits of a proposal to realign. The political costs for EMS governments associated with a realignment outweighed central bank concerns over the increasingly inflexible EMS.

As the September crisis illustrates, it takes more than central bank action to see a comprehensive cooperative agreement. Not surprisingly, in such a complex negotiating game, governments, not independent central banks, can actively scuttle cooperative monetary agreements. The resulting combination of Bundesbank and federal government preferences made finding a mutually agreeable and cooperative solution difficult if not impossible.

Franc Fort Under Pressure

Following the destructive events of Black September, the Bundesbank articulated its vision of Europe's future, one that amounted to a monetary survival of the fittest.[49] While the Bundesbank expressed public support for the goals of economic and monetary union in accordance with Maastricht, it expressed doubt about the effectiveness of the economic convergence criteria in the treaty. The bank also cited the lack of clarity about the treaty's weak provisions on political union, a union that might provide a democratic foundation of support for the goals of a single European currency and central bank. Rejecting the hope that all members of the EU could proceed together toward EMU, Schlesinger insisted that there would be no compromise in Europe with the bank's domestic objective of achieving price stability. Countries were welcome to try to fix their currencies to the DM, but it would be up to them to make the "right choice" among various economic policies that ensured their economic fundamentals—inflation, international competitiveness, and public finances—were in order.

The Bundesbank's tough talk was backed up with tough policy. When the Spanish peseta and the Portuguese escudo were both devalued by 6 percent on November 22, 1992, the Bundesbank resisted further pressure to cut interest rates and refused to compromise its strict anti-inflationary monetary policy. Even with a slight easing of German interest rates through the spring of 1993, the EMS experienced continuing stability problems. These problems were heightened by ongoing dollar-DM tensions brought on by the election of Bill Clinton in November 1992, the fear of the incoming president's potentially inflationary domestic agenda, the upcoming French parliamentary elections in March, and inward-looking German politicians and central bankers. The Irish punt was devalued by 10 percent on February 1, the Spanish peseta was devalued another 8 percent, and the escudo another 6.5 percent on May 14, 1993.[50] The Bundesbank offered only limited intervention support for these currencies, although on February 4 the bank did make an effort to ease the pressure within the EMS with an unexpected lowering of the Lombard rate a half point to 9 percent and the discount rate by a quarter point to 8 percent. Bundesbank officials indicated the rate cut was aimed primarily at domestic actors as well as the bank's concern with the ERM. Nonetheless, those countries perceived to be outside a developing "hard core" of the ERM faced an uncertain and Darwinistic monetary and exchange rate environment.

Instead, the link between the franc and the DM became the central focal point for ERM relations and the overall survival of the EMS between September 1992 and August 1993. Following the crisis in September, a franc devaluation would have been seen as an even larger blow to the political prestige of President Mitterand and to Prime Minister Bérégovoy, who made the *franc fort* the center of his economic policy. Moreover, a franc devaluation would also have demonstrated that the ERM was operating perversely by creating the conditions for the depreciation of a currency, the franc, which in terms of current economic fundamentals deserved to be stronger than the DM. The first major test of the link was the intense speculative attack on the franc following the weak *"oui"* in the

September 20 French referendum on the Maastricht Treaty. In spite of sound economic fundamentals, such as low inflation, stronger growth, and healthier government finances than those of Germany, the Bundesbank and the Bank of France had to buy Fr 160 billion in concerted intervention to curb the first post–Black September speculative wave.[51]

That initial attempt to support the franc indicated a significant turning point in Bundesbank policy. Although the Bundesbank appeared reluctant, even outright adamant, in its opposition to any large-scale intervention efforts that might influence German money supply, the bank and the government were extremely willing to commit substantial political and financial support to the French. The two central banks coordinated their policies closely; for example, the Bundesbank provided the French with a generous swap line. While the Irish, Danish, Norwegians, and Swedes experienced similar pressure, the Bundesbank was not willing to extend its generous French package to them. Moreover, the February 4 decision by the Bundesbank to lower its rates came largely in response to the intense pressure from the French on Kohl and the Bundesbank. Schlesinger noted the importance of the cuts for the future of the EMS. "We hope this unfriendly game sometimes called dominoes, in which speculators pick on one currency after another, has finally come to an end."[52] The French finance ministry responded that the German move was seen by the French as a gesture that should help the EMS get some stability back.

Between September 1992 and August 1993, a great deal of conjecture surfaced on the motives behind the tight Franco-German monetary axis. Most of this conjecture focused on the possibility of a rapid acceleration of monetary union centering on a quick jump to Stage 3 of the Maastricht Treaty.[53] Such speculation was supported by a private meeting between Kohl and Mitterand two days after the French vote on Maastricht. The conjecture was concretely supported by the close cooperation between the Bank of France and the Bundesbank in propping up the franc. Moreover, Jacques Delors's suggestion that "others may take the lead" in European monetary integration if some just looked for alibis (implying the British) added further fuel to the speculation. Finally, the ongoing, sometimes nasty, recriminations between the British and the Germans over each other's conduct during the September crisis indicated a sharp divergence of opinion over who would (Germany and France) and would not (the Italians and the British) be involved in the future European monetary union.[54]

How did the French gain the needed monetary and political support of the Germans? The French government's economic objectives since Mitterand's macroeconomic volte-face in 1983 and its rigid support of the *franc fort* policy were primarily launched to put an end to soaring budget and trade deficits, rising inflation, and repeated devaluations. This policy soon worked and became the centerpiece of France's gradual conversion to market economics in the official political and economic establishment. The *franc fort* policy also became the official starting point for all subsequent French goals concerning the future of the EU. With the success of the *franc fort* policy, French politicians, buttressed by a broad public support and consensus for the policy, could more easily move forward with such far-reaching agreements as the 1985 program for a Single European Market (codified in the Single European Act of 1986) as well as proposing large sections of the plan for economic and monetary union incorporated into the Maastricht Treaty.

More important, perhaps, were the larger political ramifications of the *franc fort* policy and France's relationship to Germany. The policy developed within French politicians the confidence and assurance that they could compete on an equal economic level with the Germans. The French had always known that they were economically weaker than the Germans but maintained a certain political dominance through France's possession of nuclear weapons and its permanent seat on the UN Security Council. Symbolized by the close relationship of Chancellor Kohl and President Mitterand, each nation believed that further European integration and monetary union, in particular, would benefit both countries absolutely. Although Mitterand initially hesitated in support of quick German reunification, both he and Kohl quickly realized that German reunification within the boundaries of the EU and the emerging structures of a federal Europe with one currency could only enhance each country's position in the world. The problem for the French was that the *franc fort* policy became more than an economic policy decision. It soon became a political symbol of French energy and fortitude. If the franc were forced to exit the ERM or face a large devaluation, the damage to the public support for Maastricht would be incalculable and would also raise the possibility of divisions in the governing conservative coalition in France.[55]

Furthermore, the Bundesbank's generous support of the French was based on the belief that the French had made a credible commitment to the so-called coronation theory of EMU. According to the coronation theory, EMU would result after a long process of convergence of national economic and monetary policies. By attaching the franc closely to the value of the DM and the Bundesbank's monetary policies, the French soon became a credible member of the convergence club. As the tensions mounted in 1992–1993, the Bundesbank did not have the resources to provide unlimited support to all EMS currencies, only to those members who belonged to the ERM convergence club. In addition, the French were not only importantly monetarily but politically as well, as France's participation in EMU was essential to the entire process of European integration. As some analysts have speculated, Germany may have seen the opportunity in September to "purge" the EMS's hard core of uncommitted or other "soft currencies."[56] The Bundesbank could finally create a monetary union more in line with its own coronation model. Finally, the Kohl government and Bundesbank's position toward exchange rate stability and European integration converged on the Franco-German axis, cemented upon political and monetary cooperation. Despite the exit of the British and Italians, the German monetary authorities indicated through late 1992 and into 1993 their continued willingness, namely, extensive central bank coordination and intervention in addition to the rate cuts on February 4, March 18, and April 21, 1993, to sacrifice a measure of domestic autonomy for their French partners all in the name of EMU.[57]

The Widening of the Trading Margins

Despite the Bundesbank's gradual reduction in interest rates, tensions within the existing EMS group of countries again resurfaced strongly by the summer of 1993. Increased calls arose among some members, including former member Great Britain, of the EMS to fundamentally alter the operation of the system or disband it altogether. An influential group of economists argued that the turmoil in the currency markets and the broader crisis of unemployment in Europe—12.5 percent in France, 22 percent in Spain, more than 3 million in Germany—provided enough evidence that the EMS had become profoundly counterproductive.[58] Even with the Italians and British out of the system, the inflexible EMS mechanism of intervention continued to be strained due to the continued dominance of the Bundesbank's high interest rate policy and France's *franc fort* policy. There were even serious discussions concerning the replacement of the DM by the franc as the anchor currency in the ERM as a series of interest rate reductions led by the French pushed French short-term interest rates below the Germans.[59]

Such speculation over the role of the franc as the new anchor currency of the EMS never caught up with actual events. With money-supply growth figures in Germany still running over 7 percent, above the Bundesbank's 4.5–6.5 percent target for 1993, and with inflation running at an annual rate of 4.3 percent through July, the Bundesbank could not have been expected to save the EMS with an interest rate cut at the last meeting before the bank's summer pause. On July 30, the Bundesbank did cut the Lombard rate by a half a point, from 8.25 percent to 7.75 percent, but as some analysts stated, the cut was purely symbolic and would only cause irritation at best.[60] The narrow easing of rates, including the small reduction of the securities repurchase (repo) rate to 6.95 percent, did not save the EMS. In fact, it helped trigger a renewed crisis. The markets were looking for more. Following the Bundesbank's decision on Thursday morning, the rest of Thursday and Friday saw European central banks spending an estimated DM 75 billion (U.S.$43 billion) propping up weak currencies. The Bundesbank alone, it was estimated, spent up to DM 60 billion on ERM intervention for the week, although efforts were made to sterilize the impact of the extra liquidity.

In the absence of a realignment of exchange rates, the refusal of the Bundesbank to lower rates as much as others wanted produced the subsequent high-powered ministerial meeting that spawned, in the words of Wim Kok, Dutch finance minister, "the worst but one solution."[61] The minimum point of agreement was that the ERM and its central parity grid had to be preserved. The institutions of the EMS had to be maintained, whatever the political or economic costs to most of the participating member countries, including Germany. The main difficulty, though, was France's absolute refusal to accept a devaluation of the franc and the Bundesbank's staunch insistence—supported by the Kohl government—that it could not be expected to provide unlimited intervention. At one point, though, the Germans and the French appeared to have achieved a compromise solution in which the Germans, who preferred to see the margins of fluctuation widened, agreed to leave the ERM.[62] As soon as the Netherlands as well as Denmark, Belgium, and Luxembourg found out about the plan, they balked and stated their intentions to pull out of the ERM as well, despite the immense French pressure placed on the Dutch to break their link to the DM. However, with Delors personally opposing the German exit—which would have been seen as a fatal blow to Maastricht—and the Dutch holding firm, the talks returned to a widening of the bands. Moreover, all participants could not picture a future credible EMS with France sitting all alone in the ERM with Spain and Portugal.

Recognizing that the future of the EMS and EU depended on a Franco-German solution, and wanting to break the logjam, Germany proposed that the French widen their fluctuation bands to approximately 6 percent, with an implicit promise, made more credible by the appearance of Schlesinger and the Bundesbank vice president, Hans Tietmeyer, at the bargaining table, that the Germans cut their interest rates. The French refused the offer, interpreting it as a de facto devaluation of the franc and placing it among the EMS's second tier, Spain and Portugal. In addition, the French were extremely hesitant to test the margins at 6 percent. Finally, after numerous variations on currency bands and particular currencies, a solution was found: a fluctuation band of about 15 percent for all currencies except the DM and the Dutch guilder.[63] The aim was to disguise a de facto French devaluation as well as the de facto suspension of the system. Nevertheless, the monetary institutions of the EU had survived. Despite extremely difficult circumstances, a minimum level of cooperation had emerged.

Clinton, the G7, and a Global Approach to Economic Growth

The election of Democrat Bill Clinton to the presidency put on hold any movement on the international monetary front until a February 1993 G7 meeting of finance ministers. Moreover, the global economic situation was dominated by many of the same problems facing the United States and its partners over the prior year: the global economy stuck in recession or subpar growth; ongoing disputes over trade and GATT, persistent U.S. trade deficits with Japan (in 1992, a then record U.S.$133 billion); and, finally, the deteriorating economic situation in the republics of the former Soviet Union. In order to address these problems, the Clinton administration was set on pursuing a more cooperative and consensus-oriented approach toward international macroeconomic coordination and moving away from the Sinatra doctrine of 1992. With a new young and active president in the White House and an experienced negotiator in the Treasury Department in the person of Lloyd Bentsen, there existed room for optimism that G7 cooperation would prosper.

Despite the rhetoric about "bold experiments" in the field of international cooperation, the Clinton "solution" to problems at home and abroad was based on the same old precepts of earlier U.S. administrations, in particular, trying to solve domestic problems through pressure on G7 partners. The Clinton administration had promised that it would seriously deal with the persistent budget deficits through a comprehensive tax-and-spending plan and that it was also interested in a stimulus package that would boost job growth and economic opportunities. What was not clear was whether Clinton could deliver. Instead, the United States looked to its European and Japanese partners for similar measures that would give a quick boost to global economic growth, and with it the demand for U.S. products. According to other G7 nations, such U.S. claims remained dubious, the pressure familiar. For the Japanese, this meant a return of U.S. pressure for a massive stimulus package at home as well as a lower dollar to stimulate U.S. exports. Bentsen's early attempts to "talk" down the dollar reflected for many Japanese politicians the return of "dollar politics." With Japanese interest rates at record lows and with an unusually strong Japanese recession limiting the amount of import goods bought by Japanese consumers, the Japanese, for their part, were not initially inclined to view the U.S. pressure positively. The finance ministry's fear of budget deficits constrained any effort of the Japanese government to push for a major stimulus package.

The same could be said of the Germans. Continued to be burdened by the massive costs of reunification and the inability to build a credible plan or concept for the financing of the entire process, Waigel pleaded at the special February G7 meeting of finance ministers that the Germans required further time to deal with their unique problems. Waigel also maintained that the Germans were in the process of consolidating their finances and reducing the government's deficits, which would, in turn, ease the pressure on the Bundesbank to lower interest rates. The Bundesbank, however, was not as optimistic as Waigel. The Bundesbank continued to hear U.S. voices, in addition to the European voices, demanding lower interest rates, yet the bank sought at every point to redirect the pressure onto the federal government.[64] The Bundesbank's Hans Tietmeyer asserted that the bank was interested in lowering interest rates, but that it would only come about if all the G7 governments could control their fiscal deficits and public debt.[65] In fact, in 1993 the Bundesbank had already begun to cautiously and incrementally lower interest rates. The debate centered on the pace (too slow for many, too fast for some) and degree (not enough for some, too far for others) of reduction.

A G7 informal meeting in February that had been called together by Clinton did not result in any new or spectacular growth initiatives. Although the talks were described as harmonious and the ministers agreed that growth with low inflation was the primary objective of all the participants, the main result of the meeting was the recognition that each nation did not want to institute a cooperative economic program. Such an approach was fine for the Germans. With the dollar-DM exchange rate somewhat stabilized (DM 1.70 to the dollar) after the historic lows of the past fall, German industry could again re-evaluate its exporting position and competitiveness given the earlier difficulties it had faced.[66] In terms of German interest rates, Norman Lamont predictably demanded reductions, but the other G7 members were more hesitant to call immediately for a Bundesbank reduction. Waigel could thus assert after the meeting that German monetary policy had not faced any major complaints or accusations.[67] The participants were more intent on hearing how the Kohl government would develop a comprehensive budget and finance package for reunification. Given the difficulties within the EMS over the previous five months, the G7 ministers were skeptical about a broad multilateral cooperative effort to deal with each nation's own particular concerns. The impact of the turmoil in the EMS was now felt in the G7 bargaining arena.

The April G7 IMF/World Bank meeting helped restore some of the credibility to the entire G7 process of international cooperation.[68] The G7 finance ministers did manage to put their names to mutually reinforcing measures designed to return the world economy to faster growth and less unemployment. They also broadened their efforts to coordinate economic policy to include long-term issues such as labor market reform and curbing health care costs. More far-reaching, perhaps, was the decision by the interim committee to appoint a referee, the IMF, to blow the whistle and cry foul if any country's economic and exchange rate policies threatened to create currency turmoil and upset the international community's efforts to achieve greater growth. The measure, however, had little teeth in terms of enforcement. Nonetheless, contacts among G7 countries had intensified since Clinton took office (the April meeting was the third high-level meeting in as many months), and an improved measure of communication and conference calls had been implemented. Horst Köhler described G7 efforts at cooperation as "Sinatra-Plus."

By the time of the July Tokyo G7 annual summit meeting, the economic policies in the G3 countries were seen as headed toward balance. The United States had taken concrete steps, through the closest of votes in Congress, to reduce its budget deficit through a comprehensive tax-increase and spending-reduction program; meanwhile, Clinton's stimulus package was put on hold. In response to U.S. movement on its own deficits, as well as ongoing U.S. pressure, the Japanese had finally announced, but not yet implemented, a fiscal stimulus package to boost its economy. It still remained to be seen, however, whether the Japanese would follow through on the plan. The Bundesbank had embarked on its program of cautious but infrequent interest rate reductions, including the cut in interest rates in April and, more dramatically, just a week before the G7 summit. The July interest rate reduction of the Lombard rate from 8.5 percent to 8.25 percent and the discount rate from 7.25 percent to 6.75 percent appeared, in particular, to be aimed directly at the G7 community and the Clinton administration, although no official statements from German monetary authorities conceded as much.[69]

Despite the optimism and the appearance of some German monetary sensitivity, the summit focused intently on the meager economic and job growth in the industrialized economies and the avenues each country could take separately to increase employment. The participants called for a number of measures to encourage noninflationary growth, but the summit was overshadowed by Clinton's efforts to secure Japanese concessions in bilateral trade talks with the United States. For the Europeans, the most serious risk remained high interest rates, which as the OECD stressed in its annual report for 1993, were much higher than domestic economic conditions warranted.[70] The Bundesbank and Kohl government—politically paralyzed at home and under pressure within the European arena—were not in a position to offer any further dramatic or meaningful concessions other than what had been agreed to at the earlier April G7 meeting or in the bank's own incremental reduction of interest rates. The lack of genuine G7 efforts to build upon the April efforts only exacerbated the tensions within Europe and indicated the weak base and less than credible foundation of G7 coordination. The Germans were not ready to offer any painful concessions to the G7.

Conclusion

Following the August transformation of the EMS and the inconclusive G7 summit in July, the French and Germans sought to patch up their differences and defend their policies, especially the criticism aimed at the Bundesbank. Waigel and his new French counterpart in the finance ministry, Edmond Alphandery, met together with their respective central bank presidents for a session of the Franco-German economic council. Each went to great lengths to state the avowedly temporary nature of this decision and that the decision to widen the bands had been the result of cooperative solutions suggested by each country. Alphandery stated, "I want to lay to rest all these rumors about the so-called deterioration in Franco-German relations. . . . I can testify that during this period of tension on the markets, the Franco-German couple once again proved its solidity."[71] Waigel stated that Germany would be sticking to Maastricht and that Franco-German support of the EMS remained the "central building block of this."[72]

However, the French prime minister, Edouard Balladur, was not so diplomatic and explicitly blamed high German interest rates for precipitating the crisis and claimed that the French government's willingness to cooperate by agreeing to the widening of the bands ultimately saved the EMS. John Major labeled the timetable to monetary union as "totally unrealistic," and that there remained "no prospect" of Britain returning to the EMS "in the near future," while the now former chancellor of the Exchequer, Norman Lamont, described Maastricht as "a bit of a fossil."[73] For George Bush and then Bill Clinton, the lack of German movement on the monetary front seemed to indicate that the independent Bundesbank was strictly dictating German monetary policy.

Does the Bundesbank deserve the blame? Could Bundesbank policy have reacted differently to the 1992–1993 crisis? Wolfgang Filc has found that the Bundesbank reacted more switfly by lowering interest rates during similar recessionary periods in Germany.[74] As compared to 1975 and 1982, when inflation rose at an annual rate of 5.9 percent and 5.3 percent and GDP rates were at –1.3 percent and –1.1 percent, respectively, the Bundesbank was able to lower short-term interest rates within a year by 6 percent in 1975 and 4 percent in 1982. With inflation lower in 1993 (4.1 percent) and GDP growth lower (–2 percent), the Bundesbank had dropped short-term rates by only 2 percent from fall 1992 to July 1993. Based on these comparisons, Filc contends that the Bundesbank had plenty of room to drop rates more rapidly. However, one can also argue convincingly that with the speed of reunification, the unpredictable monetary consequences of the entire restructuring process in the east, and the government's unclear plans on how to pay for it all, it was inevitable that the Bundesbank, traditionally a conservative institution, would pursue a cautionary path. In addition, the "hidden" effect of the worldwide recession due to the reunification boom (in 1991, GDP growth at 4.5 percent for the year in Germany as compared to −0.7 percent for the United States) also made accurate forecasting difficult, if not unrealistic.

One could also argue that the Bundesbank should have considered the larger European and international dimensions of its policy with greater precision.[75] First, the economic integration and interdependence of goods, services, and financial markets within Europe have generated a new set of demands upon German monetary policy. These demands cannot and should not be ignored or swept aside by Bundesbank officials. Monetary stability within Germany is increasingly a function of the monetary stability and the productive capacity of all of Europe. One can argue that as the German economy goes, so does the European economy. Today, however, as the European economy goes, so does the German economy. Although the relationship is not symmetrical—indeed, this is the central point in criticisms of German monetary policy—each is dependent, in some part, upon the other. Monetary stability and the productive capacity of Europe cannot be seen in strict isolation of each other.

Second, the anchor currency within any semi-fixed or fixed monetary system must acknowledge, if not actively accept, its responsibilities in terms of providing liquidity to the system and a credible, stability-oriented anchor. If the anchor currency does not take on its responsibility, undoubtedly a difficult and demanding task, the monetary regime will not last and ultimately collapse. The parallels to the Bretton Woods system are striking and hint at the necessity of a leading monetary power assuming the economic burdens and political responsibilities to ensure stability in the system.[76] These two factors do not mean that the Bundesbank should have disregarded its domestic stability-oriented policies. As noted previously in the analysis of Bundesbank policy, these remained the bank's predominant goals. However, the strict domestic orientation in terms of the indicators the Bundesbank examined before making policy decisions could have played a lesser role in its final calculations.

For their part, Bundesbank officials appeared confident that their policies were the right ones for Germany, Europe, and the global economy.[77] German monetary authorities stress, and this analysis supports the view, that they cooperated with their European partners as much as could have been expected given the narrow range of possible proposals acceptable to either the Bundesbank or government. This analysis points to the importance of a particular form of German monetary and European cooperation. German monetary authorities often were willing to accommodate their policies on behalf of maintaining the bottom-line credibility of European integration, European institutions, and the Franco-German political and economic axis upon which European integration has been built. The Bundesbank did reach a breaking point in terms of the persistent dilemma between domestic policy autonomy and exchange rate stability. However, they did go to great lengths during September 1992 and August 1993 to minimize the impact of their policies. The evidence is also clear that the German monetary authorities did make significant efforts to adjust their own policies on behalf of the Europeans, either through a realignment, which would have hurt the already depressed German business community, central bank intervention—especially in support of the French franc—or, as the Bundesbank points out, their lowering of interest rates throughout 1993. Cooperation and accommodation at the European level was forthcoming from the Germans. The built-up pressures within Germany following reunification, the static perceptions of European actors, including the German government, and the structural and global disruptions associated with the decline of the dollar ultimately overwhelmed whatever cooperative measures were taken to counteract these pressures.

Furthermore, the Bundesbank did seek to arrange a general realignment of the EMS currencies in return for a reduction in German interest rates but was rebuffed at first by its own government and then by the other EMS governments. As such, the governments of the EMS deserve a large share of the blame for the lack of cooperation surrounding the various negotiations. As this chapter has demonstrated, it takes more than central banks to secure an acceptable international monetary agreement to all the parties involved in the negotiations. By denying a request to realign, however, the demands by the French, British, or Italians for unlimited Bundesbank intervention in support of their currencies soon became incompatible with the Bundesbank's commitment to domestic monetary stability. It should not have been forgotten that the commitment of a central bank, especially the politically powerful and independent Bundesbank, to unlimited foreign exchange intervention would run counter to its primary domestic obligation of safeguarding the value of the DM. In other words, although a central bank might commit to intervention before the fact, it could have strong incentives to renege afterward if such intervention violated its primary domestic obligation. With the guarantee made by the government of Chancellor Schmidt to then Bundesbank president Emminger at the time of the EMS's creation in 1978–1979 that the Bundesbank could invoke its right to limit interventions on the grounds that it would threaten price stability, it was only a matter of time before the Bundesbank played its hand. The limits of the willingness of the Bundesbank to subjugate domestic monetary autonomy to exchange rate stability had been reached.

Notes

1. The idea of using lyrics from Frank Sinatra's famous song to describe G7 policy cooperation stems from a *Financial Times* assessment of the problems facing G7 members as they attempted to resolve their own divergent national problems.

2. After the signing of the Maastricht Treaty in December of 1991, the European Community became known as the European Union, or EU. However, formal status as the EU would wait until November 1993. For my purposes, I will use "EU" starting the analysis in this chapter.

3. Interview with the author in Bonn, September 1993.

4. That adjustments would be required until full monetary integration took place seems to have been discounted by finance ministers, politicians, and some central bankers in Europe.

5. As one Bundesbank official stated in an interview, the markets finally forced the politicians to act. See also the interview with Rudiger Dornbusch who states that only "speculators can bring crazy finance ministers to reason." "Wir brauchen die Spekulanten," *Der Spiegel*, no. 32, August 1993.

6. The concept of the "hard core" of the ERM is used to identify those nations whose currencies are less subject to speculative pressures within the ERM, nations better able to sustain their currencies' parity to the DM. The Benelux countries and Germany are commonly referred to as the hard core, although the French and Danes are often included in this bloc. However, the French and Danes were certainly subjected to intense speculative pressure during the period under investigation.

7. Deutsche Bundesbank, *Annual Report 1990* (Frankfurt/Main), p. 66.

8. Such a view was confirmed by interviews with German finance ministry officials who indicated that they, perhaps in hindsight, did not take the Bundesbank seriously enough.

9. Conservative government accounts of the economic costs of reunification suggest that over a ten-year period, U.S.$190 billion a year will be transferred directly from west to east Germany in addition to the U.S.$60 billion in the form of government subsidies, namely, unemployment, wage subsidies, and employment-creation efforts.

10. Interview with Bundesbank official, May 1994.

11. "Kein Druck auf Bonn wegen der hohen Zinsen," *Süddeutsche Zeitung*, January 26, 1992. German labor unions reacted negatively and sharply to the international pressures for wage restraint.

12. For a view that the Garden City meeting was far from "a success," see Karl Grün, "Delammationen zum Wirtschaftswachstum," *Börsen Zeitung*, January 27, 1992. Grün focused his criticisms primarily on the problems of G7 cooperation.

13. "Warning for World Economies," *Financial Times*, February 3, 1992.

14. Ibid.

15. "G7 Nations Disagree on Right Route to Growth," *Financial Times*, April 26, 1992.

16. The spring of 1992 had seen intense union pressure, especially from public service workers, to secure their wage demands ranging between 4 percent and 6 percent.

17. See Brady's comments and analysis of the G7 meeting in "They Prefer Bush, But Not Enough," *International Herald Tribune*, April 28, 1992.

18. Interview with Bundesbank official, September 1993.

19. "German Officials Bristle at U.S. Economic Criticism," *Los Angeles Times*, April 20, 1992. Köhler's comments were aimed at U.S. treasury undersecretary David Mulford, who had stirred the pot by saying that German economic policies were hurting all of Europe and the global economy. Köhler added that Mulford's comments should "be rejected in form and content."

20. See the analysis of Peter Norman, "Caught in the Eye of the Storm," *Financial Times*, May 26, 1992.

21. See Bundesbank comments on the impact of the Danish referendum in "Stunde der Mark," *Wirtschaftswoche*, June 11, 1992.

22. See the review, "The Basket-Case Summit," *The Economist*, July 4, 1992.

23. See the analysis of the problems facing Bush in "G-7 Leaders Bring Discord to Summit," *Los Angeles Times*, July 6, 1992.

24. "The Troubles of the G7," *Financial Times*, July 3, 1992.

25. Before the July summit, currency analysts and traders expected the Bundesbank to lower rates in response to U.S. pressure at the summit. "Watch for the DM to weaken this summer" was the watchword among some currency handlers, yet the opposite was about to happen. See James Flanigen's analysis in "As the G-7 Gathering Goes, So May Go the U.S. Economy," *Los Angeles Times*, July 5, 1992.

26. Interview with Horst Köhler, *The International Economy*, September/October 1992, p. 39.

27. See the analysis in *Der Spiegel*, "Das ist alles Spekulation," August 30, 1992.

28. The term "fault line" was first used by John Major to describe the pressures that were developing within the EMS.

29. Organization for Economic Cooperation and Development, *OECD Economic Surveys: United Kingdom*, Paris, 1993, pp. 36–40.

30. In contrast, facing similar pressure, Swedish monetary authorities raised short-term interest rates from 8 percent to 24 percent on September 8, then to 75 percent and again to a staggering 500 percent at the height of the currency turmoil of Black Wednesday.

31. Many observers have commented that the meeting was a blatant political use of office by Lamont and an overall embarrassing point in ECOFIN meetings. After Lamont apparently pounded his fist on the table demanding unilateral cuts from the Germans, Schlesinger nearly walked out of the meeting. Ludlow characterizes the meeting as having a "disastrous impact" upon ECOFIN and

> from then on he [Lamont] was widely regarded as unfit to exercise the presidency. In a period of extreme disquiet, not to say danger, on the foreign exchanges, the Community was therefore obliged to operate with a president of ECOFIN whom nobody inside and as a result, nobody outside could take seriously.

Peter Ludlow, "The UK Presidency: A View from Brussels," *Journal of Common Market Studies* 31, no. 2 (June 1993), pp. 250–251.

32. The German position is revealed in "Black Wednesday Massacre," *The Guardian*, November 30, 1992. Such a view was supported by the author's own interviews with Bundesbank and finance ministry officials.

33. Probably as a result of the tumultuous ECOFIN meeting of a week before, the ministers' discussions took place on the telephone, which precluded another face-to-face debate on the whole EMS and a fundamental realignment. The final chance to save the existing system had been lost.

34. Reading some of the headlines following the Bundesbank decision, one would have thought that Schlesinger had saved Europe from catastrophic disaster. However, within Germany, the Bundesbank came under intense pressure and criticism for having sacrificed the stability of the DM to the European *Inflationsgemeinschaft*. Schlesinger did admit that "external pressures" played a significant role in the bank's decision but stated that the rate cut fit well with the bank's gesture to Bonn to bring about more moderate fiscal and wage policies. See "Germany's Small Rate Cuts Dampen Euphoria," *Financial Times*, September 15, 1992. For a taste of the German criticism, see "DIHT-Präsident sieht die Unabhängigkeit der Bundesbank gefährdet," *Handelsblatt*, September 15, 1992.

35. See the discussion in "Black Wednesday Massacre," *The Guardian*, December 1, 1992.

36. See the analysis in "The Monetary Tragedy of Errors That Led to Currency Chaos," *Financial Times*, December 11, 1992. One could also suggest the option of an immediate devaluation or reinstitution of capital controls. Neither of these two options were, from the British view, even worth considering.

37. The communiqué also noted the decision of the Italians to "abstain" temporarily from the ERM and the devaluation of the peseta by 5 percent. The Italians had the intention of resuming membership in the ERM, which they did in 1997.

38. See the analysis in "The Monetary Tragedy of Errors That Led to Currency Choas," *Financial Times*, December 11, 1992.

39. "Waigel: Kein Anpassungsbedarf mehr," *Süddeutsche Zeitung*, September 23, 1992.

40. Bush had even gone so far at the annual IMF/World Bank meeting to suggest that one way to alleviate turmoil in the currency markets would be to use a market basket of commodities, including gold, to help determine the value of major currencies. Although Michel Camdessus, managing director of the IMF at the time, welcomed the proposal for further study, Schlesinger gave the idea a quick brush-off.

41. See the analysis in Dietrich Zwätz, "Sündenfall nationalstaatlicher Einzelgänge in der Siebener-Gruppe rächt sich jetzt." *Handelsblatt,* September 22, 1992.

42. "Currencies on the Verge of a Nervous Breakdown," *The Economist*, May 5, 1992.

43. See Deutsche Bundesbank, *Annual Report 1990* (Frankfurt/Main), p. 66.

44. In fact, as one Bundesbank official indicated in an interview, "Lower German interest rates back in September 1992 or August 1993 would not have saved the EMS. The fundamental problem of diverging national policies and French refusal to contemplate a realignment would not have been eliminated by the Bundesbank lowering the discount rate by a quarter or half point."

45. The British government's announcement of the central rate for the pound preempted what should have been a confidential negotiation between the UK and the other EMS members. Hans Tietmeyer, the Bundesbank representative to the EC's Monetary Committee argued that the pound should come in at a lower rate in order to be sustainable over the long term. Tietmeyer's ominous warning proved prophetic.

46. See Pöhl's comments in "Pöhl Throws a Gauntlet," *Financial Times,* January 23, 1990.

47. Interview with the author in Bonn, September 1993.

48. Pöhl, "Pöhl Throws a Gauntlet," *Financial Times*, January 23, 1990.

49. See the analysis in "The Bundesbank Begins to Make Its Voice Heard" and "Schlesinger Gives Warning on Common Currency Rules," *Financial Times*, December 2, 1992. See also the discussion in "Conservatives Hold Sway at Bundesbank," *Wall Street Journal*, November 29, 1992.

50. Following the August suspension of the narrow bands, Spanish officials expressed dismay over the lack of support that the peseta had received throughout the previous year. They stated that they did not want to leave the EMS. "Stalwart Spain Suffers Sense of Betrayal," *Financial Times*, August 3, 1993. The Germans responded by stating that realignments must now remain a viable policy option to provide the pressure-release valve in the EMS. See Johan Wilhelm Gaddum's comments in "Realignments müssen ein Sicherheitsventil bleiben," *Handelsblatt,* October 1, 1992.

51. Schlesinger sought to verbally stabilize the franc.

52. See the analysis and comments in "Schlesinger Yields to Pressure from All Sides," *Financial Times*, February 5, 1993. See also the analysis in "Shoot-Out at the Currency Corral," *Financial Times*, February 6/7, 1993.

53. See the discussion in "High Speed to EMU Begins to Gather Steam," *Financial Times,* September 27, 1993; Peter Norman, "ERM Upheaval Seen Hastening Two-Speed Europe," *Financial Times*, November 25, 1992. See also "Europa nach dem Sturm," *Die Zeit*, September 21, 1992.

54. During the particularly heated week in early February 1993, Schlesinger stated bluntly in front of a London audience that critics of German interest rates were "ignoramuses," and Pierre Bérégovoy commented that the British were "going down a dead-end path." The Germans and the French were even intent on aligning against British criticism. See David Marsh and Lionel Barber, "Shoot-Out at the Currency Corral," *Financial Times*, February 6–7, 1993.

55. French politicians certainly faced domestic criticism from French exporters who complained about their loss of competitiveness relative to their British and Italian rivals. See the analysis in "Five Easy Pieces: European Currencies," *The Economist,* February 6, 1993.

56. There is no explicit evidence that can confirm this speculation. In interviews, Bundesbank and finance ministry officials deny such a purge scenario. However, such is the view of some British observers who point to the pattern of public statements made by Bundesbank officials before the crisis exploded on September 15–16. These statements included references to pound devaluations. See Ivo Dawney and Andrew Fisher, "Britain Points Finger at Germany," *Financial Times*, September 17, 1992, p. 1; see also Barry Eichengreen and Charles Wyplosz, "The Unstable EMS," *Brookings Papers on Economic Activity*, no. 1 (1993), p. 112.

57. The Bundesbank again lowered its discount rate to 7.5 percent on March 18 in response to domestic and European factors, according to bank officials. The move was "a continuation of a policy of gradual interest rate reductions." *Wall Street Journal*, March 19, 1993. According to some German analysts, the Bundesbank had strayed far from its independent position. See the letter to the editor by Joachim Scheide, "Bundesbank," *The Economist*, June 26, 1993. *The Economist* also offered its editorial support for the bank, "Don't Blame the Bundesbank," June 12, 1993.

58. Oliver Branchard, Rudiger Dornbusch, Stanley Fisher, Franco Modigliano, Paul A. Samuelson, and Robert Solow, "Why the EMS Deserves an Early Burial," *Financial Times*, July 29, 1993.

59. See the discussion in Otmar Issing, Peter Bofinger, and Karl Friedrich and A. Unterberg, "Zeitgespräch: Die Leitwährungsrolle der D-Mark im EWS," *Wirtschaftsdienst*, no. 73 (1993).

60. "Frankfurt Dives for Cover from Flak," *Financial Times*, July 31/August 1, 1993.

61. The Bundesbank had sparked additional rumors that a discount rate cut would be forthcoming after cutting the repo rate almost to the discount rate floor on the Wednesday before the council meeting. This action was met with no public explanation, which, in turn, fueled the frenetic instability of the markets. The events that transpired at the meeting on August 1 are captured accurately in "How the Ministers Agreed: ERM Bands Produce Sort of Harmony," *Financial Times*, August 3, 1993.

62. Such an argument was made in the editorial section of the *Financial Times*, July 30, 1993, "Bleak Summer for the ERM," which suggested that a

realignment at that point in time offered no realistic prospect for relief. "A better solution might be for Germany to recognize that it—not France or Denmark—is the country with structural problems and so needs, temporarily, to leave the ERM." On the point of the Germans' offer to leave the ERM, German finance minister Waigel stated in later interviews that there had been no suggestion that they leave the ERM.

63. The communiqué read: "This measure of limited duration is in response to speculative movements, which are exceptional in amount as well as in nature. . . . The ministers and governors therefore reaffirm support for the current parities and are confident that the market rates will soon approach these parities again."

64. See the revealing interview with Horst Köhler in which he indicates the government's interest in seeing interest rates drop in order to revive the lame European economy. Köhler is very careful in the interview, despite the questioning techniques of *Der Spiegel*'s editors (who saw a *Zinskrieg* [interest rate war] under way), to respect the Bundesbank's independence. Nonetheless, one can sense from the interview the government's desire to see the Bundesbank perhaps move with more speed on the interest rate front. See "Stabilität um jeden Preis?" *Der Spiegel*, January 31, 1993.

65. "Die G7 streben die Koordination ihrer Wirtschaftspolitik an," *Frankfurter Allgemeine Zeitung*, February 26, 1993.

66. See the evaluation of the exchange rate disturbances for German industry in "Three Men and a Recession," *Financial Times*, March 4, 1993.

67. "Inflationsfreies Wachstum als Ziel," *Frankfurter Allgemeine Zeitung*, February 28, 1993.

68. See the analysis of Peter Norman, "From Sinatra to Sinatra-Plus," *Financial Times*, May 3, 1993.

69. Schlesinger did stress that the decision to lower rates would ease pressures within the EMS, especially upon the French franc. The German economics minister, Günter Rexrodt (FDP), who had recently replaced Jürgen Möllemann, was more to the point. He said that rate cuts "will help to improve conditions for economic growth in Germany and other European nations." See the analysis and comments in "Bundesbank Cuts Rates to Combat Slowdown," *Financial Times*, April 23, 1993; "Bundesbank Cuts 2 Key Interest Rates," *Los Angeles Times*, April 22, 1993.

70. The OECD suggested a decisive Bundesbank rate cut of at least 2 percentage points or a political deal to release Europe's economies from Bundesbank control. Although there was no sign that this would happen at the Tokyo summit, less than four weeks afterward, the latter had occurred. See the analysis in "Still Waiting at the G7 Table," *Financial Times*, July 2, 1993.

71. "In Their Hands?" *The Economist*, August 7, 1993.

72. "EC Governments Strive to Contain Differences," *Financial Times*, August 3, 1993. The architects of the EMS, former chancellor Schmidt and French president Valery Giscard d'Estaing, issued a statement saying the agreement was tantamount to suspending the EMS. "This solution may offer some practical advantage only if it remains an adjustment phase of limited duration."

73. Ibid.

74. See the analyses of Wolfgang Filc, "Bundesbank, Konjunktur und EWS," *Wirtschaftsdienst*, no. 9 (1993), p. 467, table 2.

75. Claus Noe, "Kalkulierter Abschwung?" *Die Zeit*, August 20, 1992; Rüdiger Pohl, "Eine stärkere Aussenorientierung der deutschen Geldpolitik," *Wirtschaftsdienst*, no. 4 (1993).

76. For a comparison of the EMS with Bretton Woods, see the analysis of Peter Loedel, "German Monetary Policy, EMS Turmoil and European Integration:

Monetary Cooperation After 'Imperfect' Hegemony?" *Collected Proceedings of the Institute of Western Europe's Conference on the Shape of New Europe* (New York: Institute on Western Europe, Columbia University, 1994), pp. 351–392.

77. It should be noted that not all Bundesbank officials agreed with the course of action taken by the Bundesbank over 1992–1993. The Landeszentralbank president of the Rhineland-Palatinate and Saarland, Hans-Jürgen Koebnick (SPD), saw the need for a quicker reduction in interest rates in 1993 as "reasonable and desirable." See the comments of politicians and interest associations, "Nur SPD und DGB für eine Zinssenkung," *Handelsblatt*, May 4, 1993.

6

Dollar Crises and Halting Steps Toward Economic Monetary Union, 1994–1995

> That it now became serious about the abolition of the D-Mark . . . created in me quite a stir, and many of us rubbed our eyes in disbelief. . . . The advantages for Germany are difficult to discern, likewise the substantiation that the new ECU will be as stable as the D-Mark.
>
> —Wilhelm Nölling, former *Land* central bank president of Hamburg, quoted in *Die Bundesbank: Geschäfte mit der Macht*

The tripartite pressures and influences on German monetary policy would again reveal themselves dramatically through 1995. The focus of pressure came from the dollar as it skidded from one crisis to the next. With a falling dollar and corresponding German-U.S. conflict, tensions within the EMS were inevitable. However, with the newfound Bundesbank autonomy provided by a restructured EMS, European monetary politics remained relatively stable. More problematic for the Europeans were the details of EMU that still required the attention of negotiators.

On the domestic front, a mixed record of economic news greeted the Germans. The German economy began its slow climb out of recession. From a distressed –1.9 percent annual rate of GDP in 1993, the annual rate of GDP growth stood at a respectable 2.5 percent by the end of 1995. Unemployment, however, rested at about 3.5 million, a post–World War II high that would increase to more than 4 million by the end of 1995. The Council of Economic Experts predicted ongoing economic stagnation in its annual report, and many commentators speculated on the termination of the Kohl government heading into the super-election year 1994. *Der Spiegel* reported on the "end of an era" as the chancellor's power ebbed under a sinking economic ship of state, a Germany "under strain."[1] Kohl tried to counter his attacks and issued a government "Report on Securing Germany's Economic Future," which cited inflexible labor laws, high-paid workers, and lack of entrepreneurial zeal. Despite Kohl's own exhortations, the corporatist and federal structure of the government prevented any quick adjustment.[2]

The Bundesbank rejoiced in the increased autonomy provided by the widening of the ERM trading margins. Compared with the hundreds of billions of DMs the Bundesbank had used to intervene and prop up EMS currencies in the year-long EMS crisis, the Bundesbank only intervened to the tune of DM 52.3 billion for the entire period of December 6, 1993, to December 5, 1994.[3] In the Bundesbank view, there was "no alternative to the wide margins for the time being,"[4] a view shared by the German government and most other European nations. This autonomy helped pave the way for the Bundesbank to pursue a steady reduction in interest rates that would, by the end of 1995, drop to their lowest levels since 1988. After the near collapse of the EMS, the Bundesbank's interest rate reductions through 1994–1995 would mark the welcome beginning of a two-year period of relative European monetary calm. Despite some pressure on noncore EMS currencies, a similar volatile period comparable to the year-long European monetary crisis of 1992–1993 would not return. Exchange rate stability within fairly narrow trading margins for those currencies participating in the EMS would be the norm.

Despite the monetary calm, many issues still needed to be addressed about the future of EMU. With deadlines looming, the devilish details of EMU would have to be negotiated. By 1995, the German government would relaunch efforts on negotiating the final components of EMU. These efforts would focus on timetables, transitions, and a "stability pact" proposed by German finance minister Theo Waigel. Waigel's attempt to tighten the convergence criteria led many analysts to conclude that he was now advocating the Bundesbank line and that EMU would be delayed indefinitely. But Kohl's single-minded determination to push EMU kept the EMU train moving forward.

On the international front, the dollar bounced from one crisis to the next, left abandoned by the Clinton administration in its trade policy with Japan and battered by the Mexican peso crisis. The Germans responded to U.S. pressure to cooperate on exchange rate management in characteristic fashion. The Bundesbank and government pointed to U.S. economic problems, primarily the twin deficits on trade and the budget, as the source of international monetary tension. In fact, the Germans would step up their level of criticism of the United States to points not heard since 1987. Moreover, disputes over international governance mechanisms, particularly the IMF, which was celebrating its fiftieth anniversary in 1994, often overshadowed minimal efforts at international monetary cooperation. The weakness of international monetary governance structures climaxed with the German-led decision by European members of the IMF to abstain from the Mexican bailout plan launched by the United States. Not only was the exchange rate program of Bretton Woods long dead, but to many, the spirit of cooperation had finally died along with it.

Monetary Calm Returns

Despite the persistent criticism of the Bundesbank that was left over from the EMS fiasco of August, the Bundesbank did not lower its political or economic visibility. In fact, with its new president, Hans Tietmeyer, providing strong political direction,[5] the Bundesbank raised its visibility on the German and European landscapes. In part, the Bundesbank could pursue such a policy because it continued to follow a steady path of interest rate reductions that slowly eviscerated the criticism of the summer. By October 21, the Bundesbank had lowered interest rates seven times during the year, culminating in the discount rate at 5.75 percent and the Lombard to 6.75 percent, both down about 3 percent for the year. According to the Bundesbank, the "stability outlook" had brightened, Bundesbank code indicating that inflation was coming under control. With negative growth and a combined German-European recession, it was not surprising that monetary conditions proved welcoming to interest rate reductions.

The Bundesbank, however, did not ease up on other political controversies. In its November *Monthly Report,* the bank criticized the government's policies on the EU. Specifically, it noted the government's role as paymaster to the EU and raised the issue of appropriate burden sharing in managing regional tasks, two issues the government quickly addressed within the context of the next scheduled intergovernmental conference. In its December *Monthly Report,* the bank urged the government to reduce the public deficit of 7 percent of GDP, far above the acceptable Maastricht level. Furthermore, Tietmeyer made it clear to the government that it would be wrong to solve German economic problems through exchange rate manipulation. Although devaluation had perhaps helped British and Italian exporters, the negative consequences of currency manipulation were, in the Bundesbank's view, prohibitive.

On EMU the Bundesbank's policies continued to set the tone in Europe. Tietmeyer, in a speech to the European Parliament, argued that Europe needed a stable DM.[6] Tietmeyer also argued that the "monetary policy of the anchor currency country must be geared primarily to achieving price stability at home, because this is the only way in which lasting stability throughout the system can be safeguarded."[7] Many of Europe's governments shared this vision as they continued to regard a firm peg to the DM as an end in itself, rather than as a means to an end. *The Economist,* however, argued that Europe's economies should pursue lower interest rates, delinking policy from the informal peg to the DM. Given that the fear of rising inflation had been eliminated by the economic slowdown across Europe, countries could build on the track record of low inflation within the wider trading bands and then make the leap directly to monetary union.[8] But few nations ventured far from a policy that might damage their hard-earned credibility. The Bundesbank continued to set the boundaries for European monetary policy.

The Europeans did have something to celebrate, however. The EU heads of state met at the end of October at a special summit in Brussels to commemorate the official ushering in of the EU. The November 1, 1993, EU starting date was important on two counts. First, the German Constitutional Court had ruled that the Maastricht Treaty could proceed, for it was compatible with the democratic principles of the Federal Republic. Second, and more significant, the EU heads of state decided to locate the site of the EMI in Frankfurt. Tietmeyer stated that Frankfurt offered "good conditions for the independence of the European Central Bank" and that "the daily political controversies dominating at seats of parliament" would be less noticeable in Frankfurt.[9] Although not a major point of contention or heated bargaining, the decision to locate the EMI in Frankfurt proved a major psychological victory for the Bundesbank. Echoing the debate involving Adenauer's call in the 1950s for the Bundesbank to reside in Bonn, Frankfurt provided the proper background to the development of a European *Stabilitätsgemeinschaft* based on an independent EMI outside of the political sphere of Brussels.

On the international front in the fall of 1993, the dollar-DM relationship was primarily buffeted by some unease in U.S.-Japanese trade relations for which the Germans voiced some concern. Overall, however, the U.S. economic recovery helped bolster the dollar (as did mid-August interventions by the Federal Reserve) and ease German-U.S. monetary tension. The link to the DM and global GATT negotiations also played a role in securing U.S.-German cooperation. A rising dollar was thought to improve the chances of a successful outcome of GATT negotiations. A weaker DM (operating parallel to the weakening yen) might ease pressure on the French franc. This would, in turn, render Franco-German ties stronger within the EU, easing the way for the Germans to pressure France to commit to a GATT agreement. Despite the room for optimism, no one quite knew what the U.S. policy on the dollar was. Would the dollar be weaker to fight the U.S. trade deficit? Or stronger, befitting the stature and strength of the U.S. economy? The markets would soon provide an answer that the Clinton administration and the G7 were unwilling to give.

Under such conditions, the state of the G7 as an institutionalized forum for cooperation and governance once again came under intense scrutiny. One of Germany's leading G7 negotiators, Horst Köhler, argued that the G7 should be revitalized.[10] The G7 monetary governance structure was becoming trivialized to the detriment of global monetary cooperation. Köhler suggested that the institutional aspects of G7 cooperation required systematic change. First, more active central bank participation in the finance minister and deputy-level discussions on exchange rates and surveillance could be encouraged. Second, the IMF could be more integrated into G7 discussions on macroeconomic surveillance. Third, one country could be assigned, perhaps for a year at a time, certain responsibilities on organizational issues, such as handling invitations, setting agendas, writing papers, and so on. Such a process would add a more bureaucratic and institutionalized decisionmaking process to international monetary governance. Finally, a secretariat could be established to give some institutional and informational memory to monetary negotiations. In sum, G7 monetary discussions could be streamlined, the muddling-through process of G7 governance eliminated, and superficial issues avoided. Heads of state could then focus on the major political and economic challenges.

Köhler's views were not necessarily shared by the Bundesbank.[11] Yes, the Bundesbank fully supported active central bank participation in G7 deliberations. In fact, the Bundesbank already maintained such an influential position within the German delegation to G7 negotiations. A more active voice of other G7 central bankers might add some reality to the discussions. However, while the Bundesbank saw nothing fundamentally wrong with streamlining the efficiency of meetings, they were not interested in institutionalizing stronger decisionmaking procedures at the G7 level. Cooperation, when necessary and if forthcoming, could be done as it had been done in the past—largely ad hoc and in response to specific crises. The Sinatra doctrine still prevailed, and the Bundesbank was singing the tune. The stage was set for another dollar-led international monetary drama.

Dollar Tension and Election-Year Monetary Politics

January 1, 1994, marked the onset of the second stage of Maastricht with the establishment of the EMI. With the respected Alexandre Lamfalussy at its head, the institute replaced the Committee of EC Central Bank Governors as one of the leading EU-level bodies of decisionmaking and cooperation. More important, a major election year (*Superwahljahr*) in Germany, the biggest election year in post–World War II Germany, was now under way. Kohl was intent on avoiding controversial European monetary questions.[12] The focus for Kohl was on combating unemployment, a focus that benefited from Bundesbank policy. Despite missing its monetary targets for 1992 and 1993 and concerns over wage increases and threatened strikes by IG Metal in early 1994, the Bundesbank continued to lower interest rates. The Bundesbank's moves, one could argue, supported Kohl's re-election chances and continued to add to the stability in the EMS. As a result, European monetary politics would not surface as a major issue in the elections.

Instead, the focus of deutsche mark politics would be on the DM-dollar relationship. With the new year, the dollar began to experience some turbulence in the international arena brought on by ongoing U.S.-Japanese trade conflicts. A strengthening yen was adding pressure for DM appreciation, which further eroded Germany's export competitiveness, the sole job creator in the economy. In February, shortly before a G7 summit, the Bundesbank lowered the discount rate by a half point, giving some indication that international issues were affecting monetary decisions.[13] The DM stabilized in the range of DM 1.65–1.75 to the dollar. At the G7 meeting in Frankfurt in late February, the primary topic for discussion was the U.S.-Japanese trade conflict and the effect it was having on currency markets. According to Bundesbank and government officials, Germany was pursuing an appropriate monetary policy given the domestic and international situation. The United States and Japan would have to address their concerns bilaterally, rather than through the G7.

At a March G7 jobs summit in Detroit, Kohl pushed the idea of labor force flexibility and open trade. With unemployment now exceeding 4 million and continued losses for the CDU in local and *Land* elections in the spring of 1994, Kohl was intent on job creation. Bill Clinton was intent on job creation as well as resurrecting the locomotive theory one more time while the United States called for lower interest rates in Europe, the implicit target again being Germany. Waigel, in turn, predictably argued that the lowering of interest rates in Germany must first be "earned" and was dependent on inflationary developments. Apparently, the Bundesbank was listening to the United States and Kohl and not to Waigel as the bank continued to cut interest rates through April. The Bundesbank noted that the latest rate drop was due, in part, to DM appreciation.[14] With inflation under control and with long-term bonds standing at around 6 percent, one could argue that the Bundesbank was gearing its policy toward economic growth and dollar stabilization. Some German economists and commentators criticized the Bundesbank as too focused on exchange markets.[15] The Bundesbank, caught between Kohl and the dollar, could not find a safe middle ground. At least Europe posed few dilemmas for the bank.

At the G7 summit meeting in April, Tietmeyer could point to relative positive developments in inflationary pressures (moderating at an annual rate of just less than 3 percent), which suggested a possible continuation of interest rate cuts. U.S. monetary diplomacy, as unsubtle as always, continued to publicly call for further rate cuts from the Germans. Resenting the U.S. pressure, the Bundesbank had already lowered rates on April 14, just ten days before the summit. Nevertheless, in May, the Bundesbank lowered rates again, the eleventh time since the highs of 1992; the discount rate now stood at 4.5 percent and the Lombard rate at 6 percent. The Bundesbank could not be faulted by anyone—Kohl, the Europeans, or the United States—for its policy.

As the Bundesbank continued to pursue a policy aimed at reviving the German economy and Kohl's electoral chances, reducing European monetary pressures, and relieving pressure on the dollar, the United States revived its policy of dollar neglect vis-à-vis the G7 and the international monetary system. As volatility in the currency markets heated up in late April, the Federal Reserve and Bank of Japan intervened heavily in currency markets to shore up the dollar. The Germans were not active participants in the efforts nor was the G7 actively involved in addressing a problem with global monetary implications. Without German or G7 cooperation and with Secretary of the Treasury Lloyd Bentsen citing "volatile" and "disorderly" markets as the primary cause, the United States finally had to significantly intervene on its own in the markets. In addition, the Federal Reserve slowly raised interest rates to deal with potential domestic inflationary pressures and the stumbling dollar. Bentsen tried to lay out a strong U.S. dollar policy by arguing that the administration saw no "advantage in an undervalued currency."[16] But Bentsen's statements were seen as late in coming and as disingenuous because the Clinton administration earlier had argued that the best way to fight the trade deficit with Japan was through the "appreciation of the Japanese yen."[17]

On the back of U.S. dollar neglect, considerable turmoil continued to rock the international currency markets. Foreign investors were reducing their purchases of U.S. bonds and stocks based on a lack of confidence in the U.S. economy, inflation, deficit reduction, and the U.S. commitment to GATT. In a rare showing of monetary cooperation, a one-day concerted effort of seventeen central banks, including the Bundesbank, was undertaken to prop up the staggering dollar. Although G7 finance ministers had informally agreed in April to cooperate loosely in foreign exchange markets, this intervention was, in fact, a response to the *failure* of earlier intervention efforts and G7 governance. Some commentators sarcastically suggested that a G-17 had emerged, replacing the G7, with leading monetary actors such as Portugal now helping to uphold the value of the dollar. In any interpretation, the decline of G7 and G3 monetary leadership was certainly evident.

Ultimately, however, it would take efforts by the Germans to help stabilize the value of the dollar. Comments by Hans Tietmeyer, that too strong an appreciation of the DM against the dollar was not in the interest of Germany's economy, provided the psychological boost to the dollar.[18] The Bundesbank was careful to note that the president's comments were aimed not in the interest of the global economy, rather at Germany's interests. If anybody wanted lower interest rates, the government would have to cut budget deficits. Yet the Bundesbank continued to lower rates, with a carefully calculated May 11 decision that helped the dollar, maintained Germany's all-important export sector, and kept Kohl's electoral chances alive.

From the German standpoint, with the DM acting as an important anchor to global monetary stability, there was not much to be done other than to criticize U.S. policy and commend German monetary policy. In late April, Tietmeyer gave a wide-ranging speech to the American Council on Germany in New York in which he assessed global and European monetary governance and the domestic monetary situation in Germany.[19] The tripartite link was again evident in his conceptualization of the issues facing Germany. He first argued that the trend of internationalization and globalization in international capital markets was likely to continue together with the corresponding greater potential for volatility in the markets. The goal of maintaining exchange rate stability could therefore only be attained if the Bundesbank secured the progress already achieved in combating inflation at home and preserving confidence in the DM. Tietmeyer connected the triangle by arguing that monetary union in Europe and stable international exchange rates could only come about by closer monetary convergence in line with the Bundesbank's policy. In other words, the United States should converge its policy more in line with the German model that it had exported to Europe.

Building on Tietmeyer's less than supportive view of U.S. policy, the respite from the dollar crisis of May was temporary. As the dollar fell below the historic 100 yen level, the DM strengthened considerably. With the DM hovering around the 1.75 range at the beginning of the year and now dropping to 1.58 by the end of June, the Germans demanded more U.S. action. Responding to German criticism and the pressure of the markets, Bentsen issued a statement suggesting that "a stronger dollar is better for our economy and better for the world's economy."[20] Moreover, Bentsen noted that the dollar was not a tool of U.S. trade policy. The markets, however, distrusted the administration; the dollar continued to drop the next day. The volatility prompted Edward Bernstein, an adviser to Harry Dexter White at Bretton Woods, to urge a system of semi-fixed exchange rates with the dollar fluctuating between DM 1.60 and 1.75. Others urged further interest rate increases to strengthen the dollar, which the Federal Reserve had already raised four times so far that year and would, by the end of 1994, raise the federal funds rate from 3 percent to 5.5 percent. There was also further pressure on the Bundesbank to lower rates or sell DMs for the dollar. Some Bundesbank members seemed to advocate lower rates for domestic reasons,[21] but many analysts feared that the Bundesbank might actually raise rates in response to new signals that the German economy was strengthening.[22] Germany and the United States were again in the position of pursuing policies counter to the interests of global monetary stability.

As the dollar crisis indicated, fifty years after the Bretton Woods summit, the international monetary system was certainly ready for a renewed effort of leadership and cooperation. Would the G7 summit in Naples provide the cure for an ill dollar and a monetary governance structure without any real leaders?[23] Clinton, in particular, faced mounting criticism for his lack of foreign economic policy. Clinton's trade plan, "Markets 2000," unveiled on the first day of the summit fell flat, criticized as overly aggressive and premature following the GATT negotiations. Moreover, with misguided stress on the "value of the dollar" as a solution to U.S. trade problems, Clinton had repeated the mistakes of earlier administrations, specifically those of Jimmy Carter, Reagan, and Bush. All would eventually learn that monetary unilateralism did not work, that working with the Germans rather than against them was conducive to monetary cooperation, and that avoiding dollar rhetoric would go far to ease global monetary instability.

Unfortunately, the Naples summit would not prove that any lessons had yet been learned. Clinton stated shortly before the summit that the United States would not intervene to support the dollar. The G7 communiqué omitted any mention of volatility in currency markets. Instead, the focus remained on employment issues. With a general economic upswing, most participants were not willing to make strong commitments one way or another on monetary policy. A "Plan of Action" was issued that called for G7 leaders to make structural improvements in education, vocational training, and flexibility in labor markets. The IMF, OECD, World Bank, and future World Trade Organization (WTO) would work together to promote jobs. The employment rhetoric did nothing to reassure the markets. In fact, it merely added to the instability. Shortly after the summit's conclusion, the dollar fell to new lows against both the yen and the DM.

By midsummer, the dollar stood at 1.53, the lowest it had stood since October 1992. Even Waigel sought to stabilize the dollar by supporting Clinton's decision at the Naples summit not to "overreact" to the declining dollar.[24] Clinton welcomed the support of the Germans. On a two-day visit to Germany after the G7 summit, Clinton encouraged Germany to broaden its role as a world leader and supported Kohl's efforts to calm German and European fears of a more assertive, reunited Germany. The Germans warmly welcomed such comments, and Kohl agreed by stating that Germany cannot be a country "with the kind of reputation and prestige we claim for ourselves if we do not fully accept our responsibilities and fulfill our obligations."[25] But it was not the responsibilities and obligations of the

Germans that the markets were concerned about; rather, the fundamental leadership responsibilities of the United States were the concern.

In late September, an opportunity for a serious re-evaluation of the international monetary governance structure (and the norm of monetary unilateralism) arose. The IMF/World Bank meeting in Madrid officially celebrated the fiftieth anniversary of Bretton Woods. The visionaries at Bretton Woods would have been pleased by the extent of the global integration and free markets and the collapse of communist and statist economies, but they would not have been pleased with the extent of monetary instability and lack of cooperation to stabilize exchange rates. Certainly the times had changed, but the IMF had relinquished its role as the governing agent for exchange rates and instead was playing the reactive role in various monetary meltdowns from Russia to Mexico. For all intents and purposes, the IMF had become a funnel of funds to transitioning and developing economies. Surveillance, whether through the IMF or G7, had all but evaporated.

The U.S. and German governments were not intent on subordinating monetary autonomy to a renewed global scheme on exchange rate stability. The various plans on reforming the international monetary governance structure advocated in Madrid or elsewhere would all fall on the deaf ears of policymakers.[26] Former Federal Reserve president Paul Volcker's plan called for greater harmony among G7 nations in fiscal and monetary policies and stronger coordination of their activities in order to avoid exchange rate volatility. Other plans suggested a G3 concert on exchange rates as a result of declining U.S. leadership within the G7 or the IMF.[27] The Bundesbank's position on these issues, shared by the government, was that "the creation of formal exchange rates target zones for the major currencies . . . would not be appropriate for strengthening the indispensable confidence of the markets. Such a monetary system would lack a 'nominal anchor' if monetary stability were not safeguarded in those countries which have major international currencies."[28] According to the Bundesbank, there existed no monetary leader capable of exerting global monetary governance over the markets. For its part, the German government was unable and unwilling to assume political leadership. As long as these conditions prevailed, target zones or other exchange rate regimes would not work.

Shortly after the IMF meetings, the United States relaunched efforts to pressure Japan on trade. This time, having learned a lesson, the administration sought to comfort financial markets. The dollar rhetoric was gone. As a September 30, 1994, trade deadline with Japan approached, Secretary Bentsen sent top administration officials to Wall Street to talk to currency traders, the new masters of the international monetary system. Stability in the exchange markets had momentarily returned. Evaluating the earlier dollar turmoil, it appeared that Germany and the United States were, in fact, pursuing policies conducive to stabilizing the dollar-DM relationship. Germany was lowering interest rates and the United States was raising rates. Moreover, both nations, albeit Germany significantly less so, had engaged in central bank intervention to push the dollar down. The problem was that each nation was arguing that their actions were addressing domestic interests, rather than international concerns. National interest still prevailed as the guiding norm of international monetary politics. There appeared to be the framework (the G7) for cooperation, but neither country was politically willing to commit. Ritual G7 communiqués on coordination meant nothing as long as each country justified actions in the name of national interest. The foundation for global monetary stability remained fragile.

A Core Europe? A German Plan for Europe

Through the late summer and fall of 1994 as the Germans assumed the presidency of the EU, a major debate erupted over what a future Europe would resemble.[29] A study by CDU's party chief and Kohl ally, Wolfgang Schäuble, argued as its main thesis that a strong core of European nations was crucial to keeping the EU strong and vital.[30] A European core of nations would also prevent centrifugal pressures from destroying the EU. As Schäuble would clarify, "We cannot set the pace of European integration according to the slowest ship."[31] Schäuble's controversial thesis, it should be noted, had been codified in the Maastricht Treaty, signed, and ratified by all EU member states. As the monetary pillar of Maastricht dictated, some states would likely not be part of EMU as defined by the convergence criteria. Those nations that were ready would thus form a core Europe. Under the code of "variable geometry," Schäuble thought to expand the idea of a core monetary Europe to imply a broad understanding of a politically united Europe led by France and Germany.

Chancellor Kohl remained largely silent as Schäuble's thesis rocked European capitals. Although one would assume that Kohl was aware of Schäuble's ideas and gave the green light for the study's publication, Kohl sought to avoid personal connection to the debate. With the election coming up, Kohl did not want the German public to focus too intensely on the Kohl-DM-EMU connection. More specifically, he did not want the German public to think that the DM would be sacrificed for all-European unity.[32] Only those qualified for EMU would be able to join an exclusive monetary club. Naturally, the Bundesbank favored Schäuble's thesis. Tietmeyer explained, "The citizens of the EU have confidence in [EMU's] success only if the conditions are met; they must be taken seriously."[33] Such a view was confirmed at an ECOFIN meeting in Lindau, Bavaria, in September where, attempting to bypass the controversy on the core Europe issue, finance ministers emphasized that the conditions for EMU be upheld, even though Luxembourg was the only country that could meet the criteria at the time. Support from France also helped solidify the core Europe model envisioned in the convergence criteria.

Elsewhere, the core Europe proposal met with mostly negative reviews. Kohl's foreign minister, Klaus Kinkel (FDP), rejected the plan's implications for dividing Europe. Although it was not clear that Kinkel had any real authority for European policy, the foreign minister stated that it did not fit into Germany's European policy.[34] Ever searching for a campaign theme, the SPD tried to exploit the core Europe controversy, to little avail. Neither the FDP nor SPD provided an alternative vision or plan for Europe, as the issue would not have any decisive role in the upcoming elections. Recognizing that they were the implied "targets" of Schäuble's thesis, the southern tier of EU nations, Italy in particular, regarded the core Europe proposal as counter to the entire spirit of European integration. How could Italy, a founding member of the European Community, not be an integral part of such an important historical step as EMU? The UK remained muted, for its policy was one that implied a Europe of various speeds. The issue of a two-speed, or core Europe, would continue to haunt the negotiations over EMU for the next three years.

The debate over a core Europe or even EMU had also not fully resonated with the public. EMU remained an elite-driven idea. There existed a large division of opinion between policymakers and the public on the need for a single currency. In a poll of European citizens commissioned by *Financial Times,* most Europeans did not anticipate the single currency arriving by the year 2000.[35] In Germany, only 8 percent of respondents believed that a single currency was "very likely" in at least three EU member countries by the end of the century. Moreover, 60 percent of German respondents favored a looser arrangement between independent states rather than the more integrated Europe envisioned through Maastricht. Public opinion was turning sharply against Maastricht and a single currency.[36] A long process of engagement and education would be necessary. Schäuble's clarifications on the core Europe were part of such an effort to educate the Germans, but the public remained skeptical.

At the December ECOFIN meeting in Brussels, the core Europe issue was debated but was not part of any formal negotiations. More significant, the ministers decided to continue the wide currency bands. The Germans supported the measure because they believed that Europe had achieved greater monetary stability with the wider trading margins. More significant, speculation from the DM-dollar tension earlier in the year had largely been avoided; the broader trading margins had provided the requisite flexibility to EMS members. The Bundesbank did begin to question whether the trading margins, at roughly 15 percent, would remain for the two-year period leading up to EMU, but that question remained off the bargaining table for now. The Essen EU summit chaired by the Germans was notable for the lack of any real substantive negotiations or issues. Building bridges to the east and improving Europe's economy were the notable goals of the summit. Kohl spoke of a Euro-optimism, and most Europeans were eager to avoid anything controversial.

Bundestag Elections

The second all-German election of October 16 can largely be interpreted as a vote for the status quo. With a much smaller majority for the Kohl coalition, there existed no strong mandate for change. The FDP remained in the Bundestag, largely on the strength of split-ticket voters of the CDU. The SPD gained 3 percent overall, and the Greens were back in the Bundestag with 7.3 percent; the Party of Democratic Socialism (PDS) secured four direct mandate seats all in east Berlin and, with 4.4 percent of the overall vote, reserved thirty seats in the Bundestag. More significant, with the SPD retaining control in the Saarland and a minigrand coalition in effect in Mecklenburg-Vorpommern, the SPD controlled the Bundesrat, or upper house of parliament. For all practical purposes, a Grand Coalition existed, a situation that would increasingly be marked by political paralysis. The Germans were still very much a divided nation: Although economically better off by most measures, except high unemployment, eastern Germans felt a loss of community as well as political impotence; for western Germans, resentment toward their eastern neighbors had increased.[37] The difficult issues of reforming pensions, health care, labor laws, and tax policy were the real sources of the divisions. Despite Kohl's rhetoric about completing German unity and European unity, which no one could fundamentally disagree with, the divisions did not end with Kohl's re-election.

The Dollar Free-Fall and German-U.S. Conflict

The year 1995 started on a positive note in the United States, Europe, and Germany. The EMS remained stable and calm, although discussions on a core Europe still reverberated throughout Europe. Many analysts predicted a strong dollar for 1995 based on positive economic news in the United States, continued U.S. interest rate increases, and a newly empowered Republican Congress intent on balancing the budget. Germany was also slowly rebounding from recession. Annual growth for 1994 stood at 2.8 percent, and inflation was down to 2.5 percent. Unemployment levels, however, remained stubbornly high. Still fresh from his re-election, Chancellor Kohl launched a new "consensus round" of talks between unions, industry, and the government in a classic quasi-corporatist attempt to address difficult adjustment problems. Kohl could also rejoice in the closing of the Treuhand, the world's biggest holding company, with 12,370 companies when it was set up in 1990.[38] Rocked by scandal, dominated by westerners (the *Wessis*), and saddled with a debt of DM 270 billion, 91 percent of east Germans had a negative view of the institution. Investors had promised 1.5 million jobs and DM 207 billion of investment. Yet six out of ten of the 4 million originally working in Treuhand companies had lost their place of employment. The legacy of the Treuhand on Germany's public coffers and employment would be felt for some time to come.

The generally upbeat mood changed drastically, however. The Mexican peso crisis, which began in December of 1994, set off an explosion in the international monetary system. By early January, the dollar—dragged down by the falling peso—was dropping precipitously against the DM and the yen, setting the stage for a classic DM-dollar-EMS crisis. The dollar's stability hinged on several key factors: the success or failure of the international monetary bailout of the Mexicans and the possible return of the policy of dollar neglect by the Clinton administration. Some analysts also saw the potential for interest rate increases in Germany that would have further complicated exchange rate management.[39] Those in control of the markets had made up their minds; the markets were being against the dollar (and the peso) and in favor of the DM.

At the beginning of February, the crisis in Mexico sharpened as markets watched nervously at various stumbling attempts to develop an internationally agreed-upon peso-rescue package. A special G7 summit convened in Toronto to discuss a coordinated strategy, but the United States already had made its decision to move quickly ahead with a combination U.S.-IMF-BIS package of loans. The rare and decisive U.S. decision on monetary governance displeased many Clinton critics. In particular, Germany, along with other European G7 countries, withheld their vote of support in the IMF directorate for the U.S.-dictated rescue package (U.S.$17.8 billion from the IMF, U.S.$10 billion from BIS, and U.S.$20 billion from the United States). The *New York Times* called the German-led decision a "rare rebuff" of U.S. leadership. As a German official stated, "We think the package was put together with too much haste and that the member countries did not have enough time to evaluate it."[40] Although the Germans and others eventually soon came around to support the package (largely on the back of promises by the United States to support European initiatives in Russia), one of the biggest international financial crises since the Black October crisis of 1987 was again marked by U.S.-German conflict.

Inevitably, and despite the wider trading margins, tension in the EMS increased appreciably in connection with the downward slide of the U.S. dollar. With the DM strengthening 16 percent against the dollar within the first quarter of 1995, the inherent tensions within the DM-dollar-EMS triangle quickly resurfaced. The DM was being quoted at 5 percent higher against all other EU currencies, largely because of the continued political uncertainties in Mexico and upcoming presidential elections in France. Despite interventions in the market, ECOFIN decided to implement an EMS realignment with the Spanish peseta depreciating by 7 percent and the Portuguese escudo by 3.5 percent. Outside the EMS, the Italian lira and British pound also faced strong downward pressure (20 percent and 10 percent against the DM, respectively). The French franc also came under sustained pressure driven by pre-election jitters. Nonetheless, the violent exchange rate variations remained largely within the widened fluctuation bands of the EMS, and interventions in the foreign exchange markets—in contrast to previous currency crises—were kept within acceptable limits. According to the Bundesbank, the EMS retained the necessary flexibility to deal with the shock. Moreover, the effect of the money shock in Germany was negligible.[41]

The EMS realignment was a glaring example of the divergence that still existed between European countries and why EMU looked increasingly impractical and improbable. Market officials were betting that little convergence along the guidelines of the Maastricht Treaty had, in fact, occurred. The strength of the DM signaled that the Bundesbank's postunification credibility crisis was now definitely over. The DM still dominated European monetary affairs. Although this fact increased pressure for early monetary union and John Major reintroduced the ill-fated parallel currency plan, France, Belgium, Denmark, and Portugal raised their interest rates in order to stay closely aligned with the DM. The Franco-German monetary entente, in particular, showed its strength. Chancellor Kohl tried to bolster the franc by stating that the fundamentals in France were much better than what was expressed in the value of the franc.[42] The Bank of France sought to make it harder for speculators to borrow money to run a quick profit by suspending its five-to-ten-day securities-repurchase lending. The core group of EMS countries remained steadfastly unified around the DM.

In March, at a meeting of the French-American Council, German finance minister Theo Waigel urged the United States to undertake greater efforts to stabilize the U.S. currency. With the dollar clearly undervalued, the Germans demanded that the United States do whatever was "necessary to have a strong dollar,"[43] including placing pressure on the Federal Reserve to raise interest rates. Interestingly, with M3 under control, the Bundesbank lowered the discount rate from 4.5 percent to 4 percent on March 30, which helped boost the dollar by 2 percent the next day. Could the Bundesbank move be interpreted as a German signal to ease tensions in Europe and the international monetary system? The Bundesbank sought to dispel such an interpretation by issuing a lengthy statement clarifying its decision based on the "stability outlook" in Germany. Underestimating his influence, Tietmeyer also stated that he did not believe Germany's decision could significantly change currency markets.[44] But Waigel was a bit more open on this topic. He stated that the measures taken by the Bundesbank would contribute to strengthening the trust in the stability of exchange rates in the markets.[45] Realignments, interest rate movement, and some Bundesbank intervention signaled a strong German commitment to cooperating within the EMS.

Despite various efforts to stabilize the dollar, the DM dropped dramatically to a post–World War II low of DM 1.36 to the dollar. The Bundesbank and government stepped up their criticism of U.S. policy. Waigel stated that Germany could not make up for "national deficiencies" of the United States and that G7 cooperation could not be used to compensate for the problems of the U.S. economy.[46] Tietmeyer argued that "currency stabilization depends above all on countries with weak currencies. . . . They must pursue policies that create confidence."[47] In April, at a tense G7 meeting to discuss the ongoing dollar crisis, the monetary conditions for a revival of the Louvre accord were certainly present, but the political conditions were not. The participants did not agree on a large-scale concerted action. They pledged to work toward a resolution of domestic and foreign trade imbalances that would contribute to exchange rate management. But each member was acting out of self-interest. The opinion of the G7, which did not count that much on the markets, was that an orderly reversal of the dollar's decline would be proper.

The public level of German-U.S. monetary discord was remarkable. Even Chancellor Kohl entered the fray by stating that the problem lay with the United States and that U.S. unwillingness to trim its budget deficit was not acceptable.[48] Lawrence Summers, U.S. under secretary of the treasury, accused the Germans of "always saying no."[49] Tietmeyer responded by pinpointing the blame on the United States and its twin budget and trade deficits. "The problems to me are clear . . . low savings ratio, relatively high budget deficit, no absolute assurance it will come down in the long run, and a high net debtor position." Tietmeyer instructed the United States to address these points. Moreover, he argued that there was no coordinated plan on the part of the German government to criticize the United States, but he conceded that he did not remember the last time there had been such outspoken criticism of the United States. More forcefully, Tietmeyer stated, "I am not interested in interfering in the policy of the United States. I am only saying that it is important to understand what are the problems behind the dollar's low value, and that the markets are not only looking at the present problems but they are looking always as what will happen in the future." The point of Tietmeyer's statements was clear: Monetary credibility required action, not mere words.[50]

Given the peso crisis and the level of international monetary discord, discussions resurfaced on restructuring the global monetary system in coordination with reform of the IMF. Some analysts suggested a tax (the "Tobin tax," named after the Nobel Prize–winning economist) on "speculators" as a way to dampen movements in exchange markets. Several books published in the popular press indicated that the influence of central banks was waning under the pressure of international financial markets.[51] Other analysts suggested a return to fixed exchange rates or to target zones. But target zones or fixed exchange rates would have to pass three critical tests in order to be credible: (1) they would have to be flexible enough to cope with economic shocks; (2) they would have to be robust enough to convince the markets that governments were committed to defending their pegged rates; and (3) they would have to be able to combat speculators who would undoubtedly test the commitment of member states.[52] More problematical, the dilemma of cooperating by sacrificing monetary autonomy for stability in exchange markets would resurface. Were the conditions conducive for a return to Plaza or Louvre? The answer was clearly no.

Not surprisingly, the German government faced its own pressure due to the DM appreciation. The strong DM brought attention to the plight of German industry and labor concerned about competitiveness and jobs, respectively. Industrial leaders like Tyll Necker, head of the Bundesband der Deutschen Industrie, blamed U.S. policies but even leveled mild criticism at the Bundesbank.[53] German economists lowered growth expectations based on the DM value.[54] Mercedes-Benz announced that it expected a severe loss in 1995, blaming the rise of the DM and suggesting that the easiest strategy for industry would be to continue to diversify production outside of Germany. Some analysts directly blamed the Bundesbank's monetary policy.[55] Such pressure on the Bundesbank to lower interest rates met with resistance as the bank continued to place blame on the United States. In its June *Monthly Report,* the Bundesbank remained cautious and warned industry not to overreact to the crisis. In any case, the Bundesbank found itself again caught between the dollar and domestic political pressures.

Fortunately, the international monetary crisis of the spring had quieted by the summer months. The Mexican economy was in tatters, but for the moment financially stable. German-U.S. tension had subsided, and there was hope that the annual G7 summit in Halifax could repair some of the damage. The discussion on reforming the IMF carried over from the fifty-year anniversary discussions a year earlier and the G7 pledge to determine a new framework of international monetary structures needed to confront the globalized financial system. The Germans were not buying into a completely restructured global governance system and pushed for a relatively unreformed IMF. Yes, the IMF could act more strongly to develop a crisis mechanism to deal with a Mexican-style crash, and it could enhance its surveillance role over developing and transitioning economies. However, the Germans demanded greater checks and controls over the IMF and World Bank. Moreover, there existed little pressure to see these institutions retooled to govern the international monetary system on behalf of the G7. The G7's own significance and influence were increasingly in doubt.[56]

Shortly before the IMF/World Bank meeting in September, the Bundesbank lowered interest rates again by a half percentage point. At the G7 summit prior to the meeting, the Bundesbank and government were thus able to deflect any potential criticism of a German role in destabilizing the dollar. In fact, the move helped strengthen the dollar as it rose to DM 1.47. Moreover, an August 15 coordinated intervention by central banks on behalf of the dollar proved successful in pushing the dollar up 2.8 percent in one day. The United States and Japan had been undertaking bilateral measures weeks earlier by following a strategy of surprising the markets (when some markets were closed for holiday) and by going with the tide of the dollar. The Clinton administration, like earlier administrations, had learned some lessons about intervention and, more generally, dollar politics. Although it appeared that the G3 was informally at least coordinating interest rate and intervention strategies, the real course of the dollar was still determined by underlying fiscal and monetary policies aimed at domestic conditions in the United States and Germany. By September the dollar rallied to around DM 1.50 (and had again jumped back over 100 yen to the dollar) and strengthened as a result of trade progress with Japan, movement on budget deficits, and U.S. and German interest rate policy. By December, as German interest rates would reach their lowest since 1988, Germany and the United States could both point to various efforts, albeit mostly unilateral and outside the G7 framework, in restoring some confidence to the dollar and the international monetary system.

Franc Fort Under Pressure

Following the election of Jacques Chirac to the presidency of France, the markets began again to test the *franc fort* policy and the government's commitment to the convergence criteria. Chirac, who had been lukewarm in his support of EMU in the campaign, and the new prime minister, Alain Juppe, proclaimed unemployment as the Number 1 preoccupation of the French government. With promises of tax breaks and minimum wage increases, and possible tension between the government and the anti-inflationary president Jean-Claude Trichet of the newly independent French Central Bank, traders were predicting that the French government would fall short of its goals. The stability of the currency, however, had also become an objective of foreign policy and a fundamental token of France's European commitment. Kohl and Chirac met on the second day of Chirac's term to indicate the strength of the Franco-German partnership and reaffirm their commitment to EMU. The monetary partnership, despite some tension, remained strong and firm.[57]

The *franc fort* policy would continue to be put to the test by the Bundesbank and its new ally, the EMI. The Bundesbank position on the convergence criteria was straightforward:

It would be wrong to make compromises when interpreting the convergence criteria. The turmoil in the international foreign exchange markets in the first few months of this year [1995] once again graphically highlighted the connection between convergence in national economic policies and stable monetary relationships. In a world of closely interrelated financial markets and highly volatile investment capital, movements in exchange rates and interest rates increasingly hinge on the credibility of national economic policy.[58]

The EMI, in turn, would ensure that national economic policy was aimed in the proper, that is, Bundesbank-oriented, direction. In its first major report, the EMI criticized the lack of progress made by EU countries in attaining the convergence criteria. Only Luxembourg was ready to make the leap to EMU. Especially in the area of public debt and budget deficits, countries would be hard pressed to make the necessary adjustments for EMU. With commitments to cutting government spending and increasing employment, the French objectives looked increasingly irreconcilable in the eyes of the EMI.

With the first EMU deadline of January 1, 1997, fast approaching, it soon became clear that a delay would be necessary. Waigel had already indicated that the German government felt currency union would be highly unlikely by the earlier date. This position was certainly welcomed in Frankfurt. However, given the DM-dollar-EMS crisis earlier in the year and the fact that the Bundesbank still reigned supreme in European monetary politics, there were still some voices pushing for an early date. France, in particular, supported an early jump to EMU as did the European Commission. The reality, however, of the Maastricht Treaty's convergence criteria and the power of Bundesbank resistance to an early start to EMU suggested that a quick move would be politically unfeasible. Hence, the EU finance ministers agreed to delay the onset of EMU until 1999.

Five years after unification, the German economy presented a mixed picture of success and failures, problems and opportunities.[59] Not only was France under pressure, but the German government found itself facing budgetary numbers not befitting its monetary leadership. As the Bundesbank noted in its *Annual Report*, 1995 was not an easy year for the German economy. On the downside, high unemployment, budget deficits, and external pressures brought on by the volatility of global exchange markets and the temporary sharp appreciation of the DM vis-à-vis the dollar hurt German exporters and competitiveness. Fiscal deficits and government debt were still above the Maastricht criteria. On a more positive note, with inflation under control and M3 within the Bundesbank's target corridor of 4–6 percent, moderate GDP growth at an annual rate of 2.5 percent indicated some life in the German economy. Furthermore, other European countries were able to lower interest rates as their currencies generally held firm to the DM. The European economy slowly, but steadily, pulled up from the trough of 1993. But the Maastricht yoke would tighten further as the new deadline of 1999 approached.

The Transition to EMU: "Mounting Wave" or "Delayed Big Bang"?

As international and European monetary stability returned in the fall of 1995 and the decision was taken to delay EMU another two years, the question of how to make the transition to the single currency topped the agenda. Essentially two positions on the introduction of the single currency developed. The first view was supported by France and the European Commission.[60] They wanted to pursue EMU by establishing a "critical mass" of participants actively using the new currency. Labeled the "mounting wave theory," this approach envisioned governments and banks employing the single currency for a short transition period before it would be introduced to the general public. Moreover, governments would fix exchange rates on January 1, 1999, and issue all new government debt in the new currency in order to secure acceptance of the currency in international markets. With governments and banks mounting the wave early and setting the process in motion (the critical mass), businesses, workers, and the public would then find it easier to fuse onto the new currency. France, in particular, was concerned that a long transition period would unduly expose the franc to speculative pressures. Delay would strain the credibility of the new system—through currency speculation on weak EMU members—and push the boundaries of Maastricht by delaying EMU in a formal sense until mid-2002. The goal of this approach would be to have the new currency quickly percolate throughout the entire European economy.

The German government, in general, and the Bundesbank, in particular, preferred a delayed "big bang" approach. This approach envisioned locking exchange rates together, but then delaying any general use of a single currency until small banks had gotten used to the new currency and could offer single-currency services to compete with big banks. The euro, as the single currency would be called, would only exist in the ledgers of central banks after exchange rates would be fixed. Moreover, the general public would also have time to accommodate themselves to the single currency because they would still be allowed to use their own national currencies up until a final cut-off date, the "delayed big bang" of EMU, when everyone would carry euro in their pockets. In addition, the German approach sought to avoid some of the confusion of a "parallel" system inherent in the Commission's approach. To deal with the French fear of speculation during the transition phase, the Germans would offer a new twist to the EMU agreement, the stability pact, discussed in the next section of this chapter.

Interestingly, the European Commission faced opposition to its plan from one of its sister EU institutions, the EMI.[61] The EMI's blueprint for the introduction of the euro echoed in many ways the German position, especially the idea of a long transition phase to a single currency. The EMI provided the Germans with European-level governance that largely conformed to a German monetary norm. This would make it easier for the Bundesbank to influence EMU debates but also allow for the continuation of accommodation of the Bundesbank and the government to the larger goal of EMU. Tietmeyer praised the EMI's report by stating that it took into account significant German concerns, especially the concept that the single currency would only become legal tender once the people had European coins and banknotes in their pockets, that is, at the end of a transition period of up to three years. The long transition phase would allow banks, of which Germany has many, to adjust internal systems to cope with the switchover. The long switchover would imply that the DM would likely be around until mid-2002.

The compromises reached by the European Council in Madrid in December fleshed out the major conditions underlying the third stage of EMU. With Chancellor Kohl pushing hard to keep the timetable for EMU alive, the Bundesbank would have to accept some aspects of the Commission's plans. On the other side, the Bundesbank and EMI secured the option that no one but the governments would be forced to deal in euros until the final stages of the transition. Governments, however, would have to issue new debt in euros right from the start, especially issues that did not mature until after the end of Stage 3. The ESCB would conduct monetary policy in euros right from the beginning of Stage 3, January 1, 1999. The compromise also included the confirmation of the scheduled implementation of Stage 3 of EMU on January 1, 1999, in accordance with the convergence criteria and the choice of the euro as the name of the future European currency.

The changeover scenario of Stage 3 divides the time required for completely replacing national currencies into three distinct phases. Phase 1 incorporates a short interim period, beginning as soon as a decision is made on which member states qualify (to be made as early as possible in 1998 by the heads of government on the basis of the actual economic data for the year 1997) and during which the ESCB would set up operations. Following this first phase, Phase 2 would start on January 1, 1999, and last up to three years during which the single currency would be introduced progressively for book-entry transactions. Again, no one would automatically be required to use euros. Central banks would be obligated to exchange national currencies at fixed rates so as to add credibility to the union and discourage speculators. Phase 3, a period not exceeding six months, specifically envisions the issue of banknotes and coins denominated in the euro and for the recall of national money. If this phase does not begin within the three-year period (Phase 2), it will start no later than January 1, 2002. By July 1, 2002, the euro will be the sole unit of account for participating members, and the final date for use of the DM.

Stability Pact for Europe?

Around the same time as the Madrid summit was settling on a transition plan, protests in France over proposed budgetary cuts and social reforms necessary to hold France to the budget and debt levels required of Maastricht led to widespread strikes and occasionally violent protests by public employees. The French economy was nearly shut down as the markets were again testing the French government's credibility. Alain Madelin, Alain Juppe's first finance minister and committed EMU supporter, was unceremoniously dumped in September, just 100 days after taking office. Was Chirac and Juppe's government up to the task of EMU? In October, the Bank of France had to raise interest rates as the franc lost more than 1 percent against the DM in just one day. Some analysts already speculated that the crisis would push Chirac to call a snap election, which would come in May of 1997, or force him to abandon EMU. In the end, France muddled through by making compromises to unions but still sticking to EMU in principle.

In large part as a result of the French crisis, criticism began to focus more narrowly on the strict convergence criteria. Why not renegotiate the criteria and make it somewhat easier for more countries to join in 1999? More important, was the demand for price stability as a prerequisite for EMU and price stability as the overriding macroeconomic objective of a future European central bank good for Europe?[62] Many analysts both within and outside of Germany questioned whether it was necessary to export the stability culture that is Germany to the rest of Europe. Others described Germany's monetary hegemony as "German bullying," especially in regard to Waigel's push for a stability pact. Helmut Schmidt, a prominent critic of Bundesbank policy, argued that German DM nationalism was threatening not only EMU but also the entire project of European integration.[63] Some SPD politicians, most notably Gerhard Schröder, were suggesting an anti-EMU course or, at a minimum, delaying EMU indefinitely.[64] Even German businesses, especially in the important export-oriented *Mittelstand,* were not entirely behind the EMU project. A survey of over 700 businesses commissioned by the DIHT found only 55 percent supportive of EMU, with 40 percent against the plan and fully two-thirds doubting the 1999 launching date.[65]

The debate over EMU feasibility and plausibility also began to shake the facade of unity at the Bundesbank. Although the Bundesbank officially stuck to one policy on EMU, internal disputes carried unusually over into the public arena. As required politically, the Bundesbank president held firm to the bank's ongoing position on EMU, namely, that it supported the Maastricht Treaty, the convergence criteria, and, most important, the timetable. But others, including Reimut Jochimsen, president of the *Land* central bank of Northrein-Westphalia, were pushing openly for a delay of the timetable.[66] Jochimsen was certainly giving voice to others within the Central Bank Council and among many leading economists who had long held deep suspicions of EMU. There also remained considerable disappointment regarding the failure to develop political union, a position shared by all Bundesbankers. Could the Bundesbank put a halt to the EMU effort? Probably not, but the internal Bundesbank debate fueled growing resistance within the German public to the EMU project.

The controversy over another round of deutsche mark politics began in October. At the CDU party meeting in Karlsrühe, Kohl painted an apocalyptic picture of a Europe without economic and monetary integration. It would be a matter of "war and peace in the twenty-first century," he noted, adding that if the Germans and Europeans "do not act now, the ship of Europe will go adrift."[67] While well intentioned, the speech rubbed some sensitive nerves. The British government, in part, and British commentators, in particular, implied that Germany was using its monetary power to dominate European affairs. Moreover, was EMU really that critical to European stability, comparable in some way to the stability provided by NATO? In addition, Kohl's European ship was leaking as a result of the gaping holes ripped in the budget. Waigel's comments to a Bundestag parliamentary committee suggesting that Italy would not meet the criteria and thus would not be able to join the core group of EMU members upset the Italian government and dragged the lira down. As Italy was desperately and earnestly attempting to steer the Italian economy in the direction of the criteria, any unnecessary political jolts to the lira's confidence were seen as unnecessary.

It should be noted that considerable advancement had been made in most EU countries, including Italy, in terms of inflation. While the picture offered was mixed, most countries were at least moving strongly and significantly in the proper monetary direction required under the criteria. As a result, it was anticipated that more nations than were originally thought would be joining EMU. By contrast, advances in the field of fiscal policy consolidation (debt and deficits) were less than satisfactory for the Germans. Although most countries did strive to reduce deficits, only Denmark, Ireland, and Luxembourg by the end of 1995 had attained budget deficits within the Maastricht range. In terms of the gross government debt as a percentage of GDP, France and Germany came under the mark but would soon excede the 60 percent figure by early 1996. In short, while some convergence had occurred across the EU, there were a number of other areas where convergence was noticeably lacking.

Realizing that the three-year transition phase (possibly three and a half years) of EMU might offer weak currency governments an opportunity to overspend—and thereby weaken the single currency—and sensing the possibility that speculators might attack these currencies one by one, the German government felt that preventative measures were necessary. Such measures came to be called the "stability pact." According to the author of the plan, Theo Waigel, governments intending to join the single currency would have to set their deficit targets not at 3 percent of GDP, but at 1 percent. This would ensure that even during a recession, when deficits rise, they would not exceed the 3 percent called for in Maastricht. Also, a stability pact would impose disciplinary measures on countries that exceeded the 3 percent clause. An offending government would have to deposit a sum equivalent to 0.25 percent of its GDP in the ECB, the sum not to be returned until the offending country had trimmed its deficit back to less than 3 percent. If the offending country remained beyond the limit for two years, the deposit would become nonreturnable—in essence, a fine.

With the Franco-German alliance sputtering under the strain of France's own internal turmoil and cracks over timetables and stability pacts, Kohl set out to keep the push toward EMU on track. Instead of doing battle solely with the Bundesbank, Kohl had to now contend with a difficult coalition of the Bundesbank and his own finance minister. While Kohl focused on the broad picture of European integration, the Bundesbank and its ally Waigel had found common ground on the devilish details of EMU. It was Waigel who was increasingly seen as the doorman to entry into currency union, dictating terms and conditions of the transition. However, Waigel served a useful purpose for Kohl; Waigel could become the lightning rod for the inevitable attacks on deutsche mark politics. Moreover, the mechanisms requiring enforcement of the "fine" would demand closer political cooperation on fiscal policy. Ultimately that would require political union, a point that the Bundesbank and Kohl had always agreed upon. Only a federal polity (for example, a European stability council) could legitimately impose the fines necessary for the stability pact.

Other commentators interpreted Waigel's efforts as a secret Bundesbank plan to scuttle the single currency by adding new, more difficult conditions for entry. But Waigel had always publicly been pro-European and pro-EMU, and there was nothing inherent in the stability pact that necessarily contradicted this view. Waigel's efforts were probably aimed at placating the Bundesbank, shoring up conservative political support (especially in the CSU), and retaining a political wedge against the SPD, which had been trying to stir things up with anti-EMU rhetoric. With most opinion polls showing 60–65 percent of the German public against the EMU/euro concept, Waigel was Kohl's front man on ensuring that only a hard euro would replace the hard DM. As the early 1998 date approached, much more work on educating the German public would still be needed.

In the end, ECOFIN generally found Waigel's ideas acceptable, and the European Council at the Madrid summit reaffirmed the notion that a sound course of public finance must be ensured. It did not formally agree to enshrine the stability pact in any treaty revisions. Such revisions would not be worked out, literally to the last minute, until the conclusion of the intergovernmental conference (IGC) in June 1997 in Amsterdam. Further left unclear was the clarification of the institutional arrangements associated with a two-speed Europe and other external exchange rate arrangements, for example, with the U.S. dollar and the Japanese yen, that would be necessary to make the ESCB operate smoothly.

Conclusion

The period 1994–1995 included fewer formal rounds of monetary negotiations comparable to the earlier periods such as Plaza/Louvre, Basel-Nyborg, Maastricht, and the year-long EMS crisis of 1992–1993. However, a few key sets of negotiations can be identified. In Europe, the primary issue for negotiation included the realignment of March 1995 and the debate over the transition to EMU. First, it should be noted that the government was less inclined to pursue a realignment (in essence, a DM appreciation vis-à-vis the Spanish and Portuguese) because of the fear of losing export competitiveness. The concern about job growth framed the government's perception of the dollar crisis. The Bundesbank, however, realized that a realignment was necessary and proper to securing continued stability within the EMS. With central bank interventions in Europe kept to a minimum and interest rates already pushing in an EMS-friendly direction, the Bundesbank's interest in a realignment can be understood as a trade-off of a small measure of autonomy in return for securing ongoing exchange rate stability within the EMS.

The debate over the transition period to a single currency is a bit more complex. The negotiations centered less on the autonomy versus exchange rate stability definition of cooperation as used in this study. The Germans had already committed themselves to the ultimate sacrifice of autonomy, the euro. But the details of the transition to the euro did hinge on the negotiations between the Germans and other Europeans, including the Commission. Moreover, these details would have a significant impact upon the stability of the transition phase of EMU. Therefore, the Germans' pursuit of a delayed big bang (postponing the introduction of the euro until the last minute, thereby encouraging the possible speculation of the markets on weak currencies) within the context of the transition stage did indicate an initially less than cooperative approach. A compromise was found whereby the German government, under the pressure of Kohl on the Bundesbank, did commit to an even more explicit date, July 1, 2002, when the DM would cease to exist.

The international monetary arena saw ongoing sets of negotiations reflected in the repeated dollar crises, in particular during the spring of 1995. These negotiations centered on the rescue package for Mexico and various efforts to coordinate interest rate policy and market interventions. Although hard to pinpoint, it did appear that the Germans were pursuing a cooperative strategy in securing some measure of exchange rate stability. But these efforts were unilateral efforts in the name of domestic interests and not within the context of any formalized G7 round of negotiations. At least within the G7, the German government pursued a hard-line strategy of resisting any G7 efforts on rescuing the dollar. Moreover, the German rebuff of U.S. leadership during the Mexican peso crisis served as another reminder of the lengths the Germans are willing to go to serve German and European interests in global monetary governance. Finally, the level of criticism by both the government and the Bundesbank toward the United States, demanding concessions from the United States in order to stabilize the dollar, indicated the continued weakness of international governance structures. Such weakness was signified by the failure to develop any concrete plans on reforming the IMF or other mechanisms for G7 governance of the international monetary system.

Notes

1. See *The Economist*'s analysis of the German economy, "Germany Under Strain," November 10, 1993.

2. "Restructuring of East Germany, " *Financial Times*, May 4, 1994; "Model Vision: Survey of the Germany Economy," *The Economist*, May 21, 1994.

3. Deutsche Bundesbank, *Annual Report 1994* (Frankfurt/Main), p. 99. As a comparison, the Bundesbank intervened with DM 338.5 billion in 1992 and DM 283.1 billion in 1993.

4. Interview with Bundesbank official, 1994.

5. Both Tietmeyer and the new vice president, Johan Wilhelm Gaddum, had strong personal and political ties to Kohl. Some feared an even stronger political connection between the government and bank.

6. "Bundesbank President Cautions Against D-Mark Devaluation," *This Week in Germany,* December 3, 1993.

7. Hans Tietmeyer, "National Monetary Policy and European Monetary Union," *Occasional Paper Series* 23-93 (Washington, D.C.: Konrad Adenauer Stiftung, 1993), p. 11.

8. "Europe's Sinking Ship," *The Economist*, November 27, 1993.

9. "Maastricht Treaty Goes into Effect, Frankfurt Chosen as Site of European Monetary Institute," *This Week in Germany*, November 5, 1993.

10. Horst Köhler, "A Farewell Address," *The International Economy*, March/April 1993. For some additional commentary on the G7 process, see the interview with Köhler, "Germany's New Mr. Big," *The International Economy*, September/October 1992.

11. Interviews with Bundesbank officials, May 1994.
12. The splinter party, Bund Freier Burger, based its platform on the single issue of defeating EMU. The Bund did not receive much support from the German public.
13. For an analysis, see "German Central Bank Lowers Discount Rate," *New York Times*, February 18, 1994.
14. Deutsche Bundesbank, *Annual Report 1995* (Frankfurt/Main), p. 62.
15. "Gefangene der Märkte," *Der Speigel*, no. 7, 1994; "Auf den Abfallhaufen," *Der Spiegel*, no. 10, 1994. The British had given Tietmeyer the name "Lightmeyer" in reference to the Bundesbank's policies.
16. "Talk Show," *The Economist*, May 14, 1994.
17. Ibid.
18. "Central Banks Step to Defend Dollar," *Financial Times*, May 5, 1994. See also "Strengthening D-Mark Rattles the Bundesbank," *Financial Times*, May 5, 1994.
19. "G7 See Economic Recovery, Inflation in Check: Bundesbank Stays Firm on Monetary Policy," *This Week in Germany*, April 29, 1994.
20. "Bentsen Voices Strong Support for Dollar," *Los Angeles Times*, June 29, 1994.
21. "Kräftiger Zinsschritt nach unten erwünscht," *Frankfurter Allgemeine Zeitung*, May 5, 1994.
22. Wilfried Herz, "Gift für den Aufschwung," *Die Zeit*, June 17, 1994.
23. See the presummit analysis, "A Troubled Clinton, His Ratings, Currency Down, Leaves Today for 2nd G7 Summit," *Los Angeles Times*, July 5, 1994.
24. "The Dollar's Slide Show," *The Economist*, July 16, 1994.
25. "Increase Work Role, Clinton Tells Germany," *Los Angeles Times*, July 12, 1994.
26. See, for example, Jeffrey Sachs, "Beyond Bretton Woods," *The Economist*, October 1, 1994; Ronald McKinnon, "Recapturing the Lost Spirit," *Financial Times*, June 21, 1994; "Reforming Bretton Woods" (Bretton Woods Commission, Washington, D.C., 1994, mimeographed).
27. "Will the Buck Stop Here?" *The Economist*, November 12, 1994.
28. Deutsche Bundesbank, *Annual Report 1994* (Frankfurt/Main), p. 18.
29. For a balanced and broad account of the debate, see Nina Grunenberg, "Was wollen die Deutschen mit Europa," *Die Zeit*, July 18, 1994; and Christoph Bertram, "Welches Europa soll's denn Sein," *Die Zeit*, September 16, 1994.
30. Christian Democratic Union, "Thoughts on European Policy" (Bonn, Germany, 1994, mimeographed).
31. "Core Europe Proposal Draws Fire from EU Members, Opposition Parties," *This Week in Germany*, September 9, 1994.
32. *Land* elections in Saxony, Brandenburg, and Bavaria confirmed the status quo.
33. "EU: Finance Ministers—Recession Is Over, Standards for Currency Union Upheld," *This Week in Germany*, September 16, 1994.
34. "German Plan for Phased Union of Europe Provokes Controversy," *New York Times*, September 4, 1994.
35. "Euro-Poll Blow for Single Currency," *Financial Times*, June 1, 1994.
36. Wilfred Herz, "Der Streit fehlt: Die Eurowährung kommt, die Bürger sind dagegen," *Die Zeit,* September 30, 1994.
37. "A Wall of Resentment Now Divides Germany," *New York Times*, October 14, 1994.
38. See the balance sheet of the Treuhand, "Farewell Sweet Treuhand," *The Economist*, December 24, 1994. See also "Der Mohr kann gehen," *Die Zeit*, December 30, 1994.

39. "Wette auf den Streik," *Die Zeit*, March 9, 1995.
40. "European Nations Abstain on Vote for Mexican Plan," *New York Times*, February 3, 1995, p. A1.
41. Deutsche Bundesbank, *Annual Report 1994* (Frankfurt/Main), p. 99.
42. "Four Nations Raise Rates to Halt Mark," *New York Times*, March 9, 1995.
43. "German-French Economic Council Calls for Efforts to Stabilize the Dollar," *This Week in Germany*, March 24, 1995.
44. "A Surprise German Rate Cut Propels the Dollar Up 2%," *New York Times*, March 31, 1995.
45. Ibid.
46. "As Dollar Falls, Economic Powers Blame Each Other," *New York Times*, April 11, 1995. See also "U.S. and Allies Try to Prop Up the Dollar But Fail Again," *New York Times*, April 6, 1995.
47. "As Dollar Falls, Economic Powers Blame Each Other," *New York Times*, April 11, 1995, p. A1.
48. "As Wealthy Nations Meet, the New Tone Is Divisive," *New York Times*, April 24, 1995.
49. "An Eclipse for the G7," *New York Times*, April 26, 1995.
50. "U.S. Savings and Deficit Key to Dollar, German Says," *New York Times*, May 8, 1995, p. D2.
51. See, for example, Gregory Millman, *The Vandal's Crown* (New York: Viking, 1995); Marjorie Deane and Robert Pringle, *The Central Banks* (New York: Viking Press, 1995); Steven Solomon, *The Confidence Game* (New York: Simon and Schuster, 1995).
52. See, for example, the criticism of fixed rates in Barry Eichengreen, *International Monetary Arrangements for the 21st Century* (Washington, D.C.: Brookings Institution, 1994).
53. "Das Schiff ist zu hoch beladen," *Die Zeit*, April 21, 1995.
54. "Von der starken Mark Überollt," *Die Zeit*, April 14, 1995.
55. Claus Noe, "Das Problem liegt zu Hause," *Die Zeit*, April 21, 1995.
56. "Nur noch ein Witz," Thomas Hanke, *Die Zeit*, June 19, 1995.
57. "Zwei Freunde, die sich fast verstehen," *Die Zeit*, April 21, 1995; "Die Räder wechseln, die Achse bleibt," *Die Zeit*, May 19, 1995.
58. Deutsche Bundesbank, *Annual Report 1994* (Frankfurt/Main), p. 9.
59. "The Eagle's Embrace," *The Economist*, September 30, 1995.
60. European Commission, "Green Paper on the Practical Arrangements for the Introduction of the Single Currency," May 1995, Brussels.
61. The EMI is located in Frankfurt and dominated by a German staff.
62. Claus Noe, "Was heisst denn Stabilitätskultur?" *Die Zeit*, July 21, 1995.
63. Helmut Schmidt, "Deutsches Störfeuer gegen Europa," *Die Zeit*, October 6, 1995.
64. "German Socialists Question the Single-Money Canon," *New York Times*, November 2, 1995. The SPD's own finance experts, however, cautioned against such a course of action.
65. See the analysis in "Zagen and Zaudern," *Die Zeit*, October 6, 1995.
66. "Kulturkampf der Geldhüter," *Die Zeit*, November 24, 1995.
67. "Kohl Presses Case for European Integration," *New York Times*, October 17, 1995, p. A10.

7

Economic Monetary Union for Europe? 1996–1998

> On paper, the conditions for a stable European currency are fulfilled. But in reality, it must pass a testing period. In Germany, there is something like a "culture of stability" and that is exactly what Europe needs.
>
> —Former Bundesbank president Helmut Schlesinger, 1992

The period from early 1996 to the historic decision in May 1998 to launch EMU can be divided into two stages. The first stage proceeded through the summer debates of 1997, including the dramatic clash over gold revaluation and the subsequent controversy over a possible Kohl cabinet reshuffle. This stage also would find continued discussion focused on the stability pact, renegotiated as the Stability and Growth Pact in June 1997 under pressure from the new socialist government of France. Considerable uncertainty over the timetable and repeated calls for delay also punctuated the debate. However, by the fall of 1997, the debate over EMU had shifted noticeably to the second stage. The discussion was no longer focused on "if" or "when." Instead, the discussion shifted to the details of how EMU would operate, creating an "ERM II" to deal with the "outs" (as opposed to the "ins"), who would be the ECB president, and developing a governing board to possibly balance ECB independence. In short, by the end of 1997, EMU was a fait accompli.

It should also be noted that the period 1996–1998 would prove comparatively stable in terms of deutsche mark politics. The convergence criteria were pushing monetary policies across Europe considerably in a coordinated direction. Even Spain and Italy—albeit with more noteworthy problems—were moving closer to the crowning moment of EMU. As a result, there would be no major ERM/EMS crises during this period. This stability, of course, was largely based on the continued interest rate policy of the Bundesbank, a policy that pushed interest rates to historic lows. On the international front, the DM weakened considerably from the historic highs of spring 1995. By the end of 1996, the DM was back to 1994 levels, trading in the range of DM 1.70 to the dollar. While G7 officials raised some concern over the strengthening of the dollar (especially as it continued to strengthen to around DM 1.80 by the end of 1997), international attention was focused instead on the exploding Asian financial crisis. Germany would add its voice to the debate on whether a new or strengthened international system of monetary governance was needed. More important, the crisis added impetus to the final push on EMU.

The weaker DM did, indeed, serve German export interests well. But export growth did not pull Germany out of the economic doldrums. The economy continued to "Trabi" along, sputtering in two strokes rather than four. Unemployment would continue to creep upward from 3.8 million in early 1996 to nearly 5 million by the spring of 1998. The high unemployment rate of 12.6 percent in February 1998 would spark immense protests from labor unions, the SPD, and the large numbers of unemployed. The protests were aimed at the government's inability to act on a number of employment fronts. The Kohl government countered that it was seeking to push through substantial policy reforms on taxes, pensions, welfare, and labor—all designed with the intent of boosting employment. But the Kohl government's hands were tied by the delaying tactics of the SPD, especially in the SPD-controlled Bundesrat, as well as the looming deadline of EMU that demanded fiscal discipline. *Reformstau*—the inability to push through any reforms—characterized the politics of Germany. Major policy initiatives would have to be put on hold until after the September 1998 elections.

The Chorus for EMU Delay Increases

The year 1996 would start off on a positive monetary note. The Bundesbank's decision to lower the discount rate from 3.5 percent to 3 percent and the Lombard rate from 5.5 percent to 5 percent was seen as an explicit step for the struggling German economy, for relaxing potential EMS tensions, and continuing the process of weakening the DM vis-à-vis the dollar.[1] For some German analysts, the hope was that the Bundesbank's policies would send the right signal to the government to also act to support the German economy.[2] Kohl's call for an "Alliance to Work" and the development of a 50-point program to revive the economy, which grew at a meager annual growth rate of 1.9 percent for 1995, was generally greeted positively by unions and businesses. Promoting jobs and investments were items most groups could agree upon. Moreover, Kohl had promised to reduce the much-hated solidarity tax. It seemed that the old corporatist consensus would bring about the required policy changes.

Nevertheless, the Maastricht convergence criteria were working against the German government and its ambitious plans for reform. With the budget deficit pushing above the acceptable levels outlined in the critieria, Waigel found himself under heavy pressure and criticism for his finance policies. In addition, there would be no new funding initiatives to spend on ambitious employment programs. With symbolic "victories" in three *Land* elections in March, the FDP reasserted its position in the coalition debates; raising taxes was not an option with the FDP. The SPD continued to offer its cooperation but only if Kohl was willing to compromise on key parts of his domestic reforms. Although there would be some movement on labor and pension reform, the political paralysis continued. Apparently, the only option for the Kohl government was to hope for a strong economic recovery. Unfortunately, the government found its hands were bound tightly together by political and economic forces beyond its control.

Even on EMU, which Kohl thought he had under his control, the chorus for delay was singing louder.[3] A poll published in *Die Woche* indicated that 84 percent of Germans thought EMU should be delayed, with over one-half of the respondents urging that EMU should be scrapped altogether. Several members of the Bundesbank council, including the influential chief economist Otmar Issing, continued to suggest concerns about EMU, in particular, the fear that competitive devaluation from non-EMU members would hurt German exports and employment. Wolfgang Schäuble, the parliamentary leader (and key Kohl ally) of the CDU argued that sticking to the criteria would have priority over the timetable. Tietmeyer suggested that it "wouldn't be the end of the world," if keeping to the criteria meant delaying EMU. Oskar Lafontaine, parliamentary leader of the SPD, envisioned using the idea of EMU postponement in the 1998 election campaign. Gerhard Schröder, who would soon assume the leadership of the SPD going into the 1998 election, also insisted on a delay so as to ensure that every EU member could join, including Britain. Schröder also envisioned a possible delay at the spring 1998 EU summit so that social matters could be incorporated into any final EMU treaty. Kohl, along with his French partners and the European Commission, sought to counter such proposals by launching various proactive information and policy programs to push the EMU agenda. Nevertheless, European politicians were increasingly seeing EMU, in the words of Roger Boyes, as "St. Augustine saw chastity: a goal worth pursuing, but please, God, not yet."[4]

Despite the calls for delay, Kohl's determination to stick with EMU would keep the momentum moving forward. Kohl emphasized his belief that the timetable and the criteria were of *equal* importance,[5] suggesting that one should not have precedence over the other. Moreover, despite the problems and tensions that existed, it should be noted that the Bundesbank and government were working extremely close together on the EMU issue. The positions of Waigel and Tietmeyer were almost identical on all aspects of the criteria, timetable, and stability pact. Both were intent on ensuring a "hard euro club." The Bundesbank was one of the leading advocates of EMU, consistently pushing the government to attain the deficit limits and keep on track with its EMU policies. The government and Bundesbank would push a hard line in order to ensure a "hard euro." But the government was willing to hold out room for accommodation, if necessary, to keep EMU on track. Kohl would hold the trump card. He alone could offer a compromise with his European partners in the forthcoming round of negotiations, especially on the stability pact.

Adding to the complexity of the negotiating milieu, the EU launched a year-long series of IGC negotiations aimed at addressing a number of issues: qualified majority voting, the size of the commission, the powers of the European Parliament, and ongoing concerns about the democratic deficit, among many possible reforms. These complex and difficult sets of negotiations would demand the attention of the Kohl government, as some of the focus was again placed on his controversial ideas of a "federalist" Europe. Fortunately, EMU negotiations were delinked from the IGC agenda. Moreover, with the debate over "Mad Cow" disease threatening to disrupt the IGC deliberations, Kohl and Chirac were ever more determined to push, if necessary, the two-speed EMU formula.[6] France and Germany would increasingly coordinate plans to promote growth and ensured everyone that the timetable laid down in the treaty was an absolute priority for both nations.[7] The Franco-German monetary axis still carried weight within the EU.

In April, with the Kohl government increasingly bogged down over internal reforms and confronted by the calls for delay, the Bundesbank once again lowered interest rates. Taking into account internal factors and the relief afforded by exchange rates, the discount rate was lowered from 3 percent to 2.5 percent and the Lombard rate from 5 percent to 4.5 percent, the lowest levels since 1987. The timing of the move came as a bit of a surprise so soon after the December rate cut, but a welcome surprise nonetheless. Many analysts also saw the move as a political concession to Kohl. With negative first-quarter growth figures and unemployment continuing upward, the Bundesbank was offering some help. Yet it also criticized the government for not acting sooner on its policy reforms, especially labor, tax, and welfare reform. Probably dependent upon the successful completion of such reforms, Tietmeyer left open the possibility for further cuts by suggesting that the Bundesbank was taking a "wait and see" attitude on interest rate policy. He added that "we aren't talking about the end. . . . We will see if there is further room."[8]

With the Bundesbank reducing exchange rate pressures within the EMS, the finance ministers could focus on EMU. In Verona, discussions focused on the stability pact as well as on the future exchange rate system—soon to be called ERM II—for the non-euro countries. Defining the conditions for the outs would soon become one of the more contested areas of debate. The Germans, primarily the Bundesbank, insisted on a system whereby the outs would peg to the euro and thus retain the onus of maintaining the peg with little, if any, help from the ECB. Moreover, only the ECB could request a realignment of the ERM II. The UK preferred either no system (left to the outs to decide for themselves), a system that targeted inflation rather than exchange rates, or a system that had more flexibility in realignments and access to ECB intervention. Clarifying ERM II would have to wait, however; the focus of EMU negotiations would increasingly hinge on clarifying the stability pact.

Looming complications over EMU would prove the least of Kohl's problems; however, he did have the upper hand in such negotiations. By May, the domestic tension developing over the government's desire to impose budgetary discipline, reform major policy issues, and address sustained high unemployment would finally explode. Kohl's urging that something "fundamental" must change in German society fell on deaf ears. What the critics pointed toward was Kohl's plan to include a "savings" package involving reductions in payments to families with children. With the Alliance to Work project in collapse, the SPD and labor unions increased the volume of their protests. Up to 350,000 union and SPD supporters turned out for the annual May Day marches. In addition, public service employees staged repeated warning strikes. Analysts began to question whether the German model (Modell Deutschland) was cracking under the pressure to reform.[9] Was the "social" being removed from the social-market economy? Was Kohl challenging the German tradition of policy by consensus? Unions criticized Kohl's plans as "socially obscene," and Lafontaine declared Kohl's policies a "war on social justice."[10] Even the European Commission was placing pressure on Kohl by including Germany in the monitoring procedures pursuant to Article 104c (excessive deficit recommendations) of Maastricht. The pressure on the government was mounting.

The Stability Pact: Still Room for Compromise?

By the summer of 1996, Waigel's proposed stability pact would again come to occupy the center stage of EMU deliberations. To convince German public opinion on the credibility of a hard euro, Waigel called for additional measures to secure budgetary discipline. While most EMU members agreed on the need for some form of "penalty," the Commission had designed a more friendly arrangement, one that would require states to forgo regional aid if they ran deficits. Waigel's stability pact was, of course, far more draconian and indicated the distrust the Germans had of their partners. It would have required a state that ran a greater than 3 percent budget deficit to place a non-interest-bearing deposit of 0.25 percent of GDP with the ECB. If the deficits were still greater than 3 percent after two years, the deposit would become a fine and would be paid into the EU budget. With the exception of France (which gave its reserved support for the general idea of the pact) and the Netherlands, most other EU members opposed the plan.

The need to ensure the stability pact's formal status in EMU operation can be discerned from the domestic debate during the fall of 1996. A flurry of reports in German newspapers and journals, with *Der Speigel* leading the way, suggested that Germany was "going soft" on the convergence criteria. Would Germany be tempted to play with the criteria in order to ensure EMU by 1999? Ernst Welteke, president of the Landzentralbank of Hesse added to the confusion when he suggested a possible flexible interpretation of the rules, seeing them more as "reference values."[11] For his part, Waigel consistently reiterated that 3 percent meant 3 percent—not 3.2, 3.4, or 3.5 percent. Kohl reassured Tietmeyer at the occasion of Tietmeyer's sixty-fifth birthday that there would be no "rotten compromises" on EMU. German concerns were also raised by the specter that Spain and Italy, which returned to the ERM in November, were increasingly moving in a sustained direction on the criteria.[12] Spain's new prime minister, Jose Maria Aznar, reassured Kohl by rejecting the idea of weakening the criteria. Nonetheless, the German public and the Bundesbank rarely hid their distaste for EMU that would include Italy or Spain in the first wave. Ultimately for the Kohl government, EMU would sink or swim based on its anti-inflation credentials, something a stability pact could provide.

The differences in the bargaining positions were thus clear.[13] Between the Germans and their EU partners differences emerged over when the disciplinary procedures would begin, whether to include time limits for a state to correct its economic problems, how the "automatic" fines would work, as well as what the various numbers and percentages would be. A central point of contention focused on how to define a "severe recession." Obviously, the Germans wanted a narrow definition so that countries could not escape the stability provisions. Most other EU members wanted a looser definition of a recession so as to allow countries to escape the harsh conditions that would be imposed under the pact. In addition, the Commission proposed a penalty equal to 0.2 percent of GDP. Germany called for a harsher 0.25 percent penalty for each point the deficit exceeded 3 percent. Waigel and his deputy finance minister, Jürgen Stark, who was heading the negotiations, insisted that an agreement be reached. But what kind of compromise would be forthcoming?

By August, the Germans had conceded on the issue that in exceptional circumstances, member states would be allowed to exceed the excessive deficit criteria. This allowed for a compromise on the issue of time limits, a period of ten months to correct fiscal imbalances. Thereafter, the fines would be automatic but imposed only by a stability council of EMU participants. The crucial compromise of the government appeared to be the idea of allowing a state to exceed the excessive deficit criteria (a move the Bundesbank opposed) as well as what role the stability council would play (an idea the Bundesbank again was not inclined to support).[14] Thus, the final version of the stability pact agreed to at Dublin in December was a classic EMU compromise. The compromise combined a clear economic definition of a severe recession with provisions for political flexibility. A drop in GDP of 2 percent or more per year would automatically be classified as exceptional circumstances and the sanctions would not apply. A fall of between 0.75 percent and 2 percent of GDP would enable that member state to petition the Council of Finance Ministers for special status. The Council would vote by a qualified majority on whether to apply the sanctions.

The Germans had received many of their negotiating demands, but on other issues, accommodation was forthcoming. Waigel and Kohl were both satisfied with the agreement.[15] The Bundesbank's dissatisfaction with the agreement stemmed from its belief that the decision mechanism would allow potential sinners to pass judgment on the actual sinners. In such a scenario, it would be highly unlikely that any one nation would want to punish another nation for fear that the former would be judged at a later date by the latter. The bank still hoped that with the stability pact now firmly codified in treaty form, member states would still have to conform to the German monetary norm.

Theoretically, how does one read the stability pact negotiations? Did the Germans comply with the concerns of their EU partners? Or did they take a hard-line strategy? The analysis reflects a mixed interpretation. On the one hand, the imposition of the stability pact was, in effect, adding to the Maastricht EMU requirements. And the fact that the ministers would agree to the pact in Dublin in November of 1996 indicates that the Germans got what they wanted. On the other hand, there were a number of significant concessions made by the Germans, including the decision to allow member states to exceed, under certain conditions, the excessive deficit criteria. Once again, a bargain was struck that indicated the leveraged political position of the Bundesbank vis-à-vis the government and the intense focus brought about by the context of European governance processes. The Bundesbank would, however, have one last chance to demonstrate its powerful domestic political base.

Cycling in Tandem: International Monetary Calm Returns

With the easing of the international currency situation by the spring of 1996, the G7's focus was not on any concerted efforts at governance. The dollar still was somewhat weak but had been moving in the general direction advocated by G7 officials. The G7 meeting in January discussed such developments and noted its approval. In fact, there was some indication among officials that it was desirable to see the dollar continue to strengthen. Secretary of the Treasury Robert Rubin stated clearly that a strong dollar was in the best interest of the United States, a view that was shared by the Europeans, especially the Germans.[16] With an upcoming election year in the United States and the economy generally strong, the focus of G7 exchange rate management would be on the status quo. At the IMF meetings in April, the G7 ministers focused mostly on debt problems in developing countries. The Germans again resisted efforts to sell more IMF gold reserves. Moreover, when IMF director Michel Camdessus asked for over U.S.$100 billion more in new funds and special drawing rights (SDRs) funds to deal with the possibility of another Mexican-style financial crash, the Germans protested. While recognizing the possible need for such funds and supporting Camdessus's plans in general, the United States was also not too insistent on raising new funds. Domestically, the Clinton administration was increasingly facing a Congress hesitant to fund new international initiatives.

By mid-1996, the G7 economies were increasingly moving in the same direction—in terms of business cycles, stock markets, and, broadly speaking, monetary policy. Fewer major conflicts characterized G7 discussions. *The Economist* suggested that with capital controls all but eliminated, with trade liberalization the dominant goal of most nations, with stock markets increasingly correlated, and with ever-more integrated markets, regional and global business cycles were becoming highly synchronized.[17] In other words, the past pattern of diverging U.S. and German (and thus European) macroeconomic policies was becoming less and less a reality. The tensions inherent in the triangulation of deutsche mark politics were, perhaps, now fading away. Federal Reserve chairman Alan Greenspan, named "policymaker of the year" by *International Economy* magazine, was credited with steering global markets steadily through potentially unstable waters.[18] With Clinton's easy re-election in November expected, the G7 annual summit in Lyon, France, was marked by positive words and statements regarding the global economy. The G7 would continue to promote political and economic security throughout the world.

However, the U.S.-led global economic upturn had diverted attention away from the earlier disputes that had so frequently characterized G7 monetary coordination. It would be naïve to think that all earlier problems were now eliminated. By early 1997, the markets would again remind everyone that each nation's cycle was not entirely moving in the same direction. As the dollar continued to strengthen vis-à-vis the DM, some analysts suggested that German officials, including Bundesbankers, wanted the dollar to stabilize at around DM 1.50. It was clear, however, that the economic fundamentals were driving dollar values, not the rhetoric of G7, U.S., or German officials. Despite some weak efforts to steer the DM to a level stabilized around the DM 1.50 level, the value of the dollar would sharply rise by the spring.[19] Furthermore, the markets would unleash their fury upon Asian economies, again testing the ability of the international monetary governance structure to deal with a major crisis.

Moreover, the annual G7 summit in Lyon discussed the "globalization" of the international economy as if the G7 alone had this trend under their firm control. Certainly, increasing globalization would require a globalization of politics. But as global governance structures, the G7 and the IMF, for all their good intentions, were overstrained. For the European members of the G7, the communiqué issued at the summit indicated that there was not much coordination forthcoming to deal with the issue that affected them most, namely, unemployment. Despite globalization, each nation was responsible for creating new jobs and managing exchange rates. Indeed, German commentators saw through the rhetoric. The newspaper *Neues Deutschland* saw the G7 annual summit in Lyon as going down in "G7 history as the summit of good menus and elegantly phrased empty declarations. Indeed, the prescriptions of the self-proclaimed world directorship are of no use."[20] The influential *Süddeutsche Zeitung* urged the G7 to expand its horizons to include new actors. Stating that the "exclusive G7 club of self-indulgent introspection is urgently due for an overhaul," the yearly gatherings and ongoing G7 discussions would only be meaningful if the circle of participants was widened to include rising economic powers.[21] Instead of backslapping and congratulations, more careful analysis of global monetary and financial governance was needed. Yet the G7 would continue to ignore substantive governance questions.

The Continuing Concern over Budget Deficits

Despite the completion of and agreement on the stability pact at Dublin, the debate over the criteria and timetables continued. The problem centered on the likelihood of Germany, among other nations, meeting the deficit and debt levels. Out of all the possible EMU candidates, if Germany did not meet the criteria, EMU would inevitably be delayed. The continuing strains on the budget brought about by high unemployment (up to a postwar record of 12.2 percent, or 4.6 million people, in February 1997), repeated policy paralysis over tax and pension reform, and slow growth plagued the Kohl government's ability to control spending.[22] Although early budget targets indicated that Germany would fall just under the 3 percent mark, the figures would be subject to considerable controversy and reinterpretation. Another round of consensus talks aimed at consolidating the budget produced partisan bickering and stalemate. In an unusually direct statement, President Roman Herzog entered into the political debate describing the "feeling of paralysis" that had settled across Germany. Perhaps the resignation was due to the lack of a vigorous internal public debate on EMU, although the level of debate at the academic and policymaking level would later increase, albeit perhaps too late to amend Kohl's EMU plans.[23] Others feared that the DM would be dragged down by the instability generated in preparation for EMU.[24]

With EU finance ministers evaluating whether France and Germany would both achieve the criteria for EMU, Waigel stressed that the criteria were more important than the timetable. Waigel's repeated assertions that meeting the criteria would determine the time plan and that Germany would hold firm to the criteria added to the chorus within Germany pushing for postponement.[25] Did that mean then a real possibility of delay? Was the German commitment to EMU starting to fray? Yet at the same time, Waigel indicated that Germany would meet the criteria including taking additional budgetary or financial steps, if necessary, to be on the "safe side" of the Maastricht levels. The lack of clarity in the government's position and its statement on EMU was adding to the confusion and instability surrounding EMU.[26] The only explicit line of thinking and coherent voice on EMU was surprisingly coming from the Bundesbank. Tietmeyer made clear that he did not see any reason for delay and that rumors, which were unsettling the markets, were not in line with reality.[27] Moreover, the Bundesbank continued to place pressure on the government to pass its budget reforms, reduce the debt, and uncompromisingly stick to the Maastricht criteria.

The Bundesbank continued its policy of holding interest rates stable, allowing for a smooth start-up to the May 1998 EMU decision. Interestingly, for the first time, the Bundesbank announced that its monetary target for M3 would be set for a two-year period. While tightening the range from 3.5 percent to 6.5 percent, the bank would take into account the specific conditions governing German monetary policy in the run-up to Stage 3 of EMU. Against this background, the Bundesbank extended the time horizon of its monetary targeting to two years in order to contain any uncertainties about its policy in the two years prior to 1999.[28] Such a policy would enhance the credibility of the future system and anchor expectations within the exchange markets. Furthermore, the bank argued, closer "monetary policy coordination" might be necessary and that the Bundesbank's policy "could serve as a reference variable for any monetary policy coordination" that would be required in the early period of Stage 3. This would give the future ECB as smooth a start as possible.[29] It was clear that the Bundesbank saw its role as the foundation upon which a hard euro, a credible European monetary policy, and an independent ECB would be built.

With the Bundesbank providing a clear monetary path toward EMU, Kohl would decisively reinvigorate the government's position. In April, Kohl indicated that he was again running for re-election in 1998. It was clear that this would mean that Kohl would stake his leadership, political reputation, and re-election chances squarely on completing the EMU project. EMU's most forceful advocate, both in Germany and Europe, was now back in control. Kohl stated that he was running because he believed that he had a duty to do so in the current situation. Moreover, Kohl would repeatedly state that he would tie his own political fate to EMU. If there were any doubts as to Kohl's intentions, they should have now been swept aside. EMU was either going to happen on time and with Germany or the Kohl government would cease governing.

Kohl's desire to see EMU launched on time would, however, soon stumble upon political and financial roadblocks. Large May Day protests demonstrated again the fragile state of employment growth in Germany and the precarious fiscal position of the government. Furthermore, Labor's landslide victory in Britain signaled to some German observers the path that the SPD should take to victory in the upcoming German election.[30] To add to the pressure, Germany was reprimanded by EU finance ministers for falling just short on the deficit criteria. The move was driven by new government figures denoting a DM 18 billion budgetary shortfall for 1997. Kohl stressed that Germany would not borrow to finance the shortfall. Although more traditional instruments would not be used to fill the shortfall, there were other possibilities the government could pursue, including selling more government shares in Deutsche Telekom and possibly revaluing the Bundesbank's gold reserves. Waigel's suggestions for shoring up the budget gaps would shortly unleash another historic battle over deutsche mark politics and place the Kohl government's political hold on power in danger.

The Rising Dollar

Driven by the uncertainty surrounding the euro project, robust U.S. economic growth, and low German interest rates, the DM dropped to 1.68 to the dollar. The strengthening of the dollar certainly helped German exporters, but the potential volatility surrounding exchange rates did worry the G7 sufficiently to focus on currency policies and exchange rate management at its February meeting. The G7 deplored the volatility but generally welcomed the corrections in exchange rates from the spring 1995 crisis. The G7 did agree to monitor exchange markets and cooperate as appropriate but specified no action to control rates. There were also no specific discussions of each country's monetary policies. Tietmeyer did indicate that the meeting would send a signal of stability to the markets and that the DM had attained appropriate levels, trusting that the DM would stabilize at around 1.70 to the dollar.[31] The G7 and the Germans seemed genuinely satisfied with exchange rates and monetary policies.

The G7's trust that the markets would take the G7 comments as a sign of commitment would prove misguided. With Waigel indicating that the meeting could not be in any way compared to the Louvre accord of 1987, the markets took it as a signal of a weak G7 commitment to the existing exchange rate levels. Analysts pointed out that the G7 statement was not very strong and was indistinct.[32] The notion that economic fundamentals should determine the value of the DM-dollar exchange, so strongly advocated by the Germans and the United States at the G7 meeting, would now guide the markets. According to traders, the economic fundamentals were indicating that the dollar should further strengthen and that the DM should further weaken. Governance was increasingly out of the hands of policymakers and in the hands of exchange markets.

By April, the DM was trading above the G7 acceptable level of DM 1.70. Driven by the continuing uncertainty over the euro, the G7 voiced displeasure with exchange rates that could lead to large discrepancies in foreign trade. Yet again, the G7 argued that exchange rates should reflect fundamental economic data, which arguably suggested to traders that DM levels (above 1.70) vis-à-vis the dollar were appropriate. The G7 members did state that they would continue to monitor exchange rates, and act together as necessary in currency markets. Tietmeyer stressed that such action would only come about if there existed excessive currency movements. Moreover, Tietmeyer stated that the G7 was not designed for coordination or concerted action, but rather as a place to share ideas.[33] Although the increase was not excessive, the dollar was up 20 percent against the DM (compared to spring 1995 levels) by the time of the July G7 summit and would stand near 1.80 by the end of the summer.

Would the G7 finally act in Denver to stabilize exchange rates? Based on Tietmeyer's comment on the significance of the G7 and the pattern set since the early 1990s, the answer would more than likely be no. Instead, the G7 focused more on the controversy surrounding which economic model was operating effectively. The Germans had little to trumpet. The Clinton administration, however, could point to the sustained economic growth, low inflation, and low unemployment of the U.S. economy. The French characteristically defended the continental model. Chirac stated emphatically, "We have our own model and we plan to stick to it."[34] There were some other discussions aimed at lessening trade conflict between the United States and Japan and what effect that was having on the dollar.

Both nations indicated that there was interest in cooperating in currency markets, but the Germans were noticeably absent from the discussions. Expectations were certainly not high for any noteworthy G7 accomplishments. With Tony Blair new to the G7 pageantry, Chirac hamstrung by domestic politics, Kohl still reeling from the gold controversy, and Russia acting as an equal partner of the G8, the summits were increasingly irrelevant moments in global macroeconomic governance.

The Bundesbank's Last Hurrah?
The Debate over Gold Revaluation

With pressure mounting, the government formally decided that it would revalue the nation's gold reserves in order to shore up gaping holes in the budget. Specifically, the announcement that new tax revenues again fell short of projections prompted Waigel to declare in May that some specific measures would be taken to make up for the budget shortfall. In particular, Waigel suggested that the Bundesbank's gold reserves could be revalued to more accurately reflect their current market value.[35] Such a move, Waigel explained, would increase the Bundesbank's profits (estimated at around U.S.$7 billion) and, therefore, its annual, legally mandated transfer to the government. The money would be earmarked by retiring debt associated with reunification, but the increased revenues would free up additional funds that the government could use for other purposes, namely, filling budget deficits.

The Bundesbank reacted swiftly and in characteristic fashion. Supported by its legal mandate of independence, the Bundesbank issued a statement describing Waigel's plans as "interference with the direct responsibility for arranging and determining the financial statement, and as such, with the independence of the Bundesbank." Clearly, the Bundesbank construed Waigel's plans as "an attack on Bundesbank independence."[36] As one Bundesbank official suggested, "It is like printing money."[37] In addition, the revaluation plan would create the appearance of unearned profits that could not be used to fill shortfalls in budget deficits. Finally, the Bundesbank countered that the accounting change would create the "risk of diminished confidence in the stability of the future European currency." The last point was perhaps the most important. The Bundesbank, along with the government, had long cited the French plans for a political counterweight to the future European central bank and Italy's various budgetary maneuvers as indicators of the inherent difficulties in creating a stable and hard euro. With German public opinion already disinclined toward the euro, the German government's own monetary shenanigans were signs to the German public that the euro would not retain the same value and trust as the treasured DM.

Despite Bundesbank protestations, the Kohl government appeared determined to proceed with the gold revaluation. According to a statement issued by the coalition leaders, and personally authorized by Kohl, the government argued that it was merely abiding by the EMI's own rules in reassessing the Bundesbank's gold at market values. Moreover, the plan would not "interfere with the independent monetary policy of the Bundesbank," was "sensible and responsible," and would be "conservative" in scope.[38] It should be noted that the government's EMI argument was legitimate because the EMI required countries to bring their reserve estimates into line with market prices by 1999. Coalition leaders suggested that the plan was a reasonable and legitimate move to tackle the debt left over from reunification. Personal lobbying efforts by Waigel, however, in meetings with Tietmeyer failed to bring an immediate solution. The high level of negotiation was certainly unusual but not unheard of in the long history of deutsche mark politics. As such, it signified that this government-Bundesbank row would be debated in the full light of public scrutiny, a definite asset to the Bundesbank.

As a result, opposition leaders, economists, powerful interest associations, and the press leveled intense criticism on the government.[39] The SPD's fiscal and financial policy expert, Ingrid Matthäuser-Maier, called the revaluation plan "virtual robbery" and demanded the resignation of Waigel in the form of a petition to Kohl to fire Waigel, a move that later failed to receive enough votes (328–311) in the Bundestag.[40] Many other politicians noted that the move would undermine the credibility and international reputation of the Bundesbank. The Berlin-based *Die Welt* noted the significance of the Bundesbank opposition: "If even the Bundesbank, long the shining model of this autonomy, gives in, longer shadows still will hang over the Euro."[41] From *Stern* to *Der Speigel* (labeling Kohl's government the "bankrupt state") to the *Frankfurter Allgemeine Zeitung* and the *General Anzeiger*, denunciations of Waigel and the government were near universal. The Council of Economic Advisors argued that the revaluing of the Bundesbank's reserves would be improper as a sustained remedy for the shortfall in finances and that the proposal would throw the independence and the credibility of the Bundesbank into question. The Federation of German Banks (Bundesverband deutscher Banken) called for compromise in order to shore up Germany's tarnished image on international financial markets, supporting the Bundesbank's opposition to the plan.

The general public, already resistant to the idea of relinquishing the DM for the euro, found added fuel for their EMU skepticism in the government's revaluation plan. The government was skating on thin ice in its strong support for the euro, support that could not be found in the public. In a survey conducted by the Allensbach Institute, 47.4 percent of the German public noted opposition to EMU.[42] Only 26.4 percent signaled support for the euro project, with just as many Germans unclear in their position. More than 60 percent of the public had real doubts and fears about EMU; at a ratio of almost 3:1, the German public felt that there were more disadvantages than advantages to the idea of EMU. Perhaps most important, fully 45.9 percent of the public felt that EMU would have a negative impact on inflation. Also interesting, support for EMU was weakest among eastern Germans, not surprising given that they had only experienced seven years of monetary stability in the form of the DM. Now, with the government launching a direct assault on the Bundesbank's control over the DM, the public let the government know its displeasure with the gold scheme.

The accounting cosmetics were certainly well within the legal right and domain of the government but turned into a political disaster for the governing coalition. The revaluation plan was clearly a transparent attempt at cooking the books. How ironic, the critics rightfully noted, that the German government was now attempting to pursue monetary gimmickry similar to efforts in other EU countries that the German government had long chastised. Germany had, in particular, sought to isolate Italy as a nation that pursued suspect bookkeeping maneuvers, for example, raising taxes one year and refunding the amount the next year, after Italy had secured early EMU entry. Italian-German monetary relations had, as a result, been quite tense.[43] With the Bundesbank rejecting the government's first plan, a compromise was finally reached whereby gold would be revalued in 1997 and the profits turned over in 1998, perhaps too late to plug the deficit gap.[44] This time Kohl would have to surrender to the Bundesbank.

More problematical, the gold revaluation plan further shook the edges of the coalition and emboldened the opposition. The CSU's Bavarian leader, Edmund Stoiber, increasingly asserted his position as defender of the decimal point, referring to the 3 percent Maastricht cutoff. Although Stoiber's position could be attributed to internal CSU politics, he was giving voice to a common view among the German public: "The Mark is part of us. . . . What do we need a worthless new money for?"[45] Kohl also had to dispense with the popular *Land* president of Saxony, Kurt Biedenkopf, who was now arguing that the Bundesrat would have a final say in judging who could join EMU.[46] With Waigel indicating interest in raising some taxes (on oil, for example), the FDP strengthened its opposition to tax increases that might have closed the deficit. Schröder and Lafontaine both raised the level of criticism of the government's finance plans and indicated that the SPD, and implicitly, labor unions, would formally step back from supporting EMU if further cuts in welfare were instituted.

By August, Waigel's frustrations over the plan became public. In a television interview, he indicated that he had had enough of the finance ministry and that he was possibly seeking a new cabinet position. Many analysts speculated that Waigel sought the foreign minister's post, held traditionally by the FDP. If true, the move would further fragment the coalition. Once again, it was Kohl who would bring an end to the internal squabbling. Under direct pressure from Kohl, Waigel eventually indicated that he would stay in office.[47] More important, in response to the public's perceived lack of confidence in the government, the government released a forceful and eloquent statement in support of EMU. With Kohl's direct approval, the statement by prominent CDU and CSU leaders asked strongly why EMU was in Germany's economic and political interests.[48] Finally, as a result of the gold revaluation debacle, a more coherent government position on EMU was emerging.

By fall, the controversy over the gold revaluation and the subsequent internal coalition debate over EMU had largely been settled. Attention would again focus on external EMU negotiations. The Bundesbank's last stand on the gold revaluation plan would nearly bring down one of Germany's most powerful politicians but in the end had not sidetracked the push toward EMU.[49] As Olaf Sievert, a member of the Bundesbank council, could now argue, the Bundesbank had once again demonstrated its impressive independence, but it would be for the last time. What is more, the Bundesbank's independent reputation could now be securely inherited by the ECB.[50]

Revisiting the Stability Pact

The controversy over gold revaluation was inextricably linked to the events in neighboring France, further complicated by the ongoing IGC deliberations, which were heading toward a formal conclusion in Amsterdam by mid-June.[51] Chirac's call for a snap election at the beginning of May was based on the hope that a renewed and reinvigorated conservative majority would be strong enough to push through painful spending cuts or tax increases necessary to achieve the Maastricht criteria. Prior to the election, the French were suffering clearly from fiscal and monetary fatigue. Although France's budget deficit had shrunk sharply and through the *franc fort* policy, now under the firm hand of Jean-Claude Trichet, inflation had been cut to less than 3 percent, social unrest caused by sustained high levels of unemployment was making governing difficult. Yet Chirac still needed to make a few more cuts and was determined to proceed with his broader program of liberalizing the economy.

But holding the election one year ahead of schedule and framing the vote almost as a referendum on the euro was a big gamble. In the first round of elections, the center-right coalition won barely 30 percent with the left-wing parties garnering more than 37 percent. Most analysts, though, considered the chances of the conservatives to be quite strong heading into the final round. Phillipe Seguin, speaker of the Assembly and one of the top candidates as a new prime minister if the conservative coalition held power, was already speaking of adding flexibility to the Maastricht criteria. Seguin was giving voice to a segment of the voting public that would be crucial to the conservatives' hopes of securing victory. Despite the efforts of Seguin, the nightmare scenario for both Chirac and the Germans came true: socialist Lionel Jospin secured a narrow victory and would now govern in coalition with the communists.

The socialist government had several conditions that it wanted met before EMU would be implemented. First, the socialists argued that Italy and Spain should be part of the first wave of EMU members. Second, some form of governing council would have to be developed to counterbalance the independence of the ECB. Third, the euro would have to be valued more realistically vis-à-vis other currencies, especially the dollar. This concern was related to the unresolved and unclear question over how exchange rate policy would serve European interests. Finally, and most controversial, was the French desire to revisit the stability pact in order to provide a "new equilibrium" between employment and price stability. Given these conditions, Jospin demanded more time to re-evaluate the entire project.[52] Despite such tactics, it was clear that Chirac was intent on steering the government toward EMU completion and that the options for Jospin were in many ways limited. As such, the immediate focus would be on the stability pact.

The Germans underscored their commitment to resist any postponement of EMU that would result from lengthy renegotiations of the stability pact. Yet the government was intent on achieving European consensus. Klaus Kinkel, in a speech to the Bundestag, indicated that the government would go along with an employment provision in the stability pact as long as it did not mandate the creation of any new funding or subsidy programs: "We cannot accept new disbursement programs that are out of touch with the public, that can no longer be financed and that are especially burdensome on us."[53] The SPD criticized the government's "concession" as merely an attempt to water down any firm commitment to employment that most European governments wanted. The Greens considered the government's proposal a "con job." Labor unions criticized the refusal of the Kohl government to seriously consider mechanisms for tackling unemployment.

Prior to the Amsterdam summit, it soon became clear that a compromise favorable to the Germans would result. With Kohl politically weak at home due to the squabbling over gold revaluation and his defeat at the hands of the Bundesbank, Waigel would have little room to maneuver or compromise. Fortunately, the French ultimately signaled their intention of not unduly delaying EMU. Dominique Strauss-Kahn, the new finance minister, issued a statement that the French and Germans would "certainly find a solution." At the first day of the Amsterdam summit, discussion on the stability pact dominated the debate. At issue was whether the pact would be adopted as provisionally accepted at Dublin or whether it would mandate EU action to reduce unemployment. In the end, the stability pact was approved as originally agreed upon, but a new resolution was added on employment policy. The new resolution would be included in "Maastricht II." More significant, the resolutions met the Bundesbank requirement that no new job creation programs requiring additional EU expenditures be created. The resolution also echoed the German position that, whereas policy coordination at the European level was desirable, primary responsibility for employment policy would still lie with individual member states. In the end, the weak resolution on unemployment was not a real compromise, rather an attempt not to insult the new French government. Despite plodding through one crisis to the next, the Franco-German EMU motor kept the momentum moving forward.

Fleshing Out the Final Details:
Asian Crisis As Final Impetus for EMU

By the fall, the momentum of EMU was too powerful to stop. Given the dramatic events and ultimate resolution of the early summer conflicts both within Germany and Europe, the Europeans settled down to focus on finalizing the details prior to the historic May 1998 decision. Of notable importance was the decision reached by finance ministers to establish fixed exchange rates between participating currencies. Fixing exchange rates would occur at the same time as the selection of the first wave of EMU participants.[54] The goal was to keep international currency markets from playing havoc with the introduction of the euro. Furthermore, fixing exchange rates would help establish the stability and credibility of EMU right from the beginning. The Germans strongly favored such a proposal with the Bundesbank, arguing that it was an important decision for the credibility of the new system. Tietmeyer indicated that the decision to fix rates would de facto create a "piece of monetary union."[55] More specifically, policymakers would be ever more constrained in their autonomy to use monetary policy. In fact, in terms of the trade-off between exchange rates and monetary autonomy, Germany had made the full sacrifice imaginable. Germany would still set the tone of European monetary policy until the DM fully disappeared, but even the Germans would be unequivocally and automatically obligated to support the system. The euro was more or less a done deal.[56]

In order to cement the reality of fixed exchange rates and EMU, the government passed legislation laying the legal groundwork for the use of the euro in the public and commercial sectors. More important, the Bundesbank Law was reformed and passed in the Bundestag. The reforms outlined the transition of the Bundesbank into the ESCB as well as the bank's future operation within the system.[57] With the start of EMU on January 1, 1999, the Bundesbank would no longer be responsible for setting interest rates and regulating the monetary supply. The veto right of the government over the Bundesbank would also disappear. The Bundesbank could still support the general economic policies of the government, but only if it did not conflict with its duties and responsibilities vis-à-vis its support for the ESCB and the ECB's overriding priority of price stability. Although the Bundesbank would still manage the nation's financial transfers and accounts in DMs, this would, as we know, come to an end in 2002. The historic Bundesbank Law of 1957 had, forty years later, been fundamentally transformed.

Nevertheless, the Bundesbank still set the tone for European monetary policy.[58] In October, the Bundesbank raised the repo rate, the first interest rate increase since 1992. All European central banks followed suit. According to Tietmeyer, a single European monetary policy was now under way and would be built with a firm anti-inflationary foundation.[59] Demands by unions for significant pay wages pushed the Bundesbank to again suggest that risks to stability had increased and that a modest tightening was in order.[60] The budgetary situation in all countries remained tense, although nearly all EU countries—with the exception of Greece—were more than likely to attain the deficit limits. Figures published by the European Commission in October indicated fourteen possible candidates.[61] Despite being included on the list, the Italian government remained feeble as the Communist Party pulled its support out from the Romano Prodi coalition over EMU-related budgetary reductions. Prodi would be back in power a week later as the communists, severely miscalculating public support for EMU, rejoined the coalition. By the end of the fall, eleven likely EMU candidates could be identified.[62]

On the international front, the financial and monetary crisis in Thailand, South Korea, and Indonesia only further spurred interest in securing the European zone of monetary stability that the euro could provide. Waigel argued that the crisis provided a stark lesson on the merits of the euro. The euro would soon become the common response of Europe to globalization. Moreover, as the global stock markets again tumbled due to monetary crises in Asia (ten years after the 1987 crash), Waigel stated that "a stable monetary area and a large internal market" would "dampen the economic shocks of international currency and economic crises."[63] Tietmeyer saw it this way: A lastingly stable euro would grow into a major rival of the U.S. dollar in the international financial markets.[64] Many analysts, including German policymakers, also saw the real possibility that the Asian economies might delink their currencies from the dollar and link them with Europe.[65] The dollar-yen relationship—which effects the Asian economies much like the DM-dollar relationship—was too unstable. For the first time, Asian voices could be heard suggesting a more common coordinated Asian currency policy. Not surprisingly, at the September meeting of the IMF/World Bank, the G7 focused its efforts upon fighting excessive currency fluctuations in Asia. But with no firm regional plan of action and with the IMF under mounting criticism for failures in Indonesia, the hope for a lasting period of monetary stability looked slim.

By the summer of 1998, the patchwork efforts by the IMF to plug the leaking financial ship of state in South Korea, Indonesia, and Russia, which had temporarily brought some stability to global markets, had finally burst. As the stock markets dropped dramatically—the yen continued to lose value and the Russian rouble collapsed—the G7 searched in vain for a solution. President Clinton called the spreading global economic crisis "the biggest financial challenge facing the world in a half century."[66] The G7 responded in typical fashion: issuing a joint statement in September of 1998 indicating their concern over the rapidly expanding global financial volatility. As expected, the G7 did not follow through with coordinated action. The expectations of joint G7 action were dashed when Alan Greenspan indicated that there was "no endeavor to coordinate interest rates" among the G7.[67] With Chancellor Kohl caught up in the final weeks before the September 27 election, the Germans were not interested in any joint G7 effort to coordinate an interest rate reduction. Moreover, with the introduction of the euro just months away, German monetary officials did not want to send an improper message to the German public about their commitment to a strong euro. With the three leading members of the G7 politically impotent to act, calls for a "New World Order for Finance" would largely go unheard.[68]

At the same time, Germany and France were moving forward on the last two significant unresolved issues surrounding EMU: clarifying the future exchange rate policy of the EU and developing a body to coordinate macroeconomic policy.[69] France proposed an informal economic council for EMU that would coordinate information and develop common fiscal and economic policy. The French were careful to insist that it was not seeking to undermine the independence of the ECB.[70] Yet Jospin sought to fulfill one of his campaign promises on EMU so as to placate domestic opposition to continued budgetary cutbacks. Although the Germans were not interested in a formal institutional structure for such a council, Waigel indicated that the Germans would prefer an informal council much like the

G7, which "has no statutes, no secretariat, no internationally binding treaty status. And it functions."[71] From the German perspective, the G7 functioned because it never had to force the Germans to do much of anything. The same could be said of the new euro club, or council, that the French and Germans had agreed upon.[72] Despite UK protests that the new club would solely address matters of interest to all fifteen members, France and Germany saw the group discussing a broad range of issues from wage policy to budgetary matters relating to the euro.[73] Whatever the interpretation, the new G7-like forum would not have any formal power. Given the record of G7 cooperation, the Bundesbank or ECB would not have to worry about direct political pressure.

By the spring of 1998, two final hurdles toward EMU remained, one at the German level and one at the European level. Within Germany, final legislative approval from the Bundestag and Bundesrat would be needed. Shaping the legislative debates was the Bundesbank's official report and recommendations on EMU, issued at the end of March on the insistence of Chancellor Kohl. Would the Bundesbank take this final opportunity to derail EMU? Although it would be impossible at this point to slow EMU momentum or permanently derail EMU, the Bundesbank did provide a sober assessment of the rush to the euro. While noting that the adoption of the euro appeared justifiable and realizing that the selection of EMU participants ultimately remained a political decision, the Bundesbank was unexpectedly frank and blunt in its critique of the loose interpretation of the debt-GDP criteria and, specifically, Italy and Belgium. Condemning fiscal profligacy, the bank stated that "the high government debt in a number of states represents a major burden" to the future success of EMU.[74] Tietmeyer also expressed his reservations within the Bundestag's finance committee as it prepared to debate EMU. Nevertheless, the Bundesbank's guarded support for EMU actually added extra leverage to the government's and European Commission's position of an EMU of eleven members. With the Constitutional Court clearing the final legal objections to EMU, the Bundestag and Bundesrat provided their overwhelming endorsement to the currency plan. The stage was now set for the European decision on EMU.

Given Germany's strong support for EMU and the apparently united European front, the historic decision in Brussels over the weekend of May 2–3 to launch EMU should have been without controversy. Indeed, agreeing to the eleven euro members and fixing exchange rates among them proved uncontroversial.[75] But controversy would prevail at what Jacques Chirac justifiably called the "greatest collective adventure of Europe." The first controversy erupted a week prior to the summit when Waigel proposed that prospective euro nations sign a stability declaration at the summit. Among other issues already related to the ratified stability pact, the declaration would have committed nations to prioritize the use of budget surpluses for debt reduction. Waigel's efforts can be understood as reflecting Bundesbank pressure for countries such as Italy and Belgium to do more to cut their excessive stock of debt and the German public's unease with EMU. Although most prospective members had no problem with the general idea of managing public finances in line with the stability pact in the interim period prior to January 1, 1999, the attempt to tie budgetary hands even further was not universally supported. Rebuffed immediately and strongly by France, the finance minister, Dominique Strauss-Kahn, stated firmly that "every country is free to use its resources as it wants."[76] Such a philosophy prevailed as the firm statement on Waigel's proposition was not agreed upon.

The stability row was largely overshadowed by the embarrassing conflict over who would head the ECB. Chirac precipitated the crisis in late 1997 by nominating Jean Claude Trichet, governor of the Bank of France, for the ECB job. Chirac's political and symbolic move (Trichet's monetary credentials were highly regarded) irritated most of the other euro members, especially the Netherlands and its candidate, Wim Duisenberg (who was already directing the EMI), and Germany. With the French refusing to budge, a compromise was reached whereby Duisenberg was appointed head of the ECB with the informal agreement that he would voluntarily step down around the halfway point of his eight-year term. At that point, Trichet would assume the presidency of the ECB. Fearing the effect the compromise would have on the independence of the future ECB, the head of the Federation of German Industry called the agreement a "foul compromise." Tietmeyer expressed similar reservations by asserting that the compromise did not contribute to the necessary expectation that the euro would, in fact, be a supranational and depoliticized currency.[77] In the end, however, the summit had to reach a compromise. As unseemly as the agreement might have appeared, EMU had always been a strategic bargain between Germany and its European (especially French) partners. The decision of the president of the ECB was no different.

The EMU summit revealed what Lionel Barber called the "paradox of German weakness."[78] With his coalition in disarray over various campaign strategies and tactics ranging from taxes, crime, and Sudenten Germans, and with the decisive defeat of the CDU in the *Land* elections in Saxonly-Anhalt a week before the summit, Kohl's chances of winning the September 1998 Bundestag elections looked increasingly less likely. As a result, Kohl could not afford politically to have the crowning achievement of his European policies sidetracked. The row over the presidency was bad enough, but any further delay in the EMU timetable would have thrown the EMU debate more directly into the electoral campaign. Ultimately, the German government had again found room to cooperate and compromise on what can be considered the final act of a historic period in European monetary affairs and deutsche mark politics. The historic EMU summit would also be Chancellor Kohl's final act on the European front. With the defeat of Kohl and his conservative-liberal coalition to Gerhard Schröder (SPD) in the 1998 federal election,[79] Kohl's extraordinary record and historical legacy would now rest—along with the peaceful reunification of Germany—on his successful effort to secure a European Germany through the sacrifice of the DM to EMU. Attention would now shift to another stage of German, European, and international politics.

Conclusion

Once again, the Germans had driven a hard bargain on the final details of EMU. The stability pact would essentially retain many of the tough conditions initially laid out by Waigel. For the Kohl government, the stability pact was the best guarantee that the future euro would remain stable and "hard" and convince the German public of the necessity of sacrificing the DM. There existed a low level of disagreement between the Bundesbank and the government on these points. However, the German government made some critical concessions in the final stages of negotiating EMU. First, the government agreed to the inclusion into the stability pact of an exception to the excessive deficit recommendations. Moreover, government ministers, always subject to political influence, would make the decisions in regard to imposing penalties. Finally, the German government agreed to reopen negotiations on the stability pact under pressure from France. Given the strong nature of the context of bargaining, a final compliant strategy was pursued. An agreement was politically necessary to keep EMU moving forward. The end result was the rewriting of the Bundesbank Law in December of 1997 and the fixing of exchange rates in May of 1998. The Bundesbank would no longer set interest rates for Germany starting in January 1999. The dilemma between exchange rate stability and monetary autonomy had, at least for Germany, come to an end. That dilemma would now face European monetary officials, a point that Chapter 8 makes clear.

On the international front, the G7 appeared to be entering a new phase of governance. Not only was the old system of G7 exchange rate management looking increasingly weak (continuing on the pattern set for the 1990s), but the nature of international monetary governance was also changing. The G7 could now claim that it managed the international monetary system, but the political will to manage no longer existed. Of course, the Germans were not interested in managing exchange rates and were not obligated to do so. Fortunately, the period 1996–1998 was relatively stable in terms of the German-EMS-G7 triangulation and, thus, serious efforts at management were not required. One could also argue that the German monetary norm had been internalized globally. Price stability at home was the only true method of securing global exchange rate stability. In this sense, no institutionalized forms of global monetary governance were required, not now or in the future.

Nevertheless, immense changes in the international monetary governance system were under way. Intense discussion on the radical restructuring of IMF was for the first time seriously being considered. Moreover, three of the G7 members, including Germany, would soon speak with one, perhaps more powerful, voice in G7 deliberations. Asian economies were for the first time considering a regional form of monetary governance. The implications of these changes are difficult to discern. Yet the story of deutsche mark politics can illustrate both the potential for and limitations of governance—in Europe and in the global economy. It is to these issues that the concluding chapter turns.

Notes

1. With inflation at its lowest annual rate since reunification, M3 growth under control, and the DM stabilizing vis-à-vis the dollar, the Bundesbank had room to maneuver. See Deutsche Bundesbank, *Monthly Report of the Deutsche Bundesbank,* January 1996 (Frankfurt/Main). The Bundesbank also saw as desirable the lowering of the repo rate in February. The decision was due, in part, to the "persistent strength of the DM." Deutsche Bundesbank, *Monthly Report of the Deutsche Bundesbank,* February 1996 (Frankfurt/Main), p. 13.

2. "Nur Narren hoffen und Harren," *Die Zeit,* December 22, 1995.

3. "Farewell, EMU?" *The Economist,* February 3, 1996. See also "The EMU Backsliders," *The Economist,* March 23, 1996.

4. Cited in "Ready or Not, Here Comes EMU," *World Press Review,* December 1996, pp. 16–18.

5. "Germans Close Ranks to Put Off Evil Euro Day," *The Times,* September 26, 1996.

6. "The Helmut and Jacques Show," *The Economist,* April 6, 1996.

7. "EMU—What the Markets Will Tell You," *The Economist,* February 3, 1996.

8. "In Surprise of Timing, Germany Cuts Interest Rates," *New York Times,* April 19, 1996, p. D1. See also the analysis of the Deutsche Bundesbank, *Monthly Report of the Deutsche Bundesbank,* April 1996 (Frankfurt/Main).

9. "Redesigning the German Model," *The Economist,* January 27, 1996; and "Is the Model Broken?" *The Economist,* May 4, 1996.

10. Ibid. It should be noted that SPD, union, and business leaders had issued a joint statement in June supporting the euro project.

11. "EMU: No Wobblers Need Apply," *Financial Times,* September 23, 1996.

12. "Guess Who's Coming to EMU?" *The Economist,* October 5, 1996. Italy's re-entry into the ERM was hotly debated, particularly the initial rate at which the lira would be exchanged. The Italians had to accept a stronger value (990 lira to the

DM) than they wanted. The Germans feared Italian devaluation. The stronger value of the lira prompted Tietmeyer to remark, "It is certainly not a comment on Italy's qualification for monetary union." See *Handelsblatt*, November 26, 1996.

13. See the analysis of Dorothee Heisenberg, "Explaining the Dominance of German Preferences in Recent EMU Decisions," in Pierre-Henri Laurent and Marc Maresceau, eds., *The State of the European Union,* vol. 4 (Boulder, Colo.: Lynne Rienner, 1998), pp. 263–278.

14. See the analysis in "Currency Talks Snag on German Demands," *New York Times*, December 3, 1996.

15. For a good review of the government's position, see "Die Europaische Wirtschafts- und Währungsunion und der Stabilitätspakt," *Auszüge aus Pressartikeln*, September 12, 1997.

16. "Rubin Sees the Big Powers Focusing on Effect of Slump," *New York Times,* January 19, 1996.

17. "World Economy: Cycling in Tandem," *The Economist*, May 11, 1996.

18. Tietmeyer would call Greenspan "central banker of the year."

19. "Dollar Up As German Officials Say Mark Should Come Down," *New York Times*, November 13, 1996.

20. Comments of *Neues Deutschland,* June 29, 1996, cited in " . . . The G-7 Summit in Lyons," *This Week in Germany*, July 5, 1996. *Neues Deutschland* is linked to the ex-communist PDS.

21. Comments of *Süddeutsche Zeitung,* June 28, 1996, cited in " . . . The G-7 Summit in Lyons," *This Week in Germany,* July 5, 1996.

22. Kohl would call this period the "darkest" of his time in office. *This Week in Germany*, February 14, 1997. Worse was yet to come.

23. See, for example, Peter Sutherland, "The Case for EMU," *Foreign Affairs* 76, no. 1 (January/February 1997), pp. 9–15; and George Soros, "Can Europe Work?" *Foreign Affairs* 75, no. 5 (November/December 1996), pp. 8–14. In early 1998, four well-known German economists, including two former Landeszentralbank presidents, Wilhelm Hankel and Wilhelm Nölling, launched a constitutional challenge to EMU. In February 1998, 164 German economists, led by Manfred Neumann and Roland Vaubel, issued a plea for an "orderly postponement" of EMU. Although arguably persuasive in some of their detail, both efforts would prove too late in fundamentally altering the EMU debate in Germany. See the declaration at Web site http://www.united.econ.uni-bonn.de/iiw/.

24. "German Fears About EMU," *The Economist*, January 25, 1997

25. "EU Ministers Endorse German Plans for Currency Union," *This Week in Germany*, March 21, 1997.

26. Further instability was caused by the diverging predictions on who would meet the criteria. The Commission's more friendly figures saw Germany attaining the 3 percent cutoff. The IMF's figures found Germany pushing a 3.3 percent deficit for the year. Germany's own figures were subject to interpretation, depending on where one stood on the EMU debate. Ultimately, it would be the Commission's figures that would determine the final participants.

27. "Central Banks: Rumors of EMU Delay Rejected," *Financial Times*, March 4, 1997.

28. Deutsche Bundesbank, *Monthly Report of the Bundesbank*, January 1997 (Frankfurt/Main), p. 17.

29. Ibid, p. 20.

30. In fact, Labor's new leader, Tony Blair, would finally provide a more constructive British role in EU politics. Although Britain would sit out the first round

of EMU, it would ensure a smooth decision in May 1998 while Britain headed the EU presidency.

31. "G7 Summit: Bankers Put Brakes on Rising Dollar," *Financial Times*, February 20, 1997.

32. "Continued Rise in the Dollar May Compel Officials to Act," *New York Times*, February 13, 1997.

33. See the interview with Tietmeyer in "Stabilitätsgemeinshaft aus Hong Kong," *Finanz-Wirtschafts Spiegel*, September 24, 1997.

34. "The Cries of the Welfare States Under the Knife," *New York Times*, September 19, 1997, p. A1. Chirac went so far as to refuse to wear cowboy boots at the summit. German commentators did note the attractiveness of the U.S. economy. Stefan Keide, "Modernes Modell," *Handelsblatt,* September 2, 1997.

35. "Germany Set to Revalue Gold Reserve," *New York Times*, May 29, 1997. The move would also require a revision of the Bundesbank Law; the Bundesbank would then have to draw up new accounts for 1997 to enable it to hand over the cash. Not surprisingly, such a move would prove controversial.

36. "Germany: Bundesbank Row Threatens Single Currency," *Financial Times,* May 29, 1997. The Bundesbank was forced to break a news blackout surrounding its discussions to deny rumors that Tietmeyer was resigning.

37. Interview with Bundesbank official, June 1997.

38. "Bundesbank Criticizes Government Plan to Revalue Reserves as Interference," *This Week in Germany,* May 30, 1997.

39. See a representative sample of opinions in *This Week in Germany*, June 6, 1997.

40. "A Champion of the Euro Finds That All Economics Is Local," *New York Times,* June 18, 1997.

41. *Die Welt,* cited in " . . . The Bundesbank's Gold Reserves," *This Week in Germany,* May 30, 1997.

42. "Der Euro kommt," *Stern*, no. 51 (1996), p. 34.

43. "For This We're Giving Up the Deutsche Mark?" *U.S. News and World Report*, June 9, 1997.

44. "Germans' Slick Bookkeeping to Meet Euro Goal Is Scrapped," *New York Times*, June 4, 1997.

45. "Clinging to Its Past, Europe Is Warily Awaiting the Euro," *New York Times*, September 18, 1997, p. A1.

46. "Germany: EMU Divisions Hit Kohl's Party," *Financial Times*, July 29, 1997.

47. Germany: Kohl Tries to Reassert Control," *Financial Times*, August 22, 1997.

48. Wolfgang Schäuble, Michael Glos, Rudolf Seiters, and Karl Lamers, "Die Europäishce Währungsunion—Deutschland's Interesse und Verantwortung," *Frankfurter Allgemeine Zeitung*, September 17, 1997.

49. For a comprehensive postgold revaluation account, see the interview with Tietmeyer, "Europa's Himmel stürzt nicht ein," *Die Woche*, September 5, 1997.

50. "Zur Europäische Währungsunion—Das Eigentliche und der Unrat auf dem Wege dahin," *Auszüge aus Pressartikeln*, September 3, 1997.

51. For a good review of the ties between the two, see "Kicking and Screaming into 1999," *The Economist*, June 7, 1997. For a review of the accomplishments of Amsterdam, see Desmon Dinan, "Reflections on the IGC's," in Laurent and Maresceau, eds., *The State of the European Union* (Boulder, Colo.: Lynne Rienner, 1997), pp. 23–42.

52. "Budget Rules: Paris Seeks EMU Pact Delay," *Financial Times*, June 10, 1997. Around the same time, more than 300 center-left economists issued an open letter urging leaders to abandon EMU. With over 20 million European unemployed, the economists argued that a refocus on job creation should be the priority of EU leaders.

53. "Germany Ready to Compromise on EU Employment Policy," *This Week in Germany*, June 13, 1997.

54. "Getting EMU Started," *Financial Times*, September 15, 1997.

55. "Euro Go-Go," *The Economist*, September 20, 1997.

56. The domestic debate against delay was marked by the failure of Henning Voscherau (SPD) to effectively use EMU as a campaign strategy in the Hamburg *Land* elections. The SPD suffered its worst post–World War II defeat. However, in March of 1998, Schröder won a decisive victory for the SPD in Lower Saxony. His victory should not necessarily be interpreted as an anti-EMU vote but rather as a vote by the people signifying their lack of interest in the tired regime of Kohl and the CDU.

57. "Bundesbankgesetz geändert," *Börsen-Zeitung,* December 13, 1997.

58. "Buba übernimmt Euro-Zins führerschaft,*"* *VWD Finanz und Wirtschaftspiegel*, October 10, 1997.

59. "Die Währungsunion als Stabilitätsgemeinschaft," *Auszüge aus Pressartikeln,* November 3, 1997.

60. "Germany Surprises World Economies with a Rate Rise," *New York Times*, October 10, 1997.

61. "Ready or Not, Here Comes EMU," *The Economist*, October 11, 1997.

62. The eleven candidates were Germany, France, Italy, Spain, Portugal, Ireland, Luxembourg, Belgium, the Netherlands, Austria, and Finland. Denmark, Sweden, and the UK would sit out the first round.

63. "Waigel: Market Turbulence Shows Euro's Advantages," *This Week in Germany*, October 31, 1997.

64. "Continuity and Change," *Auszüge aus Pressartikeln*, September 26, 1997.

65. "Asiens Zentralbankern könnte der Euro gefallen,*"* *Börsen Zeitung*, November 22, 1997.

66. See his quote and analysis in "Clinton Seeks World Economic Action," *New York Times*, September 14, 1998. Clinton's ability to lead was strongly circumscribed by the ongoing domestic crises surrounding congressional efforts to impeach him.

67. "What Happened to Those Rate Cuts?" *New York Times*, September 18, 1998. The Federal Reserve would unilaterally lower interest rates one week later.

68. "New World Order for Finance?" *Christian Science Monitor*, September 29, 1998, p. B1.

69. The EU was also engaged in an embarrassing dispute over who would head the ECB presidency.

70. See the comments of Jean-Claude Trichet, "Solid, Glaubwürdig, und Stabil," *Die Zeit*, December 19, 1997.

71. "Waigel sieht keine Notwendigkeit für einen Eurorat," *Frankfurter Allgemeine Zeitung*, October 6, 1997.

72. "Euro-Koordination nach dem Muster der G7,*"* *Frankfurter Allgemeine Zeitung,* October 15, 1997.

73. "EU Ends Dispute Over Its Single Currency Group," *Financial Times*, December 13/14, 1997.

74. See Tietmeyer's comments in "Eingangsstatement des Praesidenten der

Deutschen Bundesbank," In *Auszuege aus Pressartikeln, Deutsche Bundesbank,* April 3, 1998, p. 1. The Bundesbank was also clear to note that Germany and France needed to do more in the way of setting their finances in order if the euro was to be as stable as the DM.

75. The value of the euro will be decided at the beginning of 1999.

76. See Lionel Barber's analysis of the summit, "European Viewpoint: The Crack Appears," *Financial Times,* Special Report on the EMU, May 4, 1998.

77. "EU Approves Currency Union," *This Week in Germany,* May 8, 1998.

78. See "European Viewpoint," *Financial Times,* May 4, 1998.

79. The SPD won 41 percent of the vote and, along with the Greens, formed the first Red-Green coalition at the national level. The election was largely seen as a vote for change after sixteen years of a Kohl-led conservative government. The concern over high unemployment also played a key role in the victory for the SPD. While the election of the SPD will likely affect how the euro will be managed within the EU, the election should not be interpreted as an anti-euro vote.

8

Conclusion: The Lessons of Deutsche Mark Politics

> Money is more than a part of the economy. Money reflects the state, politics, and culture. The Euro [however] will be a denationalized and depoliticized currency.
>
> —Bundesbank president Hans Tietmeyer, 1997

> A strong and stable Euro is a further contribution by Europe to maintaining the stability of the international monetary system and to promoting prosperity throughout the world economy.
>
> —German finance minister Theo Waigel, 1997

Theoretical Implications

This volume began with the proposition that deutsche mark politics could best be explained if we first focused our analytical eye inward and disaggregated the state into two primary actors—the Bundesbank and the government. The development, formulation, and execution of German monetary policy also incorporated an analytical and theoretical framework emphasizing the triangulation of deutsche mark politics. As this book has shown, the Bundesbank and the government often do not share the same conception of German monetary policy; they differ as to what is in the nation's monetary interest, and they respond distinctively to disparate influences. The independence of the Bundesbank gives it a powerful platform from which it can influence deutsche mark politics. For its part, the government is often faced with the choice of either succumbing to the political will of the Bundesbank or seeking to bend the bank's will in order to secure the government's objectives. It is this struggle for control over the internal and external components of German monetary policy that is deutsche mark politics.

This domestic struggle for control invariably spills over into Germany's international monetary policies, particularly the debate over cooperation, defined as a sacrifice of monetary autonomy for exchange rate stability. The framework employed in this volume suggests that a trade-off is often made between exchange rate stability and monetary autonomy and that this trade-off can be evaluated in terms of the negotiating strategies of the government. These negotiating strategies are determined by the domestic-institutional dynamics of the Bundesbank-government relationship, which is influenced by varying international governance structures. For this study, I examined the G7 and the EMS as the key governance structures that can, under certain conditions, frame the domestic debate between the Bundesbank and government on whether to cooperate. In sum, domestic institutions are linked directly to international governance structures to provide a comprehensive model for evaluation.

The negotiating strategies of the government revealed a significant amount of variation in the degree of international and European monetary cooperation. These variations largely conformed to the hypotheses set forth in Chapter 1. First, it should be stressed that on many occasions the Bundesbank and government did not subordinate autonomy for stability. Whether aimed at the G7 or EMS pressure, the Bundesbank and government were often united on a strategy of resisting any and all efforts at monetary cooperation. Cooperation that would have eased tensions within the EMS or the G7 was not always forthcoming.

Second, it is important to reiterate the importance of understanding the relative political balance of power between the Bundesbank and government. The conditions conducive to cooperation arise from the domestic institutional context of German monetary policy—the dynamic, reciprocal Bundesbank-government relationship. Specifically, I examined the degree of political influence or leverage that the government had over the Bundesbank in order to determine whether it would pursue a compliant or hard-line strategy. Did the government feel that the conditions were conducive to it using its political influence over the Bundesbank to secure exchange rate stability? Or, were there instances when the government calculated that it would not have the political leverage necessary to secure Bundesbank ratification, hence making cooperation less likely? It was certainly the case that the government felt the need to pressure the Bundesbank to support the government's negotiating strategy. However, there were other cases where the government realized that it could not circumscribe Bundesbank independence, therefore, leading the government to conclude that no compromises could be made in negotiations.

At this point, we can then begin to review the periods of cooperation and noncooperation based on the level of disagreement between the Bundesbank and government on the one hand, and whether, on the other hand, the context of the bargaining structure was weak or strong. In other words, depending on the level of disagreement and the context of the governance structure, would the government pursue a hard-line negotiating strategy (resistant to concessions on autonomy) or a compliant negotiating strategy (willingness to concede autonomy for exchange rate stability)? Would the government be willing to press the Bundesbank for cooperation? Could such pressure be amplified by the governance structure within which the government was negotiating? The hypotheses are reviewed within the context of the empirical record of deutsche mark politics.

Throughout much of the negotiations leading up to Maastricht, the Bundesbank and government were often close together on many of the details of Maastricht, especially the need for an independent European central bank with its primary goal of price stability codified explicitly in the treaty. Other areas of common agreement included the strict convergence criteria that imposed German-style fiscal and monetary constraints on Germany's partners. Moreover, both realized, albeit the Bundesbank took a bit longer, that the DM would have to be sacrificed at the crowning moment of EMU. This provided the opening for Germany's counterparts to pressure the government to impose pressure on the Bundesbank to accept various concessions. The ability to pressure the Bundesbank was also enhanced by the strong governance structure of the EU and EMS. As such, the sacrifice of the DM under Maastricht fits the conditions set out in H-1 (low level of disagreement and strong governance).

However, there were noticeable stages in the Maastricht negotiations when the Bundesbank and government disagreed considerably—for example, on whether to set a firm timetable, to allow for "flexibility" in interpreting the convergence criteria, and to impose strict penalties on excessive deficit countries. The details of exchange rate policy (as codified in Article 109) were also an area of disagreement. As a result, conditions at times more closely approximated H-3 (high level of disagreement and strong governance) at various points prior to the Maastricht Treaty. Therefore, within the context of H-3, we should have expected to see a mix of compliant and hard-line strategies. Indeed, the Germans demanded a set of tough conditions in the negotiations with their European partners: the convergence criteria and independence for the ECB. At various points prior to the Maastricht Treaty, it appeared that the German government, with Bundesbank support, was intent on setting such hard-line conditions for EMU that no country would find them acceptable. The negotiations would therefore collapse and no agreement on EMU would be forthcoming. Yet, in the end, a Maastricht compromise developed. The German government offered some notable concessions—sacrificing a measure of monetary autonomy, including the ultimate sacrifice, the DM. The German government also pursued a compliant strategy on the timetable (setting a firm date), allowing for unclear and ambiguous provisions on exchange rate policy and penalties on deficit countries, and permitting the clause on flexibility in the interpretation of the convergence criteria.

A clearer example under H-1 would include the decision to pursue a compliant strategy leading up to the Basel-Nyborg agreement on intramarginal intervention. As both the government and Bundesbank realized that the zone of European monetary stability had to be secured in the face of unrelenting U.S. and dollar pressure, the two actors were united on easing tensions within the EMS. Interest rate reductions, realignments, and the Basel-Nyborg agreement, which more tightly constrained Bundesbank autonomy within the EMS, were the preferred strategies for the Germans. The period outlined in Chapter 5, the immediate post-Maastricht era, also revealed a generally compliant strategy (H-1) from German negotiators. Although the Bundesbank raised interest rates through 1992, the status quo prevailed within the EMS. As tensions began to escalate through early September 1992, the Bundesbank and government were largely in agreement that something had to change. As a result, the Germans pursued a compliant strategy, an interest rate reduction and an offer for a general realignment of the EMS. Despite British criticism that such conditions were not acceptable or did not go far enough, the German concessions on monetary autonomy were indeed noteworthy.

Under the conditions set out under H-2 (low level of disagreement and weak governance), the government and Bundesbank were often in agreement over the approach taken toward the G7's weak governance structure. The Bundesbank and government rarely disagreed on a common strategy toward the G7. The result was often a rigorous hard-line strategy, as set by the Bundesbank, in repeated G7 negotiations. After 1988, it is hard to identify even more than a few cases involving something approximating cooperation other than occasional central bank intervention. There were no new Plaza or Louvre accords. In fact, the Germans sought concessions from the United States, repeatedly criticizing U.S. macroeconomic policy and suggesting a more Germanic approach to policy. Despite low levels of disagreement, which could lead to a more compliant strategy, a hard-line strategy prevailed. Therefore, we can single out the institutional context of the negotiations—the weak governance of the G7—as the determining factor in the hard-line strategy. International institutions did influence the government's approach to G7 negotiations.

The Plaza and Louvre accords present some interesting permutations on the government's negotiating strategy. In both cases, the government and Bundesbank agreed that something had to be done to correct exchange rate imbalances and dollar volatility. But the stark contrast in the governance structure from September 1985 to February 1987 affected the final strategy of the government. I would argue that the stronger norms of governance within the G5 still prevailed in 1985. The spirit of coordination, cooperation, and accommodation, albeit within the less than formal structure of the G5, had a powerful effect on negotiations at the Plaza Hotel. In the eighteen months that followed Plaza, the Germans were quick to shift to a hard-line strategy that the norms of G7 cooperation had markedly dissipated. The Louvre accord, I would suggest, should be considered a hard-line strategy in that it was a status quo arrangement that did not demand any overt or formal commitments. The German government and Bundesbank were now united in their opposition to pressure from the United States through the G7. As the governance structure weakened, the Germans could resist pressure to sacrifice more autonomy. In fact, as the October 1987 crash revealed, it was the Germans who were now demanding concessions from the United States, a position consistent with our understanding of hard-line strategies. This German-G7 pattern would largely continue through 1998, including the heated confrontations in the spring of 1995.

The period leading up to the August 1993 EMS crisis presents a more complicated negotiating picture. First, the government and Bundesbank were increasingly moving apart on the Bundesbank's interest rate policy. While the Bundesbank was lowering rates, the rate of decrease was coming far too slowly and was not dramatic enough to stimulate a German economy sliding into recession. Bundesbank policy was thereby furthering tensions within the EMS, especially with France. However, the Bundesbank saw a realignment of the EMS as the best way to reduce the tension, a policy that the government was initially reluctant to pursue. As a result, there existed an unusual scenario where each actor wanted to pursue a compliant strategy—the Bundesbank through a realignment and the government through stronger interest rate reductions to ease tensions—but they could not agree on the proper approach. In such a situation, I would argue that conditions under H-3 prevailed. Neither the Bundesbank nor the government was intent on conceding on their particular strategy for dealing with the crisis. As a result, the Germans (as did the French) refused to offer any concessions on monetary autonomy. As a hard-line strategy prevailed through the spring and summer of 1993, the EMS nearly collapsed. However, in the end, the decision was made to preserve the EMS albeit with widened trading margins. While retaining an element of EMS governance and retaining a commitment to EMU, and hence a constraint on monetary autonomy, the decision to hollow out the EMS should be interpreted as a mixed hard-line and compliant strategy.

As the governance structure weakened noticeably following the near implosion of the EMS in August 1993, the Bundesbank and government were ever closer in agreement on the need to secure a hard euro. Securing a hard euro would come in the form of remaining firm on the convergence criteria and adding further criteria through Waigel's stability pact. If one accepts the fact that the ultimate sacrifice of monetary autonomy had already been made, the Germans were intent on securing as much autonomy as possible in the interim period leading to 1997 at the earliest, 1999 at the latest. Not surprisingly, the Germans could again play master of monetary negotiations. In fact, through the stability pact negotiations from 1995 to 1997, many analysts believed that the Germans were seeking to add more rigorous conditions to EMU. The chorus for delay across Europe, including Germany, was growing stronger such that many saw the German strategy as undermining EMU permanently. In the end and as the final deadline on EMU approached and the formal commitment by the government to EU again influenced negotiators, the stability pact was accepted as a concession to Germany. However, with enough concessions on defining the conditions of a severe recession, for example, by the German government to its European partners, a classic EU compromise and a compliant strategy had been struck.

In general, given the description of these negotiating strategies, it is not surprising to see a pattern of German-EMS and German-G7 interaction that developed over the period 1985–1998. First, in the international monetary system, the Bundesbank, supported by the government, resisted repeated attempts to set exchange rate zones or ranges. Cooperation on other macroeconomic adjustment measures remained ad hoc in nature and only arose when such measures converged with Germany's own domestic or European monetary interests. When cooperation emerged, it tended to converge closely with the interests of German monetary authorities and demanded little in the way of an adjustment of German policy. As Bundesbank officials often repeated, at no point during the period 1985–1998 did G7 coordination demand that the Bundesbank adjust its policies to conform to the demands or pressures of the United States or the G7. There are just a few examples where German monetary authorities offered policy concessions to the G7, and these concessions demanded little in the way of sacrificing a significant measure of monetary autonomy.

In the European arena, since the Plaza accord in September of 1985, the Germans pursued a fairly steady policy of accommodating European partners in order to solidify the institutional framework of the EMS and the EU. With the eventual, and often reluctant, support of the Bundesbank, the German government was willing to accommodate its European partners in a wide area of policy: the expansion of short-term financing facilities for intramarginal interventions, wider fluctuation bands of the ERM for some EMS partners, revaluation of the DM at critical moments of the EMS, interest rate adjustments to ease tensions within the EMS, the automaticity of the final stage of EMU, and revisions to soften the stability pact. This Europeanization of German monetary policy, in the sense of accommodating policy to Europe's interests in closer monetary cooperation and European integration, has been an underlying theme in the external developments of deutsche mark politics. Despite the complications brought on by reunification and the turmoil within the EMS over the 1992–1993 period, Germany increasingly recognized that its future would lie with Europe and that Germany should strengthen its leadership position in European economic, monetary, and political affairs. Most significant, the Germans sacrificed the DM for an institutionalized European monetary option—EMU and the euro. Not only did the EMS and EU constrain Bundesbank policy, but they also provided the government with the platform to make the ultimate sacrifice of monetary autonomy—the DM. Governance in monetary affairs would now shift to a European level.

The Significance of Deutsche Mark Politics for Euro Politics

One may ask why the conclusions found in this book are important today when the DM is set to disappear in the next few years. In other words, the implications of deutsche mark politics may be interesting, but dated. In one sense, this is, of course, true. However, the underlying argument of deutsche mark politics is that European monetary politics have taken on the institutional dynamics of the German model, that is, a highly independent central bank (the ECB) obligated to pursue price stability as its primary objective within the EMU member countries. The objective of price stability is potentially constrained, however, by political institutions within the structure of the EU and external exchange rate arrangements governed by the European Council or some other body. German monetary policy has certainly become Europeanized. But European monetary politics have now become much like deutsche mark politics. Therefore, the lessons of deutsche mark politics since the early 1980s can provide some distinct lessons for European monetary officials for the future of what I label "euro politics."

Initially, the euro will be invulnerable to speculative attacks that often beset the old ERM.[1] However, a run on the euro at some point will confront the ECB with the dilemma of accepting depreciation of the euro vis-à-vis the dollar (and the inflationary impact of the depreciation) or raising interest rates that might force one or more euro countries deeper into recession, and conceivably, one might argue, out of EMU. Or, the ECB might have to engage in exchange rate politics within a reformed G7 that would require intervention to shore up the euro within various zones. Given the fact that each EMU member has forgone using exchange rates as an instrument of adjustment, conflict among euro countries and conflict between the ECB, European Council, and member countries will likely erupt. More significant, as long as member governments are sovereign,

EMU is capable of breaking apart. The decision to stick with the euro in difficult times will ultimately be a political one. Much will depend on the public's acceptance of the sacrifice of the DM, or whatever currency, for the historic leap to EMU and the euro. The member countries, the European Commission, and ECB will have to continue their public relations campaigns. Despite the claims of Tietmeyer in this chapter's introductory quote, neither the euro nor the ECB will be depoliticized. Like deutsche mark politics, the euro will be by definition politicized and, in many ways, it will still retain a nationalized context through the EU's traditional governing institutions.

In addition, the lessons of Bundesbank independence should not be lost on EU officials, EMU member countries, or the European-wide public. The ECB will be more powerful and independent than even the Bundesbank. The ECB's mandates for price stability are unambiguous. Its political independence is unquestioned. A political counterweight of any importance does not exist—the Euro Stability Council notwithstanding. The euro will thus be a challenge to all Europeans to accept the implications of a stability-oriented monetary union. More precisely, does a *Stabilitätsgemeinschaft* exist in Europe that would be willing to accept the costs of a strict price stability policy? We know that the German economic culture supported such a mandate and undoubtedly supports the same mandate for the ECB. But no such consensus or European economic culture exists across the EU. Although the Bundesbank could call upon a collective German understanding of the problems of inflation, the ECB will not be able to call upon a similar collective European understanding. As such, it will make the ECB's initial actions more difficult than the Bundesbank's own early efforts at securing public support for its price stability policies. This difficulty will be accentuated by the likelihood that the ECB will first pursue an overly aggressive anti-inflationary monetary policy in order to establish its credibility in the eyes of the markets.[2]

Closely related to the issue of independence, the ongoing problems with accountability, transparency, and "democratic deficits" that plague the EU's credibility in the eyes of the people will now focus intently on the ECB. The EU already regulates the European public in many policy arenas across Europe, but the ECB will have the most direct and profound impact on all Europeans. The ECB will soon face the searing heat of the political spotlight like no central bank has ever faced before. Will the ECB melt under such pressure? If the ECB is able to withstand such pressure, what EU institution will become the focal point for the public's demand for accountability? The newly designed forum of the stability council does not promise to be of any significance, at least initially. Neither the European Commission nor the European Parliament will likely fulfill this role.

From the earlier discussion in Chapter 2 on the merits of central bank independence, accountability in an open, democratic society is an important element of an effectively functioning political system. In Germany, at least the government served this function. If the ECB and the EU institutions fail in this function, the future of EMU and the EU may very well rest on shaky political foundations. Both the German government and the Bundesbank recognized this fact when they pushed for political union to operate in conjunction with monetary union. The Bundesbank explicitly noted the importance of political union prior to Maastricht. Specifically, the Bundesbank argued that "a Monetary Union is . . . an irrevocable sworn cofraternity—'all for one and one for all'—which, if it is to prove durable, requires, judging from past experience, even closer links in the form of a comprehensive political union."[3] Judging from the past experiences of deutsche mark politics, it will be crucial that the EU develop political union to reassure the public and provide a stable political foundation for the future operation of the EMU. Ultimately, political institutions must provide a vehicle in which the people of Europe can express their concerns, worries, fears, hopes, and anger.

Exchange rate policy for the euro also remains unclear, and the debates over clarifying it remain extremely controversial.[4] More important, the ECB and the EU will face the very same choice as faced by the Bundesbank and government: pursue monetary autonomy (albeit within the EMU member countries) or sacrifice a measure of autonomy in return for exchange rate stability vis-à-vis the dollar, yen, or some other currency. The scenario sounds like one drawn straight from deutsche mark politics: a powerful independent central bank with the goal of internal price stability pitted against an external monetary policy subject to the domain of the Council of Finance Ministers, among other EU actors. Specifically, Article 109 of the Maastricht Treaty lays down the legal relationship and general parameters between the ECB and the Council on exchange rate policy. Although not entirely clear, it is assumed that representatives of the Council hold authority to negotiate formal and informal exchange rate agreements with foreign governments under consultation with the ECB. Formal agreements that peg the euro, for example, to the dollar or yen would require a unanimous vote within the Council after it consulted with the ECB, the European Commission, and the European Parliament. As understood in the analysis of deutsche mark politics, such an arduous process of agreement or "ratification" decreases the likelihood of increased exchange rate management at the international level. Exchange rate flexibility, or European monetary autonomy at the expense of exchange rate stability vis-à-vis the dollar or yen, will likely be the result.

Nevertheless, as Henning states, if cohesive, "national governments, operating through the Council, appear to hold a strong position vis-à-vis the ECB on the matter of formal arrangements."[5] Whereas the search for consensus on exchange rate policy is required, actually attaining consensus is not required. Moreover, it is not clear which institution, the ECB, the Council, or some other institution, would determine whether an exchange rate agreement would do damage to the price stability mandate of the ECB. In Germany, the government holds the final say over such questions, which as we have seen, suggests the potential for constraints on the autonomy of the ECB. A similar scenario for the EU depends on the cohesiveness of national governments, a pattern for which the EU national governments are not often known. A final determination on how this debate will be resolved remains open.

Moreover, informal exchange rate arrangements such as those of Plaza and Louvre can be negotiated by the Council under the rubric of setting a "general orientation" of exchange rate policy. The general orientation must not, however, prejudice the primary objective of the ESCB to maintain price stability. This would suggest that the ECB would have a right to reject such an orientation, although this again is not clear and will be subject to later determination under actual practice. We have seen from deutsche mark politics that informal agreements were often limited in their impact upon the Bundesbank and that the bank found it easier to disregard such arrangements and/or frustrate any new initiatives. We can speculate that based on the theoretical understanding of governance set forth in this volume, with weak governance structures of the G7 existing today, the European Council will have a low level of political leverage over the ECB. As a result, given the difficulty in securing the ECB's support, we should expect a more hard-line strategy taken by the Council of Finance Ministers in any exchange rate negotiations. Assuming that the Council is responsible for negotiating exchange rate agreements, we should not expect any new major exchange rate initiatives in the international monetary arena.

Clarifying how exchange rate policy will be determined is undoubtedly a difficult task. If the lessons of deutsche mark politics are of any relevance, the degree of political control that the Council (or some other body) has over the ECB in the matter of exchange rate policy will be crucial to determining the full extent of ECB independence from the political fetters of exchange rate policy. The Council has only begun to detail some of the conditions that it would pursue in an exchange rate policy. As agreed to at the Luxembourg summit in December 1997, the conditions that could lead to the development of an exchange rate policy are cited as "definite exchange rate distortions."[6] These conditions were, however, not clearly defined. Nor was it determined who would decide when exactly such "distortions" demanded action. Without prejudicing price stability or the independence of the ECB, it is thought that the Council will undertake this role. With consultation with the ECB and Commission, the Council will act to formulate a policy. How this will all develop remains a bit of a mystery.

The lessons for Europe derived from deutsche mark politics will depend on the ability of EMU to function effectively in the immediate post-1999 period. Bundesbank officials believe that in order to ensure a frictionless transition from the DM to the euro, it is especially important that the euro and EMU enjoy the same prestige on international financial markets as that attained by the DM since the end of World War II. This prestige will depend on how effectively the EMU can deal with various crises, such as external shocks from dollar instability, internal shocks within certain regions, and the ongoing political question of high unemployment. The ability to deal with such crises that are certain to come will depend on the institutional and legal foundations of EMU. Will the stability pact operate as designed? Will there be a political forum to address or counter ECB policy? Will political union develop? Will the ECB, in fact, be able to withstand pressure on exchange rate policy? Like the Bundesbank, the ECB will have to be careful to decide when to fight and when to give in. Overall, though, it is not clear what the answers to these questions are. But they certainly provide a rich forum for future research. Much will be decided in the first years of EMU's operation.

Global Monetary Governance and Deutsche Mark Politics

What are the lessons of deutsche mark politics for global monetary governance? The previous discussion on the exchange rate policy of the euro hints at some initial problems. Overall, the powerful institutional framework of the EU and the EMU suggests that the development of EMU has given the Germans and the Europeans greater bargaining leverage in the global monetary balance of power. In this book, we have seen that the strengthening of the Bundesbank model of European monetary cooperation and coordination enhanced the bargaining power of German monetary authorities who then used a united European front to counteract U.S. pressure or calls for cooperation. Germany's strategy of strengthening the European monetary arena of cooperation and institution building was aimed at stabilizing Germany's important European trading and monetary zone, even if that meant a loss of domestic monetary autonomy resulting in the sacrifice of the DM. While German monetary policy was not and could not feasibly be disconnected from U.S. economic policies, Germany's bargaining position vis-à-vis the United States could be strengthened if the idea of the EU, on the back of monetary union, could be advanced. As such, the EMS and EMU should not be thought of as a complete alternative to U.S.-German cooperation (in fact, the German-U.S. relationship remains a central pillar of Germany's overarching foreign policy) but as a counterbalance to German-U.S. interaction.[7]

Indeed, the developments since the mid-1970s in the international monetary system continue to frame the larger debate on the future direction of international monetary politics. First, the decline in the global influence of the United States relative to that of Europe and the Asia Pacific region has continued the mild erosion of the U.S. dollar in international transactions. If backed by a credible monetary policy, the euro could play a more important global role. Central banks will want to hold some of their reserves in euros, and financial markets will likely conduct more transactions in the new currency. Some analysts suggest that between 30 percent and 40 percent of global financial assets will be denominated in euros.[8] This challenge to the dollar, a challenge that some commentators speculate will lead to increasing conflict between the old and new world,[9] will undoubtedly alter the monetary balance of power, a tripolar currency world. But how soon all this will occur, if at all, remains one of the great EMU unknowns.

Second, the ability of the United States, Japan, and Germany to hold down inflation without committing themselves to a system of fixed exchange rates vis-à-vis each other only solidifies the incentives of countries not to sacrifice domestic monetary autonomy to hold their exchange rates within narrow target ranges. This lesson will undoubtedly be transferred to the external operations of EMU. Finally, and most important, the increasing trilateral nature of the global monetary system where the EU, the United States, and some Asia Pacific currency regions serve larger roles as nominal anchors of regional monetary regimes introduces a tripolar orientation to the international monetary system. More flexible and looser exchange rate mechanisms and commitments between the monetary poles and increasingly tighter levels of exchange rate coordination and policy coordination around the center of the poles do not indicate a return to a centralized global monetary regime. Despite some suggestions to call together a new international monetary conference comparable to Bretton Woods,[10] all of these developments would seem to indicate that resurrecting an international monetary system does not seem likely in the immediate future. As governments recognize that international financial flows of U.S.$1.5 trillion a day often limit policy choices,[11] governments may see a greater incentive to strengthen regional monetary affairs first before tackling the international monetary system. Asian leaders interested in developing a common Asian voice and response to IMF, G7, and U.S pressure have duly noted this fact. Asian leaders would do well to study the history of EMU and deutsche mark politics.

The experiences of German monetary authorities under the Bretton Woods system continue to frame their view and, I would argue, now frame the ECB's view toward the international monetary system. Proposals to resurrect some new form of global monetary regime (a fixed exchange rate system, a gold standard, and a basket of commodities) will be met with a large measure of skepticism and rejection by the ECB. The ECB will likely not be interested in returning to a system that might undermine its efforts to maintain European price stability or the EU's efforts to solidify and enhance the processes of collective European monetary cooperation. Automaticity and supranationality, at least at the international level, are not concepts that are accepted easily among German or many European central bankers. The ECB will likely prefer not to rely on mechanical rules, obligatory standards, or automatic guidelines in external monetary affairs. Price stability and securing the value of the euro will take priority over exchange rate objectives. If it has not already, the German monetary norm will likely become the European monetary norm guiding Europe's exchange rate policy.

Some Recommendations on Global Monetary Governance

Given such factors, there are a few possible measures that might enhance the process of international monetary coordination, although, as this volume has repeatedly noted, they may prove politically difficult to implement. We should not expect any rapid movement by the ECB or the EU on formulating EMU's position within the international monetary system. However, in my view, the EU and EMU should actively promote European leadership in international monetary affairs. As noted by Theo Waigel, the euro can promote international monetary stability. This is a natural state of affairs and will, in fact, enhance Europe's international monetary power. EMU can also act to stabilize an international system of governance that is largely nonexistent, dominated by markets, and prone to bouts of instability. The process of completing EMU can reinvigorate global monetary governance. The opportunities to reform the G7 in the next few years should not be lost. The political will necessary for such an undertaking must be found.

As Henning cogently argues, the completion of EMU will raise questions for the management of virtually all the international financial and monetary organizations to which the member states of EMU, including Germany, belong.[12] Moreover, EMU more than likely could increase the number of representatives at G7 summits and the meetings of finance ministers and central bankers. Certainly the president of the ECB would have to attend. With financial, fiscal, and regulatory policy still under the sovereign domain of nation-states, it is hard to imagine each nation's representatives, at least German monetary authorities, relinquishing their role in the larger dynamic of G7 governance. In addition, how would Britain fit into any newly restructured G7, given the difficulty of devising a role for the "outs" in EMU? Replacing the G7 with another group including developing economies also does not lend itself to a more efficient, streamlined system of governance.

Instead, Bergsten and Henning suggest devising a monetary G3 consisting of the United States, Japan, and EMU, with a narrow focus on exchange rate management and monetary policy coordination.[13] Evaluating their suggestion in the context of this study, I would contend that such a forum would likely not be dismissed outright by the ECB. More than likely, the ECB's president would serve as a leading spokesperson for EMU within the G3. Although finding an appropriate political representative of the EMU countries would be difficult, the European Council could designate a political "monetary" representative to work with the president of the ECB on developing "Europe's" negotiating strategy. Such a representative may also emerge in the process of clarifying EMU's exchange rate policy. The EU, I would argue, should move quickly in this regard. However, I remain skeptical that something on this level will develop in the near future and more than likely will have to wait until after the year 2002 when the euro finally replaces national currencies and if Great Britain joins EMU.

A second more general recommendation by Bergsten and Henning, yet one not likely to occur soon, would be to develop for the G3 and/or G7 the rules approach and institutions that characterize European monetary cooperation. These rules and institutions could be transposed up to the G7 level where such rules and institutions are lacking in scope and strength. With the Plaza accord of 1985 and the Louvre accord of 1987, international economic cooperation appeared to enter into a new phase of strengthened rules, albeit without formal institutions or commitments. G7 efforts were seen at that time as a credible framework for analyzing the global effects of the policies and performances of individual countries. No new institutions were developed, but it was believed that a rules-based approach—emphasizing aggregate quantitative indicators such as real GNP growth, the average level of interest rates, and the current account position used by the IMF to gauge the impact of each nation's policies—might enhance coordination. As a result, nations could have been expected to carefully calibrate their national policies to meet predetermined G7 agreements on exchange rate targets or fiscal and monetary policy. Nevertheless, without formal and universal acceptance of fixed rates with the dollar, or possibly the euro, as the international anchor currency of the system or some other form of rules-based approach to policy coordination, international monetary cooperation did not flourish in the 1990s.

Moreover, even though a full set of economic indicators is used at the G7 level and by the IMF for central banks and government policymakers to analyze the impacts of their policies on other nations, policy coordination will continue to suffer unless such indicators can be formalized into a stronger institutional arrangement. Such an arrangement must obligate central banks and government officials to act at the system level, even when they disagree. The illusion of institutionalization at the G7 level (committees, councils, summits, and so on) gives the politicians and public alike the impression that international management exists. Some level of management does exist, but as this work has demonstrated, instability, conflict, and diverging policies predominate such management.

Finally, a re-emphasized process of G7 or G3 *macroeconomic* summitry needs to be developed. The current G7 process surrounding the IMF/World Bank meetings and the overly politicized G7 annual summits with their focus shifted from macroeconomic policy coordination to global security and political questions has proven to be ineffective in developing an ongoing process of international macroeconomic decisionmaking, rules, or regulations for the international monetary system. This would include strengthening some aspect of the G7 consultation process, for example, by giving each country for a year some responsibility for organizing meetings, handling invitations, setting agendas, writing papers, and the like. Such a move might enhance mutual trust, learning, and institutional memory. Moreover, in addition to existing G7 finance minister meetings, an annual G7 finance summit should be held separate from the traditional overly politicized G7 summits. The number of permanent representatives to this G7 finance summit could also be increased.

In sum, EMU provides an opportunity for everyone, the United States, the Europeans, the Germans, and Asian leaders to reevaluate global monetary governance structures. Old patterns of interaction characterized during the period analyzed in *Deutsche Mark Politics* will shift, leading, I believe, to a possibility for a fresh start to global monetary governance. In light of the massive financial disruptions through the summer of 1998—including monetary meltdowns in Russia, Brazil, and across Asia—and the apparent inability of international actors like the IMF or the G7 to respond effectively to such disruptions, such an opportunity should not be wasted.

Conclusion

The motivation for this book started with a narrow interest to examine the role of the DM in the German economy. The scope expanded to include the role of the central bank and government in managing Germany's monetary affairs, what I came to label deutsche mark politics. From there, the book has followed the evolving nature of deutsche mark politics to the point today where it is being replaced by euro politics. The implications of these developments were also noted for the international monetary system. Not only do I feel that such a process was politically appropriate for Germany and Europe, despite the inherent difficulties and looming problems, but Germany's influence upon global monetary politics has, in fact, dramatically increased. From the Bundesbank model of central bank independence that is being used in the developing world to the German norm of price stability governing Europe and international monetary governance, the implications and legacy of deutsche mark politics will continue despite the demise of the DM. Contrary to some critics and skeptics, the story of deutsche mark politics is one of achievement and success, peacefully attained on the international stage. Such is extremely noteworthy given the legacy of the German question. In strict monetary terms, the German question, as analyzed in *Deutsche Mark Politics,* has been answered; the answer is the euro.

Notes

1. See the analysis in "Ready or Not, Here Comes EMU," *The Economist,* October 11, 1997.
2. For a view on what monetary policy in the EMU might look like, see Wim Duisenberg, "Monetary Policy in the EMU," *Auszüge aus Presseartikeln,* December 2, 1997.
3. Deutsche Bundesbank, *Monthly Report of the Deutsche Bundesbank,* September 1990 (Frankfurt/Main), p. 1.
4. See especially the analysis of C. Randall Henning, *Cooperating with Europe's Monetary Union* (Washington, D.C.: Institute for International Economics, 1997).
5. Ibid., p. 36.
6. "Euro-Wechselkurspolitik lässt Fragen offen," *Finanz-und Wirtschaftsspiegel,* December 15, 1997.
7. While largely supportive of EMU, U.S. officials have often criticized the Europeans for becoming preoccupied ("navel-gazing") with EMU when more important issues such as enlargement of NATO and the EU remained on the agenda.
8. "Why Non-Europeans Should Care About EMU," *The Economist,* March 29, 1997.
9. See the rather overstated fears of Martin Feldstein, "EMU and International Conflict," *Foreign Affairs* 76, no. 6 (November/December 1997), pp. 60–74.
10. See the analysis of Ronald McKinnon, "Recapturing the Lost Spirit," *Financial Times,* June 21, 1994; and Judy Shelton, *Money Meltdown: Restoring Order to the Global Currency System* (New York: Free Press, 1994).
11. This is one of the arguments set forth in Robert Solomon's book, *Transformation of the World Economy, 1980–1993* (Washington, D.C.: Brookings Institution, 1994).

12. Henning, *Cooperating with Europe's Monetary Union,* p. 46. I draw heavily on Henning's perceptive analysis of the future of the G7. See also the analysis of Robert Chote, "Questions over Membership of the IMF and G7," *Financial Times,* September 9, 1997.

13. C. Fred Bergsten and C. Randall Henning, *Global Economic Leadership and the Group of Seven* (Washington, D.C.: Institute for International Economics, 1996). See also Henning's discussion in *Cooperating with Europe,* pp. 48–57.

Selected Bibliography

Andrews, David M., and Thomas D. Willett. "Financial Interdependence and the State: International Monetary Relations at Century's End." *International Organization* 51, no. 2 (summer 1997), pp. 479–511.
Baldwin, David, ed. *Neorealism and Neoliberalism: The Contemporary Debate.* New York: Columbia University Press, 1993.
Baum, Thomas. "Empirische Analysen der Bundesbankautonomie." *Konjunkturpolitik*, no. 29 (1983), pp. 163–185.
Bergsten, C. Fred, and C. Randall Henning. *Global Economic Leadership and the Group of Seven.* Washington, D.C.: Institute for International Economics, 1996.
Blackburn, Keith, and Michael Christensen. "Monetary Policy and Policy Credibility." *Journal of Economic Literature*, no. 27 (March 1989), pp. 1–45.
Burdekin, Richard. "Cross-Country Evidence on the Relationship Between Central Banks and Governments." *Journal of Macroeconomics* 9 (summer 1987), pp. 391–405.
Caesar, Rolf. *Der Handlungsspielraum von Notenbanken.* Baden-Baden: Nomos, 1981.
Cohen, Benjamin J. *Organizing the World's Money.* New York: Basic Books, 1977.
———. "The Triad and the Unholy Trinity: Lessons for the Pacific Region." In Richard Higgot, Richard Leaver, and John Ravenhill, eds., *Pacific Economic Relations in the 1990s: Cooperation or Conflict?* London: Allen and Unwin, 1993, pp. 133–158.
———. "Phoenix Risen: The Resurrection of Global Finance." *World Politics* 48 (January 1996), pp. 268–296.
———. *The Geography of Money.* Ithaca: Cornell University Press, 1998.
Committee for the Study of Economic and Monetary Union. *Report on Economic and Monetary Union in the European Community.* [Delors Report.] Luxembourg, 1990.
Cooper, Richard, B. Eichengreen, and G. Holtham, eds. *Can Nations Agree? Issues in International Economic Cooperation.* Washington, D.C.: Brookings Institution, 1989.
Destler, I. M., and C. Randall Henning. *Dollar Politics: Exchange Rate Policymaking in the United States.* Washington, D.C.: Institute for International Economics, 1989.

Deutsche Bundesbank. *30 Jahre Deutsche Bundesbank: Die Entstehung des Bundesbankgesetzes,* vom 26. Juli 1957. Frankfurt/Main, 1988.

———. *Geldpolitischen Aufgaben und Instrumente.* 6th ed. Frankfurt/Main, 1993.

Eichengreen, Barry, and Jeffry Frieden, eds. *The Political Economy of European Monetary Unification.* Boulder, Colo.: Westview Press, 1994.

Emminger, Otmar. "The D-Mark in the Conflict Between Internal and External Equilibrium, 1948–1975." *Princeton Essays in International Finance,* no. 122 (1977).

———. *Verteidigung der DM: Pladöyers für Stabiles Geld.* Frankfurt/Main: Fritz Knapp, 1980.

———. *DM, Dollar, und Währungskrisen.* Stuttgart: Deutsche Verlags-Anstalt, 1986.

Feldman, Gerald. *The Great Disorder: Politics, Economics, and Society in the German Inflation, 1914–1924.* New York: Oxford University Press, 1993.

Frey, Bruno, and Friedrich Schneider. "Central Bank Behavior." *Journal of Monetary Economics,* no. 7 (1981), pp. 291–315.

Frieden, Jeffry, Daniel Gros, and Erik Jones, eds. *The New Political Economy of European Monetary Union.* Lanham, Md.: Rowan and Littlefield, 1998.

Funabashi, Yoichi. *Managing the Dollar: From the Plaza to the Louvre.* Washington, D.C.: Institute for International Economics, 1988.

Gilpin, Robert. *The Political Economy of International Relations.* Princeton: Princeton University Press, 1987.

Goodman, John. *Monetary Sovereignty: The Politics of Central Banking in Western Europe.* Ithaca: Cornell University Press, 1992.

Hanrieder, Wolfram, ed. *Economic Issues and the Atlantic Community.* New York: Praeger, 1982.

———. *Germany, America, and Europe.* (New Haven, Conn.: Yale University Press, 1989).

Henning, C. Randall. *International Policymaking in the U.S., Japan, and Germany.* (Washington, D.C.: Institute for International Economics, 1994).

———. *Cooperating with Europe's Monetary Union.* Washington, D.C.: Institute for International Economics, 1997.

———. "Systemic Conflict and Regional Monetary Integration: The Case of Europe." *International Organization* 52, no. 3 (summer 1998), pp. 537–573.

Kaiser, Rolf H. *Bundesbankautonomie—Möglichkeiten und Grenzen einer unabhängigen Politik.* Frankfurt/Main: Rita G. Fischer, 1980.

Katzenstein, Peter. *Policy and Politics in West Germany.* Philadelphia: Temple University Press, 1987.

———, ed. *Tamed Power: Germany in Europe.* Ithaca: Cornell University Press, 1997.

Kaufmann, Hugo. "The Deutsche Mark Between the Dollar and the European Monetary System." *Kredit und Kapital,* no. 18 (1985), pp. 29–60.

———. *Germany's International Monetary Policy and the European Monetary System.* New York: Brooklyn College Press, 1985.

Kennedy, Ellen. *The Bundesbank: Germany's Central Bank in the International Monetary System.* London: RIIA and Pinter Publishers, 1991.

Krasner, Stephen, ed. *International Regimes.* (Ithaca: Cornell University Press, 1983).

Lipschitz, Leslie, and Donogh McDonald, eds. "German Unification: Economic Issues." *International Monetary Fund.* Occasional paper, no. 75, 1990. Washington, D.C.

Loedel, Peter. "Enhancing Europe's International Monetary Power." In Pierre-Henri Laurent and Marc Maresceau, eds., *The State of the European Union: Volume 4, Deepening and Widening*. Boulder, Colo.: Lynne Reinner, pp. 243–261.
Lombra, Raymond, and Willard Witte, eds. *The Political Economy of International and Domestic Monetary Relations*. Ames: Iowa University Press, 1982.
McNamara, Kathleen. *The Currency of Ideas: Monetary Politics in the European Union*. Ithaca: Cornell University Press, 1998.
Marsh, David. *Die Bundesbank: Geschäfte mit der Macht*. Munich: Bertelsmann, 1992.
Merkl, Peter. *German Unification in the European Context*. University Park: The Pennsylvania State Press, 1993.
———, ed. *The Federal Republic at Fifty*. London: Macmillan, 1999.
Milner, Helen. "International Theories of Cooperation Among Nations: Strengths and Weaknesses." *World Politics* 44, no. 3 (April 1992), pp. 466–496.
Moravcsik, Andrew. "Negotiating the Single European Act: National Interests and Conventional Statecraft in the European Community." *International Organization* 45, no. 1 (winter 1991), pp. 19–56.
Nölling, Wilhelm. *German Monetary Policy in Europe After Maastricht*. New York: St. Martin's Press, 1993.
Oatley, Thomas H. *Monetary Politics: Exchange Rate Cooperation in the European Community*. Ann Arbor: University of Michigan Press, 1997.
Overturf, Stephen. *Money and the European Union*. New York: St. Martin's Press, 1997.
Pöhl, Karl Otto. "Das Spannungsverhältnis zwischen nationaler und internationaler Währungspolitik aus der Sicht der Bundesbank." *Hamburger Jahrbuch für Wirtschaft und Gesellschaftpolitik*, no. 30 (1985), pp. 177–187.
Putnam, Robert. "Diplomacy and Domestic Politics: The Logic of Two-Level Games." *International Organization* 42, no. 3 (summer 1988), pp. 427–460.
Putnam, Robert D., and Nicholas Bayne. *Hanging Together: Cooperation and Conflict in the Seven-Power Summits*. Cambridge: Harvard University Press, 1987.
Robert, Rudiger. *Die Unabhängigkeit der Bundesbank*. Regensburg: Athenäuem, 1978.
Rohrlich, Paul Egon. "Economic Culture and Foreign Economic Policy: The Cognitive Analysis of Economic Policy Making." *International Organization* 41, no. 1 (1987), pp. 61–92.
Sandholtz, Wayne. "Choosing Union: Monetary Politics and Maastricht." *International Organization* 47, no. 1 (winter 1993), pp. 1–39.
Schmidt, Helmut. *Menschen und Mächte*. Berlin: Siedler Verlag, 1987.
Smyser, William. *The Economy of United Germany: Colossus at the Crossroads*. New York: St. Martin's Press, 1992.
Stares, Paul, ed. *The New Germany and the New Europe*. Washington, D.C.: Brookings Institution, 1992.
Sturm, Roland. "The Role of the Bundesbank in German Politics." *West European Politics* 12, no. 2 (1989), pp. 33–50.
Tsoukalis, Loukas, ed. *The Political Economy of International Money*. London: RIIA, 1985.
von Arnim, Hans Herbert. "Die Deutsche Bundesbank—Pfeiler der Demokratie." *Zeitschrift für Wirtschaftspolitik* 37, no. 1 (1988), pp. 51–63.
von Bonin, Konrad. *Zentralbanken zwischen funktioneller Unabhängigkeit und politischer Autonomie*. Baden-Baden: Nomos, 1979.

Webb, Michael. *The Political Economy of Policy Coordination: International Adjustment Since 1945*. Ithaca: Cornell University Press, 1995.
Woll, Arthur. "Zur Unabhängingkeit der Deutschen Bundesbank." In Volker Nienhaus and Ulrich van Suntum, eds., *Grundlagen und Erneurung der Marktwirtschaft*. Baden-Baden: Nomos, 1988.
Woolley, John T. *Monetary Politics*. Cambridge, UK: Cambridge University Press, 1984.

Index

Adenauer, Konrad, 46, 57
Alesina, Alberto, 41
Asia: financial crisis in, 225–226, 230
Association for the Monetary Union of Europe, 98
Association for the Protection of German Savers, 99

Baker, James, 14, 68–70, 73, 89n43, 103; October 1987 market crash, 83
Bangemann, Martin, 104
Bank der deutschen Länder (BdL), 46, 56–57
Bank for International Settlements (BIS), 21, 192
Bargaining strategies, 24; compliant vs. hard line, 25–26, 27tab; definition of, 24–25
Basel-Nyborg agreement, 80–83, 238
BdL. *See* Bank der deutschen Länder
Bentsen, Lloyd, 167, 185–186
BIS. *See* Bank for International Settlements
Brady, Nicholas, 129, 131–132, 150–151
Brandt, Willy, 57
Bretton Woods: collapse of, 12, 16, 161; comparison to EMS, 171; constraint on Germany, 76, 146–147; fiftieth anniversary, 187–188; fixed exchange system, 4; and G7, 181; resurrection of, 246–247
Britain: and EMU, 101, 108–109; exit from EMS, 155–157

Bundesbank, 6–7; constitutionality of, 47–50; and convergence criteria, 196–197; credibility of, 40, 42–43; and ECB, 113–114; and ECU, 89n54; and EMU, 94, 99–100, 102, 114–115, 161–162, 128, 181, 243; and federalism, 49–50; financial independence, 52–54; relationship to the G7, 183; goals and objectives, 10tab, 39–40; gold revaluation debate, 219–223; independence, 40, 41–42; instruments of, 53; internal divisions on EMU, 201; law, 11, 45, 49, 52–54, 81; personal independence, 49–51; and Plaza Accord, 70–72; policy after GEMU, 147–149; political independence, 45–49; revisions of law, 225; as a scapegoat, 158, 170–172; terms of office, 51
Bundestag, 47–48; elections, 191, 227
Bush, George, 14, 104–105; benign neglect of, 149–151, 154; on EMU 124–125

Calleo, David, 37
CDU. *See* Christian Democratic Union
Central Bank Council, 30n7, 48–49, 51, 63n40, 77, 81
Chirac, Jacques, 196, 227; and ECB, 97; and EMS, 77; and G7, 218; and May 1997 election, 222–223. *See also* France
Christian Democratic Union (CDU), 57, 79, 189

257

Christian Socialist Union (CSU), 79, 140n104, 221–222
Clinton, Bill, 14; and the G7, 144, 162, 167; in Germany, 187; and Asian crisis, 226
Cohen, Benjamin J., xv, 15, 75, 253
Cooperation, 15–16, 237–240
Core Europe, 119–120, 173n6; and Bundesbank, 101, 162, 210; and German government, 189–191
Coronation theory, 94, 102, 128, 164–165
Council of Academic Advisors, 109
Council of Economic Advisors, 220
Craig, Gordon, 37
CSU. See Christian Socialist Union

Delors, Jacques, 98
Delors Plan, 96
Delors Committee, 97, 100–101, 109–112
Deutsche mark politics, x, 2; and economic culture, 36–38; Europeanization of, xiv, 75–79; and G7, 245–247; lessons of, 235, 250; model, 5; significance to Europe, 241–245; triangulation of, 7–10

ECB. See European Central Bank
ECOFIN. See European Council of Finance Ministers
ECU. See European currency unit
EFTA. See European Free Trade Area
EMI. See European Monetary Institute
Emminger, Otmar, 12, 35, 172, 254
EMS. See European Monetary System
EMU. See European Monetary Union
Erhard, Ludwig, 57
ERM. See Exchange Rate Mechanism
ESCB. See European System of Central Banks
Euro, 1, 198–200, 202, 211; and the deutsche mark, 245; and the dollar, 246–247; and European Central Bank, 241–243; and "Europolitics," 241; exchange rate of, 244; and France, 223; gold revaluation plan, 219–221
European Central Bank (ECB), 1, 93, 102, 113, 127–128, 182; comparison to Bundesbank, 52; control over exchange rates, 127; controversy over president, 227–228; implications for Europe, 241–245; and stability pact, 227–228
European Council of Finance Ministers (ECOFIN), 120, 193; control over exchange rates, 127, 243; and Delors Committee, 101; and ECB, 114; and the EMS, 19–20, 22, 155, 158, 174n31
European currency unit (ECU), 1. See also Bundesbank
European Free Trade Area (EFTA), 81
European Monetary Institute (EMI): creation of, 183; operation of, 196–197, 199
European Monetary System (EMS), xi, 2, 8–10, 12, 77; operation of, 18–21; realignments in, 77–78, 158–161, 193; widening of the margins, 165–166; yearlong crisis, 145–150; zone of monetary stability, 12
European Monetary Union (EMU): transition to, 198–200; delay of convergence criteria, 215–217
European System of Central Banks (ESCB), 50, 199, 225
Exchange Rate Mechanism (ERM), 18–20, 54, 80, 102, 146; ERM II, 207, 211; September 1992 crisis, 155–157

Federal Republic of Germany, 2, 46; economic miracle, 2; Federal Constitutional Court, 47, 182, 227; *Grundgesetz*, 37, 46; *Rechstaat*, 2, 38, 46
Federal Reserve, 73–75, 104–105, 115; and G7, 131–132; intervention by, 154, 185, 214, 226; and October 1987 market crash, 83
FDP. See Free Democratic Party
France, 18, 94; Bank of, 114; DeGaulle's franc crisis, 57, 65n60; elections in, 222–223; EMS realignment, 77; *franc fort* policy, 20, 146, 159, 161–165, 196; Franco-German Economic Council, 96; and G7, 107; referendum on Maastricht, 162–163; relations with Germany, 13, 11, 96, 170, 193, 210, 224;

strikes, 200, 222; and trade, 71. *See also* Trichet, Jean-Claude; Mitterand, François; Chirac, Jacques
Free Democratic Party (FDP), 79, 104, 190, 209, 221
Funabashi, Yoichi, 79, 254

GEMU. *See* German Economic and Monetary Union
Genscher, Hans-Dietrich, 94, 96, 109
German Economic and Monetary Union (GEMU), 2, 93, 108, 112–113, 143*tab;* impact on Germany, 143, 173*n*9; and EMU, 120–121
German monetary norm, 40, 117, 199, 230, 247
Goodman, John, 45, 47, 254
Governance, 4, 17–18; weak and strong forms, 23–24
Greenspan, Alan, 214. *See also* Federal Reserve
Group of Seven (G7), x, xi, 4, 8–10, 16, 54; definition of, 31*n*16; and fixed exchange rates, 116; and GEMU, 117–118; Gulf War, 129–130; Mexican peso crisis, 192–193, 195; operation of, 21–24; reforms of, 247–249. *See also* Summits, G7 annual

Hard ECU. *See* Britain; Major, John
Henning, C. Randall, 243, 247, 248, 253–254
Hitler, Adolf, 56

IGC. *See* Intergovernmental conference
IMF. *See* International Monetary Fund
Intergovernmental conference (IGC), 210; Amsterdam Summit, 222–224. *See also* Maastricht
International Monetary Fund (IMF), xv, 4–5, 21–22, 105, 192, 194–195; reforms of 187–188, 214
Italy, 112, 190, 201, 225, 235–236; Rome EMU Summit 120–122; on two-speed Europe, 125

Japan: Baker-Miyazawa Accord, 75, 87*n*26; Bank of, 185; pressure from United States, 149, 167

Kaiser, Rolf, 47, 254
Katzenstein, Peter, 84, 254
Keynes, John Maynard, ix, 39
Kinkel, Klaus, 190, 223
Kloten, Norbert, 97
Kohl, Helmut, xi, 2, 6, 13, 47, 70; elections, 179, 187, 191, 217, 228–229, 234*n*79; on EMU, 109–110, 209; and Europe, 93, 109–110; gold revaluation plan, 220; political union, 114–115; relations with France, 111, 164. *See also* Christian Democratic Union
Köhler, Horst, 125, 151; views on G7, 153, 169, 182–183
Krönungstheorie. See Coronation theory

Labor Unions: and EMU, 98, 138*n*60
Land central banks, 49–52
Leigh-Pemberton, Robin, 101, 150
Louvre Accord, 14, 22, 79–80, 107, 195, 238–239

M3, 10, 43, 31*n*21, 61*n*20
Maastricht, 95, 198, 201, 213; convergence criteria, 126, 193; and a core europe, 189; Danish referendum, 152; debate over delay, 144, 149, 155, 159, 160; ECB, 127–128; French referendum, 161–162; and German policy, 237–238; Maastricht II, 224; Treaty, 119, 122, 129, 216. *See also* Core Europe
Major, John, 155, 170, 193
Mitterand, François, 107, 110, 162–163. *See also* France

Noelle-Neumann, Elizabeth, 38
Nölling, Wilhelm, 179, 255

OECD. *See* Organization for Economic Cooperation and Development
Organization for Economic Cooperation and Development (OECD), xv, 21, 70, 103, 169, 187

Padoa-Schioppa, Tommaso, 98
Plaza Accord, 68–72, 107, 195; and German bargaining strategies, 238–239; governance, 16, 22

Pöhl, Karl-Otto, 6, 51; and Bundesbank independence, 42, 62n33; and ECB, 93; and the EMS, 78, 80, 160; on EMU, 99–100, 102, 119; exchange rate policy, 11, 67; and the G7, 83, 132; and GEMU, 112, 123; and Helmut Schmidt, 59

Public opinion: of EMU 99, 110, 138n60, 141n118, 147, 198, 200, 202, 221; gold revaluation debate, 220–221; of the Maastricht Treaty, 128; timetable, 198, 209; and Treuhand, 192

Reagan, Ronald, 68–69, 74
Reichsbank, 55–56
Rubin, Robert, 214

Schacht, Hjalmar, 55–56
Schäuble, Wolfgang, 189; core Europe plan, 209
Schiller, Karl, 57, 128
Schlesinger, Helmut, 1, 11, 124, 133, 147, 156; on EMU, 207
Schmidt, Helmut, 11–12, 14, 51, 98, 172, 200, 255; conflict with Bundesbank, 57–59
Schröder, Gerhard, 200, 209, 221; election of, 229, 233n56
SEA. *See* Single European Act
Sinatra doctrine, 144, 167–169, 172n1, 183
Single European Act (SEA), 82, 86n15, 164
Smyser, William, 37
Socialist Democratic Party (SPD), 128, 208–209, 211; election victory, 229, 234n79; gold revaluation debate, 220–221
SPD. *See* Socialist Democratic Party
Stabilitätsgemeinschaft, 99, 242
Stability and Growth Law, 39

Stability and Growth Pact, 180, 200–203; Bundesbank view of, 213; and European Commission, 213; and France, 222–224; penalties of, 212
Stoltenberg, Gerhard, 67; and EMS, 78; and G7, 80, 83, 103, 106; and Plaza Accord, 70, 72
Strange, Susan, 37
Summers, Lawrence, 41, 194
Summits, G7 annual: Denver, 218–219; Halifax, 195; Houston, 118; London, 132; Lyon, 214–215; Munich, 152–153; Naples, 187; Paris, 107; Tokyo, 75, 169; Toronto, 104; Venice, 80. *See also* Group of Seven

Thatcher, Margaret, 101, 118. *See also* Britian
Thiel, Elke, 45
Tietmeyer, Hans, 50–51, 100, 148; on a core Europe, 189, 227; and EMU, 181; and euro, 235; and United States, 186, 194. *See also* Bundesbank
Trichet, Jean-Claude, 196, 222, 228
Two-speed Europe. *See* Core Europe

Volcker, Paul, 74, 188. *See also* Federal Reserve
Von Arnim, Hans Herbert, 3, 255
Von Bonin, Konrad, 47, 255

Weimar Republic, ix, 2, 37, 55–56
Werner Report, 98
Waigel, Theo, 94; and G7, 117, 150, 151, 167–168; gold revaluation debate, 219–222, 235; and stability pact, 180, 194, 200–203, 211–213. *See also* Christian Socialist Union
Woolley, John, 42, 45, 256

About the Book

Why is Germany prepared to sacrifice the deutsche mark for European Monetary Union? Peter Henning Loedel's novel analysis, incorporating domestic, European, and global aspects of German monetary policy, suggests that the institutional relationship between the Bundesbank and the federal government, together with Germany's bargaining strategies toward European and global monetary-governance structures, can provide the answer to the deutsche mark puzzle.

Examining the record from 1985 through May 1998, Loedel challenges common conceptions of the Bundesbank's independence. He also explores the ability of external structures to affect German monetary decisions. His presentation of political and economic forces offers fresh insight into the factors shaping German monetary politics and the future of European Monetary Union.

Peter Henning Loedel is assistant professor of political science at West Chester University, West Chester, Pennsylvania. He is editor (with Mary McKenzie) of *The Promise and Reality of European Security Cooperation: States, Interests, and Institutions*.